Kenneth Hyltenstam (Ed.)
Advanced Proficiency and Exceptional Ability in Second Languages

Studies on Language Acquisition

Edited by
Peter Jordens

Volume 51

Advanced Proficiency and Exceptional Ability in Second Languages

Edited by
Kenneth Hyltenstam

DE GRUYTER
MOUTON

ISBN 978-1-5015-1697-9
e-ISBN (PDF) 978-1-61451-517-3 e-ISBN (EPUB) 978-1-5015-0048-0
ISSN 1861-4248

Library of Congress Cataloging-in-Publication Data
A CIP catalog record for this book has been applied for at the Library of Congress.

Bibliographic information published by the Deutsche Nationalbibliothek
The Deutsche Nationalbibliothek lists this publication in the Deutsche Nationalbibliografie; detailed bibliographic data are available on the Internet at http://dnb.dnb.de.

© 2018 Walter de Gruyter Inc., Boston/Berlin
This volume is text- and page-identical with the hardback published in 2016
Typesetting: RoyalStandard, Hong Kong
Printing and binding: CPI books GmbH, Leck
♾ Printed on acid-free paper
Printed in Germany

www.degruyter.com

Preface

Research on the acquisition and use of second languages has developed into a vibrant field of investigation over a period of almost fifty years. The multifaceted nature of the area, its breadth and depth, is reflected in a rapidly expanding set of field establishing artifacts: specialized scientific journals for second language research, continuously emerging textbooks and introductions to the field, several large handbooks, professional associations with regular international and national conferences, departments and academic positions, etc. Present day globalization with massive migration has made it more evident that not only widely used languages such as English, French, German, Russian, and Spanish are learnt and used as second languages. An ever increasing diversity of second languages appear on the pages of scientific articles today, as does a growing number of learner and user populations. The current plethora of competing and overlapping – or totally independent – theoretical approaches to specific questions or subfields may be seen as a sign of immaturity of the field, but simultaneously, this is a stimulating way forward for an area that is intrinsically cross-disciplinary. Like language in general, second languages are acquired and used by individuals in a societal context, i.e. second languages are fashioned by both internal cognitive and psychological conditions and external societal micro- and macro-determinants.

This book focuses on learners who have accomplished a no less than enviably advanced proficiency level in one or more second, or additional, languages. They find themselves in the uppermost categories of any proficiency scale; many of them cannot be distinguished from first language users of the language. Some exhibit exceptional language learning abilities, while others are just anyone who have needed or wanted to learn as much as possible of a new language. This broad category of second language users is still under-researched and is therefore interesting in itself, but it also has the potential to contribute with new theoretical insights into what the acquisition and use of second language is all about.

The chapters of the book give an extensive review of current knowledge on their individual topics. They typically go a long way to explain not only the actual research achievements on advanced second language users in their areas, but also provide a firm theoretical and methodological basis for the scientific understanding of specific research results. For example, the chapters on the lexicon and formulaic language give brief but succinct presentations of what is generally known about these areas in linguistics at large. Therefore, the book serves well as a source of knowledge not only for the research community, but also for students of all undergraduate and graduate levels.

All the contributors of this book have participated in a long-term research programme at Stockholm University, High-Level Proficiency in Second Language Use, financed by Riksbankens Jubileumsfond, the Swedish Foundation for Humanities and Social Sciences (grant M2005-0459). The writing of this book was made possible by the grant. We gratefully acknowledge the Foundation's support.

Kenneth Hyltenstam
Stockholm
January 2016

Table of contents

Preface —— v
Contributors —— viii

Kenneth Hyltenstam
Introduction: Perspectives on advanced second language proficiency —— 1

Lars Fant
1 Pragmatic markers in high-level second language use —— 15

Inge Bartning
2 Morphosyntax and discourse in high-level second language use —— 43

Camilla Bardel
3 The lexicon of advanced L2 learners —— 73

Britt Erman, Fanny Forsberg Lundell & Margareta Lewis
4 Formulaic language in advanced second language acquisition and use —— 111

Alan McMillion & Philip Shaw
5 Reading proficiency in advanced L2 users —— 149

Kingsley Bolton
6 Linguistic outsourcing and native-like performance in international call centres: An overview —— 185

Kenneth Hyltenstam
7 The polyglot – an initial characterization on the basis of multiple anecdotal accounts —— 215

Kenneth Hyltenstam
8 The exceptional ability of polyglots to achieve high-level proficiency in numerous languages —— 241

Subject index —— 273

Contributors

Camilla Bardel
Department of Language Education
Stockholm University

Inge Bartning
Department of Romance Studies and Classics
Stockholm University

Kingsley Bolton
Language and Communication Centre
Nanyang Technological University, Singapore

Britt Erman
Department of English
Stockholm University

Lars Fant
Department of Romance Studies and Classics
Stockholm University

Fanny Forsberg Lundell
Department of Romance Studies and Classics
Stockholm University

Kenneth Hyltenstam
Centre for Research on Bilingualism
Stockholm University

Margareta Lewis
Department of English
Stockholm University

Alan McMillion
Department of English
Stockholm University

Philip Shaw
Department of English
Stockholm University

Kenneth Hyltenstam
Introduction: Perspectives on advanced second language proficiency

1 Objectives of this volume and its chapters

This book is about success and spectacular accomplishment in second language acquisition (SLA). Most people who have experienced acquiring a second language (L2) know that the command of a new language does not come altogether easily. Second language acquisition is a complex and often laborious enterprise, and, in brief, represents a vast challenge. It goes on for many years, and the learner often feels that the task never becomes entirely accomplished. Compared to the fluency, lexical access, and intuition for what is an accurate expression that the learner has in his/her first language, the obstacles felt during second language use may be both tiring and irritating. The complicated nature of second language acquisition is, perhaps, perceived more clearly by older, or adult learners than by young learners, but the complexity of the task is in no way to be dismissed even in the case of child L2 learners.

Despite this, a large proportion of learners, both migrants and foreign language students, successfully achieve advanced-level proficiency in their second language. The first set of chapters in this volume, chapters 1–5, provides a detailed account of how second languages are used at this level. Individual chapters describe high-level L2 use in terms of discourse pragmatics (chapter 1), grammar (chapter 2), lexicon (chapter 3), and formulaic language (chapter 4). Both oral and written corpus data are referred to as well as experimentally elicited data. One of the chapters specifically discusses the issue of reading comprehension at the advanced level of L2 proficiency (chapter 5) and is thus based on perception data. The wider context examined in this chapter is academic content teaching through English to students for whom this language is an advanced L2. All the chapters also discuss the reasons why high levels of proficiency are reached successfully in some situations, but are difficult to attain in others.

The second set of chapters, chapters 6–8, discusses more spectacular examples of second language achievement. One example (chapter 6) concerns a group of L2 speakers who demonstrate a remarkable ability to use a second language efficiently and proficiently in their working life, namely employees in transnational call centres. The chapter displays conversations and negotiations carried out in

Kenneth Hyltenstam, Stockholm University

this context and tells us about the social macro- and micro-conditions that surround the particular L2 achievement required by call centre staff. The other example, treated in two chapters (chapters 7 and 8), is that of polyglots, i.e. individuals who have learnt not just one or two second languages to an advanced level, but rather, an astonishingly high number of them. We are here talking about people who are highly proficient in at least six languages (cf. Hudson 2012). Such manifest polyglots, who may succinctly be labelled second language learners par excellence, are scrutinized from myriad angles. The reason that two chapters are devoted to the issue of polyglotism is the fact that astonishingly little has been written about this phenomenon (cf. Erard 2012). The first of these two chapters (chapter 7) deals with the non-academic literature on polyglots. Through a compilation of more or less detailed reports about nearly one hundred polyglots and an analysis of recurring observations and patterns to be found in these materials, this chapter provides a first approximation of the social, psychological, cognitive and linguistic qualities that can be said to characterize polyglots. The second of the two chapters (chapter 8) reviews the few scientific studies of polyglots that have been published. In addition to reporting the results presented in these studies, the chapter goes into some depth in accounting for the different theoretical frameworks that have informed these analyses. Chapter 8 arrives at a more nuanced picture of the present knowledge of polyglot characteristics and sets the scene for future research in this area.

The authors of all the chapters shared the ambition of providing an extensive theoretical background to each of their individual topics. In the chapters of the first section on advanced L2 proficiency, this aim is spelled out in a clarification of the analytical tools that are being employed in current research in discourse pragmatics, morphosyntax, the lexicon, and formulaic language as well as the theoretical concepts that are employed in studies of reading comprehension at an advanced L2 level. The same goal holds for the chapters in the second section that exemplify specific cases of exceptional L2 use.

2 Some terminology related to advanced or high-level L2 proficiency

The definition of L2 proficiency levels is central to all practices of language assessment. The purpose of L2 language tests may be to define specific language requirements for jobs, educational programmes, continued language courses, or, in the political realm, for being accepted as a citizen. Or their purpose may be to certify levels of achievement (summative assessment), or to identify a learner's strengths and weaknesses as a basis for continued educational planning and support (formative assessment). The labels employed by different organizations and agencies concerned with foreign or second language assessment and education are often similar along dimensions such as 'low–high' or 'weak–strong/good'. For example, in the internationally recognized TOEFL tests (www.ets.org/toefl/institutions/scores/interpret), levels are labelled Low, Intermediate, and High for skills in Reading and Listening and Weak, Limited, Fair, and Good for skills in Speaking and Writing. The levels specified by the ACTFL (American Council on the Teaching of Foreign Languages) are Novice, Intermediate, Advanced, Superior, and Distinguished (ACTFL 2012) with the major levels of Advanced, Intermediate, and Novice subdivided into High, Mid, and Low sublevels. In Europe, the CEFR scale (Common European Framework of Reference for Languages, Council of Europe, 2001) has gained widespread application in many countries. The three major levels of Basic, Independent and Proficient are each divided into two sublevels, thus resulting in the six grade scale shown below:

A – Basic User
    A1 – Breakthrough
    A2 – Waystage

B – Independent user
    B1 – Threshold
    B2 – Vantage

C – Proficient user
    C1 – Effective operational proficiency
    C2 – Mastery

The stages or levels defined in these administrative contexts often have a terminological resemblance with developmental stages defined in SLA research on the basis of empirical L2 data. L2 acquisition obviously proceeds as a continual development from a point where no proficiency in the L2 exists up to a level that is often termed 'ultimate L2 attainment'. When researchers divide the developmental continuum into labelled phases or stages, this does not, of course, mirror any pre-existing reality. It is nothing but a methodological procedure for making a complex situation more tangible. The stages or steps that are specified in various attempts at systemizing L2 development, as for example in Processability Theory (Pienemann 1998) or other interlanguage frameworks (e.g. Bartning and Schlyter 2004), are often defined in terms of emergence or frequency of target-like use of specific grammatical features.

The correlation between the proficiency levels defined by the language assessment establishment and SLA research is not necessarily obvious. While the levels specified in SLA research frameworks are specified on empirical grounds, i.e. from accumulated data of L2 development, the levels specified in the language assessment contexts referred to above are created by experienced experts on language teaching and assessment who have developed a sense for what can be expected from learners at different levels in their language learning career. Attempts at investigating and discussing the formal correlation between SLA stages and, for example, the stages suggested in the CEFR framework, are scarce, an exception being Bartning, Martin, and Vedder (2010). In that volume, Forsberg and Bartning (2010) contend that even if it is difficult to correlate the stages of the two frameworks directly, "morpho-syntactic deviances [...] yield significant differences between CEFR levels up to B2" (p. 151). Hulstijn (2010), however, explicitly notes that "CEFR levels do not constitute steps towards native-speaker proficiency" (p. 237), which makes a correlation between its levels and SLA levels not viable to start with.

The chapters of the present volume are specifically interested in what happens in situations where L2 learners attain a level of ultimate attainment that is equal to or close to that of native speakers. As opposed to what is the case in L1 acquisition, L2 acquisition is characterized by ample individual variation as to the level of ultimate attainment. Ultimate attainment refers to an 'endstate', which in the case of L1 acquisition per definition is synonymous with adult nativelike command of the language. In L2 acquisition, in contrast, the level of ultimate attainment should not be conceived as 'nativelike' (which, however, is a common misinterpretation, cf. Birdsong 2004: 82), but may range from nativelike or near-native proficiency at the top to any lower level along the continuum. Various factors that are involved in the reason for a certain learner ending up at his/her specific ultimate attainment level have been discussed. An ultimate attainment level already at a low level of proficiency may depend on social segregation from other speakers of the language (lack of exposure, lack of opportunity) or lack of adequate strategies to cope with second language input as may be the case for adult L2 learners with a limited educational background etc. A variety of such factors has been investigated, where age of onset (i.e. the biological and social changes that correlate with age growth) seems to be the most prominent one.

Ultimate attainment is here understood as a phenomenon characterized by stabilization. In the L2 literature, the notion of stabilization is used to characterize a temporary plateau in language development without any specification as to whether development will continue/restart or not. Stabilization is often preferred to the notion of fossilization, which carries the assumption of a permanent discontinuation of development (Long 2003). The concept of stabilization is more in line with massive observations that L2 development, or change, generally does not cease totally, even if changes may be very slow, and at times not target-directed (Long 2003: 511).

The chapters in this volume employ a set of terms for easy reference to different aspects of L2 proficiency in the upper sections of the proficiency continuum. First of all, the notions of 'high-level proficiency' and 'advanced level proficiency' are used without specificity – and interchangeably – to cover exactly this, the upper sections of the proficiency continuum. On some occasions, as in chapter 2, the term 'advanced' has a specific meaning, namely, when it is used in a theoretical framework on L2 development, in which the term is used to distinguish smaller but formally defined sections of the continuum.

As noted above, in typical L1 acquisition that continues into adulthood, i.e. without being interrupted, for example, by migration to a non-L1 linguistic environment, the level of ultimate attainment per definition equals native L1 proficiency (see Table 1). While the dimension low–advanced proficiency is not relevant or used about L1 development, in the L2 context, that dimension is often intertwined with another non-congruent dimension of language proficiency, namely the non-native–nativelike dimension. Table 1 illustrates how the terms of the two dimensions may be combined. Advanced L2 proficiency covers (1) 'nativelike L2 proficiency', i.e. proficiency levels among L2 users who are, in fact, equal to those of native speakers[1]; (2) 'near-native L2 proficiency', i.e. a level that is close to but not exactly nativelike (L2 speakers at this level are not easy to distinguish from native L1 speakers in everyday oral communication, but differences may be more salient when speakers are faced with demanding linguistic tasks (Hyltenstam and Abrahamsson 2003)); and (3) non-native L2 proficiency, i.e. proficiency levels among speakers who are clearly identified as non-natives in everyday oral communication although being at an advanced level of L2 proficiency. This is the case with a majority of all those late L2 learners who have a noticeable accent but who, communicatively/functionally, are on a level that allows them to operate as efficiently in their L2 as any L1 speaker, both in their professional life and in their everyday environment.

---

[1] There is an ongoing debate on the notion of 'native speaker' as such, and particularly about the standard for comparing native L1 data and L2 data. It is beyond the scope of this introduction to go into that debate, but see Bylund, Abrahamsson, and Hyltenstam (2012) and Birdsong and Gertken (2013).

Table 1: Terminology for proficiency levels in L1 and L2

L1	L2
Native	Nativelike Advanced level
	Near-native Advanced level
	Non-native Advanced level
	Non-native Intermediate level
	Non-native Low level

3 Studies of advanced L2 proficiency

Although advanced or high-level proficiency in second languages is an integrated part of the practices of language education, language assessment procedures and curriculum planning, it has received comparatively little attention in theoretical/empirical L2 research. As of 2013, an SLA handbook entry on 'advanced language proficiency' stated that "the field does not yet have a sufficiently comprehensive theoretical basis for understanding advanced language, much less advanced language use" (Byrnes 2013: 506). Compared to the understanding that has been gained about the early and intermediate stages of L2 development, the body of knowledge on advanced second language acquisition and use is rather limited. Nevertheless, in the last two decades quite substantive research has been carried out on this matter.

Two focus areas, in particular, can be pointed out as central to this research. One area comprises research related to factors that can explain variation in ultimate attainment, especially questions and hypotheses generated by the notion of a 'critical period' for language acquisition – in L2 research currently more often couched in the notion of 'sensitive periods' (see Granena and Long 2013a). This includes attempts at falsifying/confirming the hypothesis as well as general challenges to the whole idea of critical/sensitive periods. The second area aims at identifying the characteristic features of advanced L2 use. This focus is a continuation of the long-standing research tradition on developmental stages or acquisition sequences in initial and intermediate stages of L2 acquisition.

3.1 Research on critical/sensitive periods of language acquisition

Among the many concerns that have been attended in the first of these areas are (1) the correlation between the level of ultimate attainment and the age of onset of acquisition (AO); (2) the frequencies with which L2 ultimate attainment is similar, or even identical, to that of native speakers; (3) whether observations concerning the age limitations of L2 learning ability can be given a biological maturational constraints interpretation or whether social or cognitive changes that go together with increasing age are more reasonable explanations; and (4) what other factors determine the level of ultimate attainment for individual learners such as length of residence in the L2-speaking environment, chronological age, language learning aptitude, and cross-linguistic influence (for overviews, see Abrahamsson 2013; DeKeyser and Larson-Hall 2006; Hyltenstam 2012; Muñoz 2013).

As to the correlation between AO and ultimate attainment in a second language, it has for a long time been an established fact that younger starters outperform older starters in ultimate attainment (Long 1990): "The inverse relationship between AO and achievement is one of the most widely attested and widely accepted findings in SLA" (Granena and Long 2013b: IX). It is also clear, however, that this correlation holds only for AOs up to the mid-teens (Abrahamsson 2012: 201).

With regard to the incidence of nativelike ultimate attainment in L2 learners, studies present widely different results. The differences can be explained, to a large extent, by different research methodologies and by the individual research questions that are being investigated. A three-way distinction in discussions about the incidence of nativelikeness among L2 users is that between 'self-identified nativelikeness', 'perceived nativelikeness', and 'scrutinized nativelikeness' (Abrahamsson and Hyltenstam (2009: 259). As for self-identified nativelikeness in late AOs, in a study by Piller (2002), 37% of the participants (27 out of 73) themselves "claimed that they had achieved high-level proficiency in their L2 and could pass for native speakers in certain contexts" (p. 186). Although the participants' average age of first natural exposure to the L2 was 20.9 years, most of them had been exposed to the same language as a foreign language much earlier, on average at the age of 11.7 years. In studies of perceived nativelikeness, i.e. how native speakers of a language perceive the degree of nativelikeness in L2 speakers, figures are generally lower. Abrahamsson and Hyltenstam (2009: 272) present an incidence of 6% for perceived nativelikeness among learners with AOs beyond puberty (operationalized as ≥12), whereas 62% of those with AOs before puberty (operationalized as ≤11) were perceived as nativelike, i.e.

they passed for native speakers. As for scrutinized nativelikeness, i.e. when the L2 data from highly proficient speakers are analyzed in detail, Abrahamsson and Hyltenstam (2009) report that "only a few of the early learners [9%] and none of the late learners [0%] exhibited actual, linguistic nativelikeness across a broad range of tasks when their performance was scrutinized in detail" (p. 287). Others have claimed considerably higher incidences, also for late learners. For example Birdsong and Molis (2001) found that more than 20% of the late learners (defined as those with AO ≥17 years) performed within the native-speaker range on a grammatical judgement test. However, a closer look at statements like this often reveals either, as in this particular case, that the test itself was too simple to distinguish between high proficiency levels, i.e. the test had ceiling effects, or that only a few features of the L2 were analyzed in detail.

Several of the chapters in this book review results of research showing that even near-native L2 users who clearly pass for native speakers and who have been residents for many years (sometimes up to three decades) in a country where their L2 is the dominant language (France, Spain, the UK) differ slightly but significantly from native speakers in discourse, formulaic language, lexicon, and grammar when scrutinized in detail. In many of the cases discussed, the L2 users had studied his/her second language (English, French, or Spanish) as a foreign language at school and at the university level before experiencing natural exposure to it.

The issue of how to interpret age differences – as reflecting biologically determined maturational constraints or other social, psychological or cognitive changes – is an unresolved question, and it is not the focus of any of the chapters of this volume. Suffice it to say here that different researchers hold rather incompatible views. However, after a thorough analysis of the arguments put forth in the pro and con debate of maturational explanations, Long (2013: 34) concludes that "age effects are one of the most widely attested and widely accepted findings in SLA, with maturational constraints their likely cause".

Several factors other than AO have been proposed as candidates for explaining differences in ultimate L2 attainment, length of residence (LOR) in the L2 environment, age at testing, and L1 use being the most important ones. Undoubtedly all these factors contribute to defining the individual's level of ultimate attainment, but statistical analyses show that AO is by far the most important factor (DeKeyser and Larson-Hall 2005; Long 2013). Studies show that correlations between AO and ultimate attainment among adult learners are strong and statistically significant, while factors such as LOR have a low and often insignificant rate of correlation (see e.g. Abrahamsson 2012).

A factor that has been investigated extensively over the last decades is that of language learning aptitude (cf. Granena 2013). DeKeyser (2000), DeKeyser

Alfi-Shabtay, and Ravid (2010) and Abrahamsson and Hyltenstam (2008) have indicated that high levels of aptitude are a necessary condition for reaching near-native proficiency in adult L2 acquisition. The latter study also indicates that aptitude plays a role for the level of ultimate attainment even in child learners. Results presented by Granena (2013) show an interaction between aptitude and the modality in which language testing is carried out. In her study, aptitude scores correlated more positively with language measures that allowed "participants time to reflect on language correctness and language structure" (p. 200), i.e. to draw on explicit knowledge or language awareness.

3.2 Characteristics of advanced L2 proficiency

The second of the two focus areas we mentioned above concerns the characteristic features of advanced L2 proficiency. Issues investigated here comprise (1) the grammatical, lexical, and discourse features that continue to exhibit instability at advanced levels, (2) the extent to which there is a discernible systematic development still going on at the advanced level, and, relatedly, (3) the notion of 'stabilization', i.e. "a state of L2 development where fluctuation has temporarily ceased" (Ellis 2008: 30). One approach to defining language learner outcomes is in terms of the complexity, accuracy/correctness, and fluency (CAF) of L2 performance (Housen, Kuiken, and Vedder 2012).

At very advanced levels, in particular at near-native or nativelike levels, the degree of accuracy is high – which explains why native listeners often cannot distinguish this L2 use from native language use – but still significantly different from the level of accuracy among native speakers. Errors are not limited to complex grammar but also involve areas of grammar that may be considered simple and even create problems at initial and intermediate levels. Gender selection, agreement morphology, and basic word order are examples of such structures. Hyltenstam (1992) showed that although extremely low, grammatical error frequencies in both oral and written production data from near-native L2 users were significantly higher (0.3–1.0 errors per 100 running words) than in data from native speakers (0.1–0.4 per 100 running words). Similarly low frequencies were found for lexical errors. A reasonable interpretation of the background for such very low error frequencies is that they are not generally due to a lack of representation of L2 morphosyntactic or lexical regularities but are instead due to processing difficulties. (This does not exclude that some errors have a representational cause.) This interpretation is supported by research showing that the morphosyntactic error frequency in oral L2 data from very advanced speakers is higher in rhematic parts of utterances (65–76 errors in corpora of 22,000–32,000 words) than in thematic parts (4–10 errors in the same corpora), as compared to native speakers who had 6 errors in the rhematic part of utterances and 0 errors in thematic parts in a 25,000 word corpus (Bartning, Forsberg Lundell, and Hancock 2012). The processing load is generally higher in the rhematic part of a sentence, where the speaker is creatively constructing new information, than in the thematic part, where given information is produced. The chapters of this volume illustrate this phenomenon extensively, showing that low, almost negligible, frequencies of errors are reported from various linguistic levels, including the lexicon, grammar, discourse, and, in particular, formulaic language.

Another feature is over- and under-use of certain features of L2 compared to native language use. Ädel and Erman (2012) found that very frequent 'lexical bundles' in native English such as *this would suggest that* and *there appears to be* were underused in academic writing by Swedish advanced L2 learners of English. This under- and over-use is discussed in detail, particularly in chapters 1 (discourse) and 4 (formulaic language).

Several researchers have investigated the extent to which various linguistic features are dissimilarly sensitive to reaching full nativelike status at advanced or near-native L2 levels (Sorace 2003; Hopp 2009). Antonella Sorace has examined the hypothesis that structures at the interfaces of syntax and semantics as well as syntax and discourse pragmatics are more vulnerable and consequently less likely to be acquired completely than structures that are not affected by such interfaces (for an overview, see Sorace 2011). She suggests that optionality, i.e. variability between forms that converge with and diverge from those of native speakers, may potentially be permanent. The interactions between morphosyntax and discourse pragmatics is again treated extensively in chapters 1, 2 and 4 of the present volume.

Small but significant differences between advanced L2 users and native speakers are not seen only in their language production. Research on speech perception in noise is a case in point where massive research shows that non-native speakers have greater difficulties than native speakers. Whereas advanced L2 speakers perform as native speakers in quiet conditions, they fall significantly below native speakers when the signal is deteriorated by noise (for an overview, see Tabri, Smith Abou Chacra, and Pring 2010). This result is repeated even for near-native speakers, i.e. in populations consisting of L2 users who cannot easily be distinguished from native speakers in their speech production (Hyltenstam and Abrahamsson 2003).

Acknowledgments

I am deeply grateful to Lamont Antieau for reviewing my English writing – efficiently and rapidly as always – here and in chapters 7 and 8.

References

Abrahamsson, N. 2012. Age of onset and ultimate attainment of L2 phonetic and grammatical intuition. In: N. Abrahamsson & K. Hyltenstam (eds.), *High-level L2 Acquisition, Learning and Use*. Thematic issue of *Studies in Second Language Acquisition*, 32/2. 187–214.
Abrahamsson, N. 2013. The critical period. In: P. Robinson, (ed.), *Routledge Encyclopedia of SLA*. London: Routledge. 146–151.
Abrahamsson, N. & K. Hyltenstam. 2008. The robustness of aptitude effects in near-native second language acquisition. *Studies in Second Language Acquisition*, 30/4. 489–509.
Abrahamsson, N. & K. Hyltenstam. 2009. Age of onset and nativelikeness in a second language: Listener perception versus linguistic scrutiny. *Language Learning*, 58/2. 249–306.
ACTFL 2012. *Proficiency Guidelines*. American Council on the Teaching of Foreign Languages.
Ädel, A. & B. Erman. 2012. Recurrent word combinations in academic writing by native and non-native speakers of English; a lexical bundles approach. *English for Specific Purposes*, 31/2. 81–92.
Bartning, I., F. Forsberg Lundell, & V. Hancock. 2012. On the role of linguistic contextual factors for morphosyntactic stabilization in high-level L2 French. In: N. Abrahamsson & K. Hyltenstam (eds.), *High-level L2 Acquisition, Learning and Use*. Thematic issue of *Studies in Second Language Acquisition*, 32/2. 234–267.
Bartning, I., M. Martin, & I. Vedder (eds.). 2010. *Communicative Proficiency and Linguistic Development. Intersections between SLA and Language Testing Research*. Eurosla Monographs Series, 1.
Birdsong, D. 2004. Second language acquisition and ultimate attainment. In: A. Davies & C. Elder (eds.), *Handbook of Applied Linguistics*. Malden, MA: Blackwell. 82–105.
Birdsong, D. & L. M. Gertken. 2013. In faint praise of folly. A critical review of native/non-native speaker comparisons, with examples from native and bilingual processing of French complex syntax. *Language, Interaction and Acquisition*, 4/2. 107–133.
Birdsong, D. & M. Molis. 2001. On the evidence for maturational constraints in second-language acquisition. *Journal of Memory and Language*, 44. 235–249.
Bylund, E., N. Abrahamsson, & K. Hyltenstam. 2012. Does first language maintenance hamper nativelikeness in a second language? A study of ultimate attainment in early bilinguals. In: N. Abrahamsson & K. Hyltenstam (eds.), *High-level L2 Acquisition, Learning and Use*. Thematic issue of *Studies in Second Language Acquisition*, 32/2. 215–241.
Byrnes, H. 2013. Advanced language proficiency. In: S. M. Gass & A. Mackey (eds.), *The Routledge Handbook of Second Language Acquisition*. London: Routledge. 506–521.
Council of Europe, 2001. *Common European Framework of Reference for Languages: Learning, Teaching, Assessment*. Cambridge, UK: Cambridge University Press.
DeKeyser, R. M. 2000. The robustness of critical period effects in second language acquisition. *Studies in Second Language Acquisition*, 22/4. 499–533.

DeKeyser, R., I. Alfi-Shabtay, & D. Ravid. 2010. Cross-linguistic evidence for the nature of age effects in second language acquisition. *Applied Psycholinguistics*, 31/3. 413–438.

DeKeyser, R. & J. Larson-Hall. 2005. What does the critical period really mean? In: J. F. Kroll & A. M. B. de Groot (eds.), *Handbook of Bilingualism: Psycholinguistic Approaches*. Oxford: Oxford University Press. 88–108.

Ellis, R. 2008. *The Study of Second Language Acquisition* [2nd edition]. Oxford: Oxford University Press.

Erard, M. 2012. *Babel No More. The Search for the World's Most Extraordinary Language Learners*. New York: Free Press.

Forsberg F. & I. Bartning. 2010. Can linguistic features discriminate between the communicative CEFR-levels? A pilot study of written L2 French. In: I. Bartning, M. Martin, & I. Vedder (eds.), *Communicative Proficiency and Linguistic Development. Intersections between SLA and Language Testing Research. Eurosla Monographs Series*, 1. 133–158.

Granena, G. 2013. Reexamination of the robustness of aptitude in second language acquisition. In: G. Granena & M. Long (eds.), *Sensitive periods, language aptitude, and ultimate attainment*. Amsterdam: Benjamins. 179–204.

Granena, G. & M. Long 2013. Introduction and overview. In: G. Granena & M. Long (eds.), *Sensitive Periods, Language Aptitude, and Ultimate Attainment*. Amsterdam: Benjamins. IX–XV.

Hopp, H. 2009. The syntax-discourse interface in near-native L2 acquisition: Off-line and on-line performance. *Bilingualism: Language and Cognition*, 12/4. 463–483.

Housen, A., F. Kuiken, & I. Vedder (eds.). 2012. *Dimensions of L2 Performance and Proficiency: Complexity, Accuracy and Fluency in SLA*. Amsterdam: Benjamins.

Hudson, R. 2012. How many languages can a person learn? In: E. M. Rickerson & B. Hilton (eds.), *The Five-Minute Linguist. Bite-Sized Essays on Language and Languages*, 24. Sheffield: Equinox. 102–105.

Hulstijn, J. H. 2010. Linking L2 proficiency to L2 acquisition: Opportunities and challenges of profiling research. In: I. Bartning, M. Martin, and I. Vedder (eds.), *Communicative Proficiency and Linguistic Development. Intersections between SLA and Language Testing Research. Eurosla Monographs Series*, 1. 233–238.

Hyltenstam, K. 1992. Non-native features of near-native speakers. On the ultimate attainment of childhood L2 learners. In: R. J. Harris (ed.), *Cognitive Processing in Bilinguals*. Amsterdam: Elsevier Science. 351–368.

Hyltenstam, K. 2012. Critical period. In: C. Chapelle (ed.), *Encyclopedia of Applied Linguistics*. Wiley-Blackwell. DOI: 10.1002/9781405198431.wbeal0285.

Hyltenstam, K. & N. Abrahamsson. 2003. Maturational constraints in SLA. In: C. J. Doughty & M. H. Long (eds.), *Handbook of Second Language Acquisition*. Oxford: Blackwell. 539–588.

Long, M. 2003. Stabilization and fossilization in interlanguage development. In: C. J. Doughty & M. H. Long (eds.), *Handbook of Second Language Acquisition*. Oxford: Blackwell. 487–535.

Long, M. 2013. Maturational constraints in child and adult SLA. In: G. Granena & M. Long (eds.), *Sensitive Periods, Language Aptitude, and Ultimate Attainment*. Amsterdam: Benjamins. 3–41.

Muñoz, C. 2013. Age effects in SLA. In: P. Robinson (ed.), *Routledge Encyclopedia of SLA*. London: Routledge. 12–16.

Pienemann, Manfred. 1998. *Language Processing and Second Language Development: Processability Theory*. Amsterdam: John Benjamins.

Piller, I. 2002. Passing for a native speaker: Identity and success in second language learning. *Journal of Sociolinguistics*, 6/2. 179–206.

Sorace, A. 2003. Near-nativeness. In: C. J. Doughty & M. H. Long (eds.), *Handbook of Second Language Acquisition*. Oxford: Blackwell. 130–151.

Sorace, A. 2011. Pinning down the concept of "interface" in bilingualism. *Linguistic Approaches to Bilingualism*, 1/1. 1–33.

Tabri, D., K. M. Smith Abou Chacra, & T. Pring. 2011. Speech perception in noise by monolingual, bilingual and trilingual listeners. *International Journal of Language and Communication Disorders*, 46/4. 411–422.

Lars Fant
1 Pragmatic markers in high-level second language use

1 Introduction

Communicative proficiency in L2 use is a vague and multi-faceted notion which, although it undoubtedly needs to be unpacked in its manifold dimensions, has considerable psychological relevance as a holistic concept to both laymen and scholars. Establishing theoretical models for analysing communicative proficiency and defining the various sub-skills involved are indeed central concerns, not only for second language research, but also in psycho- and neurolinguistics and in many other linguistic sub-disciplines, as far as both theoretical study and applied investigation are concerned. For applied studies in the field of L2 learning, finding operational parameters for measuring L2 communicative proficiency must be considered a fundamental objective.

Studies on the acquisition and use of L2 grammar are considerably more abundant in the literature than work devoted to other fields of linguistics, among which the pragmatics of the second language was for a long time a neglected area. One field which combines a structural, lexical and a pragmatic approach is the study of pragmatic markers, which has been intensely investigated in past decades, but, as regards L2 use, has not been in scholarly focus until fairly recently.

Very advanced or near-native L2 use is an area which has received considerably less attention than the analysis of early acquisition in second language research. Not surprisingly, the use of pragmatic markers among very advanced or near-native L2 users is quite a recent concern with relatively few studies carried out so far. The study by Altenberg and Tapper (1998) stands out as a forerunner, although this field has in more recent years been represented to a great extent by work produced within the programme 'High-Level Proficiency in Second Language Use' at Stockholm University, such as Hancock (2007), Hancock and Sanell (2010), Hancock (2012), Fant and Hancock (2013), or Fant (2015).

Pragmatic markers can be investigated from many perspectives. One important aspect is their form/function mapping. Although pragmatic markers are not formally complex, in the sense that they hardly ever show any morphological alternation, their syntax and their often subtle meanings are, more often than

Lars Fant, Stockholm University

not, complex and thereby difficult to acquire, since there hardly exists any one-to-one relation between form and function. These properties contribute to the blurring of form-function mappings in L2 acquisition. Another aspect of pragmatic markers regards their role in creating discourse cohesion. Connective particles and markers of reported speech are directly concerned with macro-syntactic organization and the stratification of speech, and with the movement between different levels of discourse. Also, discourse boundary markers are essential for the speaker to be able to perform naturally in everyday conversation.

The definition and subcategorization of the class of pragmatic markers is a much debated issue. In this chapter, no particular stance will be taken as regards the overall taxonomy. Instead, three functional categories will be focused on: own-communication management, interaction management and argumentation management (section 2).

The use of certain classes of pragmatic markers directly affects fluency; thus, the class of meta-discursive markers is mainly involved with the regulation of speech fluency as well as turn-taking and feed-back management. Furthermore, an accurate use of all types of pragmatic markers can be regarded as contributing to idiomaticity in a wide sense. Different ways of understanding the notions of fluency and idiomaticity will be briefly discussed (sections 3 and 4), whereupon the topic of what causes non-targetlike traits to persist in the performance of highly proficient or even near-native L2 users will be addressed (section 5).

Thereupon, a case study will be presented in which features of the discourse produced in an interaction event taking place in Spanish between two native and two non-native (Swedish) highly proficient participants will be examined and interpreted in terms of idiomaticity and targetlikeness in the non-native participants' production (section 6). Insights following from the overview on research addressing pragmatic markers, idiomaticity, fluency and ultimate attainment will be combined with conclusions suggested by the case study in order to formulate new research questions and indicate needs for future research (section 7).

2 What categories could count as 'pragmatic markers'?

A beloved child is, as we know, liable to receiving many names. The category of words referred to by the philosopher John Locke in *An essay concerning human understanding* (1690, edited in 1959 by A.C. Fraser) as 'particles' – in modern times extended to include not only words but multi-word expressions – has been called many names: 'pragmatic markers' (preferred e.g. by Fraser 1996; Jucker and Ziv 1998; Aijmer and Simon-Vandenbergen 2006), 'pragmatic particles' (e.g. Östman 1995), 'discourse particles' (e.g. Hansen 1998), 'discourse markers' (e.g. Schiffrin 1987; Beeching and Detges 2014), or simply 'particles' (Wierzbicka 1986), just to mention the most common terms used in English, with a variety of terms in other languages. The question of how to label this category – more often than not perceived as rather a fuzzy one – is far from being an uncontroversial issue. It is closely connected with the question of how the category should be defined, which, in turn, also depends on what is to be exactly understood by key terms such as 'pragmatic' and 'discourse/discursive'.

The interest in the field throughout the past century has grown in what could be described as geometrical progression: after a few early representatives (among which Denniston's 1934 work on particles in Greek deserves special mention) there is a marked rise of interest taking place in the 1970s, and a virtual explosion in the 1990s and onwards. A number of comprehensive studies and volumes have been dedicated to the issue – e.g. the earlier mentioned study by Schiffrin (1987) or the Jucker and Ziv (1998) volume – as well as work offering broad views on the phenomenon in specific languages, e.g. Brinton (1996) for English, Hansen (1998, 2008) for French in a diachronic perspective, Dostie (2004) for Canadian French and Martín Zorraquino and Montolío (1998), or Martín Zorraquino and Portolés (1999), for Spanish.

Along with work which takes this broad perspective, there is a large number of studies devoted to specific items, or to limited sets of items, written in and/or dealing with a wide array of languages among which English is no longer overrepresented, e.g. the work by Fischer (2006), Aijmer and Simon-Vanderbergen (2006), Drescher and Frank-Job (2006) and Lauwers, Vanderbauwhede, and Verleyen (2010).

Some definitions of the category are broader than others. Schiffrin (1987) regards discourse markers as 'contextual coordinates' which create 'discursive coherence' (Schiffrin 1987: 330), and a similar stance is taken by Redeker (1990), who talks of these markers as linguistic expressions "used to signal the relation of an utterance to the immediate context" (Redeker 1990: 367). Fraser (1990) has a more restricted view, considering pragmatic markers as signals of "how the speaker intends the message following to relate to the foregoing discourse" (Fraser 1990: 394).

This latter definition brings the class close to what is commonly referred to as 'connectives' or 'connectors', while excluding e.g. expressions referring to the formulation or reformulation of speech, as do (more often than not) such English expressions as *you know* or *I mean*. In fact, connectives have so far been the most widely represented object of study in the field of second language acquisition and use of pragmatic particles. Granger and Tyson (1996), who investigated the underuse, overuse and misuse of connectors by French learners of English is one of the most representative studies in this domain; subsequently Granger (2002) has widened the scope by including five sub-corpora of L2 learner language, viz. with Dutch, French, German, Italian and Spanish learners. An important finding is that transfer plays a role in overuse (for instance, the overuse of in fact and indeed could be transfer of en fait from French. Similar conclusions were drawn by Hancock (2000) for advanced Swedish speakers of L2 French (above all the use of *mais* 'but' and *parce que* 'because').

If a wide definition of pragmatic particles is chosen, the object of study would be all kinds of expressions that are not an integrated part of the core syntactic or propositional argument structure, and which in some sense or another contribute to discursive and dialogic coherence. This perspective allows the inclusion of expressions that refer to formulation or reformulation and repair; however, it far from settles the issue of what should, and what should not, belong to the general class. The syntactic restriction 'not being part of the core syntactic structure' could, for instance, be questioned. What about adverbial expressions such as actually, which may or may not be syntactically integrated (compare *he actually told me that* and *he told me that, actually*), or the Germanic modal particles (such as Swedish *ju*, German *doch*, Danish *da*, Dutch *wel*, etc.), which are formally defined as being allotted a specific syntactic slot in the sentence? Clearly, however, even when these markers are embedded in surface syntax, they are not integrated in the propositional content of the utterance. In actual practice, different scholars follow different principles in treating these and other borderline cases.

The extent to which propositional/referential/core lexical meaning should be taken into account is another controversy among scholars. As an example, Schiffrin (1987: 63) and Redeker (1990: 1145) take opposite stances here, the former being more inclined towards including core meanings. From a historical linguistics perspective, in any case, this is bound to be a central concern. Traugott (1982) in a seminal article on the semantic and pragmatic aspects of grammaticalization claimed that lexical items take a unidirectional route from 'propositional' to 'expressive' meanings passing through 'textual' meanings. Hansen (1998, 2008) has developed this idea while providing detailed accounts of the ways in which expressions endowed with a clear propositional meaning develop into predominantly pragmatic markers which lend illocutionary force to a contiguous string; in a further development, both core semantic component and the pragmatic meaning will eventually erode and give rise to purely meta-discursive functions. This is what has happened, for instance, to French adverbs such as *b(i)en* or *enfin*.

The distinction between illocutionary and meta-discursive functions can readily translate into a distinction between markers considered to be 'argumentative' in nature and such markers as are involved in speech-planning, i.e. as part of the formulation and reformulation processes. The latter category has been treated by Levelt (1983) and later on accounted for extensively by Allwood, Nivre, and Ahlsén (1989), who coined the term 'speech-management markers'. Both studies include expressions such as mm or uh, which traditionally have not been attributed morphemic status but have rather been considered as 'vocalizations', a view rejected by Allwood et al (1989). In their study, speech management markers are divided into expressions of 'choice', including pre-formulation and hesitation markers, and expressions of 'change', which cover the category of reformulation markers.

Pre-formulation and hesitation markers have also been named 'editing markers' (Erman 2001; Denke 2005), in contradistinction to what Erman (2001) calls 'pragmatic markers' in a restricted sense, which roughly equals 'connectives'. The question is, admittedly, whether pre-formulation and hesitation can be regarded as contributing to discursive coherence strictly speaking, or as signaling the relation of utterances to their immediate context, and thereby qualifying as 'pragmatic' markers in Schiffrin's (1987) or Redeker's (1990) sense. Undeniably, they do the work of ensuring surface coherence by avoiding disruption in speech. Arguably, however, not only markers of pre-formulation, hesitation and reformulation, but also information-organizing expressions such as *incidentally, furthermore, first(ly)... second(ly),* or *on the one hand...on the other hand* could be considered instances of speakers' management of their own production. If these types are included, the category of speech management markers would no longer be restricted to spoken discourse but also include writing, which means the term 'speech management' becomes less accurate. This is, in fact, the reason why the scholars who originally coined this term have renamed it at a later stage 'own-communication management' (Allwood, Ahlsén, Nivre, and Larsson 1997), which will also be the term used henceforth in this chapter.

Along with argumentative and own-communication management markers, there is a third functional category that deserves special focus, namely markers of feedback or intersubjective management. Corresponding phenomena have been treated by several scholars under various headings, albeit seldom as a subcategory of discourse/pragmatic markers (particles). One extensive study which deserves special mention is Allwood, Nivre, and Ahlsén (1991), which treats feedback phenomena as indispensable components of dialogue. The feedback class contains several subcategories, such as feedback-givers (including back-channeling devices and minimal responses such as *aha, yeah, sure*), feedback-claimers (e.g. *isn't it? right?*), and attention claimers (e.g. *hey, look, listen*). From a pragmatic marker perspective, these devices for intersubjective/interpersonal management have often gone unnoticed by scholars, have been only partially dealt with, or have been misleadingly labelled. Thus, for instance, Martín Zorraquino and Portolés (1999) refer to all three subcategories simply as 'conversational markers', while feedback-claimers have been listed by Fraser (1996) under the somewhat confusing heading 'declarative-based hybrids'.

The present author regards pragmatic markers as devices for implementing different forms of 'modalization' in discourse (Fant 2005, 2007, 2011; Fant and Harvey 2008). In that framework, modalization is seen as a process which establishes scalar differences in various discourse domains, such as epistemicity (degree of credibility attributed to the utterance by the sender), formulation accuracy (degree of precision attributed by the sender to her/his formulation) and intersubjectivity (degree of common ground attributed by the speaker to her/his own, or to the interlocutor's, utterance, Fant 2011). Although modalization can be implemented by other means than pragmatic markers, most if not all pragmatic markers are used for modalization purposes. Thus, argumentative markers (henceforth AM) can be seen as epistemicity or evidentiality devices by assigning degrees of credibility to an utterance. Own-communication markers (henceforth OM), in turn, are largely speaker instruments for assigning degrees of formulation accuracy, and, finally, most interaction management markers (henceforth IM) are tools for assessing degrees of intersubjectivity.

The three highlighted categories – argumentation markers (AM), own-communication management markers (OM) and interaction management markers (IM) – may not cover all instances of pragmatic markers but most certainly include the vast majority of them. They are the categories focussed on in the case study included in section 6 of this chapter. It should be emphasized, however, that these are functional classes which typically include given lexical items from an onomasiological perspective, which is to say that they should not be interpreted semasiologically, as listings of particular lexical items. This has to do with the fact that individual pragmatic markers more often than not are multi-functional[1], which is to say that not only can one and the same item (type) belong to separate functional categories depending on the context, but also that one and the same occurrence may combine two or several functions in the given context. A marker such as *of course* will, for instance, do the work

---

[1] This is a point of controversy among scholars. Thus Östman (1995: 101–103) vividly argues against the idea of multifunctionality among pragmatic markers. See also Denke (2005: 63).

of a feedback giver (interaction management), either in isolation (*Will you be at work tomorrow? – Of course, why do you ask?*), or in combination with yes (*Will you? – Yes of course*). In the same context, however, of course also acquires an argumentative function by adding credibility to the response utterance. In other contexts, of course will have only an argumentative value – and not necessarily one that strengthens the speaker's line of argumentation. In an utterance such as of course we never thought of it that way, a concession granted to the interlocutor's stance is a more likely interpretation.

In sum, a series of classificatory systems for pragmatic/discursive markers (particles) have been proposed by a number of scholars. These systems may seem contradictory but become largely compatible once we start looking beyond terminology. Which categories are to be excluded or included remains, however, an issue where no consensus has hitherto been attained. The classification suggested here, which is based on a communicative-needs perspective, will be further discussed in connection with the case study accounted for in section 6.

3 Fluency and pragmatic markers in L2 performance

Pragmatic markers are undoubtedly an indispensable tool for enhancing performance and fluency both in L1 and L2 speech. The notion of fluency is, however, far from being unequivocal. In an early seminal study, Fillmore (1979) conceptualized fluency broadly, including both 'local' abilities, such as producing long stretches of talk with few disruptions, and more 'global' abilities, such as getting messages across in a coherent manner, and knowing what expressions to select in a wide range of contexts. In this latter sense, Fillmore's understanding of fluency comes close to that of idiomaticity manifested in e.g. Fillmore et al (1988).

Both Fillmore (1979) and Pawley and Syder (1983) have focused their attention on fluency in speech, where such phenomena as hesitation markers, filled or unfilled pauses, repairs and frequent use of 'fillers' have often been considered indicators of disfluency in non-native speech. An important forerunner as concerns L2 use of pragmatic particles used for enhancing fluency is the psycholinguistics-based study by Towell, Hawkins, and Bazergui (1996) concerning advanced French L2 learners' access to frequent pragmatic markers in French ('organizers' and 'fillers') which are part of the procedural knowledge and thus contribute to fluency. Also Trosborg (1995) in a study addressing L2 English evaluates these and similar phenomena positively as 'communication strategies' used for building up a so-called strategic competence in L2 learners by means of which they can overcome difficulties in word searches and construction selection. On the other hand, an L2 speaker's relative overuse of these strategies could again be regarded negatively as a manifestation of imperfect fluency.

It deserves mentioning, in this context, that pragmatic markers are not a frequent token of (second or foreign) language instruction but more often than not seem to be acquired incidentally (Paradis 2009), in contrast to most grammar and much vocabulary in contexts of language teaching (which is not to say that there are no good arguments for teaching pragmatics, including the use of pragmatic marker, in the classroom; for a clarifying discussion on this issue, see Bardovi-Harlig 2001). This circumstance can be seen as facilitating the comparison between L1 and L2 use, given that the 'instruction effect' is largely neutralized as an interfering factor.

The focus on L2 learning in connection with fluency may have obscured the fact that also L1 users may vary considerably in their skills. From this perspective, hesitation markers, repairs or fillers, far from being considered mere signs of disfluency (i.e., as tokens of imperfection), may be understood as tools by means of which both L1 and L2 speakers normally regulate their flow of speech, namely as 'own-communication management' devices in the terms of Allwood et al (1997). These devices can have more far-reaching effects, since the regulation of speech flow may serve purposes in the domain of politeness or impression management, particularly as mitigation tools. Trosborg's (1995) SLA-related communication strategies could then be reconceptualized as strategies for all language users, the difference between L2 and L1 speakers consisting of the range of devices used, their frequencies, and the degree to which they bear marks of targetlike (=idiomatic) selection.

Regarding fluency as a variable with expected ranges both for L1 and L2 users would, among other things, lead us to conclude that, in order to assess the fluency of a (hopefully well-defined) set of L2 users by comparing it to that of native users, fairly large populations will have to be investigated. In turn, a plausible hypothesis following from this would be that fluency in an individual's second language performance may well depend on, and correlate positively with, the fluency of their L1. Strong support for this hypothesis has been found e.g. by Towell and Dewaele (2005), and Mirdamadi and de Jong (2014).

The degree to which non-native speakers are fluent, technically speaking as objectively measured through a set of parameters, does not necessarily have to coincide with the extent to which they are perceived as such. An overuse of hesitations, repairs and other tokens of disfluency may well go unnoticed if the L2 speaker's production is targetlike in other respects, e.g. phonetic accent, lexical diversity, or syntactic complexity. Rather, such speakers will not be seen as distinct from L1 speakers who would manifest disfluent speech (about native speakers' ability to discriminate near-natives from natives in perception tests, see e.g. Abrahamsson and Hyltenstam 2009: 266–279).

In a study on language teachers' perception of fluency in foreign language students (Kormos and Dénes 2004), the authors found that phenomena such as accuracy or lexical diversity were more important in the assessment of fluency than local disfluency phenomena of the mentioned kind. Similar conclusions were reached by Bosker, Quené, Sanders, and de Jong (2014).

Fluency is, after all, a multi-faceted notion which somehow resists unequivocal operationalizing. There are quite a few fluency measures, such as speech rate, mean length of runs, mean syllable duration, mean pause duration, and number of silent pauses per time unit, just to name a few. A 'high' on the three latter measures would then relate to lack of fluency, whereas a high speech rate and a high mean length of runs would be positive indices of fluency which take a more holistic stance on speech production. A terminological suggestion would be to refer to one type as 'disfluency phenomena' and to the other, in line with de Jong and Perfetti (2011), as 'proceduralization phenomena'.

4 Idiomaticity and pragmatic markers in L2 performance

Pawley and Syder (1983) have addressed both fluency and idiomaticity as constituting puzzles for linguistic theory. The authors, who see a close connection between the two phenomena, refer to idiomaticity as 'targetlike selection' while claiming, with regard to fluency, that the vast number of lexical phrases and 'sentence stems' (=formulae) that native speakers know is also what will surface as targetlike fluency in their language use. They admit, however, that the connection between phrases/stems and fluency is only a claim and "can be tested only be examining spoken discourse" (Pawley and Syder 1983: 214).

Defining idiomaticity as 'targetlike selection', as do Pawley and Syder (1983), implies a broad view of the issue, which is based on the semantic value of 'idiom(atic)' as "linguistic usage that is grammatical and natural for native speakers of a language" (definition given in Collins English Dictionary, 1995 ed.). A much-quoted study by Sinclair (1991), in which the 'idiom principle' is seen as opposed to what has later been termed the 'open choice principle' (Erman and Warren 2000), concludes that since expressions of the former kind are easier and more economical to process, they will also be preferred by native speakers. This is perhaps the most important assumption that underlies the restricted conceptualization of idiomaticity, which in turn constitutes the basis for a whole linguistic sub-discipline devoted to formulaicity and multi-word expressions[2], with important theoretical work such as Erman and Warren (2000), Wray (2002) or Schmitt (2004). For a discussion on uses of formulaic language in highly proficient L2 users, see also Erman, Forsberg Lundell, and Lewis (this volume).

Formulaic expressions have indeed been an important concern in SLA research since the 1990s. Weinert's (1995) study is an early seminal work. Granger (1998), which addresses formulaic expressions in writing, is another early important contribution to the field. A high proportion of earlier as well as later studies are based on large corpora, e.g. Grant (2003) and Wiktorsson (2003).

Undoubtedly, formulaic language covers a substantial portion of what can be regarded as idiomaticity phenomena. An alternative – or, at least, complementary – approach is offered by the school of construction grammar: constructions formed in accordance with targetlike use may indeed be regarded as manifestations of idiomaticity. Warren (2005), who embraces a broad view on idiomaticity, suggests a general classification model according to which not only targetlike selection of expressions is taken into account but also all that "which one has to know over and above rules and words" (Warren 2005: 35), the latter formulation sharing the perspective taken by Fillmore, Kay and O'Connor (1988) on the English formula let alone. Three categories of phenomena are included in Warren's classification: information-organizing patterns (text level), clausal idioms (sentence level) and collocations (phrase level).

Warren's (2005) model is helpful in order to reach a global understanding of the notion of idiomaticity. While the categories 'clausal idioms' and 'collocations' can be seen as covering the area of formulaic language in her model, the concept of 'information-organizing patterns' may be in need of further specification. By including the suggested construction grammar perspective, a broad sense of idiomaticity could be said to encompass targetlike (1) construction choice, (2) routines of information packaging, and (3) command of formulaic expressions. In the case study of section 5, the third area – formulaicity – will be one of the topics addressed.

Not only with regard to fluency, but also to idiomaticity, restricted understandings should be kept separate from broader ones. A broad view on idiomaticity would lead to including comprehensive phenomena such as construction

---

[2] Different terms are used to cover the notion of formulae or multi-word expressions. Thus, e.g., Erman and Warren (2002) use 'prefabricated expressions' and Granger (1998) uses 'prefabricated patterns'.

choice, or information selection and packaging in e.g. event construal, whereas the narrower view would focus on formulaicity alone. For the study of non-native as well as native use of pragmatic markers, the latter perspective is arguably the most relevant. Denke's (2005) work on pragmatic markers in English L2 shows interesting differences between native and non-native use of the markers *you know*, *well* and *I mean* in monologic speech. The natives of her study use the markers in a varied way, whereas the non-native speakers use them primarily as hesitation ('editing') markers.

5 Pragmatic performance in highly proficient L2 users

Studies in L2 pragmatics have shown that pragmatic markers are not always acquired in ways that adequately reflect usage in the target language. In Yoshimi's (2001) study on L2 learners' use of the Japanese narrative-structuring markers *n desu*, *n desu ne* and *n desu kedo* (these markers, according to the framework presented in section 2, would constitute combined interaction management and own-communication management markers), the subjects succeeded well in using at least some functions of *n desu*, the cognitively least complex marker of the three, while the two more complex markers were less effectively used overall. Another example is Siegal's (1994) study of American students learning Japanese in an immersion situation, where one subject would avoid using honorifics belonging to specific speech registers (see also Siegal 1996).

A justified question, in connection with the notions of fluency and idiomaticity, is whether the use of pragmatic markers in general, or at least specific subcategories of pragmatic markers, constitutes a particularly sophisticated domain of L2 learning which is not fully acquired until late, if at all. In this respect, Fant and Hancock (2013) and Fant (2015) have shown subtle limitations in the production of highly proficient (Swedish) speakers of L2 French and Spanish: elaborate uses of frequent pragmatic particles, albeit represented to a certain extent in the non-native speakers' production, are not at all as frequent among them as among the native speakers. This indicates something which could be called 'cautiousness' on behalf of the non-natives, who seem to prefer sticking to more conventional uses.

The above question, in turn, evokes a more general issue, viz. which domains of language structure and use offer such resistance to learners that they will reach a full command of them only at very late stages, if at all (for an overview, see Bartning this volume).

In connection with cognitive explanations for what can be seen as shortcomings in L2 use, it may also prove fruitful to include findings by proponents of so-called 'task-based language teaching', to the effect that the nature of the task performed by L2 learners in settings of formal instruction may have far-reaching effects on their performance. The 'cognition hypothesis' suggested by Robinson (2005) predicts that more complex tasks will yield more accurate and more complex L2 performance, and that interactivity (dialogic tasks) will increase the level of accuracy. Task variation in language teaching is interesting in the sense that it points at a very basic variable in human communication, namely that of genres or activity types. The extent to which L2 users would manifest various degrees of complexity, accuracy and fluency depending on which real-life genre or activity type they are momentarily engaged in is a research field in need of further exploration.

Does the impressive amount of evidence for cognitive obstacles to L2 development – in particular in terms of maturational constraints (Abrahamsson and Hyltenstam 2009) – leave any room for social-psychological or sociocultural explanations regarding limited endstates? The answer is a qualified yes: contributions to this effect are to be found in the research area of L2 pragmatic development, particularly in studies addressing individual differences (for an overview of such studies, see Kasper and Rose 2001: 275–303). Social identity, including effects of age and gender, must be regarded as an important component in language learning (Ochs 1993). Also, such mixed social and psychological phenomena as motivation and social-psychological distance are factors that deserve to be taken into account at all levels of second language acquisition, including very advanced stages. One hypothesis which has found some empirical support concerns the degree of affiliation to (or acculturation into) the target community, or, from a motivation studies perspective, the degree of 'integrative' motivation (Dörnyei 1990, 2010); these factors will affect the degree to which L1 practices will be retained or new L2 practices will be acquired. Examples of this strand of research are Schmidt's (1983) developmental study on 'Wes', a Japanese user of L2 English, or Kim's (2000) doctoral dissertation on Korean subjects learning English in the US. The role that motivation plays for the extent to which, and ways in which, students of L2 Japanese pay attention to pragmatic features in Japanese has been investigated by Takahashi (2001), who found that the students' success in noticing these features depended more on motivation than on variables of linguistic proficiency.

Siegal's (1994, 1996) earlier mentioned work on Americans learning Japanese in Japan, a study based mainly on naturalistic data, gives revealing insights about sociological and psychological factors which may influence L2 learners' pragmatic performance. In a conversation that 'Mary', one of the subjects in this study, had with her teacher, the subject deviated in several regards from what, in a Japanese monocultural setting, would be regarded as the expected behaviour for a woman and for an academic supervisee, and this happened in spite of her being an otherwise highly proficient speaker. The author suggests that her subject, rather than being unaware of the appropriate politeness strategies, chose not to put them into practice since that would have amounted to denying her self-image. In this sense, an identity construal built on primary socialization may become an obstacle to targetlike behaviour in certain situations, or with regard to specific linguistic items.

Other factors, too, may contribute to behaviour and practices in L2 users which are not fully accommodated to L1 patterns. L2 users who live in a bilingual and bicultural environment may develop specific mixed or intercultural styles in their linguistic and discursive practices; several reports of this effect have been given, among others Clyne (1994), Blum-Kulka (1997), and House and Kasper (2000). Another factor is to do with native speakers' expectations of non-natives. These may be expected to behave in a more conformist manner than natives; in fact, the mere perception of the interlocutor as a foreigner may trigger such expectations. Natives may even prefer non-natives to act 'like foreigners' and reject – overtly or covertly – certain types of targetlike behaviour detected in their non-native interlocutors. For reports on such effects, see Siegal (1994) and Iino (1996).

Finally, returning to the issue of high-level L2 use of pragmatic markers, the question remains: what do we know today from studies that focus directly on the learning and use of pragmatic markers, especially when the L2 is culturally not as distant from the L1 as Japanese is from English? In Denke (2005), the non-native subjects studied, who could best be described as mid-advanced learners (corresponding to levels B2 or C1 in the CEFR system; Council of Europe 2001), had a comparatively targetlike command of a number of markers, a majority of which pertained to a colloquial register. However, the fact that the frequencies in L2 speakers exceeded, more often than not, those of the L1 English subjects shows that the L2 participants used a number of colloquial markers (e.g. *y' know* or *I mean*) as communication strategies in formulation search, or even as 'fillers'. Lindqvist (forthc.), whose subjects are largely intermediate-level learners of Spanish reaching the B1 level in the CEFR system (Council of Europe 2001) who were recorded at two occasions during a four-month stay in Spain, reports a less frequent and less diversified use of meta-discursive markers in her participants than in the native speakers they interact with, and, as far as the developmental process is concerned, coins the principle 'one at a time and in as many functions as possible'. This is to say that pragmatic markers tend to be learned in a specific order, that each newly learned marker tends to become overused, and that each tends to overshadow the previously learned. An interesting issue, then, is which pragmatic marker subcategories will be most easily used in a targetlike way among highly proficient L2 speakers.

6 Highly proficient L2 speakers' use of pragmatic markers in interaction with L1 speakers: a case study

What will highly proficient L2 users' performance be like in a setting where they interact with native speakers in a professional activity where high verbal proficiency is required and in which both native and non-native participants are under pressure to deliver good results? The event analysed in this section can hopefully give us a few hints about what the strengths and weaknesses of very proficient non-native users in spontaneous interaction may be, as well as to what extent, and in which respects, their production can be perceived, and understood, as targetlike.

The data under study is a video-recording and transcription of a simulated negotiation[3] carried out in Spanish, in Spain, between a "team" of two Spanish and a "team" of two Swedish business people. Each team consisted of a female and a male participant in their early forties, all with a solid professional background where formal negotiations are an important ingredient. The members within each team knew each other well and across the teams, the respective members had had earlier professional contacts. The Swedish participants stood out as highly proficient users of Spanish: not only had they received previous instruction in the language at university level but they also had been working in Spain for several years and were well integrated into Spanish society. They can arguably be described as near-native L2 users with a proficiency level on relevant measures reaching the C2 level of the CEFR scale (Council of Europe 2001). Among other things observed, the Swedish participants were found to make remarkably few formal mistakes: altogether 18 grammatical inaccuracies were found, which yields a frequency of 0.76 per 100 words – a low figure indeed for L2 speakers (for the native participants, the corresponding figure was 0.11 inaccuracies per 100 words).

---

[3] For a broad overview of role play and simulations as pragmatic tasks, see Félix-Brasdefer (2010), and Bardovi-Harlig (2013). For a discussion on the validity of using role play in data collection, see also Fant (1992).

The simulated situation was one where a "Research department" of a supposedly multinational industry is confronted with the "Development department" in order to decide when to time the launching of a new product. The respective parties were expected to have goals and interests that were not quite easy to align. In fact, in this event, at the end of a 35-minute long encounter, the parties had only managed to agree on one point: to meet again a few days later "after consulting the engineers and the sales department". The atmosphere can be described as friendly while highly competitive and argumentative, and all participants were found to make an elaborate use of their professional negotiation skills.

During the 35 minutes that the encounter lasted, 5,866 words were produced, of which 59% were produced by the native team and 41% by the non-native team. This imbalance between the teams did not reflect any deficiency in the Swedes' command of Spanish but rather the 'sociology' of the event, with one Swedish negotiator taking a leading part while the other acted as a support, whereas the Spanish negotiators had a more equal distribution of turns and were more competitive among themselves.

6.1 Fluency, complexity, idiomaticity

One divergence between the parties was found that could be naturally interpreted as reflecting differences in fluency level, viz. that the non-native participants produced more than twice as many speech-planning sequences as did the natives (covering 274 as compared to 119 words). This comparatively high frequency of speech-planning moves – albeit hardly perceivable by a non-trained bystander – could well indicate that the L2 speakers experience some obstacles in formulating themselves. The situation is one where the participants are expected to argue convincingly for their cause, and it would hardly be surprising that communicative stress of this kind would affect non-native speakers more negatively than native speakers. On the other hand, the non-native participants' more frequently occurring speech-planning moves could also be regarded as a communication strategy (Trosborg 1995; see section 3). Since we have no control data with the same subjects under more relaxed circumstances, we cannot, however, ascertain that this albeit limited lack of fluency would not characterize their L2 performance overall.

An interesting observation regards the natives producing a strikingly higher amount of off-turn sequences (= utterances produced without the speaker having been granted the turn by the floor-holding speaker, see Sacks, Schegloff, and Jefferson, 1974, or Edelsky, 1981); thus, 180 words were produced off-turn by the natives as compared to 29 by the non-natives. In particular, the native participants tended to give feedback signals off-turn, which can be seen as a floor-seizing strategy. This difference could give rise to various interpretations: one is that non-natives can be expected to behave in a more canonical and rule-observing manner with regard to a number of parameters, among which turn-taking is one; another is that internalized cultural patterns make Swedes behave in a more rule-respecting way than Spaniards with regard to turn-taking (cf. Fant 1989 and 1995, Fant and Grindsted 1995a and 1995b, Villemoes 1995 and 2003, Bravo 1998).

If the L2 speakers' fluency could be interpreted as not attaining the L1 speakers' level, then what about complexity? Although no measurement was undertaken of syntactic complexity at sentence level, some indications can be given regarding complexity at text level. Thus, each team's production of turns and turn-constructional units (TCUs) roughly parallels that of their word production, which is to say that their similar words-per-turn and words-per-TCU ratios reflect similar levels of discourse complexity. This, in turn, points at a high degree of proceduralization in the non-native participants' speech, which should be seen in contrast to disfluency manifestations such as the earlier-mentioned higher rate of speech-planning moves, or disruptive events as reported below, (6.2.B).

In order to assess the lexical proficiency of the Swedish participants, two criteria were added, namely lexical density, and formulaicity. A sample of 1,000 words of speech from each team (altogether. 2,000 out of 5,966 words) was then extracted from the mid-section of the event while excluding its beginning and end. With regard to their lexical density, these samples were practically identical: the lemma/token ratio was 0.244 for the natives and 0.237 for the non-natives, and their distribution on frequency bands was also very similar.

As for the level of formulaicity (or 'idiomaticity' in a restricted sense, see section 4), multiword expressions were identified in both samples. The expressions were subdivided into three groups, in line with the analysis proposed by Erman and Warren (2000): referential/denotative, grammatical, and discursive formulae. Here again, the overall figures are practically identical for both groups, not only with regard to overall type/token ratio but also the ratios for the three subcategories.

Could it be the case, then, that the non-native speakers' level of idiomaticity equaled that of the native speakers? The answer would be a somewhat qualified yes. The non-natives produced a small though not entirely negligible amount of non-idiomatic formulae ("attempted" formulaic expressions, in the terms of Yorio 1989 and Lewis 2008), viz. 3.4% of the total amount. Secondly, a divergence between the groups could be perceived regarding the length of the referential formulae: the natives produced a larger number of longer formulae, consisting of 4 words or more, than did the non-natives (14 vs. 10).

6.2 Use of pragmatic markers

In the above-mentioned 2 × 1,000 word sample, three categories of pragmatic markers were identified and counted: interaction management markers (IM), own-communication management markers (OM) and argumentation markers (AM). Overlaps between the categories are not uncommon. Expressions such as *claro* 'of course' and *exactamente* 'exactly' function more often than not as feedback givers (=IM) and argumentative intensifiers (=AM) at the same time. Also, a marker such as *bueno* 'well' can be a minimal response (=IM), a hesitation marker (=OM) and a signal of distance-taking (=AM), depending on the context, or even combined in one and the same token. A consequence of this multifunctionality, in the current context, is that the same occurrence may at times be listed twice or more, under separate headings.

A. Interaction management. IM markers can be either initiative moves (feedback and attention claimers) or response moves (feedback givers). The latter can be divided into turn-initiating minimal responses and turn-internal back-channeling expressions. Depending on context, most types of response markers can function in either way (e.g. *sí* 'yes', *ya* 'okay', or *mhm*). The figures show that the distribution of types is very similar between the groups, while the token frequencies are not: altogether, the natives produced 49 IM markers distributed over 16 types, as compared to 29 IM markers (12 types) for the non-natives. The most salient difference between the groups thus consists of the intensity of the interpersonal/intersubjective management performed.

A less conspicuous though quite interesting feature is that attention claimers – which should be considered to possess stronger initiatory properties than feedback claimers – were produced only by the native participants. Furthermore, a semantic analysis of the markers shows that only the native participants produced intensifying responses such as *hombre* 'man', *por supuesto* 'sure, of course', or *exactamente* 'exactly'. Conversely, only the non-natives produced concessive and mitigating expressions such as *bueno sí* 'well yes' or *sí bien* 'yes okay then'. Whether this is to be ascribed to differences in linguistic competence, cultural preferences, or simply the dynamics and role-distribution of this particular event remains an open question; earlier research on the communicative behaviour of Scandinavian and Spanish negotiators (Fant 1989, 1995; Fant and Grindsted 1995a, 1995b; Villemoes 1995, 2003) would, however, lend support to a cultural explanation.

B. Own-communication management. With regard to OM markers, the overall divergence between natives and non-natives is by no means spectacular, the main difference being the type/token ratio, which is clearly lower for the non-natives (0.24) than for the natives (0.47), which means the former use a wider array of markers. This may be interpreted as reflecting a lower degree of idiomaticity in the non-natives since these may be more uncertain about which expression is to be preferred, or the most conventionally used, in a given context type (cf. Blum-Kulka, House, and Kasper 1989; see also Forsberg Lundell and Erman 2012).

Salient differences can be found in the distribution of specific OM sub-categories. As for hesitation/repair markers, the non-native participants produced 31 tokens distributed over 5 types, whereas the natives produced only 10 tokens and 4 types. This result in well in line with the finding in section 5.1 which indicates a higher degree of disfluency in the non-natives. It does not, however, indicate that the underlying speech planning capacity of the non-native would be inferior, since we cannot know the extent to which these negotiators, acting out of socio-pragmatic motives such as unwillingness to impose, chose to make extensive use of hesitations, repairs, reformulations or other mitigating markers of formulation accuracy. To complicate the issue further, this may not even be a matter of more or less conscious choice, but an effect of applying automatized conversational routines, which, in turn may vary considerably among individuals.

With regard to intensifying OM expressions, there were clear divergences between the groups: the Swedes produced only one token (*claro* 'of course'), in sharp contrast to the Spaniards' 18 tokens distributed over 8 types. Once again, the Spaniards' tendency of maximizing the affirmative and affective force of their verbal contributions is opposed to the Swedes' tendency of keeping a low emotive profile. Here, as with regard to IM initiatives, earlier findings (e.g. Fant 1995, 2006; Villemoes 1995) lend support to cultural explanations.

As a yardstick of disfluency, an alternative to counting occurrences of verbal OM markers is to consider disruption at word- or utterance level. Four types of micro-events were taken into account: (1) false starts, (2) self-interrupted and repaired words or expressions within a turn-constructional unit (TCU), (3) repaired whole turn-constructional units, and (4) abandoned turns. Altogether, disruptive micro-events took place more than three times as often in the non-native as in the native participants' speech (69 occurrences as compared to 22) with largely the same proportion in all four sub-types (appr. 3 to 1). Once again we find that the highly proficient non-natives in our case study are more disfluent than the natives. Moreover, disruptive phenomena of this kind could hardly be attributed to strategic choice as would many occurrences of 'fillers' such as *uh* or *I mean*.

C. Argumentation management. The AM markers were subdivided into three main classes: (1) intensifying (e.g. *realmente* 'really') and mitigating (e.g. *quizá* 'perhaps') expressions; (2) connectives which indicate the direction of an argumentative move (additive as in *también* 'also', adversative as in *pero* 'but', causal as in *porque* 'because', or conditional as in *en caso de que* 'provided'); (3) evidential expressions, consisting of either co-referentials, which locate the source of argumentative moves in the preceding discourse (e.g. *entonces* 'then', *por eso* 'for that reason'), or exophoric markers, which locate the source of argumentative moves outside the immediate co-text (e.g. *obviamente* 'obviously', *sabemos que* 'we know that').

Altogether, the native negotiators were shown to produce more than twice as many tokens (239/102) and almost twice as many types (80/47) as the non-natives. The most striking difference was to be found in the category of intensifiers, with the natives producing eight times as many occurrences as the non-natives (42/5). The same explanation could be given here as for the intensifying expressions of the IM and OM categories.

An aspect which becomes more relevant in connection with AM markers than with the other two classes is what could be labelled 'cognitive complexity' (Fant and Hancock 2013; Fant 2014). It makes sense assuming that the more complex the type of expression, the greater the challenge will be for a L2 learner to master it, and the greater the likelihood of imperfect learning. The AM sub-categories could in fact be conceived of as a hierarchy of cognitive complexity, ranging from 'low' (intensifiers and mitigators) via 'mid' (connectives) to 'high' (exophorics), provided cognitive complexity is seen in virtue of the degree of immediacy to be inferred between the pragmatic marker and the unit it operates on. Thus, intensifiers and mitigators operate on an intra-clausal or even phrasal level, whereas connectives operate on an inter-clausal, and co-referentials on an inter-sentential level. Exophorics, finally, make reference to assumed knowledge which is unexpressed in the immediate co-text and which oblige speakers to conceptualize information as generally known (e.g. *obviamente* 'obviously'), shared with the hearer (e.g. *como bien sabes* 'as you may well know'), or known only by themselves (e.g. *lo que pasa es que* 'what happens is that'), and can therefore be said to operate on the encompassing text level.

This 'cognitive complexity hypothesis' could well match the discrepancies found between the native and the non-native participants. Thus, with regard to AM markers, there seem to be reasons for testing the 'cognitive complexity' hypothesis in future research based on a larger amount of data. Needless to say, other parameters will have to be considered, too. Social-psychological and cultural factors – in particular preferences for different argumentative styles – can be expected to be relevant, not only for the selection and use of AM markers, but also for other types of pragmatic markers, and for information packaging and organisation in general.

6.3 Discussion of the findings

Although this case study is based on very limited data which do not permit any generalizations to be drawn, it does, however, provide some hints capable of affording hypotheses for future research.

With regard to features such as formal accuracy, complexity, lexical density and formulaicity, the non-native participants in this event largely seem to behave like their native counterparts. Their rate of disfluency clearly exceeds that of the natives, although their proceduralization capacity in terms of words per TCU, or TCUs per turn, does not appear to be inferior.

With regard to their use of pragmatic markers, the non-native participants resemble their native counterparts to different degrees depending on which specific subcategory is involved. In their use of IM markers they behave in a less intense and more mitigating manner than their native counterparts, and they also produce less off-turn back-channeling than the natives. All these features could be accounted for by cultural explanations and are not necessarily representative of L2 performance in general.

As regards OM markers, more visible differences appear. The non-natives produce considerably more hesitation and repair markers than the natives, which seemingly reflects a lower fluency level, although this difference could again be ascribed to cultural preferences. Also, their greater use of mitigators and more restricted use of intensifiers may be interpreted as reflecting underlying cultural patterns.

AM markers are the category which yields the most salient discrepancies. Here, both token quantity and type density are considerably lower in the non-native than in the native participants. Intensifiers are much less frequent in the speech of the non-native participants, which again may be explained in terms of cultural preferences. Furthermore, if the relation between intensifying/mitigating, connective, co-referential and exophoric AMs is understood as representing a rising scale of cognitive complexity, the non-native speakers' underuse of the more complex categories could be interpreted as reflecting a shortcoming in their L2 command.

A hypothesis to be tested in future research could be that IM markers are more easily acquired for production purposes than OM markers, which in turn are more easily acquired than AM markers. If this scale is corroborated, various explanations could be suggested, one of which would involve levels of speech-planning. IM markers, and to a large extent also OM markers, mainly depend on local planning. Local speech-planning devices presumably constitute highly routinized and entrenched strategies in both native and non-native speakers and will often surface as 'fillers'. Although many AM markers undoubtedly can be used as 'fillers', an accurate use of most AM markers requires planning at a global level, which is to say that not only formulating but also conceptualizing activity will be involved, and more extensive strings of speech will be comprised. Presumably, speech-planning is cognitively more demanding on a global than on a local level, since more elaborate and comprehensive routines have to be activated. Global planning could therefore be expected to constitute more of a challenge to L2 than to L1 speakers, and when speakers fall short of global planning, their formulation of argumentative markers is likely to get impaired (all, of course, seen in relative terms).

Shortcomings in global planning will also affect local planning and give rise to hesitations, reformulations or self-interruptions, leaving TCUs or whole turns unfinished. Both phenomena – a less elaborate use of argumentative devices, and inadequate fluency – are clearly manifest in the speech of the non-native participants of this case study, which lends support to the claim that even highly proficient non-native users may have difficulties in attaining the planning capacity characteristic of L1 users.

7 Desiderata, questions and hypotheses for future research

Given a plausible typology of pragmatic markers while taking into account parameters such as idiomaticity and fluency, what do we know about the non-native use of these expressions? More specifically, considering the state of present-day knowledge of endstates and obstacles to targetlike attainment, what can be said about the degree to which very proficient or even near-native speakers and writers can be expected to use various classes of pragmatic markers in a targetlike manner? Frankly speaking, fairly little, and certainly less than what we know in the domain of morphology, syntax, information structure, or even pragmalinguistic routines.

More studies will be needed regarding both the development of pragmatic markers in learners and advanced or near-native use. Elaborating the semantic analysis of individual markers, as well as of groups and classes, is also among the desiderata for future research, since, if we do not know enough about components and complexity in markers, we will have difficulties in formulating hypothesis about what will, and what will not, constitute learning difficulties. More generally speaking, since research on pragmatic markers has been pursued on observational and descriptive levels, or for purely classificatory purposes, more theoretical work providing explanations for their occurrence and use is called for. In particular, more psycholinguistically or cognitively oriented studies will be necessary in order to find out e.g. how pragmatic markers are processed in L1 users, and whether this happens in different ways in L2 users.

Task and genre variation is another important domain for future research: in which ways will different activity types, tasks and genres afford different behaviour, and different levels of proficiency, in non-natives (see e.g. Bardovi-Harlig 2013)? Could it, for instance, be hypothesized that a non-native speaker, when put under pressure to perform rapidly and accurately, will do better than in a more relaxed kind of task? Or is it the other way round? Or is there considerable individual variation to be found in this respect?

Given that certain findings in L2 pragmatics point to sociocultural and sociopragmatic factors, such as identity defence and established politeness routines in the L1 (see e.g. Félix-Brasdefer 2008), as obstacles to learning L2 patterns, intercultural aspects deserve to be examined more closely, and in a wider range of L1/L2 combinations. A plausible hypothesis would be that sociocultural divergences with regard to pragmatic routines in general, and the use of discursive particles in particular, would be more serious obstacles to targetlike behaviour than would typological-structural differences.

The question of which research orientations would be most suitable for the kind of studies involved would certainly benefit from more discussion. In this regard, one parameter is what Ellis (1994) refers to as hierarchical (theory-driven) vs. concatenative (research-question based) research. Although a good mixture of both should be regarded as desirable, generally speaking, the relative lack of theoretical work in the domain of pragmatic markers indicates a need for more theoretical-driven research.

As a result of the discussion on types of research, types of data, cognitive vs. sociocultural approaches, and the importance of task/genre variation, a number of question-hypothesis pairings emerge. One concern is which general categories of pragmatic markers are easier or more difficult to acquire. The results from the included case study suggest that for highly proficient users, interaction management (IM) markers do not constitute any greater difficulty (although that remains to be proven, also for other L1/L2 pairs than Swedish/Spanish). Own-communication management (OM) markers appear to present somewhat greater difficulties for learners, although it can be suspected that in the language pair at stake (Spanish L2/Swedish L1), routinized socio-pragmatic preferences in the L1 may play an important part. Argumentative (AM) markers, finally, seem to constitute the greatest challenge even to highly proficient L2 users, although the complexity inherent in this category would require a more fine-grained analysis of the features and feature combinations involved.

Corollary questions concern the various sociocultural factors that may constitute obstacles to learning, and, on the other hand, what cognitive features and mechanisms may account for why some pragmatic markers are scarce in L2 production, and what makes "difficult" markers difficult. One hypothesis would indicate the degree of semantic-cognitive complexity as a determining factor, although it could be objected that the concept of semantic-cognitive complexity would have to be made clearer. The degree of transferability of the marker from the L1 involved constitutes another natural hypothesis; here, in turn, transferability is a concept which would require further analysis.

A question following from insights about ultimate attainment is whether one could trace any clear tendencies as regards stabilization in the acquisition of pragmatic markers (cf. Long 2003; Romero Trillo 2002). And it could indeed be questioned whether stabilization in this and other domains of sophisticated proficiency would not be characteristic of "prototypical" L1 users, too.

Finally, an important research question concerns whether there exists a general tendency among even highly proficient L2 users towards limiting their repertoire of pragmatic markers, in particular the argumentative markers? The hypothesis that this would depend to a considerable extent on individual differences seems plausible but leaves the question open as to which aspects will be more, and which will be less, liable to individual variation.

Acknowledgements

I am deeply indebted to Victorine Hancock and Inge Bartning for their useful advice regarding the contents and scope of this chapter.

References

Abrahamsson, N. & K. Hyltenstam. 2009. Age of onset and nativelikeness in a second language: Listener perception versus linguistic scrutiny. *Language Learning*, 58/2. 249–306.
Aijmer, K. & A.-M. Simon-Vandenbergen (eds.). 2006. *Pragmatic Markers in Contrast*. Oxford: Elsevier.

Allwood, J., J. Nivre, & E. Ahlsén. 1989. Speech management. On the non-written life of speech. *Gothenburg Papers in Theoretical Linguistics*, 58. University of Gothenburg, Dept. of Linguistics.

Allwood, J., J. Nivre, & E. Ahlsén. 1991. On the semantics and pragmatics of linguistic feedback. *Gothenburg Papers in Theoretical Linguistics*, 64. University of Gothenburg, Dept. of Linguistics.

Allwood, J., E. Ahlsén, J. Nivre, & S. Larsson. 1997. *Own Communication Management. Kodningsmanual.* University of Gothenburg, Dept. of Linguistics.

Altenberg, B. & M. Tapper. 1998. The use of adverbial connectors in advanced Swedish learners' written English. In: S. Granger (ed.), *Learner English on Computer*. London: Addison Wesley Longman. 80–93.

Bardovi-Harlig, K. 2001. Evaluating the empirical evidence: Grounds for instruction in pragmatics. In: K. R. Rose & G. Kasper (eds.), *Pragmatics in Language Teaching*. Cambridge: Cambridge University Press. 11–32.

Bardovi-Harlig, K. 2013. Developing L2 Pragmatics. *Language Learning*, 63. 68–86.

Bartning, I. This volume. Morphosyntax and discourse in high-level second language use.

Beeching, K. & U. Detges. 2014. Introduction. In: K. Beeching & U. Detges (eds.), *Discourse Functions at the Left and Right Periphery: Crosslinguistic Investigations of Language Use and Language Change*. Leiden: Brill. 1–23.

Beeching, K. & U. Detges (eds.). 2014. *Discourse Functions at the Left and Right Periphery: Crosslinguistic Investigations of Language Use and Language Change*. Leiden: Brill.

Blum-Kulka, S. 1997. *Dinner Talk*. Mahwah, NJ: Erlbaum.

Blum-Kulka, S., J. House, & G. Kasper. 1989. *Cross-Cultural Pragmatics: Requests and Apologies.* New Jersey: Ablex.

Bosker, H. R., H. Quené, T. Sanders, & N. H. de Jong. 2014. The perception of fluency in native and nonnative speech. *Language Learning*, 64/3. 579–614.

Bravo, D. 1998. 'Face' y rol social: Eficiencia comunicativa en encuentros entre hablantes nativos y no nativos de español. *REALE*, 9/10. 11–41.

Brinton, L. 1996. *Pragmatic Markers in English: Grammaticalization and Discourse Functions. Topics in English Linguistics*, 19. Berlin: Mouton de Gruyter.

Bylund, E. 2009. Effects of age of L2 acquisition on L1 event conceptualization patterns. *Bilingualism: Language and Cognition*, 12/3. 305–322.

Clyne, M. 1994. *Intercultural Communication at Work*. Cambridge: Cambridge University Press.

Council of Europe. 2001. *Common European Framework of Reference for Languages: Learning, Teaching, Assessing*. Cambridge: Cambridge University Press.

Collins English Dictionary. 1995. 3rd updated edition.

Denke, A. 2005. *Targetlike Performance. A Corpus Study of Pragmatic Markers, Repair and Repetition in Native and Non-Native English Speech*. Doctoral dissertation, Stockholm University.

Denniston, J. D. [1934]1978. *The Greek Particles*. Second Edition. Oxford: Clarendon Press.

Denniston, J. D. 1990. Conceptualizing motivation in foreign-language learning. *Language Learning*, 40/1. 45–78.

Denniston, J. D. 2010. Researching motivation: from integrativeness to the ideal L2 self. In: S. Hunston & D. Oakey (eds.), *Introducing Applied Linguistics*. London: Routledge. 77–84.

Dostie, G. 2004. *Pragmaticalisation et marqueurs discursifs. Analyse sémantique et traitement lexicographique*. Bruxelles: De Boeck, Duculot.

Drescher, M. & B. Frank-Job (eds.). 2006. *Les marqueurs discursifs dans les langues romanes. Approches théoriques et méthodologiques*. Bern: Peter Lang.

Edelsky, C. 1981. Who's got the floor? *Language in Society*, 10. 383–421.

Ellis, N. C. 2008. Usage-based and form-focused language acquisition: The associative learning of constructions, learned attention, and the limited L2 endstate. In: P. Robinson & N. C. Ellis (eds.), *Handbook of Cognitive Linguistics and Second Language Acquisition*. New York: Routledge. 372–405.

Ellis, R. 1994. *The Study of Second Language Acquisition*. Oxford: Oxford University Press.

Erman, B. 2001. Pragmatic markers revisited with a focus on *you know* in adult and adolescent talk. *Journal of Pragmatics*, 33. 1337–1359.

Erman, B., F. Forsberg Lundell, & M. Lewis. This volume. Formulaic language in advanced second language acquisition and use.

Erman, B. & B. Warren. 2000. The idiom principle and the open choice principle. *Text*, 20/ 1. 29–62.

Fant, L. 1989. Cultural mismatch in conversation: Spanish and Scandinavian communicative behaviour in negotiation settings. *Hermes Journal of Linguistics*, 3. 247–265.

Fant, L. 1992. Analyzing negotiation talk – authentic data vs. role play. In: A. Grindsted & J. Wagner (eds.), *Communication for Specific Purposes/ Fachsprachliche Kommunikation*. Tübingen: Gunter Narr. 164–175.

Fant, L. 1995. Negotiation discourse and interaction in a cross-cultural perspective: The case of Sweden and Spain. In: K. Ehlich & J. Wagner (eds.), *The Discourse of International Negotiations*. Berlin: Mouton de Gruyter. 177–201.

Fant, L. 2005. Discourse perspectives on modalisation: the case of accounts in semi-structured interviews. In: A. Klinge & H. H. Müller (eds.), *Modality: Studies in Form and Function*. London: Equinox. 103–121.

Fant, L. 2006. National cultural norms or activity type conventions? Negotiation talk and informal conversation among Swedes and Spaniards. *SYNAPS*, 19. Bergen: Bergen Business School. 1–22.

Fant, L. 2011. Modalización discursiva en el diálogo oral. In: L. Fant & A. M. Harvey (eds.), *El diálogo oral en el mundo hispanohablante*. Madrid: Iberoamericana Vervuert. 119–138.

Fant, L. 2015. El uso de *entonces* e *igual* en hablantes nativos y no nativos de español chileno. In: G. Engwall & L. Fant (eds.), *Festival Romanistica: contribuciones-contribution-contributi-contribuções. Studies in Romance Languages*, 1. Stockholm: Stockholm University Press. 198–218.

Fant, L. & A. Grindsted. 1995a. Conflict and consensus in Spanish vs. Scandinavian negotiation interaction. *Hermes Journal of Linguistics*, 15. 111–141.

Fant, L. & A. Grindsted. 1995b. Responses to value mismatch in intercultural negotiation interaction. *Text*, 15/ 4. 561–588.

Fant, L. & V. Hancock. 2013. Marqueurs discursifs connectifs chez des locuteurs de L2 très avancés: le cas de *alors* et *donc* en français et de *entonces* en espagnol. In: M. Borreguero Zuloaga & S. Gómez-Jordana Ferary (eds.), *Marqueurs du discours dans les langues romanes: une approche contrastive*. Limoges: Lambert Lucas. 317–335.

Fant, L. & A. M. Harvey. 2008. Intersubjetividad y consenso en el diálogo: análisis de un episodio de trabajo en grupo estudiantil. *Oralia Análisis del discurso oral*, 11. 307–332.

Félix-Brasdefer, J. C. 2008. *Politeness in Mexico and the US: A Contrastive Study of the Realization and Perception of Refusals*. Amsterdam: Benjamins.

Félix-Brasdefer, J. C. 2010. Data collection methods in speech act performance: DCTs, role plays, and verbal reports. In: A. Martínez-Flor & E. Usó-Juan (eds.) *Speech Act Performance: Theoretical, Empirical and Methodological Issues*. Amsterdam: Benjamins. 41–56.

Fischer, K. 2006. *Approaches to Discourse Particles*. Amsterdam: Elsevier.

Fillmore, C. J. 1979. On fluency. In: C. J. Fillmore, D. Kempler, & W. Wang (eds.), *Individual Differences in Language Ability and Language Behavior*. New York: Academic Press. 85–101.

Fillmore, C. J., P. Kay, & M. O'Connor. 1988. Regularity and idiomaticity in grammatical constructions: The case of 'let alone'. *Language*, 64. 501–538.

Forsberg Lundell, F. & B. Erman. 2012. High-level requests: a study of requests in long-residency users of English and French and in native speakers. *Journal of Pragmatics*, 44. 756–775.

Fraser, B. 1990. An approach to pragmatic markers. *Journal of Pragmatics*, 14. 383–395.

Fraser, B. 1996. Pragmatic markers. *Pragmatics*, 6. 167–190.

Granger, S. 1998. Prefabricated patterns in advanced EFL writings: collocations and formulae. In: A. P. Cowie (ed.), *Phraseology: Theory, Analysis and Applications*. Oxford: Clarendon. 145–160.

Granger, S. & S. Tyson. 1996. Connector usage in the English essay writing of native and non-native EFL speakers of English. *World Englishes*, 15. 17–27.

Grant, L. 2003. *A Corpus-Based Investigation of Idiomatic Multiword Units*. Doctoral thesis, Victoria University of Wellington.

Hancock, V. 2000. *Quelques connecteurs et modalisateurs dans le français parlé d'apprenants universitaires. Cahiers de la recherché*, 16. Doctoral dissertation, Stockholm University.

Hancock, V. 2007. Quelques éléments modaux dissociés dans le paragraphe oral dans des interviews en français L2 et L1. *Journal of French Language Studies*, 17. 21–47.

Hancock, V. 2012. Pragmatic use of temporal adverbs in L1 and L2 French: Functions and syntactic positions of textual markers in a spoken corpus. In: C. Lindqvist & C. Bardel (eds.), *The acquisition of French as a second language: New developmental perspectives/ L'acquisition du français langue seconde: nouvelles perspectives développementales*. Special issue of *Language, Interaction and Acquisition*, 3/1, 29–51.

Hancock, V. & A. Sanell. 2010. Pragmaticalisation des adverbes temporels dans le français parlé L1 et L2: étude développementale de *alors, après, maintenant, déjà, encore* et *toujours*. In: L. Roberts, M. Howard, & M. O'Laoire (eds.), *EUROSLA Yearbook*, 10. Amsterdam: Benjamins. 62–91.

Hansen, M.-B. Mosegaard. 1998. *The Function of Discourse Particles. A Study with Special Reference to Spoken Standard French*. Amsterdam: Benjamins.

Hansen, M.-B. Mosegaard. 2008. *Particles at the Semantics/Pragmatics Interface: Synchronic and Diachronic Issues: A Study with Special Reference to the French Phrasal Adverbs*. Amsterdam: Elsevier.

House, J. & G. Kasper. 2000. How to remain a non-native speaker. In: C. Riemer (ed.), *Kognitive Aspekte des Lehrens und Lernens von Fremdsprachen. Festschift für Willis J. Edmundson zum 60. Geburtstag*. Tübingen: Narr. 101–118.

Iino, M. 1996. *Excellent Foreigner! Gaijinization of Japanese Language and Culture in Contact Situations – an Ethnographic Study of Dinner Table Conversations between Japanese Host Families and American Students*. Doctoral Dissertation, University of Pennsylvania (available in *Dissertations Abstracts International*, 57, 1451).

de Jong, N. & C. Perfetti. 2011. An experimental study of fluency development and proceduralization. *Language Learning*, 61/2. 533–568.

Jucker, A. & Y. Ziv (eds.). 1998. *Pragmatic Markers: Descriptions and Theory*. Amsterdam: Benjamins.
Kasper, G. & K. Rose (eds.). 2001. Pragmatic development in a second language. *Language Learning*, 52, Supplement 1.
Kim, I.-O. 2000. *Relationship of Onset Age of ESL Acquisition and Extent of Informal Input to Appropriateness and Nativeness in Performing Four Speech Acts in English: A Study of Native Korean Adult Speakers of ESL*. Doctoral dissertation, New York University (available in *Dissertations Abstracts International*, 61, 1265).
Kormos, J. & M. Dénes. 2004. *Exploring Measures and Perceptions of Fluency in the Speech of Second Language Learners*. On-line publication. Budapest: Eötvös Loránd University.
Lauwers, P., G. Vandenbauwhede, & S. Verleyen (eds.). 2010. *Pragmatic Markers and Pragmaticalization: Lessons from False Friends*. Special issue of *Languages in Contrast*, 10.
Lenneberg, E. 1967. *Biological Foundations of Language*. New York: Wiley & Sons.
Levelt, W. J. M. 1983. Monitoring and self-repair in speech. *Cognition*, 14. 41–104.
Levelt, W. J. M. 1989. *Speaking: From Intention to Articulation*. Cambridge, MA: The MIT Press.
Lewis, M. 2008. *The Idiom Principle in L2 English. Assessing Elusive Formulaic Sequences as Indicators of Idiomaticity, Fluency, and Proficiency*. Doctoral dissertation. Stockholm University.
Lindqvist, H. Forthcoming. *Marcadores metadiscursivos en el español hablado L2: fluidez y participación conversacional*. Doctoral dissertation. Stockholm University.
Locke, J. [1690]1959. *An Essay Concerning Human Understanding*. Edited by A. C. Fraser. New York: Dover.
Long, M. 2003. Stabilization and fossilization in interlanguage development. In: C. J. Doughty & M. H. Long (eds.), *Handbook of Second Language Acquisition*. Oxford: Blackwell. 487–535.
Martín Z., M. Antonia, & E. Montolío (eds.). 1998. *Los marcadores del discurso*. Madrid: Arco Libros.
Martín Z., M. Antonia, & J. Portolés. 1999. Los marcadores del discurso. In: I. Bosque & V. Demonte (eds.), *Gramática descriptiva de la lengua española, tomo 3: Entre la oración y el discurso* (capítulo 63). Madrid: Espasa Calpe. 4051–4213.
Mirdamadi, F. S. & N. H. de Jong. 2014. The effect of syntactic complexity on fluency: Comparing actives and passives in L1 and L2 speech. *Second Language Research*, 31/1. 105–116.
Ochs, E. 1993. Constructing social identity: A language socialization perspective. *Research on Language and Social Interaction*, 26. 287–306.
Östman, J.-O. 1995. Pragmatic particles twenty years after. In: B. Wårvik, S.-K. Tanskanen, & R. Hiltunen (eds.), *Organization in Discourse. Proceedings from the Turku Conference, Anglicana Turkuensia*, 14, University of Turku. 95–108.
Paradis, M. 2009. *Declarative and Procedural Determinants of Second Languages*. Amsterdam: Benjamins.
Pawley, A. & F. Syder. 1983. Two puzzles for linguistic theory: targetlike selection and targetlike fluency. In: J. C. Richards & R. W. Schmidt (eds.), *Language and Communication*. London: Longman. 191–226.
Redeker, G. 1990. Ideational and pragmatic markers of discourse structure. *Journal of Pragmatics*, 14. 367–381.
Robinson, P. 2005. Cognitive complexity and task sequencing: Studies in a componential framework for second language task design. *International Review of Applied Linguistics*, 43. 1–32.

Romero Trillo, J. 2002. The pragmatic fossilization of pragmatic markers in non-native speakers of English. *Journal of Pragmatics*, 34/6. 769–784.

Schiffrin, D. 1987. *Pragmatic Markers*. Cambridge: Cambridge University Press.

Sacks, H., E. A. Schegloff, & G. Jefferson. 1974. A simplest systematics for the organization of turn-taking in conversation. *Language*, 50. 696–735.

Schmidt, R. 1983. Interaction, acculturation, and the acquisition of communicative competence: A case study of one adult. In: N. Wolfson & E. Judd (eds.), *Sociolinguistics and Language Acquisition*. New York: Newbury House. 136–174.

Schmitt, N. (ed.). 2004. *Formulaic Sequences: Acquisition, Processing and Use*. Amsterdam: Benjamins.

Siegal, M. 1994. *Looking East: Learning Japanese as a Second Language in Japan and the Interaction of Race, Gender and Social Context*. Doctoral dissertation, University of California, Berkeley.

Siegal, M. 1996. The role of learner subjectivity in second language sociolinguistic competency: Western women learning Japanese. *Applied Linguistics*, 17. 356–382.

Sinclair, J. 1991. *Corpus, Concordance, Collocation*. Oxford: Oxford University Press.

Takahashi, S. 2001. The role of input enhancement in developing pragmatic competence. In: K. R. Rose & G. Kasper (eds.), *Pragmatics in Language Teaching*, 171–199. Cambridge: Cambridge University Press.

Towell, R. & J.-M. Dewaele. 2005. The role of psycholinguistic factors in the development of fluency amongst advanced learners of French. In: J.-M. Dewaele (ed.), *Focus on French*. Clevedon: Multilingual Matters. 210–239.

Towell, R., R. Hawkins, & N. Bazergui. 1996. The development of fluency in advanced learners of French. *Applied Linguistics*, 17/1. 84–119.

Trosborg, A. 1995. *Interlanguage Pragmatics: Requests, Complaints, and Apologies*. Berlin: Mouton de Gruyter.

Villemoes, A. 1995. Culturally determined framework priorities in Danish and Spanish business interaction. In: K. Ehlich & J. Wagner (eds.), *The Discourse of International Negotiations*. Berlin: Mouton de Gruyter. 177–201.

Villemoes, A. 2003. *Negociar a lo español*. Aarhus: Systime.

Warren, B. 2005. A model of idiomaticity. *Nordic Journal of English Studies*, 4/1. 35–54.

Weinert, R. 1995. The role of formulaic language in second language acquisition: A review. *Applied Linguistics*. 16/2. 180–205.

Wierzbicka, A. 1986. Introduction. *Journal of Pragmatics*, Special issue on 'Particles', 10/5. 519–534.

Wiktorsson, M. 2003. *Learning Idiomaticity: A Corpus-Based Study of Idiomatic Expressions in Learners' Written Production. Lund Studies in English*, 105. Lund University.

Wray, A. 2002. *Formulaic Language and the Lexicon*. Cambridge/New York: Cambridge University Press.

Yorio, C. 1989. Idiomaticity as an indicator of second language proficiency. In: K. Hyltenstam & L. Obler (eds.), *Bilingualism across the Lifespan*. Cambridge: Cambridge University Press. 55–72.

Yoshimi, D. R. 2001. Explicit instruction and JFL learners' use of interactional pragmatic markers. In: K. R. Rose & G. Kasper (eds.), *Pragmatics in Language Teaching*. Cambridge/New York: Cambridge University Press. 223–244.

Inge Bartning
2 Morphosyntax and discourse in high-level second language use

1 Introduction

Most of SLA research in the 1970s and 1980s described early or intermediate stages of acquisition with a focus on identifying developmental sequences in grammar, phonology and lexicon (cf. Doughty and Long 2003; R. Ellis 1994, 2008; Larsen-Freeman and Long 1991; Klein and Perdue 1997). Focused studies of advanced levels of language proficiency started later. Coppieters (1987) was among the first, followed by many others in the 1990s and later (e.g. Ioup, Boustagi, El Tigi, and Moselle 1994; Bongaerts 1999; Birdsong 1992, 2003, 2006; Hyltenstam and Abrahamsson 2003; Bartning 1997; Muñoz and Singleton 2011). Hyltenstam, Bartning, and Fant (2005) point out that knowledge about higher stages, i.e. stages where speakers may appear as if they had stopped developing their L2 proficiency even though learning is still going on, is less elaborated than for lower stages. One of the important questions that researchers ask concerning these higher stages is which features found in native use are still undergoing development at the very advanced levels of second language use.

It has been claimed that very advanced speakers have often already acquired the grammatical features of the L2. Researchers claim that what is lacking is native-like preferred patterns of discourse organization. The present chapter takes as its point of departure observations that indicate that the very advanced/near-native L2 speaker has not yet automatized or acquired various discourse features, but also that some fine-grained purely grammatical phenomena are still undergoing development towards nativelikeness (cf. Hyltenstam 1992; Birdsong 2006; Lardiere 2007; Sorace and Serratrice 2009; Hopp 2010; Montrul 2004). The study makes the hypothesis that these late grammatical features may be predicted by their acquisitional 'history', their internal relationships and also contextual factors.

This chapter focusses on the development and use of morphosyntactic and discursive features in advanced/near-native varieties, in particular in L2 French with different L1s. It also seeks to identify possible interfaces between discourse and morphosyntax. As will be shown, morphosyntactic difficulties typically occur in certain discursive/syntactic contexts that create vulnerable areas where

---

Inge Bartning, Stockholm University

the learner has difficulties in finding adequate command in the performance of accurate solutions.

The outline of the chapter is as follows: the chapter starts with a short presentation of the developmental continuum elaborated for spoken L2 French by Bartning and Schlyter (2004) (section 2). The stages of this continuum will be used as a point of departure for a current state-of-the-art of the literature about grammatical and discourse features in (very) advanced learner usage and about the possibility to attain nativelikeness (section 3). The chapter then offers a short presentation of recent findings in this field of research (section 4). Lastly, a concluding section explores some potentially explanatory factors in order to better understand nativelike achievement in L2 (section 5).

2 Development of grammatical and discursive features towards near-native levels

The issue of developmental stages and sequences has been prominent for a long time – and especially at the beginning of SLA research (Sharwood Smith and Truscott 2005). In this section there will first be a short presentation of one developmental scheme, i.e. Bartning and Schlyter's developmental stages from 2004. Section 2.2 focuses on some relevant morphosyntactic features giving their acquisitional history in order to better understand the 'near-native' features (cf. section 4 below). Similar summaries of the six stages have already been published in Bartning (2009: 17–18, 2012a: 12–14); Forsberg Lundell and Bartning (2010: 155–157); Ågren, Granfeldt, and Schlyter (2012: 102).

2.1 The developmental perspective in SLA with an illustration of stages proposed for French L2

Drawing on earlier results presented in Bartning (1997), Bartning and Schlyter (2004) proposed a six-stage continuum for the acquisition of French L2. It comprises the following stages: 1. initial, 2. post-initial, 3. intermediate, 4. advanced low, 5. advanced medium, and 6. advanced high. The groups were true beginners, secondary school students, university students, future teachers, doctorate students and control groups of native speakers. The developmental continuum is based on developmental sequences of 25 features/criteria found in two longitudinal corpora with approximately 80 recordings of both formal or semi-formal and 'natural' spontaneous speech from Swedish-speaking learners of French.

The main morphosyntactic criteria used to delineate the six stages were (p. 283): type of utterance structure (nominal, verbal non-finite or finite) (Klein and Perdue 1997); verbal morphology and development of finiteness (Schlyter 2003); subject-verb agreement; subject and object pronouns (Granfeldt and Schlyter 2004); temporal and modal systems (Kihlstedt 1998); negation; noun phrase morphology, e.g. gender, adjective-noun agreement (Granfeldt 2003; Bartning 2000); and subordination (Hancock 2000; Kirchmeyer 2002).

These developmental sequences have been organized in successive stages and each stage can be seen as constituting a cluster of co-existing features or a grammatical/discursive 'profile' of a learner at a given moment in her/his interlanguage development. An example of such an order is the developmental sequence of TMA (Tense, Mode, Aspect) with the following implicational scale: the present > the perfect (*passé composé*) > the imperfect (*imparfait* of *être* 'be', *avoir* 'have') > the periphrastic future > the imperfect on lexical verbs > the conditional and the subjunctive > the pluperfect.

2.2 Summary of the six developmental stages in L2 French as presented by Bartning and Schlyter (2004)

The following section presents all six stages in order to illustrate the development of the different features. For this short presentation we have selected the following phenomena: utterance structure, finiteness, verb morphology, TMA, negation, noun phrase morphology, gender marking and some discourse phenomena.

- *The initial stage* (stage 1) is characterized by nominal utterance structure, utterances with some formulae, bare nouns but also some determiners; very little verb morphology is used; but non-finite verb forms *je *manger* 'I eat/ate'), preverbal negation and some finite verb forms. This means that grammatical morphemes are not all together absent (cf. the pre-basic and basic varieties as presented in Klein and Perdue 1997).
- *The post-initial stage* (stage 2) contains both non-finite and finite utterance structure, polyfunctional 'base' forms (the present for the past and the future, etc.), some inflection on verbs and adjectives, paratactic utterance structure but also the emergence of some subordination. Irregular verbs in the 3rd person sing/plur appear but in different NTL (non-target like) non-finite (*ils *partir* 'they leave') and finite forms (*ils *prend* 'they take') and in obligatory contexts. The *imparfait* appears on stative verbs. If gender is marked at all at these two first stages, it may either be the use of a default value for each of the two possibilities (masculine/feminine) or the overuse of the masculine forms.

- *The intermediate stage* (stage 3), which is more systematic and regular, with a more or less finite utterance structure but still a simple IL (interlanguage) system, contains the present tense, the *passé composé* (which may correspond to both the 'perfect' and the 'preterite') and the future, mostly the periphrastic future. The non-finite forms still persist but become less frequent. The 1st person plural and (in principle) 3rd person plural of frequent verbs such as *avoir* 'have', *être* 'be', and *faire* 'do' are marked, but for the same irregular verb the learner continues to use, multiple co-existent forms of the polyfunctional present: the non-targetlike non-finite form (*je *manger*) and the non-targetlike finite form (*ils *prend* 'they take') in competition with some rare target language forms. The first appearances of the subjunctive emerge at this stage. French double phrasal negation is more or less acquired at this stage in combination with a finite verb. Non-targetlike forms on determiners and adjectives persist as far as gender agreement is concerned.
- At *the low advanced stage* (stage 4) the typical structures of French grammar emerge: the clitic pronoun before the finite verb, the conditional, the pluperfect and the subjunctive – the last three in isolated cases. These more complex forms still appear mainly where syntax is not complex (Kirchmeyer 2002); however, not all contexts are systematically marked by the right forms. Most non-targetlike non-finite forms of regular verbs have disappeared. The non-targetlike short forms for 3rd person plural of irregular verbs *ils *prend* 'they take' continue to exist alongside the targetlike form; there is overuse of the simplified present form for past tenses and some forms of the future tenses (Kihlstedt 1998). There is also significant overuse of the connectors *mais* 'but' and *parce que* 'because' (Hancock 2000). Negation is used in its different variants (*ne... jamais* 'never', *ne... rien* 'nothing'). The masculine gender on determiners and adjectives is overused, and there is more TL gender agreement on the definite determiner than on the indefinite. The masculine form in gender agreement of adjectives is overused.
- At *the intermediate advanced stage* (stage 5) inflectional morphology develops notably and becomes more or less functional. Gender and adjectival agreement are still problematic. There is elaborate macro-syntactic use of *parce que* 'because' in complex utterances and multi-propositional subordination increases as in native speech. There are contracted sentences with infinitives and gerunds. In subject-verb agreement there are still some residues of non-marked 3rd person plural on irregular verbs (*ils *prend*) but 3rd person plural does not cause problems (*ils sont, ont, vont*). As in native French

speech, telic verbs are even used in the imperfect, static verbs in the perfect. There is now mostly TL use of the future, the conditional, the pluperfect and the subjunctive. There might be some overuse of the perfect (*passé composé*) for the pluperfect. There are still problems with gender agreement on preposed adjectives (Bartning 2000).
- Finally, at *the high advanced stage* (stage 6) inflectional morphology stabilizes slowly, even in multi-propositional utterances. There is some degree of utterance packaging, ellipsis and integrated propositions (*le gérondif*), properties that show that the user can now manage to handle several levels of information at the same time in the same utterance. There is almost native-like use of connectors *enfin* 'at last, finally, in short', and *donc* 'thus, so' (Hancock 2004, 2007) and of relatives and causal clauses. There is mostly TL use of 3rd person plural present tense of irregular verbs and TL use of the subjunctive but still not in fragile zones in e.g. complex syntax/discourse.

The fact that the developmental continuum is very similar across different types of learners, whether 'formal' or 'natural', indicates that it is not arbitrary or dependent on external factors. It should also be emphasized that these stages are based on the oral proficiency of Swedish learners of L2 French: the first four stages were confirmed by Granfeldt (2007), and stages 1–4 by Ågren (2008) for written French L2 with new groups of Swedish-speaking students. Interestingly, later international studies have confirmed – with surprisingly high correspondence – the proposed stages also for speakers of other L1s: stages 4–6 were confirmed by Housen, Kemps, and Pierrard (2009) for Dutch-speaking students and by Bolly (2008) for Dutch and English-speaking students of written L2 French and, finally, the advanced stages in written tests by Anglophone university students by Labeau (2009). (For a computational implementation of the six stages, see work by Granfeldt (2007); Granfeldt and Nugues (2007); for a recent synthesis and different applications of the six stages, see Ågren et al. (2012).[1]

---

[1] It must be underlined that the six morphosyntactic/discursive stages proposed by Bartning and Schlyter (2004) have not been conceived in the same manner as the six pragmatic stages of the European CEFR scale which takes as its point of departure learners' communicative needs (cf. Council of Europe 2001). See however Forsberg and Bartning (2010).

2.3 The status of some grammatical features in French interlanguage used in the continuum of Bartning and Schlyter (2004)

In order to better understand the emergence and development of some grammatical forms across the continuum, the analysis below will show the status of some of the most important forms. It is important to emphasize that the features of the different morphosyntactic criteria are of very different kinds; they have different developmental status since they are part of complex form-function relations in the developing interlanguage. We propose that there are two main types of forms (or 'features') *A-forms*: simplified targetlike interlanguage forms, often polyfunctional, and *B-forms*: non-targetlike idiosyncratic forms. We call the A-forms *developmental* in the sense that they emerge, change and, before disappearing, develop into more complex forms; their forms, but not functions, are simplified targetlike forms. They exist as authentic forms in the target language. The B-forms, idiosyncratic and transitory, emerge and disappear eventually in the interlanguage system. These forms do not exist in the target language but in the interlanguage.

Types of A-forms: These forms develop slowly and become more complex, often having pragmatic and lexical precursors (adverbs like 'yesterday', 'tomorrow', 'maybe' etc.). This is typical of the emerging TMA system, e.g. past tense and modal markers. For example, even though the present tense form is a polyfunctional, simplified substitute for many other 'hidden' tense functions, it is nevertheless a TL form. Example (1) illustrates an A-form in the present as a substitute for *imparfait*.

(1) *Il remplissait (SIM I:mhm) et je croyais que c'était déjà quelqu'un qui* **connaît** *(connaissait) déjà très très bien la personne qui traduisait* ('he completed it and I thought that it was someone who *knows* very very well the person who translated')

Another example of the A-type is the *passé composé* for the pluperfect (see below 3.1).

Types of B-forms: The B-forms are always non-targetlike forms in the target language:
- Non-targetlike forms of gender markers on determiners and adjectives (**un image* 'a picture', *une *petit ville* 'a small town').
- Non-targetlike verb forms in subject-verb agreement of the 3rd person plural of irregular verbs: the short singular form, *ils *prend* 'they take'. As will be shown in section 4, it takes a long time for this over-generalized form to disappear, if at all in certain contexts.

These overgeneralized forms of irregular verbs are created in analogy with the regular verb pattern of the first conjugation verbs (-*er*) in French (over 90% of the verbs) where the singular and plural are identical in speech (silent morphology) but different in written language ([il parl] for both *ils parlent* and *il parle* 'they talk, he talks'); hence the form *ils *prend* 'they take' is produced. Or, as Bybee (2008: 224) puts it, '[...] the more frequent forms of the paradigm have stronger representations in memory and thus can be used as the basis for constructing the other forms'.

Some B-type forms fall into a class that we call transitory. They are always non-targetlike. Some of these forms are extensively used at the beginning, typically at stages 1–3. For example, at the beginning of acquisition, there are non-finite verb forms ending in -*er* as a default form: *je donner* 'I give, I gave' in finite positions. This idiosyncratic form is supported by high input frequency for many different orthographic forms, pronounced in the same way, namely [e]: -*é* (past participle), -*er* (infinitive), -*ez* (present, 2nd person plural and imperative), -*ai* (future), -*ais* (*imparfait* and conditional).

The idiosyncratic B-forms disappear at different stages. Forms that disappear at early stages are the negation markers, stages (1–2): *ils *non prendre* for *ils ne prennent pas* 'they do not take'. Other forms disappear very late, if at all, particularly the short form *ils *prend* 'they take', and the short forms (masculine) of adjectival gender agreement marking: *une *petit ville* 'a small town' (see section 4).

After having analysed the sub-corpora of early acquisition in Bartning and Schlyter (2004), we have more knowledge about the developmental status of the forms. Let us again take *ils *prend* 'they take', which is a 'singular' form instead of a 'plural' one. As shown above, it appears early in both natural and formal learners (stage 2) and is still used very late, at stages 5–6 and beyond. It is thus a 'steady' French idiosyncratic feature formed by overgeneralization processes, presumably due to high frequency input effects.

The developmental history of these forms from the longitudinal corpora shows that their presence in the advanced varieties is not isolated random phenomena (e.g. slips of the tongue) but are rather predictable and consistent morphosyntactic and morpho-phonological features in certain contexts. Thus the forms *ils *prend* (an idiosyncratic transitory B-form) for *ils prennent* 'they take' and *il chante* 'he sings' (polyfuntional targetlike A-form) for *il a chanté* 'he sang' are still present in very advanced learners' production as will be demonstrated in section 4.

The following state-of-the-art section will investigate other recent studies of the very advanced learner in French L2, but also in other L2s.

3 A current state-of-the-art of very advanced learner varieties – resources and obstacles

In the following we present an overview of a selection of recent literature on the advanced learner and ultimate attainment as well as the domains of features that tend to develop late in the acquisitional process, so called 'late features', suggesting typical resources and obstacles of the advanced or near-native L2 user. The relevant domains are morphosyntactic and discourse organization features sometimes identical, sometimes similar to those presented in the Bartning and Schlyter continuum and in high-level proficiency presentations. The survey also accounts for studies grounded in various theoretical orientations, such as functionalistic, UG, processing, corpus linguistic, sociolinguistic and pragmatic perspectives. In this overview we try to account for several L2s, not only French, even though there is a certain bias towards French L2. (For overviews of the acquisition of grammar in French L2, see also Herschensohn 2006 and Véronique, Carlo, Granget, Kim, and Prodeau 2009). For more extensive accounts of late features in morphosyntax and discourse and in sociolinguistics (cf. Dewaele (2004), pragmatics and speech production/fluency (cf. Towell, Hawkins and Bazergui 1996; Towell and Dewaele 2005), see Bartning (2009, 2012a). For a collection of studies on information structure in advanced SLA, see Dimroth and Lambert (2008). Mention should also be made of the electronic database of French Learner Language Oral Corpora (FFLOC), which contains some groups of advanced learners (see Rule 2004). For advanced/near-native use of multiword sequences, see Erman, Forsberg Lundell, and Lewis this volume and for the use of discourse markers, see Fant this volume. (A similar overview has earlier been presented in Bartning 2012b.)

3.1 Tense, Mood and Aspect (TMA) as late features

Mastery of the forms and functions in the L2 acquisition of temporality is a classical threshold to overcome. As many researchers have previously noticed, adult learners of SLA never seem to reach a native-like level of discourse organization in the temporal domain (e.g. Hickmann 2005; Lardiere 2007; Leclercq 2009; Kihlstedt 1998; Howard 2005, 2012a, b). Our knowledge about how the L2 learner expresses reference to time has, however, been greatly enriched within the last 15 years. For an overview of the acquisition of TMA, see Howard 2012a and Labeau 2009. Earlier research, e.g. Bardovi Harlig (2000, L2 English) proposed three developmental stages: 1. a pragmatic stage, 2. a lexical stage and 3. a morphological stage. The learners encompassed by this proposal were, however, not advanced. The same stages were found in the above mentioned ESF-programme concerning early learners referring to past time (cf. Perdue 1993).

Howard (2005, 2009a, b, 2012a) and Labeau (2005, 2009) both report new insights into the acquisition of TMA in French L2 at advanced levels by revealing a rich morphology and complex learner solutions. Howard (2005) examines, for instance, the use of the pluperfect when it expresses the meaning of 'reversed order' in advanced French L2 and also the 'last acquired' uses of imperfect in French L2. The study concludes that because of its functional and cognitive complexity the pluperfect is learnt late even though learners express the same temporal functions via lexical and pragmatic devices much earlier. Labeau (2005, 2009) explores the relevance of the Aspect Hypothesis (Andersen 1991), which originally was formulated for Spanish L2 tense-aspect acquisition by naturalistic learners. Labeau investigated data from the use of French tense/aspect system by advanced English-speaking learners in an instructed environment (61 university students at different levels in written and oral tasks) as compared to that of native speakers. The hypothesis is that, *grosso modo*, learners acquire tense and aspect according to the inherent lexical aspect of the verbs (in French and Spanish), so that, for example, the *imparfait/imperfect* is first learnt for atelic events (e.g. stative verbs, with no endpoint: *elle se promenait dans la rue* 'she was walking in the street') and the *passé composé/preterite* for telic events (activity, achievement verbs, with an endpoint; *elle a cassé la tasse* 'she broke the cup'). These results suggest that further factors, such as event type, pragmatics, grounding, and discourse structure, affect the advanced stages of perfective and imperfective past tense acquisition. Labeau (2009) also shows several subtle native speaker (NS) uses of French imperfect, usually not acquired by non-native speakers (NNS). These researchers also confirm that the pluperfect hardly occurs in French learner language, the present perfect being the main marker of the reversed order in the learners' discourse (Howard 2005, 2012a).

The results mentioned above show that the TMA system is fertile ground for exploring the highest levels of L2 acquisition and proficiency (cf. also Leclercq and Howard, 2015).

3.2 Subject-verb agreement and verb morphology

As we have seen, verbal morphology and subject-verb agreement are well-known as vulnerable zones in L2 acquisition (Lardiere 2007; Hopp 2010). Although they are regarded as easy to teach and thus are sometimes believed to be easy to acquire, the fact is that they are seldom acquired to native-like levels (see section 4 below). In Bartning (2005) some late features, such as the use of the subjunctive and 3rd person plural subject-verb agreement in the present of irregular verbs, are compared in different groups of the InterFra corpus and for different tasks (beginners, secondary school students, university students and doctoral students; in narrations and interviews). It is striking that at the higher levels 3rd person plural agreement is 'later' and thus more 'difficult' to automatize than the subjunctive, especially in complex syntax (for a discussion, see McManus, Tracy-Ventura, Mitchell, Richard and Romero de Mills 2014). Factors, such as frequency effects, type/token relations, the stem bases of irregular verbs and syntactic complexity play an important role. For example, salience and identical forms in the subjunctive paradigm are facilitating factors (*qu'il fasse, qu'ils fassent* 'that he/they will do it').

Ågren (2005, 2008, 2009; Ågren et al. 2012) investigated VP and NP morphology of number marking and agreement in written L2 French of Swedish students at high school level in the fifth and sixth year of French as compared to L1 writers of the same age (16–17 years). The L2 writers were placed at stage 4 of the continuum proposed by Bartning and Schlyter (2004). Ågren's results show that the L2 learners had less difficulty than the L1 group with the silent number agreement (the ending *-nt* being silent in French *ils parlent* 'they talk') on regular verbs (2008). Ågren also confirms the findings of Bartning (1997, 2005) that irregular verbs with stem alternations in the 3rd person plural are vulnerable areas. The problem, thus, is not the plural ending -nt as such, but the stem alternation.

In studies about complexity, accuracy and fluency (CAF) and their interrelatedness it has been confirmed that accuracy, and especially accuracy with respect to agreement, both verbal or nominal, is an important remaining problem area also in very advanced spoken French L2 (see Housen and Kuiken 2009; Bulté and Housen 2012; Bartning et al. 2012).

3.3 Gender and Noun phrase morphology

Gender assignment and gender agreement are important ingredients in the fragile part of the very advanced learner's repertoire. Over the last fifteen years, there has been an explosion of studies (e.g. Bartning 2000; Granfeldt 2003; Carroll 1999, 2005; Holmes and Segui 2005; Hawkins 2004). An early study of gender is Chini (1995: 139) who proposed an implicational scale for the acquisition of gender agreement for Italian L2: personal pronouns > definite articles > indefinite article > attributive adjectives > predicative adjectives > past participles (see also Gudmundsson, 2013 for Italian L2). In her longitudinal study of the development of gender on adjectives and determiners from beginners to very advanced learners in the InterFra corpus, Lindström (2013) confirms earlier results in the literature on gender agreement: a tendency to overuse the masculine form, earlier correct gender agreement of the definite determiner than of the indefinite, agreement of adjectives after that of determiners. Lindström's results speak in favour of a continuous, though never complete, slow and variable acquisition of gender in French L2 by Swedish speaking learners, following individual variational paths over time, as it were, rather than a linear increase in development (cf. Larsen-Freeman 2007).

Ågren's study of Swedish learners of L2 French (2008) indicates that in written French L2 number marking in NP morphology is more complex than in verb morphology. Plural agreement is less correct in the NP in French L2 than number marking in subject-verb agreement, even though in Swedish, adjectives also agree in number with nouns. In the L2 texts that she examined, Ågren found that number agreement on adjectives was most correct in post-position. Bartning (2000) found the same tendency for gender agreement in advanced learners of oral French: the preceding noun seems to be a more solid basis for selecting an appropriate adjective form than the determiner, the cues of which are too arbitrary to rely on. Again type/token frequency effects, transfer and activation patterns are evoked as relevant factors in these differences. (For a recent study of written NP morphology with learners from stages 1–4 of the continuum, see Ågren et al. 2012.)

There is a current debate of how gender in French L2 (and L1) is learnt: some studies show that phonological cues to gender in word endings may help acquisition. This is the case for Tucker, Richard, Lambert, and Rigault (1969) for L2 acquisition and Tucker, Richard, Lambert, and Rigault (1977) for native speakers. According to other authors native speakers more often rely on lexical associations (Holmes and Dejean de la Bâtie 1999). Carroll (1999) also found that early L2 learners are sensitive to word endings. Along the same lines Holmes and Dejean de la Bâtie (1999) showed that the L2 learner needs cues, whereas native speakers memorize the gender of nearly all individual words. According to DeKeyser (2003: 330), changes that take place in more advanced stages of L2 learning can often be modelled as a gradual change in sensitivity to different cues.

3.4 Discourse markers and discourse organization

Discourse markers, discourse organization and information structure are also key areas in the study of resources and barriers of the very advanced learner.

Discourse phenomena were also studied in the continuum of Bartning and Schlyter (2004), e.g. discourse markers such as *donc* 'so, thus', *enfin* 'finally, at last, in short' and conjunctions such as *parce que* 'because'.

There are a number of perspectives in the investigation on connectors and discourse markers: one concerns fluency as a speech production strategy; another is the form/function mapping of discourse markers and their role in creating discourse cohesion. Still another has a quantitative/contrastive perspective as a starting point, and relates to the form/function mapping approach. The first perspective is represented by Towell, Hawkins, and Bazergui (1996) in their psycholinguistic study of advanced French L2 concerning learners' access to recurrent discourse markers (and *formulae*) as *organizers* and *fillers* which is part of the procedural knowledge and thus contributes to fluency. As an example of the second perspective, let us mention Denke's (2005) work about pragmatic markers in English L2 which shows interesting differences between NS and NNS in their use of *you know, well, I mean* in monologic speech. NS use the markers in a varied way, whereas NNS use them primarily as editing markers (hesitation markers).

The third perspective is the quantitative one which is adopted by the Louvain group. Typical areas of research are connectors as shown by Granger (2002), using the ICLE corpus (International Corpus of learner English). Since 1990 these projects have yielded a wealth of studies on connectors and discourse markers (often in advanced learner language, e.g. Granger and Tyson (1996), who investigated the underuse, overuse and misuse of connectors by French learners of English. The authors suggest that transfer plays a role in overuse, e.g. the overuse of *in fact* and *indeed* could be transfer of *en fait* 'actually' from French.

Hancock (2000), in her thesis on textual structure, connectors (above all *mais* 'but') and epistemic markers in spoken French of Swedish advanced learners, found that *parce que* 'because' as an introducer of parenthetical utterances was a property of very advanced spoken French L2. She also found that *donc* 'so, thus' and *enfin* 'finally, at last' are typical features of advanced French by the fact that they signal different levels of textual structure as natives do (Hancock 2007).

For further results concerning discourse markers and modalization strategies, see Fant this volume.

3.5 Discourse organization and syntactic complexity

Discourse complexity has been analysed by Hancock (2007) in the context of a model proposed by Morel and Danon-Boileau (1998). In this context Hancock analysed the utterance structures with the analytical tools of *preambles* and *rhemes*, the preamble being the thematic part of the utterance and the rheme the part with new information. The preamble thus belongs to the left peripheral elements as presented in Beeching and Detges (2014). Hancock (2007) investigated highly frequent modalizing adverbs (*peut-être* 'maybe', *vraiment* appr. 'indeed, really') in NS and very advanced NNS speech showing that these adverbs, as a late feature, appear in the preamble following NS preferred patterns. These studies show the interplay between discourse organization, complex syntax, intonation and information structure. Concerning syntactic complexity (subordination) and discourse organization, Hancock and Kirchmeyer (2005) investigated features of advanced and very advanced varieties of the InterFra corpus. The results show that advanced learners use fewer autonomous relative clauses than native speakers. For other studies of syntactic complexity and hierarchization in advanced French L2, see Bartning and Kirchmeyer (2003) and for English L2 by German and French speakers, see Lambert, Carroll, and von Stutterheim (2003). In a similar way Chini (2003) compared German advanced learners' use of subordination in narratives in their L2 Italian to that of NS Italian, and found, not surprisingly, that subordination among the NNSs was less integrated in the utterances and less hierarchical.

Still another important area of discourse organization is scope phenomena such as negation and additive/restrictive particles (see Benazzo 2005; Sanell 2007). Sanell's longitudinal study suggests a developmental sequence for negation and scope particles (*aussi* 'also', *seulement* 'only', *encore* 'still/more', *déjà* 'already') in French L2. The developmental sequence agrees with earlier results for French negation. What is new, however, is the results for semi-negation and the late appearances of *rien* 'nothing', *personne* 'nobody' as subjects and objects, as well as *aucun* 'no (one)', *ne ... que* 'only', *ne... plus* 'no longer' and *ne pas* + infinitive ('not'). The last acquired negations at high levels are *ne pas* + infinitive, *ne...plus* 'no longer', *ne...personne* 'nobody', *personne ne...*'nobody', and the 'last' particles are the temporal *encore* 'still' and *déjà* 'already', whereas additive and restrictive *aussi* 'also' and *seulement* 'only' are early markers. Sanell (2007) draws on earlier work by Benazzo (2000, 2005) on advanced Italian, English and German learners of French L2 and their use of additive and temporal particles. Advanced learners succeed in integrating the particles in the utterance structures, whereas beginners use them in the margins of the utterances and only on adjacent focalized constituents.

3.6 Perspective taking and information structure

Important discourse research has been carried out in the last decade, with several of the central papers included in Hendriks (2005) dealing with the following L2s: German, French, Italian, Spanish, English, Polish and Chinese (see Dimroth and Lambert 2008). In this cross-linguistic volume edited by Hendriks (2005), Noyau, De Lorenzo, Kihlstedt, Paprocka, Sanz, and Schneider (2005) investigate the conceptualization and verbalization of complex event representations in texts by means of two key aspects, namely, granularity (the degree of temporal partitioning of a situation) and condensation (the degree of hierarchical organization of event structure). The authors show that there are two different strategies of embedding events into a global text structure: linearization, based on temporal consecutiveness, which goes with a high degree of granularity and low condensation, and aspectualization, based on a hierarchical structure (perfectivity vs imperfectivity, causality, etc.) which goes with a lower degree of granularity and higher condensation. These studies converge in showing how speakers are guided by their L1 to adopt a particular perspective in discourse planning.

Perspective taking was also investigated in work by Carroll, Murcia Serra, Watorek, and Bendicioli (2000); Von Stutterheim (2003); Lambert (2006) and Lambert, Carroll, and Von Stutterheim (2008). It remains an intractable hurdle even at the final levels of L2 learning. In exploring narratives by very advanced or near-native speakers of L2 English, French and German, compared to NS of the same languages, Von Stutterheim and Lambert (2005: 228) examine what events learners select for verbalization and how they present the events selected. Analyses of the selection and structuring of information in L1 English, French and German texts show *preferred sets of options* for expressions that are influenced by specific combinations of the grammatical means in L1. Comparisons with second language learners show that they tend to maintain the basic selection pattern of their source language. The fact that this type of knowledge at the macro level is deeply rooted and difficult to reorganize may arise from the need for L2 speakers to discover, piece by piece, not only the function performed by each grammatical feature but also its link with other grammatical features. The results of Von Stutterheim and Lambert show that it is language-specific principles of information organization, i.e. language-specific preferences for perspective taking, that guide learners in structuring events (see also Bylund 2007 for cross-linguistic differences in Swedish and Spanish concerning grammaticized aspect on event conceptualization processes). To sum up, these discourse features represent barriers at very high levels of proficiency and are often language specific rather than universal.

4 A research project on late oral L2 French

In order to further investigate features pertaining to levels of high proficiency in French L2 a database was established which consisted of recordings by

10 Swedish-speaking adults who were 'near-native'/very advanced speakers' having lived in France (Paris) for 15–30 years. They were 40–60 years old, lived in bilingual families and also worked in bilingual settings (Swedish-French). The tasks submitted to the informants were interviews in French, retelling of cartoons and video films, and grammatical judgement (GJ) tests. The corpus also included 8 native French speakers of roughly the same age and background in the same type of tasks. For an updated description of the InterFra corpus, see www.su.se/romklass/interfra.

The following two definitions of the 'near-native speaker' and the 'advanced learner' were used as a starting-point for investigations and discussions: "By a 'near-native' speaker we mean someone who is perceived, in normal oral interaction, as a native speaker, but who can be distinguished from native speakers in some feature when their language is analysed in greater linguistic detail. By an 'advanced' second language learner/user we mean a person whose second language is close to that of a native speaker, but whose non-native usage is perceivable in normal oral or written interaction" (Hyltenstam et al. 2005: 7; Abrahamsson and Hyltenstam 2009). Although these operationalizations call for precisions and evidence, they can conveniently be used as a point of departure.

4.1 Morphology and syntactic/discourse complexity

The first qualitative impressionistic analyses of this group showed that they all use advanced target language features in their oral French, such as complex utterances as in (2) with a high number of constituents and words in their preambles (in bold), before the rhematic part is uttered.

(2) *[Preamble]* **mais / c'est vrai que / par exemple / par rapport à la Suède / en hommes femmes / un homme /** *[Rheme] c'est un homme* 'But / it is true that / for example/ compared to Sweden / when it comes to men and women / a man he is a man'

These informants also often have the same repertoire of discourse markers as native speakers (*donc* 'so, thus', *du coup*, appr. 'because of', *en fait* 'actually, in fact'); they use advanced TMA markers (e.g. pluperfect, subjunctive) and highly complex syntactic and discursive utterances (integrated structures like the gerund and reported speech); they are fluent and use idiomatic expressions, multiword sequences (e.g. *ça roule tout seul*, appr. 'it all works fine') (cf. Forsberg 2008).

What is striking, however, is that these 'near-natives' may use some of the persistent non-targetlike features of intermediate and advanced learners of stages 3, 4, 5 and 6 above, namely, in subject-verb agreement and in gender agreement of determiners and adjectives (see 2.2). Such features are illustrated in example (3) below.

(3) *euh ils on:t # je pense que ça fait partie de mon vécu aussi pour moi une langa- # enfin ce que les Français ils **dit** [disent]* 'they have # I think that it is a part of my experience also for me a language # well that is what the Frenchmen say'.

This morphosyntactic stabilization in advanced/very advanced speakers' production has been noted before (Bartning 2005, 2009): the morphosyntactic deviances could be predicted to appear in certain vulnerable areas in certain contexts, namely not in the preamble but in the rhematic part of complex utterances. As can be seen in example (3), non-target-like subject-verb agreement forms are produced in complex utterances (here in a relative clause).

The contextual factor is not the only one, however. The cases are still more complex, we think, because they involve the morpho-phonological competitive distinctions that are strongly dependent on input frequency and entrenchment of the users' systems (cf. N. Ellis 2006). Forms such as *ils *dit* ('they say'), *ils*prend* ('they take') may be the effect of 'deeply entrenched rivals' (cf. Sharwood-Smith and Truscott 2005: 237), where these 'rivals' are persistent reoccurring competitive forms occurring in identical contexts in the interlanguage at the same time: e.g. *ils *prend, ils *prendre, ils prennent* 'they take'). These cases may suggest different variation patterns in L1 and L2 with different explanations and origins of similar forms: the L2 features may be 'developmental' coming from interlanguage whereas the L1 forms are caused by synchronic variation of the norm in the target language. There is an interesting parallel to draw here. According to the studies by Mougeon and Beniak (1995) concerning variation in Canadian oral French the form *ils *dit* 'they say' coexists with *ils disent* 'they say'. What they have in common is the dependence on input frequency relations.

Another typical late feature from these investigations (Bartning 2009) is the acknowledged difficulty of gender agreement on articles and adjectives, as exemplified in (4).

(4) *j'étais à l'école de journalisme première année ensuite ***un année** aux Beaux Arts* 'I was at the school of journalism first year then one-MASC year-FEM at the Art School'

The majority of contexts that attract gender errors require the indefinite feminine determiner in the context of nouns with initial vowels (ex. 4). As stated above, we now know that gender on determiners is a problematic feature in French L2, from the very start to late levels, if it is ever learnt at all. These special contexts, however, to our knowledge, have not previously been examined in detail. The fact that the elided definite determiners before nouns beginning with vowels (*l'école* 'the school') do not reveal anything about gender may be one of the causes (cf. Holmes and Segui 2005; Ågren et al. 2012).

4.2 Discourse complexity

The first preliminary discourse investigations of these new data show the following results.

As shown above, information structure with the distinctions theme (preamble)/ rheme are fruitful areas for the study of very advanced French L2. It is also well-known that left dislocation has been highlighted as a frequent and typical property of spoken French (e.g. Lambrecht 1994; Morel and Danon-Boileau 1998; Beeching and Detges 2014). Furthermore, there are several studies of left dislocation as an interesting domain for the study of late acquisition of French (cf. Donaldson 2011). If we enlarge the scope of analysis, Hancock and Kirchmeyer (2009) observe that left detachment with two or more modal or thematic elements is more frequent in interviews with native and near-native speakers than with advanced learners, as in (5):

(5) [Theme:] ***c'est vrai que / mon mari /avec ses copains/*** [Rheme:] *il se moque de moi* 'it's true that my husband with his mates / he teases me'

It seems then that some aspects of left dislocations could be relevant features in characterizing discourse complexity at very late stages in French. In the same vein, it has also been shown that both the number of words and the number of the constituents in the preambles could be an interesting measure of discourse complexity since NSs produce more constituents in this part of the utterance (see Hancock 2007; Bartning et al. 2012).

In the new project this domain will be an important area of study. An example of four constituents in the preamble is here illustrated by a NNS speaker in (6):

(6) [Theme:] ***comme / par exemple / j'sais pas / un matin /*** [Rheme:] *je suis partie...* 'as / for instance / I don't know / one morning / I left...'

There are other areas that seem fruitful to the study of discourse complexity in very advanced L2 French, namely the use of adverbs. Hancock and colleagues have investigated central adverbs (*peut-être* 'maybe', *vraiment* 'really, indeed', *aussi* 'also', *seulement* 'only') through the stages from beginners to near-native speakers in interviews, and the following features were found: the discourse function of *vraiment* for emphasis (initial position) does not appear until stage 6, where it also starts to develop as a discourse organizing marker (Hancock and Sanell 2009). This is another example that shows that the developmental perspective turns out to be important for the understanding of 'late' features. In the same vein, Hancock and Sanell (2010) studied the use of six temporal adverbs at different developmental stages of L2 French, even the very advanced/ near-native stages, and proposed an order of acquisition of the adverbs as pragmatic markers. The acquisition of time seems to precede all the other functions of the markers, although the advanced learners had not fully acquired some aspectual uses of the adverbs.

5 Towards a theoretical understanding of ultimate attainment at the highest levels and concluding remarks

Let us once more return to examples (3) and (4) above of the non-targetlike forms of subject-verb agreement and gender agreement in section 4.1. As mentioned, such examples of verb agreement and gender problems are not merely slips of the tongue, they are too systematic to be so categorized, and, indeed, they are found in several different speakers. They are systematic in the sense that their presence in certain contexts seems predictable based on French interlanguage development and syntactic complexity as shown in this chapter.
– Could these tendencies be explained by what Birdsong (2005: 323) calls "inevitable reflexes of bilingualism" where one effect "is a specific L1 effect whereby performance in a given L2 is differentially affected by properties of various L1s." Birdsong's statement could be applied to these L2 users: Swedish has no subject-verb agreement and much less complex verb morphology than French. Furthermore, transfer effects take place at all stages in L2 development. Sorace (2003: 144) proposes the notion of 'optionality' to explain the divergence between NNS and NS grammars, for example the influence of English L1 on Italian L2 preverbal subjects where near-natives overuse overt subjects in L2 Italian, Italian being a pro-drop language.

N. Ellis (2006: 100) also refers to L1 transfer as a possible late strategy by saying: "and it is this L1 entrenchment that limits the end state of usage-based SLA". In the synthesis above we saw that Noyau et al, Von Stutterheim, and Lambert have shown to what extent the L1 still influences the L2 production, a fact that confirms the reflexes of bilingualism or transfer from the L1.

- Another factor may be the degree of markedness of the features (Hyltenstam 1984): the more complex and marked, the less automatized a feature is throughout its development. A marked form is said to be less frequent, morphologically and syntactically more complex, and its form less 'basic' and 'natural'. Learners often acquire unmarked forms before marked forms, as in the case of the relative pronoun accessibility hierarchy. If this hierarchy is taken to reflect the degree of markedness of relative pronoun functions, then the degree of markedness correlates with the order of acquisition (R. Ellis 1997: 70). The pattern of verb morphology in French is a good candidate for marked/unmarked forms, at least on the basis of the frequency criterion since 90% of French verbs belong to the 1st verb group (ending in *-er*) with the regular inflection having identical forms in the 3rd person singular/plural present *il/ils joue(nt)* 'they play'. Thus the irregular forms like *ils prennent* 'they take' would be candidates for marked forms (e.g. stem vowel change, final consonant pronounced, low frequency of paradigm pattern compared to frequency of verbs of the 1st conjugation).
- It would also be interesting to investigate the notions of 'simple' and 'complex' structures. In our view the morpho-phonological final consonant opposition in 3rd person singular/plural of irregular verbs (*ils *sort/sortent* 'they go out') and gender agreement in adjectives (*fort/forte* 'strong') in oral French would be good candidates for a supposedly morpho-phonologically complex feature. The notions simple and complex must, however, be more thoroughly investigated and defined (cf. Bulté and Housen 2012). As mentioned above and stated in the literature, simple structures are sometimes exemplified by subject-verb agreement because it is said to be an easy feature to teach and thus believed easy to learn. Our data show contrary results. Perhaps one could evoke factors like 'language change' here: if *ils prennent* 'they take' is complex, the form *ils *prend* would be a simplified alternative because complexity is not easily conserved when the communicative value becomes low. Thus, as suggested by Mougeon et al 1995 concerning the tendency in Canadian French, there might be an ongoing change in contemporary oral varieties of French.
- Are these findings language–specific features, revealing the impact of the source and target languages involved, or are they features of language

universals? As has been shown in the SLA literature, there are a number of steps in developmental progression, some of which may be universal while others seem specific to particular languages. Klein and Perdue (1997) proposed the Basic variety for the first phase of development of a SL, and it is supposed to be universal (pragmatic principles, certain information structure devices, reliance on lexical means with no inflection). Further developments after this initial phase show the impact of (source and target) language-specific properties during acquisition (Hickmann 2005), e.g. in discourse and information structure as the studies by Von Stutterheim, Carroll, Lambert, and Noyau have shown (section 3.2.3). Having examined the literature and our own empirical research concerning the set of late features presented in sections 3 and 4 above, it seems to us now that typical features of the advanced and very advanced/near native varieties rather show language specific properties. At the same time, we see that languages with rich morphology, e.g. the Romance languages, offer the same type of morphosyntactic obstacles to all advanced learners, e.g. grammaticalization features in time reference, subject-verb agreement, NP agreement, reference to entities, and pronominalization. These are features that are inherent to these languages and whose development depends on their complicated intrinsic relationships and dependencies.

- Discourse markers also have common features across languages, but they differ in nature. Connectors and discourse markers, as well as modality markers such as markers of reported speech, concern macro-syntactic organization and stratification of speech, i.e. movement between different layers of discourse. Discourse boundary markings are essential for the speaker to be able to perform naturally in everyday conversation. To a great extent discourse markers seem to be acquired incidentally (cf. Paradis 2004) and used in an automatized way in real time production. Their acquisition seems to depend largely on their frequency in the input and its quality. Though discourse markers are not complex with respect to form, their syntax, word order (position in information structure) and subtle semantic/pragmatic functions are often much more complex and difficult to acquire as there is no one-to-one relation between form and function. These properties contribute to the blurring of form-function mappings in L2. (For further reading, see Fant, this volume.)

These late features lead us to propose two other important factors, namely input frequency and the distinction between implicit and explicit knowledge.
- First, as we previously pointed out, there are areas in very late acquisition which are typically sensitive to frequency effects, above all verb morphology,

gender distinctions, connectors and discourse markers. As N. Ellis (2002: 143) says: "the acquisition of grammar is the piecemeal learning of many thousands of constructions and the frequency-biased abstraction of regularities within them."
– Secondly, there is the important distinction between implicit and explicit knowledge (see works by e.g. De Keyser 2003; N. Ellis 2002; R. Ellis 2005; Paradis 2004, 2009). As Paradis (2004: 58) states: "Whenever one speaks of 'learning a language late', one must be explicit as to whether one refers to implicit linguistic competence, acquired incidentally, stored implicitly, and used automatically, as is generally the case with L1 [...], or whether, in addition to possibly impoverished implicit competence, greater reliance on the use of metalinguistic knowledge in a fluent, albeit controlled manner, are [sic] also considered." Another possibility evoked by Paradis (2009) is that this could be an effect of non-automatized declarative knowledge because L2 acquisition is in its nature declarative. In contrast, R. Ellis (2005: 143) states that linguistic knowledge is tacit and implicit rather than conscious and explicit in nature, and attempts to establish operational definitions of these two constructs. He reports a psychometric study of a battery of tests designed to provide relatively independent measures of them. A factor analysis produced two clear factors. The two factors were interpreted as corresponding to implicit and explicit knowledge. Correspondingly, in our project, the conversations and narration tasks in a non-formal setting carried out by informants, e.g. those in the recent corpus, do seem to 'tap' spontaneous online spoken language, revealing, one could assume, access to the informants' implicit knowledge rather than metalinguistic knowledge. The speakers of our pilot group can probably be seen as very proficient speakers of French, but some do not seem to have automatized or proceduralized 'late' features in the tasks presented in section 4.

6 Concluding remarks

It is trivial to say that our field is growing very fast. Consequently, state-of-the-art articles are dangerous enterprises. Nevertheless this review has, hopefully, shown areas revealing resources and obstacles for the very proficient L2 speaker in second languages. The areas in question were verb phrase and noun phrase morphology, gender, subject-verb and nominal agreement, and selected discourse phenomena – all these are now classical areas when it comes to linguistic domains that present hurdles for the high level learner/user. It also showed that some of the grammatical/discursive features of French L2 already presented in the stages of the developmental continuum are still relevant at high levels according to our state-of-the-art summary. On the basis of some glimpses of these late data one can see that the participants are rather proficient speakers/users within the very highest ranges of L2 acquisition, i.e. the speakers in this group have a very rich, elaborated L2 characterized by a high quantity of formulaic sequences, several constituents of preambles, complex syntax/discourse – acquired during important lengths of residence in the TL country. However, it will be necessary to pursue our investigations of the resources and obstacles in the very advanced/near-native productions in greater detail, in parallel with native speaker performance.

What also seems necessary is to increase the number of measures, tests and informants in order to get a richer picture of these proficient speakers: e.g. to discover whether they can be perceived as native speakers and qualify as 'near-natives'. It will also be important to investigate their lexical competence as manifested, for instance, by lexical richness and formulaic sequences, their fluency and language aptitude, and finally their syntactic complexity. The age factor has not been discussed in this study – a very important issue for the informants of the group who all started their L2 acquisition after puberty. In order to investigate late acquisition of morphosyntax and information structure it looks promising to scrutinize in more detail the syntactic/discursive contexts where the deviances occur, viz. a narrow analysis of the contexts where these vulnerable areas with several barriers are to be found.

Acknowledgements

I am very grateful to my colleagues Victorine Hancock and Lars Fant. Victorine for all her valuable contributions and comments on this chapter and Lars for his relevant critical remarks and great support.

References

Abrahamsson, N. & K. Hyltenstam. 2009. Age of onset and nativelikeness in a second language: Listener perception versus linguistic scrutiny. *Language Learning*, 58/2. 249–306.
Ågren, M. 2005. La morphologie du nombre dans le système verbal en français L2 écrit. L'accord de la 3e personne du pluriel. *Perles*, 20. 131–150.

Ågren, M. 2008. *À la recherche de la morphologie silencieuse. Sur le développement du pluriel en français L2 écrit. Études romanes de Lund*, 84. Doctoral Dissertation, Lund University.

Ågren, M. 2009. L'apprenant avancé est aussi un scripteur avancé. In: E. Labeau & F. Myles (eds.). *The Advanced Learner Varieties: The Case of French*. Bern: Peter Lang. 149–172.

Ågren, M., J. Granfeldt, & S. Schlyter. 2012. The growth of complexity and accuracy in L2 French. Past observations and recent applications of developmental stages. In: A. Housen, F. Kuiken, & I. Vedder (eds.). *Dimensions of L2 Performance and Proficiency. Complexity, Accuracy and Fluency in SLA*. Amsterdam: John Benjamins. 95–120.

Andersen, R. 1991. Developmental sequences: the emergence of aspect marking in second language acquisition. In: T. Huebner & C. A. Ferguson (eds.). *Crosscurrents in Second Language Acquisition and Linguistic Theories*. Amsterdam: Benjamins. 305–324.

Bardovi-Harlig, K. 2000. *Tense and Aspect in Second Language Acquisition: Form, Meaning and Use*. Oxford: Blackwell.

Bartning, I. 1997. L'apprenant dit avancé et son acquisition d'une langue étrangère. Acquisition et interaction en langue étrangère. *AILE*, 9. 9–50.

Bartning, I. 2000. Gender agreement in L2 French – pre-advanced vs. advanced learners. *Studia Linguistica*, 54/2. 225–237.

Bartning, I. 2005. 'Je ne pense pas que ce soit vrai.' Le subjonctif : un trait tardif dans l'acquisition du français L2. In: M. Metzeltin (ed.), *Hommage à Jane Nystedt*. Wien: Cinderella Miscellannea. 31–48.

Bartning, I. 2009. The advanced learner variety: ten years later. In: E. Labeau & F. Myles (eds.), *The Advanced Learner Varieties: The Case of French*. Bern: Peter Lang. 11–40.

Bartning, I. 2012a. Synthèse rétrospective et nouvelles perspectives développementales. Les recherches acquisitionnelles en français L2 à l'université de Stockholm. *Language, Interaction and Acquisition*, 3/1. 7–28.

Bartning, I. 2012b. High-level proficiency in second language use: morphosyntax and discourse. In: M. Watorek, S. Benazzo & M. Hickmann (eds.). *Comparative Perspectives on Language Acquisition. A Tribute to Clive Perdue*. Bristol: Multilingual Matters. 170–188.

Bartning, I., F. Forsberg, & V. Hancock. 2012. On the role of linguistic contextual factors for morphosyntactic stabilization in high-level L2 French. In: N. Abrahamsson & K. Hyltenstam (eds.), *High-level L2 Acquisition, Learning and Use*. Thematic issue of *Studies in Second Language Acquisition*, 32/2. 243–267.

Bartning, I. & N. Kirchmeyer. 2003. Le développement de la compétence textuelle à travers les stades acquisitionnels en français L2. *AILE*, 19. 9–39.

Bartning, I. & S. Schlyter. 2004. Itinéraires acquisitionnels et stades de développement en français L2. *Journal of French Language Studies*, 14. 281–299.

Beeching, K. & U. Detges. (eds.). 2014. *Discourse Functions at the Left and Right Periphery. Cross-linguistic Investigations of Language Use and Language Change*. Leiden: Brill.

Benazzo, S. 2000. L'acquisition de particules de portée en français, anglais et allemand L2. Études longitudinales comparées. University of Paris 8/ VIII/ Freie Universität, Berlin.

Benazzo, S. 2005. Le développement des lectes d'apprenants et l'acquisition de la portée à distance en L2. *AILE*, 23. 65–93.

Birdsong, D. 1992. Ultimate attainment in second language acquisition. *Language*, 68. 706–755.

Birdsong, D. 2003. Authenticité de prononciation en français L2 chez des apprenants tardifs anglophones: analyses segmentales et globales. *AILE*, 18. 17–36.

Birdsong, D. 2005. Nativelikeness and non-nativelikeness in L2A research. *IRAL*, 43. 319–328.

Birdsong, D. 2006. Age and second language acquisition and processing: A selective overview. In: M. Gullberg & P. Indefrey (eds.), *The Cognitive Neuroscience of Second Language Acquisition*. Oxford: Blackwell. 9–49.

Bolly, C. 2008. *Les unités phraséologiques: un phénomène linguistique complexe?* Doctoral Dissertation, Louvain-la-Neuve, UC Louvain.

Bongaerts, T. 1999. Ultimate attainment in L2 pronounciation: The case of very advanced late L2 learners. In: D. Birdsong (ed.) *Second Language Acquisition and the Critical Period Hypothesis*. Mahwah, N.J.: Lawrence Erlbaum. 133–159.

Bulté, B. & A. Housen. 2012. Defining and operationalizing L2 complexity. In: A. Housen, F. Kuiken, & I. Vedder (eds.). *Dimensions of L2 Performance and Proficiency. Complexity, Accuracy and Fluecy in SLA*. Amsterdam: John Benjamins. 21–46.

Bybee, J. 2008. Usage-based grammar and second language acquisition. In: P. Robinson & N. Ellis (eds.), *Handbook of Cognitive Linguistics and Second Language Acquisition*. New York: Routledge. 216–236.

Bylund, E. 2007. Procesos de conceptualización de eventos en español y en sueco: diferencias translingüísticas. *Revue Romane*, 43/1. 1–24.

Carroll, M., J. Murcia Serra, M. Watorek, & A. Bendiscioli. 2000. The relevance of information organization to second language acquisition studies. *Studies in Second Language Acquisition*, 22. 441–466.

Carroll, S. 1999. Input and SLA: adults' sensitivity to different sorts of cues to French Gender. *Language Learning*, 49. 37–92.

Carroll, S. 2005. Input and SLA: Adults' sensitivity to different sorts of cues to French gender. *Language Learning*, 55. 79–138.

Chini, M. 1995. Un aspect du syntagme nominal en italien L2: le genre. *AILE*, 5. 115–142.

Chini, M. 2003. Le phénomène de la jonction interpropositionnelle dans la narration en italien L2: entre agrégation et intégration. *AILE*, 19. 71–106.

Council of Europe. 2001. *Common European Framework of Reference for Languages: Learning, Teaching, Assessing*. Cambridge: Cambridge University Press.

Coppieters, R. 1987. Competence differences between native and near-native speakers. *Language*, 63. 544–573.

DeKeyser, R. 2003. Implicit and explicit learning. In: C. J. Doughty & M. H. Long (eds.), *Handbook of Second Language Acquisition*. Oxford: Blackwell., 313–348.

Denke, A. 2005. *Nativelike Performance. A Corpus Study of Pragmatic Markers, Repair and Repetition in Native and Non-Native English Speech*. Doctoral dissertation, English department, Stockholm University.

Dewaele, J.-M. 2004. The acquisition of sociolinguistic competence in French as a foreign language: an overview. *Journal of French Language Studies*, 14. 301–319.

Dimroth, C. & M. Lambert. 2008. La structure informationnelle chez les apprenants L2. *AILE*, 26/Special issue. 5–10.

Donaldson, B. 2011. Left dislocation in near-native French. *Studies in Second Language Acquisition*, 33. 399–432.

Doughty, C. J. & M. H. Long (eds.). 2003. *Handbook of Second Language Acquisition*. Oxford: Blackwell.

Ellis, N. 2002. Frequency effects in language processing. *Studies in Second Language Acquisition*, 24. 143–188.

Ellis, N. 2006. Cognitive perspectives on SLA. The Associative-Cognitive CREED. *AILA Review*, 19. 100–121.

Ellis, R. 1994. *The Study of Second Language Acquisition*. Oxford: Oxford University Press.
Ellis, R. 1997. *Second Language Acquisition*. Oxford: Oxford university press.
Ellis, R. 2005. Measuring implicit and explicit knowledge of a second language. *Studies in Second Language Acquisition*, 27. 141–172.
Ellis, R. 2008. *The Study of Second Language Acquisition*. 2nd ed. Oxford: Oxford University Press.
Erman, B., F. Forsberg Lundell, & M. Lewis. This volume. Formulaic language in advanced second language acquisition and use.
Fant, L. This volume. Pragmatic markers in high-level second language use.
Forsberg, F. 2008. *Le langage préfabriqué. Formes, fonctions et fréquences en français parlé L2 et L1*. Bern: Peter Lang.
Forsberg F. & I. Bartning. 2010. Can linguistic features discriminate between the communicative CEFR-levels? A pilot study of written L2 French. In: I. Bartning, M. Martin, & I. Vedder (eds.), *Communicative Proficiency and Linguistic Development. Intersections between SLA and Language Testing Research. Eurosla Monographs Series*, 1. 133–158.
Granfeldt, J. 2003. L'acquisition des catégories fonctionnelles. Étude comparative du développement du DP français chez des enfants et des apprenants adultes. *Études romanes de Lund*, 67. Lund University.
Granfeldt, J. (ed.). 2007. Studies in Romance bilingual acquisition – age of onset and development of French and Spanish. *Perles*, 21. Lund University.
Granfeldt, J. & S. Schlyter. 2004. Clitisation in the acquisition of French as L1 and L2. In: P. Prevost & J. Paradis (eds.), *Acquisition of French : Focus on Functional Categories*. Amsterdam: Benjamins. 333–370.
Granfeldt, J. & P. Nugues. 2007. Évaluation des stades de développement en français langue étrangère. *TALN 2007*, Toulouse.
Granger, S. 2002. A bird's-eye view of learner corpus research. In: S. Granger, J. Hung, & S. Petch-Tyson (eds.), *Computer Learner Corpora, Second Language Acquisition and Foreign Language Learning*. Philadelphia, PA: John Benjamins. 3–33.
Granger, S. & S. Tyson. 1996. Connector usage in the English essay writing of native and non-native EFL speakers of English. *World Englishes*, 15. 17–27.
Gudmundsson, A. 2013. *L'accordo nell'italiano L2 di studenti universitari svedesi: uno studio sull'acquisizione del numero e del genere in una prospettiva funzionalista*. Doctoral Dissertation, Stockholm University.
Hancock, V. 2000. *Quelques connecteurs et modalisateurs dans le français parlé d'apprenants universitaires*. Cahiers de la recherché, 16. Doctoral dissertation, Stockholm University.
Hancock, V. 2004. L'emploi de *donc* chez des apprenants avancés: intono-syntaxe et fonctionnements dans la chaîne parlée. *Stockholm Studies in Modern Philology*, 13. 99–121.
Hancock, V. 2007. Quelques éléments modaux dissociés dans le paragraphe oral dans des interviews en français L2 et L1. *Journal of French Language Studies*, 17. 21–47.
Hancock, V. & N. Kirchmeyer. 2005. Discourse structuring in advanced L2 French: The relative clause. In: J.-M. Dewaele (ed.), *Focus on French as a Foreign Language*. Clevedon: Multilingual Matters. 17–35.
Hancock, V. & N. Kirchmeyer. 2009. Compétence discursive des apprenants avancés et quasi-natifs: étude du marqueur polyfonctionnel de *vraiment*. *Information Grammaticale*, 120. 1–9.
Hancock, V. & A. Sanell. 2009. The acquisition of four adverbs in a learner corpus of L2 French: focus on late stages. *Discours: Revue de linguistique, psycholinguistique et informatique*, 5/1. 1–27.

Hancock, V. & A. Sanell. 2010. Pragmaticalisation des adverbes temporels dans le français parlé L1 et L2: étude développementale de *alors, après, maintenant, déjà, encore* et *toujours*. In. L. Roberts, M. Howard, M. Ó Laoire & D. Singleton (eds.), *EUROSLA Yearbook*, 10. Amsterdam: Benjamins. 62–91.

Hawkins, R. 2004. The contribution of the theory of Universal Grammar to our understanding of the acquisition of French as a second language. *Journal of French Language Studies*, 14. 233–255.

Hendriks, H. (ed.). 2005. *The Structure of Learner Varieties*. Berlin: Mouton de Gruyter.

Herschensohn, J. 2006. Review article Français langue seconde: from functional categories to functionalist variation. *Second Language Research*, 22/1. 95–113.

Hickmann, M. 2005. Determinants in first and second language acquisition: person, space, time in discourse. In: H. Hendriks (ed.), *The Structure of Learner Varieties*. Berlin: Mouton de Gruyter. 231–262.

Holmes, V. M. & B. Dejean de la Bâtie. 1999. Assignment of grammatical gender by native speakers and foreign learners of French. *Applied Psycholinguistics*, 20. 479–506.

Holmes, V. & J. Segui. 2005. Assigning grammatical gender during word production. *Journal of Psycholinguistic Research*, 35/1. 5–30.

Hopp, H. 2010. Ultimate attainment in L2 inflection: performance similarities between non-native and native speakers. *Lingua*, 120. 901–931.

Housen, A., N. Kemps, & M. Pierrard. 2009. The use of verb morphology of advanced L2 learners and native speakers of French. In: E. Labeau & F. Myles (eds.), *The Advanced Learner Varieties: The Case of French*. Bern: P. Lang. 41–61.

Housen, A. & F. Kuiken. 2009. Complexity, accuracy and fluency in second language acquisition. *Applied Linguistics*, 30. 461–473.

Housen, A., F. Kuiken, & I. Vedder. 2012. Complexity, accuracy and fluency. Definitions, measurements and research. In: A. Housen, F. Kuiken, & I. Vedder (eds.), *Dimensions of L2 Performance and Proficiency: Complexity, Accuracy and Fluency in SLA*. Amsterdam: Benjamins. 1–20.

Howard, M. 2005. The emergence and use of the plus-que-parfait in advanced French interlanguage. In: J.-M. Dewaele (ed.), *Focus on French as a Foreign Language*. Clevedon: Multilingual Matters. 63–87.

Howard, M. 2009a. Expressing irrealis in L2 French: a preliminary study of the conditional and tense-concordancing in L2 acquisition. *Issues in Applied Linguistics*, 17/2. 113–135.

Howard, M. 2009b. Short- versus long-term effects of naturalistic exposure on the advanced instructed learner's L2 development: a case study. In: E. Labeau & F. Myles (eds.), *The Advanced Learner Varieties: The Case of French*. Bern: P. Lang. 95–123.

Howard, M. 2012a. From tense and aspect to modality: the acquisition of future, conditional and subjunctive morphology in French L2. In: E. Labeau & I. Saddour (eds.) *Tense, Aspect and Mood in First and Second Language Acquisition*. Amsterdam: Rodopi. 201–223.

Howard, M. 2012b. The advanced learner's sociolinguistic profile: On issues of individual differences, second language exposure conditions and type of sociolinguistic variable. *The Modern Language Journal*, 96/1. 20–33.

Hyltenstam, K. 1984. The use of typological markedness conditions as predictors in second language acquisition: the case of pronominal copies in relative clauses. In: R. W. Andersen (ed.), *Second Languages. A Cross-Linguistic Perspective*. Rowley, Mass: Newbury House. 39–58.

Hyltenstam, K. 1992. Non-native features of near-native speakers: on the ultimate attainment of childhood L2 learners. In: R. J. Harris (ed.), *Cognitive Processing in Bilinguals*. Amsterdam: North Holland. 351–368.

Hyltenstam, K & N. Abrahamsson. 2003. Maturational constraints in SLA. In: C. J. Doughty & M. H. Long (eds.), *Handbook of Second Language Acquisition*. Oxford: Blackwell. 539–588.

Hyltenstam, K., I. Bartning, & L. Fant. 2005. High Level Proficiency in Second Language Use. Research program for Riksbanken Jubileumsfond. Stockholm university. http://www./biling.su.se/~AAA.

Ioup, G., E. Boustagi, M. El Tigi, & M. Moselle. 1994. Reexamining the critical period hypothesis: a case study in naturalistic environment. *Studies in Second Language Acquisition*, 16. 73–98.

Kihlstedt, M. 1998. *La référence au passé dans le dialogue. Étude de l'acquisition de la temporalité chez des apprenants dits avancés de français. Cahiers de la recherche*, 6, Doctoral dissertation, Stockholm University.

Kirchmeyer, N. 2002. *Étude de la compétence textuelle des lectes d'apprenants avancés. Aspects structurels, fonctionnels et informationnels. Cahiers de la recherche*, 17. Doctoral Dissertation, Stockholm University.

Klein, W. & C. Perdue. 1997. The basic variety or: Couldn't natural languages be much simpler? *Second Language Research*, 13/4. 301–347.

Labeau, E. 2005. Beyond the aspect hypothesis. Tense-aspect development in advanced L2 French. *EUROSLA Yearbook*, 5. 77–101.

Labeau, E. 2009. An imperfect mastery: the acquisition of the functions of *imparfait* by Anglophone learners. In: E. Labeau & F. Myles (eds.), *The Advanced Learner Varieties: The Case of French*. Bern: P. Lang. 63–92.

Lambert, M. 2006. Pourquoi les apprenants adultes avancés ne parviennent-ils pas à atteindre la compétence des locuteurs natifs? In: G. Engwall (ed.), *Construction, acquisition et communication. Études linguistiques de discours contemporains. Acta Universitatis Stockholmiensis. Romanica Stockholmiensia*, 23. Stockholm: AWE International. 151–171.

Lambert, M., M. Carroll, & C. von Stutterheim. 2003. La subordination dans les récits d'apprenants avancés francophones et germanophones de l'anglais. *AILE*, 19. 41–69.

Lambert, M., M. Carroll, & C. von Stutterheim. 2008. Acquisition en L2 des principes d'organisation de récits spécifiques aux langues. *AILE*, 26. 11–29.

Lambrecht, K. 1994. *Information Structure and Sentence Form: Topic, Focus and the Mental Representations of Discourse Referents*. Cambridge Studies in Linguistics, 71. Cambridge: Cambridge University Press.

Lardiere, D. 2007. *Ultimate Attainment in Second Language Acquisition: A Case Study*. Mahwah, NJ: Erlbaum.

Larsen-Freeman, D. 2007. The emergence of complexity, fluency, and accuracy in the oral and written production of five Chinese learners of English. *Applied Linguistics*, 27/4. 590–619.

Larsen-Freeman, D. & M. Long. 1991. *An Introduction to Second Language Acquisition Research*. New York: Longmann.

Leclercq, P. 2009. The influence of L1 French on near-native French learners of English. In: E. Labeau & F. Myles (eds.), *The Advanced Learner Variety: The Case of French*. Bern: Peter Lang, 268–291.

Leclercq, P. & M. Howard. 2015. The Morphological Expression of Temporality on the Verb in French as a Second Language / L'expression morphologique de la temporalité sur le verbe en français langue seconde. *Language, Interaction and Acquisition*, 6/1. 1–14.

Lindström, E. 2013. *L'acquisition du genre en français L2 – développement et variation. Cahiers de la Recherche*, 50. Doctoral dissertation, Stockholm University.

McManus, K., N. Tracy-Ventura, R. Mitchell, L. Richard, & P. Romero de Mills. 2014. Exploring the acquisition of the French subjunctive: Local syntactic context or oral proficiency? In: P. Leclercq, A. Emonds, & H. Hilton (eds.), *Measuring L2 Proficiency. Perspectives from SLA*. Bristol; Multilingual Matters. 167–191.

Montrul, S. 2004. *The Acquisition of Spanish. Morphosyntactic Development in Monolingual and Bilingual L1 Acquisition and in Adult L2 Acquisition. Series on Language Acquisition and Language Disorders*. Amsterdam: John Benjamins.

Morel, M.-A. & L. Danon-Boileau. 1998. *La grammaire de l'intonation. L'exemple du français*. Paris: Ophrys.

Mougeon, R. & É. Beniak. 1995. Le non-accord en nombre entre sujet et verbe en français ontarien : un cas de simplification? *Présence francophone: L'oralité*, 46. 53–65.

Muñoz C. & D. Singleton. 2011. A critical review of age-related research on L2 ultimate attainment. *Language Teaching*, 44/1. 1–35.

Noyau, C., C. de Lorenzo, M. Kihlstedt, U. Paprocka, G. Sanz, & R. Schneider. 2005. Two dimensions of the representation of complex event structures: granularity and condensation. Towards a typology of textual production in L1 and L2: In: H. Hendriks (ed.), *The Structure of Learner Varieties*. Berlin: Mouton de Gruyter. 157–201.

Paradis, M. 2004. *A Neurolinguistic Theory of Bilingualism*. Amsterdam: Benjamins.

Paradis, M. 2009. *Declarative and Procedural Determinants of Second Languages*. Amsterdam: John Benjamins.

Perdue, C. 1993. *Adult Language Acquisition: Cross-Linguistic Perspectives* (2 vol.). New York: Cambridge University Press.

Perdue, C. 2000. Organizing principles of learner varieties. *Studies in Second Language Acquisition*, 22. 299–305.

Rule, S. 2004. French interlanguage oral corpora: recent developments. *Journal of French Language Studies*, 14. 343–356.

Sanell, A. 2007. *Parcours acquisitionnel de la négation et quelques particules de portée en français L2 chez des apprenants suédophones. Cahiers de la recherche*, 35. Doctoral dissertation, Stockholm university.

Schlyter, S. 2003. Development of verb morphology and finiteness in children and adults acquiring French. In: C. Dimroth & M. Starren (eds.), *Information Structure, Linguistic Structure and the Dynamics of Learner Language. Studies in Bilingualism*. Amsterdam: Benjamins, 15–44.

Sharwood-Smith, M. & J. Truscott. 2005. Stages or continua in SLA: a Mogul solution. *Applied Linguistics*, 26/2. 219–240.

Sorace, A. 2003. Near-nativeness. In: C. J. Doughty & M. H. Long (eds.), *Handbook of Second Language Acquisition*. Oxford: Blackwell. 130–151.

Sorace, A. & L. Serratrice. 2009. Internal and external interfaces in bilingual language development: Beyond structural overlap. *International Journal of Bilingualism*, 13. 195–210.

von Stutterheim, C. 2003. Linguistic structure and information organisation. In: S. Foster & S. Pekarek Doehler (eds.), *EUROSLA Yearbook*, 3, 183–206.

von Stutterheim, C. & M. Lambert. 2005. Cross-linguistic analysis of temporal perspectives in text production. In: H. Hendriks (ed.), *The Structure of Learner Varieties*. Berlin: Mouton de Gruyter. 203–230.

Towell, R., R. Hawkins, & N. Bazergui. 1996. The development of fluency in advanced learners of French. *Applied Linguistics*, 17. 84–119.

Towell, R. & J.M. Dewaele. 2005. The role of psycholinguistic factors in the development of fluency amongst advanced learners of French. In: J.-M. Dewaele (ed.), *Focus on French as a Foreign Language*. Clevedon: Multilingual Matters. 210–239.

Tucker, G. R., W. E. Lambert, & A. Rigault. 1969. Students' acquisition of French gender distinctions: a pilot investigation. *IRAL*, 7/1. 51–55.

Tucker, G. R., W. E. Lambert, & A. Rigalut. 1977. *The French Speaker's Skill with Grammatical Gender: An Example of Rule Governed Behaviour*. The Hague: Mouton.

Véronique, D., C. Carlo, C. Granget, J.-O. Kim & M. Prodeau. 2009. *L'acquisition de la grammaire du français, langue étrangère*. Paris: Didier.

Camilla Bardel
3 The lexicon of advanced L2 learners

1 Introduction

In recent years, the study of L2 vocabulary learning has developed considerably, and new methods for investigating aspects of L2 users' vocabulary are constantly being explored. Knowledge of words is regarded as crucial not only for the possibility to communicate, but also in reading comprehension and in teachers' judgements of students' overall proficiency. This chapter is an outline of some of the most important fields of research within L2 vocabulary learning, addressing some questions regarding high-level proficiency of L2 vocabulary, namely the following:

- How can high-level proficiency of vocabulary knowledge be observed and measured?
- How proficient can an L2 user become when it comes to vocabulary?
- Has nativelike attainment been attested in L2 vocabulary acquisition?
- What are the respective roles of internal and external factors such as prior language knowledge and frequency in the input?

In an attempt to answer these questions, some of the most relevant research on L2 vocabulary learning will be reported. A special interest is taken in studies on advanced L2 learners, and some examples from the research project *Aspects of the advanced French and Italian L2 learner's lexicon* will be given (Lindqvist, Bardel and Gudmundson 2011; Bardel and Lindqvist 2011; Bardel, Gudmundson and Lindqvist 2012). This project investigated the oral production of advanced learners, i.e. learners that have been defined as advanced on the basis of other criteria than vocabulary knowledge. Apart from being a general overview of the study of L2 vocabulary learning, this chapter aims at discussing some aspects of vocabulary knowledge that this research project deals with, and that can be studied in oral production, namely cross-linguistic influence and lexical richness, trying to capture what characterizes the advanced L2 learner's vocabulary.

Camilla Bardel, Stockholm University

2 Second language vocabulary learning: Background

During the 1980s and 1990s, it was often and rightly pointed out that the study of L2 vocabulary learning and teaching had long been neglected (cf. e.g., Carter and MacCarthy 1988; Coady and Huckin 1997; Laufer 1997; Singleton 1999). Research on vocabulary was then attracting new interest and today its importance is recognized as central in linguistics as well as in language education and in studies on both first and second language acquisition (Treffers-Daller, Daller, Malvern, Richards, Meara, and Milton 2008: 269–270). This is reflected in the number of volumes and special issues on vocabulary learning that have been published during the last decades (e.g., Read 2000; Malvern, Richards, Chipere, and Durán 2004; Daller, Milton, and Treffers-Daller 2007; Milton 2009; Jarvis and Daller 2013; Bardel, Lindqvist, and Laufer 2013). Nevertheless, the claim that "ways of measuring the size and nature of the L2 lexicon offer a challenge to researchers" (Long and Richards 1997: ix) is still valid (cf. Daller, Milton, and Treffers-Daller 2007). This is indeed not due to a lack of studies on L2 acquisition of vocabulary, but it is probably rather a consequence of the complexity of the whole research area and the multi-faceted character of word knowledge. In fact, an overall theory of L2 vocabulary learning and knowledge is still missing, and studies on the topic are typically very specialized, focusing on certain aspects of word knowledge (Singleton 1999: 5; Chacón-Beltran, Abello-Contesse, and Torreblanca-López 2010: 2–3). A fundamental problem for vocabulary research is that "vocabulary is less amenable to generalization than closed systems like grammar or phonology" (Laufer 1997: 140). However, as Laufer (1997: 141) also notes, although "vocabulary is not a closed rule-governed system", it is still characterized by certain regularities, both formally and functionally.

Learning, knowledge and use of L2 vocabulary are today at the centre of attention of different linguistic research domains. Areas of interest are knowledge of idioms and collocations, the construction of valid and reliable testing methods for examining lexical complexity and the role of frequency in vocabulary learning, just to mention some. Research regarding the organization and structure of the mental lexicon – often described with metaphors such as the *web of words* or the *lexical network* of the individual's mind (Daller, Milton, and Treffers-Daller 2007; Wilks and Meara 2007) – also includes a vast number of studies of cross-linguistic influence.

3 High-level L2 proficiency vis-à-vis the native speaker's proficiency

High-level proficiency is here used as the superordinate term for categories of language proficiency of advanced, very advanced and even 'near-native' or 'nativelike' speakers of an L2. In this framework, the labels *advanced*, *near-native* and *nativelike* are employed to characterize L2 users that can be said to be located at the highest end of a developmental continuum, as far as proficiency is concerned, and in comparison with native speakers of the target language (TL). Similar labels frequently occur in the literature on Second Language Acquisition (SLA), but are not always clearly defined, or are differently defined in different contexts. In the current research program, the following definitions are adopted: A native speaker is the archetypical first language speaker who has learnt the language in question as L1 and continued to use it regularly throughout the lifespan. A nativelike speaker of a specific language is someone who, in all respects, uses this language like a native speaker, and who is perceived as native even when her/his language is scrutinized in detailed analysis, in spite of the fact that the language in question is not that person's L1.[1] By a near-native speaker we mean someone who is perceived as a native speaker by native speakers, in normal, oral everyday interaction, but who can be distinguished from native speakers when her/his language is analyzed in greater linguistic detail (Hyltenstam and Abrahamsson 2003; Abrahamsson and Hyltenstam 2008, 2009). By an advanced L2 learner/user, we refer to a person whose L2 is close to that of a native speaker, but whose non-native usage is perceivable in normal oral or written interaction.

Using the native speaker as a benchmark is common in studies on SLA, although it is an approach that has been discussed with scepticism by many, see for instance Cook (2002, 2003), Davies (2003), Birdsong (2005). As Cook has pointed out (2003: 3), native speakers are not necessarily monolinguals, and as soon as a native speaker comes into contact with an L2, something happens to the L1: "the L2 user's knowledge of his or her first language is in some respects not the same as that of a monolingual" (Cook 2003: 5). It is, however, theoretically and empirically motivated, both from a cognitive and a linguistic point of view, to investigate how close the L2 learner can come to the native speaker's

---

[1] This definition of the nativelike L2 speaker is a theoretical construct, and while there are examples of L2 users that reach a near-native level, nativelike L2 users are yet to be found (Abrahamsson and Hyltenstam 2008, 2009). In their studies, Abrahamsson and Hyltenstam found L2 learners of Swedish who had reached such high proficiency that they were assumed to be native Swedes by Swedish L1 speakers; nevertheless, they scored lower than a control group of native speakers in a variety of language tests and tasks.

abilities. Furthermore, as the native speaker's level is the implicit aim for many L2 learners, the perspective of the native speaker's proficiency seems reasonable from the point of view of language education as well, for example in order to find out whether it is a realistic goal for students and teachers (for an interesting discussion of the native speaker as a model in assessment and SLA, see Davies 2003: 171–197). When it comes to vocabulary it is important to be aware of the fact that this is an area of language that is – maybe more than any other – characterized by variation among L1 speakers as well, depending on various social, situational and cognitive factors such as education and literacy, context, memory, concentration, level of formality, etc. Vocabulary knowledge varies not only among L2 learners at different levels of proficiency, but also among native speakers. We will return to the L1 speakers' vocabulary in further sections.

In the project referred to earlier, studies have been carried out on Swedish students of French and Italian who have been defined as advanced or very advanced on the basis of both language external and internal criteria as well as general judgements of teachers and researchers. Some of these students are so advanced that they pass for native speakers in certain situations (Pauletto and Bardel submitted). The working hypothesis has been that it is possible for L2 speakers to become 'nativelike' in the domain of vocabulary, and this has also been possible to show in certain aspects of this domain, such as lexical richness (cf. section 7).

4 Words and word knowledge

In this section, we will address some basic questions that are worth some discussion when studying vocabulary knowledge. What does it mean to know a word in all its respects? What is actually a word? How do we define and delimit the lexical domain of a language with respect to other linguistic domains? What do we mean when we say that someone has a large or a rich vocabulary? Furthermore, if we want to study the L2 learner with high-level proficiency: What does it mean to have a near-native or a nativelike vocabulary? What does the native speaker know in terms of vocabulary: how many words and how many aspects of these words?

From an educational point of view, it may be interesting to think about what the L2 user needs in terms of lexical knowledge in order to use the L2 successfully (cf. Nation 2001). What should the learner and the teacher focus on in the learning process? What does the learner really need to know in order to reach a high proficiency level when it comes to vocabulary?

Given the extreme size and complexity of a language's lexical domain, it may seem impossible for an L2 user to attain near-native, let alone nativelike, proficiency in the L2. Still, it is a well-known fact that the native speaker adds new lexical knowledge to his or her mental lexicon all the time, even in adulthood. New word forms and new meanings of old words enter our native languages and our L1 mental lexicons continuously. According to Paradis (2009), vocabulary knowledge is sustained in the human brain by declarative memory, independently of whether the words belong to a person's L1 or L2. Thus, it seems reasonable to assume that people can also develop their L2 vocabulary continuously. However, the question is not only whether the L2 learner can become nativelike as regards lexical breadth (i.e. the number of words known) or size (the number of words used) but also if she/he can achieve nativelike deep knowledge of individual words (see section 4.2.4). As pointed out by Aitchison (2003: 12), it is part of a human's lexical ability to use words in creative and innovative ways, and there seems to be no reason to assume that this ability is less developed when it comes to an L2. Then again, we also know that many aspects of lexical knowledge, such as the ability of stylistic variation between registers for instance, vary among native speakers as well as L2 users. Therefore, theoretically, the limits for attaining near-native proficiency might not be fixed, but determined by individual factors.

4.1 What is a word?

A word can be described as a set of properties or features, i.e., semantic, phonological, morphological, syntactical and orthographical features (Singleton 1999: 8–38). A first and simple definition might be one based on graphic aspects, and indeed, a string of letters that express a semantic content and is divided from other strings of letters by spaces is normally regarded as a word. However, contextual and syntactical factors challenge this definition, and multi-word units give rise to new meanings of words when these appear together. The role of context is central also when interpreting single word forms. Most words have more than one meaning and we interpret the meaning according to the (linguistic as well as extralinguistic) context that the word appears in. In summary, the semantic relations between words are complex and their interpretation and use require sensitivity with regard to the context. It is also worth pointing out that the contextual factors that determine the meaning of words – single word forms and multi-word units – differ between languages, a fact that makes the bi- or multilingual mental lexicon extremely complex. Words differ from each other as to their formal and functional structure within or between languages. A word can be formally more or less complex (single or multi-word units, compounds or not compounds), it can have one or several meanings, and it can be more or less tied to certain pragmatic functions.

Another important definitional issue is how words that form a text should be counted, when we are interested in finding out how many words an individual speaker or writer uses in a particular text. Words can be counted as *types* or *tokens*. By counting types a word form is counted only once. By counting tokens every running word in the text is counted. Therefore, in the text *Today I know what I didn't know yesterday*, the word *know* occurs as one type but two tokens. Other times one may want to count all the forms that appear of a word, for instance all different verb forms, as one base word, i.e., as a *lemma*. The lemma consists of a headword and its inflected forms. In the text *We don't know what he knows* the two words *know* and *knows* are two forms of the lemma *know* (cf. e.g., Singleton 1999: 10; Nation 2001: 7–8, Daller et al. 2007: 2–3). Lexical *size* (I will use this term for the number of words used in a text) is often measured in lemmas but sometimes also in types or tokens. There are different measures that are used in attempts to quantify the degree to which the vocabulary of a text is large and varied (see section 7.1). However, in many studies on lexical size, richness and diversity, especially as far as English is concerned (e.g., Laufer and Nation 1995), the *word family* is also used as a counting unit. "A word family consists of a headword, its inflected forms, and its closely related derived forms" (Nation 2001: 8). For instance, *know, knew, knowledge, unknown* are all members of the same word family. A complicating part when the lexical profile of a text is calculated is that many of the words in the text appear both as single words and as parts of multi-word units, as well as with different meanings. This raises questions about how to count these words (cf. section 7.2).

4.2 Word knowledge

4.2.1 Vocabulary knowledge and use

The framework of this overview is one that comprises vocabulary *knowledge* and *use*, taking an interest in what L2 learners know about vocabulary, and how they make use of this knowledge. There are many different aspects of vocabulary that can be observed in order to investigate vocabulary use and assess vocabulary knowledge. *Size, width, breadth* and *depth* are fundamental aspects of vocabulary. They can be approached in different ways, and sometimes these terms, which denote different aspects of the lexicon, are used with slightly different meanings.

In the previous section we saw that the definition of a word is far from simple because of the complex nature of words. As a natural consequence of the inherent complexity of words, vocabulary knowledge is multi-faceted. As noted by Vermeer (2001: 218) increasing interest in vocabulary both in L1 and L2 acquisition research has raised the awareness that knowledge of words is multidimensional and that it comprises various types of knowledge. The learner must acquire several lexical aspects in order to achieve complete knowledge of a word and of its relations with other lexical units, i.e., in order to establish a functioning network between units in the mental lexicon. There is no single process involved in learning an individual word in its completeness, and this has been pointed out by several researchers (e.g., Ellis 1997; Laufer 1997; Melka 1997; Moon 1997; Nation 2001; Read 2004). As Cook (1991a: 118) explains, the task of vocabulary learning implies an enormous amount of detailed knowledge about the individual word, what it means, and how it is used. Summing up previous linguistic analysis of what a word is, Laufer (1997: 141) has made explicit how lexical knowledge implies many different aspects and dimensions, on the one hand formal characteristics such as acoustic, graphic, morphological and syntactic aspects, and on the other, aspects of meaning, pragmatics and discourse:

- Form (spoken and written i.e., pronunciation and spelling)
- Word structure (morphology)
- Syntactic pattern of the word in a phrase and sentence
- Meaning (referential – including multiplicity of meaning and metaphorical extensions of meaning; affective – the connotation of the word; pragmatic – the suitability of the word in a particular situation)
- Lexical relations of the word with other words (e.g., synonymy, antonymy, hyponomy)
- Collocations

All these aspects can be more or less well known. The more advanced a learner, the more aspects of a word are likely to be known, and the more developed the different aspects of the word. For example, more meanings of a polysemic word are likely to be known, more synonyms, more collocations and idiomatic expressions mastered. As is noted in the first point, word knowledge can refer to both written and spoken language. From an educational point of view, the mastery of orthography is naturally an important aspect of lexical competence, but in accordance with the primacy of speech over writing (cf. Linell 2005), orthography must reasonably be viewed as a system of its own, which may or may not be mastered, independently of oral competence.

Moreover, knowledge of all the aspects of a word can be either *productive* or *receptive*, or both (Nation 2001: 23–59). In reception, it is not always necessary to have a very developed notion about a particular word in order to understand it; interpreting the meaning of a word form does not require the same recalling and processing capacities as the production of the word when various aspects of the word must be readily accessible and available to the speaker (Bogaards 2000: 493, Enström 2004: 176–177, Daller et al. 2007: 4ff). When the word appears in a context, the learner will at times be able to resort to guessing strategies, or inferences (Haastrup 1991), and thereby understand it even if her/his knowledge of the word is basically poor.

It is clear that the distinction between receptive and productive knowledge is important and that when testing learners' knowledge of vocabulary one must be aware of the fact that receptive knowledge of a word does not necessarily tell us that a learner can also produce it in a given moment. However, as has been pointed out by Melka (1997), it is wise not to see the receptive-productive aspects as a dichotomy, but rather as a continuum, since the degree of knowledge of individual words varies in the L2 vocabulary. In production, for instance, complete knowledge of all the aspects of a word is not given just because a word is used correctly in a certain context. In summary, it is often the case that a learner has partial knowledge of a word both from a productive and a receptive point of view.

Receptive and productive knowledge are both necessary foundations for conversational interaction between interlocutors, "the most primordial and universal setting for speech" (Levelt 1989: 29). As Levelt (1989: 30) points out in line with many others, conversation regulates and ritualizes social relations, and it is fundamental for the L2 user to be able to do just this. In conversation, turn-taking and cooperation as well as text regulation are central functions that are expressed lexically. Consequently, the interactional ability is an aspect of the advanced L2 user's lexical competence that should not be neglected (cf. Bardel 2004; Fant this volume).[2]

4.2.2 Memory

Memory is a crucial aspect of vocabulary knowledge. It happens regularly that one cannot recall the form of an intended word at the moment of production,

---

[2] It is interesting to note that in the *Common European Framework of Reference for Languages* (Council of Europe 2001), interaction is regarded as a separate linguistic ability in addition to oral and written reception and oral and written production.

although one has knowledge of it. This problem is related to processing and also affects L1 speakers in 'tip of the tongue' states (Levelt 1989: 320–321). Conversely, forgetting the meaning of a word form also happens to everyone (Meara 1996), even in the L1 if the word is rarely encountered. In such cases, there can still be partial knowledge of the word so that the input is somehow possible to decode; aspects of knowledge can be recalled during reception, especially if inferring from the context is feasible. The native speaker relies on his or her complete knowledge of the linguistic system in order to interpret the meaning of lexical units in different uses. In L2, a limited knowledge of the whole linguistic system will make L2 learners less efficient than native speakers in using context, at least until they achieve a high level of L2 proficiency (Nagy 1997: 79). There is however nothing that speaks against the possibility of L2 learners achieving such a level of proficiency and then be able to make use of context in a way that approaches that of native speakers.

4.2.3 L1 word knowledge

Laufer (1997: 142) points out that all the aspects of a word listed by her and reported above are rarely known to the learner, who often has a partial knowledge of the word. As a matter of fact, this is also sometimes the case for native speakers. Leaving aside the fact that certain words can be completely unknown to L1 speakers, layers of meaning of polysemic words might be obscure also to the native speaker. It is part of native speakers' linguistic competence to know how to use wide-ranging words appropriately, but many meanings are connected to technical use of the language and are known mostly by people working in special fields (cf. Dijkstra 2003: 18). In some cases, new meanings appear in non-standard varieties of a language, for example in adolescent varieties. As mentioned earlier, polysemic development is part of language change, and all co-existing meanings of a certain word are not always as frequently used as others. Consequently, they may not be understood and are certainly not used by all native speakers. Also, other semantic relations may be unknown to native speakers, such as synonymy, antonymy etc. These are problems that may be due to an imprecise understanding of the meaning of words, especially rare words. Another domain where native speakers can find difficulties is spelling. Variation in lexical competence may be related to literacy skills (cf. Singleton 1999: 46–47). Moreover, multilingual individuals often experience influences in their L1 from their L2 at the level of form-meaning overlapping and use of collocations (cf. e.g., Laufer 2003). Multilinguals' susceptibility to cross-linguistic influence makes their lexicon particular in some respect when compared to the monolingual native-speaker norm, which in its turn raises some serious question marks in relation to the very idea of the native speaker as a benchmark for lexical acquisition.

4.2.4 The relationship between breadth and depth

Researchers tend to see the knowledge of words mainly from two perspectives, *breadth* and *depth*.[3] Breadth of the vocabulary refers to "the number of words for which the person knows at least some of the significant aspects of meaning" (Anderson and Freebody, 1982: 92–93) or "the number of words a learner knows regardless of how well he or she knows them" (Daller et al. 2007: 7).[4]

By depth, on the other hand, a more detailed qualitative knowledge about the single word is referred to, or to put it simply, "how well particular words are known" (Read 2004: 211). As Read points out, this definition is too generic to serve the purposes of research in, and assessment of, vocabulary knowledge (cf. Gyllstad 2013 for a critical discussion of the notions of breadth and depth). Trying to pinpoint what researchers have in mind when investigating depth of knowledge, Read distinguishes three approaches to vocabulary learning in the literature: *comprehensive word knowledge, precision of meaning* and *network knowledge*. According to the first approach, depth covers different types of knowledge of a word, like those indicated by Laufer (1997: 141) and discussed above, which all together, if fulfilled, can be called *comprehensive word knowledge*. Read's *precision of meaning* (2004: 211) refers to "the difference between having a limited, vague idea of what a word means and having much more elaborated and specific knowledge of its meaning". It appears problematic to establish a criterion for precise knowledge. Typically, the benchmark is the adult native speaker (although even a native speaker may have a vague idea about the meaning of certain words). However, as Read (2004: 213) points out, "knowledge of specialized, low-frequency vocabulary reflects in the first instance a person's level and field of education but also their social background, occupation, personal interests and so on". Precision of meaning thus seems to be an aspect

---

[3] Cf. Daller et al. 2007:8, who combine these two with the dimension of *fluency* in their model of 'lexical space'.
[4] For a slightly different approach, the reader may want to consult Housen et al. (2008), where *width* and *depth* are discussed as two dimensions of qualitative knowledge of the single word at a micro-level, and *size* seems to correspond to 'breadth' in the way this term is used by Read (2004) and Daller et al. (2007).

of word knowledge that might be related to the degree of literacy a person has. Depth can also be understood as *network knowledge*, i.e., the incorporation of a word into the network surrounding it in the mental lexicon. Word knowledge is sometimes thought of as a network, and words as interconnected nodes. The nodes are interconnected in different dimensions, thematically, phonologically, morphologically, conceptually etc. (Vermeer 2001: 218). What Read calls comprehensive vocabulary knowledge can fluctuate, develop, and even regress in an L2 as well as in an L1. In a similar way, we can assume that the other two approaches, precision of meaning and network knowledge, refer to knowledge that can be continuously developed in L1 as well as in L2. From this point of view, there are theoretically no limitations either in L1 or in L2 on vocabulary growing and developing in depth as well as in breadth.

Although superficially very different, breadth and depth are not necessarily contrasting. According to Vermeer (2001) there is a complex interaction between breadth and depth and "there is no conceptual distinction between breadth and depth measures" (Vermeer 2001: 218), since the more the network develops around an individual word, the larger the vocabulary becomes as a whole. What is really the point when distinguishing between breadth and depth then? As Read points out, when assessing word knowledge, "[i]n order to make choices from among the range of measures available, it is necessary for researchers to have some theoretical basis for classifying them" (Read 2004: 210). Or as Bogaards (2000) expresses it:

> As lexical knowledge comes in very many forms and presents a lot of different aspects, this means that there is not one single way to measure L2 vocabulary knowledge. Different types of tests are needed to address different aspects of the lexicon and different formats may be more or less adapted to different levels of vocabulary knowledge and to different types of questions the teacher or the researcher wants to answer. (Bogaards 2000: 490)

Thus, although certain studies point at strong correlations between breadth and depth, especially for learners with high proficiency (Nurweni and Read 1999), it is important from a methodological point of view to distinguish between these aspects.[5]

4.2.5 Breadth, coverage and basic vocabularies

It should be clear from above that the mental lexicon – the individual's word-store – of the L1 as well as of any subsequently acquired language, does not

---

[5] See also Laufer and Goldstein (2004) who conducted tests of four different degrees of the link between meaning and form trying to combine breadth with depth of meaning knowledge.

consist of just a long list of words (cf. Aitchison, 2003: 26–27), but that there are layers of knowledge about each and every word. Still, it may be interesting to know how many words a language learner has some kind of knowledge of, or how many words the L2 user needs to have some basic knowledge of in order to use the language successfully. One often meets questions like: How many words are there in a language? How many words does a native speaker know? How many words does a second language learner have to learn? These are apparently questions that language learners and language users care about. In fact, as Milton (2008: 334) points out, vocabulary and its knowledge and use is countable in a particular way compared to other aspects of language. Let us therefore dwell for a moment on these quantitative questions of vocabulary learning. Certainly, as Nation (2001: 6) suggests, the most ambitious goal for a language learner is to learn everything of the language in question. However, as the author continues, not even native speakers know all the vocabulary of their language. So, how many words does a native speaker know? Certainly, as already pointed out, there are individual differences, depending on sociolinguistic factors, such as social background and education. According to Nation (2001: 9), reliable studies (e.g., Goulden, Nation and Read 1990) "suggest that educated native speakers of English know around 20,000 word families". It is important to note that these are not only native speakers, but also educated; hence this number constitutes an extremely ambitious goal for an L2 learner. According to James Milton (p.c.), English speaking undergraduates, who maybe represent the average L1 speaker better, scored about 9.000 on the same test as the one used by Goulden et al.

It might be interesting to ask *which* words an L2 learner should learn (at least to some extent) in order to become an efficient L2 user. Are some words more useful than others? According to many researchers, e.g., Nation (2001); Cobb and Horst (2004), frequency based studies show that some words are much more useful than others, basically because they are more frequently used. Only a portion of the mass of words that are present in for example a newspaper or a book occurs frequently in the text, whereas many words are quite low-frequent. The most frequently recurring words constitute a central or basic vocabulary, and they are also highly polysemic, which makes it important to know them well, that is to know many of their meanings. Interesting work has been done on lexical comprehension and its role in the reading process, showing that a basic vocabulary, consisting mainly of the most frequent words of a language, is what is basically required for reading comprehension. See Nation (2006: 61–62) for a presentation of different studies of *coverage*, i.e., "the percentage of running words in the text known by the readers" (Nation 2006: 61). "[T]he minimal ratio of known to unknown words for both reliable comprehension and new acquisition is at least 20:1, or in other words when at least 95% of the running words in the environment are known" (Cobb and Horst 2004: 17; see also Laufer and Ravenhorst-Kalowski 2010).

About how many words can be considered to belong to the basic vocabulary of a language? The ways of measuring and the results vary in studies on different languages. As for Swedish, for example, Enström (2004: 173) claims that 10,000 words (lemmas, one would presume, although this is not specified) are the most central and are those who are required for coverage of 95% of the words in a text. As far as English is concerned, something like 4,000 word families should give coverage of 95% of a text, according to Nation 2001: 147). For Italian, De Mauro (2000, 2005) has established that the basic vocabulary of the Italian language contains about 7,000 lemmas, and that it covers more than 95% of any non-specialised text.[6] And for French, the 2,000 most common word families cover 90% (Cobb and Horst 2004: 32). Among the most central words of a language we find high-frequency function words such as for instance articles and prepositions, but also the most frequently used verbs and nouns (cf. Nation 2001, 2004; De Mauro 2005). Words belonging to the basic vocabulary are often assumed to constitute the ground needed to understand most texts of a general character. However, as Enström points out (2004: 173), even if the most frequent vocabulary of the language is known, the rest of the words in a text – the low-frequent words – carry lots of important information. In fact, according to Nation (2001), for a pleasurable reading, about 98–99% coverage of the text is needed and 98% coverage is hypothesized to constitute a threshold for unassisted comprehension of an English text:

> It is useful to understand why coverage of tokens is important. Eighty per cent coverage of a text means that one word in every five is unknown (about two words per line). Ninety per cent means one in every ten is unknown (about one word per line), and 95% coverage means one in every twenty is unknown (about one unknown word in every two lines). Hirsch and Nation (1992) suggest that for ease of reading where reading could be a pleasurable activity, 98–99% coverage is desirable (about one unknown word in every 50–100 running words). (Nation 2001: 147)

So, how many words does the reader need to understand in order to achieve 98–99% coverage of a written text? Nation (2006) reports that 8,000–9,000 word families are required for this coverage when reading English literature and newspapers.

---

[6] Note that among these 7,000 lemmas De Mauro includes around 2000 lemmas that are not particularly frequent but highly present in the native speaker's mind. They are the words of every day life, that every native speaker knows, but that you may not hear often at all, such as Italian *cavatappi* (corkscrew), *solletico* (tickle) *sparecchiare* (clear the table).

5 The organization of the mental lexicon

Many basic questions regarding vocabulary knowledge still need to be solved. These concern for instance the organization of the mental lexicon and, in particular, the degree to which the L2 lexicon resembles that of the L1 and the extent to which the L2 lexicon is integrated with, or separate from, the L1 lexicon. Researchers discuss the respective roles of form and meaning in the L2 lexicon compared to those of the L1 lexicon, and whether the relation between form and meaning is qualitatively different in the L2 and in the L1 mental lexicon.

According to models of the mental lexicon, words are organized in the mind according to specific principles. In the adult L1 mental lexicon, words seem to be organized, above all, by semantic relations. Also in L2, words that are well-known are connected to other words on a semantic basis (Wolter 2001; Namei 2002). But there is also a grammatical connection between words. This can be observed in word selection errors as these often conserve the word class of the intended word (Singleton 1999: 19). Especially paradigmatically related words (e.g., hyponyms and hyperonyms, co-hyponyms, antonyms) are often exchanged in word selection errors, as has been shown in studies on slips of the tongue, i.e., the involuntary use of a word in an inappropriate function, such as *tree* instead of *flower* or *contemporary* instead of *adjacent* or utterances such as *he will arrive in a few years* when *he will arrive in a few days* was what the speaker intended to say (Poulisse 1999: 21, Aitchison 2003: 20). There are also slips of the tongue, however, that indicate that there is a phonological connection between words in the mental lexicon. Certain words that pop up by mistake are phonologically similar to the intended word, the two words starting with similar sounds, having the same intonation etc., like in *combination* for *contamination* (Poulisse 1999: 20).[7]

A key question regarding the bilingual mental lexicon is the one of integration vs. separation of the L1 and the L2. As Aitchison (2003: 255) notices, "there is no general agreement as to how the various lexicons are organized in the minds of bilingual and multilingual speakers – though there is increasing evidence for a single integrated network" (cf. Singleton 1999, 2006). Aitchison continues: "If a person knows two languages reasonably well, words are possibly subconsciously activated in both languages, then the language which is not wanted is suppressed" (cf. Green 1986). The fact that we can keep together the words we know in an L2 at all indicates that not only the L1 lexicon, but also

---

[7] Ringbom (2007: 20) defines a speech error as an error occurring when "the intended word and a semantically or phonologically similar word are stored close enough for them both to be activated in the production process, and the wrong selection is made".

the L2 lexicons involve intralexical networks of associations. This speaks in favour of the separation hypothesis. However, as Swan (1997: 174) puts it, the associative links of the L2 may be less firmly established than those of the mother-tongue, something that would explain the activation of L1 and other languages in instances of code-mixing and other phenomena of cross-linguistic influence, phenomena that as a matter of fact indicate that the systems are not entirely separated, but at least interacting or partially overlapping (Dijkstra 2003). Discussing the relationship of L1 and L2 in terms of either separation or integration appears excessively categorical, especially considering the fact that the degree to which languages are co-activated, or supressed, in multilingual speakers seems to depend on both non-linguistic and linguistic factors, for example the interlocutor, the situation, the subject of conversation, language distance, proficiency, frequency and recency effects (Grosjean 2001; Dijkstra 2003). An alternative model is Cook's integrative continuum for relating the languages in the bilingual or multilingual speaker's mind (cf. Cook 2002, 2003). According to Cook, such a continuum "does not necessarily imply the whole language system [...]; a person's lexicon might be integrated, but the phonology separate. Nor does it necessarily affect all individuals in the same way" (Cook 2003: 9).

It seems reasonable to assume that the more frequently activated, the stronger the links between words become and the more fixed the relations between nodes in the network (cf. Ellis 2002). This would mean that language users have tighter links between words belonging to a language that they use often, i.e., hear or produce themselves, and that advanced L2 learners have stronger links in their intralinguistic L2 networks.

> Finding a word in the mental lexicon can be envisaged as following a path through this complex network, with some network links being stronger than others. For well-known common words, the paths are well worn, and it is easy to travel fast. But for words used only occasionally, the paths are narrow and dimly lit. (Aitchison 2003: 244–245)

It appears logical that the semantic connections between words in the L2 mental lexicon cannot be very strong at a low level of proficiency when few words are known. Although the adult has knowledge of concepts related to the words in his or her L1, he or she has to develop new relations between concepts and L2 words. When not all semantic aspects of the TL words are known, and when partially known words are still not used in all their possible effects, semantic associations cannot be implemented in the L2. But, as shown by Namei (2002), the more the L2 mental lexicon evolves, the more its organization has the prerequisites to become like L1-like.

Relations between words in the L1 and L2 mental lexicon have been investigated in word association tests (e.g., Meara 1978; Söderman 1993; Wolter 2001; Namei 2002; Fitzpatrick 2006, 2007; Fitzpatrick and Izura 2011), mainly against the background of a number of studies on children's word associations. Studies on monolinguals have indicated that young children give more clang responses than older children, and that the number of semantic responses increases with age. In addition, studies have shown a shift from overwhelmingly clang and syntagmatically driven responses to paradigmatically driven responses at a certain point of development in the young monolingual. It is not clear to what extent the L2 mental lexicon develops in a similar way, as results from L2 studies are somewhat disparate. Meara (1978) found that at lower levels of proficiency, phonological relations dominate the network of the L2 mental lexicon. Later studies (Söderman 1993; Wolter 2001 and Namei 2002) indicate that it is a matter of development and at a word individual level: the deeper the knowledge is of an individual word, the more dominant are semantically based associations. These studies suggest that as the word becomes more integrated into the L2 system, it passes from a predominantly phonological to a more semantic profile, although the shift from clang and syntagmatic responses to paradigmatic ones is not obvious. Interestingly, Fitzpatrick (2006, 2007) found considerable variation among native speakers as to predominant response type, indicating that native speakers are not homogeneous in their word association patterns. One can conclude that depth of knowledge plays a role in word association. If words are really well known, phonology does not play a more significant role in L2 than in L1. It is not impossible for L2 learners to acquire semantic relations between the words similar to L1 speakers' word relations. It is more a matter of how well the words are known (by L1 as well as L2 speakers). Words that are well known by the L2 learner can elicit the same kind of semantically based associations as words that are well known by the L1 speaker.

In their study from 1993, Hulstijn and Tangelder observed intralingual influences in "synforms", a kind of malapropism[8] characterized by formal similarity to the target according to Laufer (1988). The study of Hulstijn and Tangelder is another example that indicates that advanced L2 learners can develop deep semantic relations between words and use the language in a way similar to native speakers, while learners at an intermediate level behave differently. The study regards difficulties to distinguish between similar words with different meanings like 'historic'/'historical' in L2 learners of English and a group of

---

8 A malapropism is defined as the "misuse of a word, in mistake for one that resembles it" (Hulstijn and Tangelder 1993: 149). They are used by L2 users as well as by native speakers and "are usually made unintentionally" (ibid.).

English native speakers. The authors underline that the study is exploratory and that strong conclusions cannot be drawn. However, their results indicate a difference in error patterns between intermediate learners on the one hand and advanced learners and native speakers on the other. According to the authors, "confusions between 'historic' and 'historical' are due to the fact that they have similar meanings rather than to the fact that they have similar forms" (Hulstijn and Tangelder 1993: 159). The authors come to the conclusion that there is a gradual development of semantic aspects of words and that native speakers sometimes are unsure about the semantics of certain words.

6 Cross-linguistic influence

The influence of the L1 is known to play a role at different linguistic levels in the L2 (phonology, morpho-syntax, lexis, pragmatics) and it affects different linguistic skills – oral and written production and reception/comprehension (cf. e.g., Swan 1997). The same goes for influence from previously acquired secondary languages in third or additional language acquisition, often referred to as L3 acquisition (cf. e.g., De Angelis 2007). It is important to keep in mind that many of the learners observed in L2 acquisition research are in fact multilinguals, that is, they have knowledge not only of an L1, but also of at least one foreign language apart from the one under study. It is only in recent years that the role of the L2 in L3 has been seriously acknowledged besides that of the L1 in studies on non-native language acquisition (see e.g., Cenoz, Hufeisen and Jessner 2001, 2003; Hammarberg 2009; Aronin and Hufeisen 2009).

Cross-linguistic influence (CLI) is relatively easy to identify at the level of vocabulary, and especially in production. In particular oral production data have been studied within the research of L3 lexicon (Cenoz 2003: 103). In production, cross-linguistic influence can take its expression in formally or semantically motivated deviances from the TL (Ringbom 2001, 2007). It can result in for example pure code-switching, that is, the insertion of entire words from one language into another, so-called false friends (errors that appear when the learner creates a correspondence between words in L1 and L2 that are phonologically similar but where the meaning is different), or word construction attempts in which lexical material from a background language (L1 or L2) is adapted to the TL at a morphological or a phonological level (Hammarberg 2009, Bardel and Lindqvist 2007). Apart from typical CLI-based errors of this sort, there is obviously also a positive effect of cross-linguistic influence from previously acquired languages on the TL. Such a positive effect (positive transfer) is not as easily detected as negative transfer, as, by definition, it does not lead to any deviances from the TL, since it appears when the learner's assumption that there are similarities between languages corresponds to actual similarities (Jarvis and Pavlenko 2008). However, it is clear that multilinguals have a certain support from the languages they already know at the level of word construction, use of cognates, etc. It is important to keep in mind that the knowledge of additional languages generally increases communicative competence, not the reverse. In order to pin down the competence of a bi- or multilingual, and to emphasize that L2 users have nothing less than knowledge of both a first and a second language, Cook (1991b, 2002, 2003) introduced the term 'multi-competence' referring to the knowledge of two or several languages in one individual's mind.

Different factors seem to stimulate activation of the languages known to the learner, of which the most frequently discussed is perhaps similarity between the involved languages (often discussed in terms of typological relations). The more closely related languages are, the more similarities there are at a lexical level (Cenoz 2003: 105–106). If a person is bilingual or multilingual, connections between words belonging to different languages are purportedly present in the mental lexicon (Herwig 2001). There are studies that indicate that similar words in different languages are easily activated in the multilingual's mind (de Bot 2004). Proficiency level in the background languages as well as in the TL is also an important factor. Studies on cross-linguistic influence at different proficiency levels clearly show that the languages are more easily kept apart the more proficient the language user is in the different languages (Poulisse 1999, Dewaele 2001, Lindqvist 2006, Bardel and Lindqvist 2007). It seems reasonable to assume that the connections between words within one and the same language are stronger at an advanced level of a language that has been and is often used than those in a language that is not, or has not been, much practiced.

As we have seen, several studies on L2 vocabulary acquisition indicate that learners focus more on formal and phonological aspects of words at an initial stage, and that deeper semantic knowledge is developed at a later stage (cf. Singleton 1999). Also from studies on CLI it seems to be possible to distinguish a development from form-based CLI in the initial stages towards more semantically driven CLI. While most studies on lexical CLI mainly deal with beginners or intermediate learners, and show mostly formal transfer such as code-switches and word construction attempts, fewer studies on CLI investigate advanced learners. A few exceptions are the studies by Lindqvist (2010a; 2012) on Swedish advanced learners of French L3; see also Bardel (2015) for an overview of data from French and Italian L3 at different levels of development. In advanced learners, not many instances of CLI are detectable, but in the few cases found semantically-based CLI is dominant when compared to formally-based CLI especially from background languages in which the proficiency level is high. According to Ringbom (2001) high proficiency in a background language is a condition for meaning based transfer to occur, and this is not surprising. As we have seen, high proficiency is necessary to develop the semantic aspects of lexical deep knowledge. Along the same line of reasoning, Ringbom claims that meaning-based transfer mainly occurs from the L1, or from an L2 of very high proficiency (cf. Lindqvist 2010a). As regards transfer of meaning, the background languages in which the learners are highly proficient seem to play an important role as a source. The role of typology does not seem decisive, although formal similarities seem to have an impact in certain cases.

Stroud (1979: 178–179) classified some different kinds of interference that involve the semantics of the word: A simple example of the phenomenon that was described as "false friends" above encountered among Swedish native speakers' L2 English, is the use of the English word *eventually* in the sense of *possibly/maybe*. The reason for this error may be the Swedish word *eventuellt*, which means 'possibly, maybe', but it can also have its source in other languages known to the speaker, e.g., Italian *eventualmente* or French *éventuellement*. Another type of instantiation of the false friend phenomenon can be found when there is a partial identity between the meanings of the words, e.g., English *ride* – Swedish: *rida*. As Stroud (1979: 213–214) points out, among the meanings of polysemic words there is often one that is perceived as more central than the others. This meaning can be shared by two languages, while the secondary meanings may not be equivalent. This can lead to an overuse of an L2 word, i.e., the L2 word is used in more senses than it has in the TL, and as a consequence, non-target like collocations can appear: While *ride a horse* has its Swedish equivalent in *rida på en häst*, to *ride a bike* is not to **rida en cykel* in Swedish, but is expressed with a verb: *cykla*. Or vice versa, it can lead to underuse of a word form, i.e., the use of the form is restricted in the interlanguage to a few senses.

This kind of partial identity causing false friend phenomena is possible also between words that are not phonologically similar, but share the same meaning in some but not all of its senses. This is observed by Ringbom (2001) in what he calls "semantic extensions", a kind of transfer based error occurring when the learner assumes that what is a homonym or a polysemous word in the TL has a meaning correspondent to what is most commonly the core meaning of the equivalent L1 (or other background) word (cf. Ringbom 2001: 62). An example reported by Lindqvist (2010a) is *chambre* (French), the meaning of which is restricted to 'bedroom'. In one of her examples, *chambre* is used in a case when the more appropriate target word would be *bureau* (office). In both Swedish and

English the words *rum* and *room* have wider extensions than in French, as they can refer to any delimited space of a building, and thus have a larger extension than *chambre*. A similar overuse of the Italian word *camera*, which means 'bedroom', is often heard in the speech of Swedish students of Italian.

Yet another kind of cross-linguistic influence at a phonological level, pointed out by Stroud again, that also involve the semantics of the word occurs when the learner assumes cognateness between L1 and L2 and simply transfers an L1 word to the TL, adapting it phonologically, e.g., Swedish *trafik* → German **Trafik* (*Verkehr*). This kind of word construction attempt often occurs when the two languages are typologically proximate and has been noticed in cross-linguistic influence from L2 to L3 (Hammarberg 2009; Bardel and Lindqvist 2007).

To sum up, the research on cross-linguistic influence has often concentrated on lower levels of proficiency where many interesting results have been found as to how L1, L2 and L3 interact on a lexical level. Less is known about cross-linguistic influence at more advanced stages of development. It would be interesting to study higher proficiency levels where the most obvious cases of code-switches and word construction attempts made out of resources from previously acquired languages are probably rare, but where one may find more subtle semantically or stylistically-driven transfer typologies.

7 How can word knowledge be assessed?

Vocabulary tests are basically used either for research or for assessing learners' vocabulary knowledge in a teaching programme. Most vocabulary tests have in common that they typically measure knowledge of individual word forms as they appear in one particular context, if any context at all. Moreover, most tests measure word knowledge at a particular point in the learner's acquisition of an L2 (Read 2004: 212), but tests can also be used at different points of development before and after a period of studies or a stay abroad, for example. As we have seen in the previous sections, there are several aspects of vocabulary knowledge, and measuring or testing all these aspects is hardly done in one single kind of test. Different types of tests are used to tap different types of word knowledge, for instance meaning and lexical relations are often tested in word association tests or other specifically designed tests on e.g., synonymy or collocational relations between words (cf. e.g., Greidanus, Bogaards, van der Linden, Nienhuis and de Wolf 2004). For an overview of different test types, see Nation (2001: 344–379) or Gyllstad (2013).

Read (2004: 209–210) defines six different kinds of tests for assessing word knowledge: The checklist (a list of words, where learners indicate whether they know each word or not); recognition items (matching of target words with other related words or definitions); recall-type items (learners should supply words deleted from texts); translation from L1 to L2 or vice versa; interviews designed to elicit different components of word knowledge; and speaking or writing tasks that yield text samples from which word counts and other measures of lexical size or richness can be made.

Examples of well-known tests that fall under the second category are the *Vocabulary Size Test* (Nation and Beglar 2007), which tests words from the 7,000 most frequent word families in English, and the *Vocabulary Levels Test*, of which there are both receptive and productive versions (Nation 2001: appendixes 2–5). Another one is Read's *word associates test* (Read 2004: 220), which is a development of the classical word association test intended to measure network knowledge.

In attempts to assess breadth of vocabulary, a selection of items that is supposed to be representative is normally tested. Tests such as the checklist, C-tests (a gap-fill test where the second half of every second word has been deleted and should be filled in by the learner), translation of vocabulary, etc., normally include a large number of items, and in order to keep the task simple and not too time-consuming, they measure only some aspects of word knowledge and do not tap depth of knowledge (see Read 2004: 210–211, for a discussion).

As for aspects of deep knowledge, different methods to test it have been suggested. The *Vocabulary Knowledge Scale* (Wesche and Paribakht 1996) is a test that aims at measuring the degree of knowledge of precision of meaning, and was used by e.g., Wolter (2001) for assessing the level of deep knowledge of individual words. Learners have to choose between five statements regarding the degree of knowledge of a particular word, and in case they choose stage four or five, they also have to give synonyms or translations or use the word appropriately in context:

1. I don't remember having seen this word before
2. I have seen this word before but I don't know what it means
3. I have seen this word before and I think it means...
4. I know this word. It means...
5. I can use this word in a sentence e.g., ...

In his discussion of existing tests, Bogaards (2000) concludes that breadth of vocabulary is an essential dimension, and that tests that measure size or breadth of vocabulary are the most common. But as he points out (p. 494–495) referring to Wesche and Paribakht (1996), tests that account for deep knowledge are also necessary, especially for advanced learners for whom it is important to acquire polysemy, collocations, pragmatic variations, etc. As observed by Wesche and Paribakht "advanced learners need depth and speed of access as well as range in their vocabulary knowledge, for ease and precision of comprehension as well as for effective composition and oral expression" (p. 26). In turning this around, these abilities exemplified by Wesche and Paribakht and by Bogaards as being important to acquire for the advanced learner could also be assumed to be characteristic of the high-proficiency levels of L2 use and prerequisites for learners in order to be defined as advanced.

In different works Bogaards (2000) and Greidanus et al. (2004) have tried to find a solid test of semantic relations and collocational knowledge. When evaluating the *Euralex French Tests* (EFT, Meara 1992), a test that tries to tap qualitative aspects of word knowledge EFT, Bogaards (2000) found that advanced learners had higher scores than native speakers on test items where meaning relationships (synonyms and hyponyms) were implied, but no significant difference between the groups was found. Areas where the natives scored significantly better than the advanced learners were fixed expressions, compounds and culturally bound items. At an individual level, difficulties were found for native speakers in certain specialized/technical vocabulary and some fixed expressions.

Greidanus et al. (2004) constructed and validated a deep knowledge test for advanced learners of French L2. They found differences between advanced and native speakers of French, but also striking differences in word knowledge within the group of native speakers, who did not answer correctly 100% of the items (Greidanus et al. 2004: 204).

The tests mentioned up to now measure the declarative knowledge of individual words (items given in a particular test) at a particular stage of acquisition. Other methods have to be used in cases where the researcher aims at finding out what kind of words are used by learners in written or spoken production (cf. the last category out of the six mentioned by Read 2004, as quoted above). Vocabulary in spoken language has for long been rather unexplored, but recently a number of studies based on corpora have appeared (e.g., Housen et al. 2008; Tidball and Treffers-Daller 2008). As pointed out by Melka (1997: 97–98), although production is the ideal form of evaluation of the size of a productive vocabulary, the data obtained with this method are restricted to the items produced by the subject. This is of course true since a corpus is finite, but then again, data that have been elicited from tests are restricted to the items chosen by the tester or the researcher.

A general aspect of L2 learners' language is the relative difficulty to access words quickly in actual use, and above all in oral production (Hilton 2008).

Even though many words may be known to the learner in all their aspects, semantics and pragmatics included, it is reasonable to assume that the processing capacity in the L2 is limited when compared to the L1, but such an assumption has to be empirically tested by comparing the fluency of very advanced learners with native speakers. As we have seen, vocabulary tests seldom focus on on-line production, and therefore we do not know much about the similarities and/or differences between highly proficient L2 users and native speakers, as far as processing is concerned. However, some recent studies indicate that there is correlation between word knowledge, as measured in various tests of vocabulary size, and the classical foreign language skills; correlations were found between size and reading comprehension by Albrechtsen, Haastrup and Henriksen (2008); Stæhr (2008, 2009) and between size and all the four skills (Milton, Wade and Hopkins 2010), cf. Milton (2013).

7.1 Lexical richness and the role of frequency

One way of measuring knowledge for research aims, either cross-sectionally or longitudinally, is to study learner corpora. In section 3.1, lexical size was defined as the number of words used in a text/production. While lexical size is purely quantitative, i.e., concerns the number of lemmas or word families in a text (written or oral), lexical *richness* is in some sense a qualitative aspect in that it says something about the character of the vocabulary of a text, and how varied it is from a lexical point of view (for an overview see e.g., Vermeer, 2004).

As Malvern et al. (2004: 3) observe, the terms 'lexical richness' and 'lexical diversity' are sometimes used synonymously. In other cases, lexical diversity is looked upon as one of several indications of lexical richness, and the latter is then used as a superordinate term. For instance, for Read (2000), students' lexical richness is composed of four different measures: Lexical density, lexical diversity (i.e., variation), lexical sophistication and number of errors. *Lexical density* is defined as the proportion of semantically full words or lexical words as opposed to function words in a text (Ure 1971, Linnarud 1986, Hyltenstam 1988, Laufer and Nation 1995). *Lexical diversity* or *variation* means "the range of vocabulary and avoidance of repetition – and is measured by comparing the number of different words with the total number of words" (Malvern et al. 2004: 3). This is traditionally done by the use of the type-token ratio (TTR) and various adaptations of the TTR, a method which has been criticized by e.g., Laufer and Nation (1995: 307) and Vermeer (2004), who suggest that frequency based methods are more valid and reliable, as opposed to type/tokens based measures. The basic problem with TTR is its sensitivity to text length. As explained by

McCarthy and Jarvis (2007: 460), "the more words (tokens) a text has, the less likely it is that new words (types) will occur". If a text is so long that certain words start to be repeated, the more frequent words will be repeated more often with respect to the infrequent words, and this tendency will increase the longer the text is. It goes without saying that most productions (oral or written) vary in length, so this problem has to be compensated for in some way. Several researchers have tried to solve the problem with text length, Malvern et al. (2004) with their D measure, an index of lexical diversity, or, more recently McCarthy and Jarvis (2010) with the MTLD.

For the measure of *lexical sophistication* researchers have considered the percentage of sophisticated or advanced words in a text (Laufer and Nation 1995: 309; see also Bardel, Gudmundson and Lindqvist 2012). As pointed out by Laufer and Nation (1995: 309–310), which words are labelled as 'advanced' will depend on each researcher's definition. I will just mention a few examples, where the criteria for defining advanced words vary: One is Linnarud (1986), who in her study of Swedish learners of English L2 used lexical words from a particular word-list designed for the 10th year of English in the Swedish school system. The list was not only frequency based, but contained also words considered of interest to Swedish learners of English (Linnarud, 1986: 45). Another one is the study of Hyltenstam (1988), who used words not included in the 7,000 most frequent Swedish words in a study of young learners of Swedish L2. A recent proposal to ingrate lexical diversity, sophistication and density in one single notion, namely lexical complexity, has been put forward by Bulté and Housen (2012); see also De Clercq (2015).

Frequency is undoubtedly a very important factor for vocabulary acquisition (cf. e.g., Ellis 1997, 2002; Nation 2001, 2006; Cobb and Horst 2004; Milton 2007). The more often a word is encountered in the input, written or oral, the more plausible it is that one will recognize it, interpret its meaning and be able to use it in one's own production (cf. Ellis 2002 for the role of frequency at different levels of language). It has even been suggested that learners acquire L2 vocabulary in order of frequency: "Whether in a classroom or a naturalistic setting, learners tend to acquire L2 vocabulary in rough order of frequency" (Cobb and Horst 2004: 17). Consequently, the use of more rare words is assumed to be a typical feature of the advanced learner's vocabulary, if compared to learners at lower levels of proficiency. It is not clear, however, exactly how important frequency is for the development of lexical richness in the learner's lexicon. Other factors definitely play a role, such as cognateness and saliency, the individual's overall proficiency level, literacy and specialized knowledge in different areas which enhances knowledge of terminology. For a discussion of the possible interaction in L2 acquisition between frequency and other factors, such as

L1 transfer, maturational constraints, Universal Grammar and the counteracting effect of learners' limits due to developmental stages, see Gass and Mackey (2002). Milton (2007) and Milton and Alexiou (2009) also discuss other input related factors, such as the thematically designed input of textbooks and word difficulty factors such as cognateness, which might determine which words are learnt or not, although probably to a lesser extent than frequency.

Laufer and Nation's (1995) *Lexical Frequency Profile* (LFP) offers one way of measuring lexical richness. In their study, Laufer and Nation used the computer program *VocabProfile* (VP) to compare the words produced by learners with words present in frequency lists based on written corpora in order to study the proportion of high frequency, academic words and low-frequent words in learners' writing. The idea of this method is to divide the vocabulary of a certain production (written text) into four frequency bands, as a measure of lexical richness. In Laufer and Nation (1995) LFP was correlated to the Vocabulary Levels Test (Nation 1983), which, as we have seen in section 6, is an established test for different levels of acquisition. The first frequency band, K1, comprises the 1,000 most common word families in English. The words in K2 are the following 1,000. The third category is *The University Word List* (UWL), which consists of 836 common words in academic texts. Words that are not present in the three categories end up in the not-in-the-list category. The program analyzes any specific text sorting its words into the three categories plus a fourth one (where the off-list words end up) and gives the proportions in the output. It is important to note that "word" in this context means word family, so that when we talk about the frequency band K1, for instance, we mean the 1,000 most frequent word families, a family comprising a base word with all its derivations and forms.

Laufer and Nation advanced two hypotheses, both of which were confirmed in their study. First, they expected the division into the frequency bands to be the same for a certain learner, independently of text type. Second, they expected the measure to be able to show differences between different proficiency levels. The underlying assumption is that a very advanced learner should have a higher proportion of words in the two categories "not-in-the-list" and the UWL than a less advanced learner. In sum, the proportions between the bands will depend on the learner's proficiency level rather than on text type.

LFP was first developed for written English texts, but there is an increasing number of studies that investigate how the method can be used for the acquisition of other languages. Cobb and Horst (2004) developed a French version of VP, *VocabProfil*, and investigated written French L2. They were followed up by Ovtcharov, Cobb and Halter (2006) and subsequently Lindqvist (2010b) who used *VocabProfil* for spoken French L2. The role of frequency in oral production has also been studied by Vermeer (2004) in his study of Dutch L1 and L2 children with a similar lexical frequency profiling method. A pilot study of spoken Italian L2 carried out by Nystedt, Bardel, and Gudmundson (2007) showed that two learners of Italian with different levels of grammatical proficiency had different lexical profiles as well: the more advanced learner (from a morpho-syntactic point of view) who had also studied for a longer period than the other one and spent several months in Italy, used a higher proportion of low-frequency words with respect to the other learner, who had a lower level of proficiency and a lower amount of exposure to the language. The abovementioned studies of learners of French (Ovtcharov et al. 2006 and Lindqvist 2010b) show that very advanced learners can have a lexical frequency profile that is similar to that of native speakers. This indicates that from a formal point of view, the L2 vocabulary can be similar to that of native speakers as far as lexical richness is concerned. This was confirmed in a study on intermediate and advanced French and Italian (Lindqvist et al. 2011), where the oral production of L2 speakers and native speakers of both languages was compared to frequency lists based on Italian and French oral data bases respectively.[9] However, it was also shown in an individual analysis of two L2 speakers of Italian that although the proportions of rare words were about the same in the two learners, many of the low-frequency words used at an intermediate level were cognates, while the more advanced learner presented a higher number of non-cognates. This theme was further explored by Bardel and Lindqvist (2011) in an in-depth study of four learners' production of low-frequency words. The study showed that cognates and so-called "thematic vocabulary" (words related to particular domains and introduced early in textbooks) constituted a relatively

---

[9] These results add information about 'active knowledge' of low-frequency words to the results reported in Arnaud and Savignon (1997), who found that low-frequency words can be acquired to an extent that comes close to the native speaker's knowledge, but at a level of 'passive knowledge'. They studied the passive knowledge of advanced French learners of English L2. For the terms 'passive' and 'active' knowledge, see Nation (2001: 24). Arnaud and Savignon came to the conclusion that advanced learners can acquire passive knowledge of rare words similar to that of native speakers. Interestingly, the same level of passive knowledge of complex lexical units (idiomatic expressions and collocations) was not found. Multi-word items, in particular metaphorical ones are generally considered difficult (cf. Moon 1997: 58). They are language specific and connected to particular sociocultural connotations and associations. According to Moon (1997: 58), "the appropriate use and interpretation of multi-word items by L2 speakers is a sign of their proficiency", but the question if L2 learners can use them in a totally nativelike way remains to be solved; see e.g. Wolter and Gyllstad 2011; Paquot 2014 for studies of traces of cross-linguistic influence in advanced learners' multi-word units. For a detailed overview of the acquisition of multi-word units see Erman, Forsberg Lundell, and Lewis (this volume).

high proportion of the low-frequency words for the less advanced learners. In order to take into account the role of cognates and thematic vocabulary Bardel, Gudmundson and Lindqvist (2012) designed a new lexical profiler, which was based on a list of words categorized into basic and advanced after having been judged by experienced teachers. Using the modified method, learners' lexical profiles were found to be more homogeneous within groups of learners at specific proficiency levels. The superiority of the new method over the purely frequency-based one was shown when comparing effect sizes.

7.2 Limitations of lexical frequency profiling methods

Although LFP and similar methods offer a handy tool for revealing lexical richness, there are some limitations to the method. First of all, with the kind of analysis achieved, one can only draw conclusions about the formal side of vocabulary knowledge. The researcher gets a list of words that the learner uses in a certain production and information about how frequent these words are in the TL, but the output does not reveal anything about *how* the words are used. Apart from the basic fact that it cannot be determined whether the learner is using the appropriate word for the concept she/he wants to express, the computer based analysis of single words (lemmas or word families) cannot account for polysemy nor for the use of multi-word units, and this means that the contextual variation which has been described by many as characteristic for word knowledge cannot be captured. This problem needs to be solved by sorting out those words that are used in a semantically incorrect way manually, before carrying out the automatic LFP analysis (Laufer and Nation 1995). Neither does the classical version of LFP, which is purely frequency-based, say anything about the role of CLI and cognates in L2 vocabulary. One needs to zoom in on single words, to look at the word forms in the productions individually and qualitatively in order to see such details and how they may differ between individuals.

It is probably also relevant here to point out a few things about lemma and word family as counting units. To say that a learner's language contains a specific lemma means that one or some forms of the lemma are found in his or her production. On the basis of a lemma count, one cannot take for granted, however, that an L2 learner has knowledge of all forms of a lemma (for instance, only some of the verb forms of a whole paradigm may be known, others not). The same problem goes for the notion of word family, and to an even higher degree. When reducing all forms of a word family to one base form, which is counted as the known word, two methodological problems arise. As pointed out by Witalisz (2007), first of all, there is nothing that says that the learner has knowledge of all members of the family just because one or some of them are found in the text. Furthermore, all family members do not have the same frequency in the input, so categorizing them into one and the same frequency band by basing the choice of band on the headword is somewhat arbitrary.

Despite these problems, the frequency-based measure of lexical richness appears to be one of the best methods at hand for getting a picture of the level of a learner's vocabulary. The methodological problems just mentioned should be possible to resolve first of all by counting lemmas instead of word families, secondly, by looking into each learner's production more carefully, taking context and semantics into account as a complement to the basic lexical frequency profiling analysis.

8 High-level proficiency of L2 vocabulary: Conclusions

As we have seen, breadth is an essential dimension of word knowledge. The more advanced the learner's variety, the more words are likely to be known. It is difficult to say how many words are known to the advanced L2 learner, but as we have seen there are estimations of how many word families a native speaker of English might have knowledge of. These figures stretch from around 9,000 up to 20,000, and maybe more, word families. It is also very important, however, to come to grips with different aspects of deep knowledge. Advanced learners need to develop, and can be expected to have developed, different aspects of deep knowledge of particular words. It still remains to be found out more precisely to what degree an individual L2 learner is capable of attaining nativelike depth. As we have seen, there are many ways of testing word knowledge. There are different tests of both declarative knowledge and online production, and of both quantitative and qualitative aspects of word knowledge. Most methods aim at testing declarative knowledge and often measure only one particular aspect of word knowledge. It is therefore difficult to get a clear picture of the whole range of lexical knowledge from breadth to depth, from receptive to productive vocabulary and covering the different abilities production, reception and interaction (but see Stæhr 2008, 2009; Milton, Wade and Hopkins 2010, for indicative results concerning the correlation between these aspects).

Can a L2 user become nativelike or near-native as far as vocabulary knowledge is concerned? As we have seen, there are studies that indicate that certain aspects of vocabulary knowledge of advanced learners are much more similar to native speakers' knowledge than that of intermediate learners, and that advanced learners come relatively close to native speakers. It is also possible to conclude from studies on the organization of the L2 mental lexicon that semantic relations become more and more nativelike with L2 development, and in some cases, certain semantic aspects of word knowledge are learnt up to a level similar to, or even better than, native speakers. What seem to be the most difficult lexical aspects to master even for advanced learners are semantico-pragmatic aspects such as e.g., collocations and knowledge related to cultural phenomena. These are areas where teachers and teaching materials can play an important role at advanced levels. We have also seen that advanced learners' knowledge of rare words can be close to that of native speakers. Nativelike attainment in L2 vocabulary acquisition has been demonstrated in some studies as to the proportion of low-frequency words. However, the method used in most studies on the role of frequency can be discussed and would benefit from completing quantitative and qualitative analyses of words that indicate deep knowledge. It remains to be seen in future research if the learners that reach a nativelike lexical frequency profile are also nativelike in their deep knowledge (e.g., semantics and pragmatics).

It seems possible to conclude that, despite obvious differences between the majority of L2 learners and native speakers, there are also important similarities between advanced L2 learners and native speakers related to the organization of the mental lexicon, possibilities to acquire semantic relations between words, and individual lexical profiles. A review of the literature in the area of vocabulary learning reveals no theoretically motivated obstacles for a learner to develop her/his L2 vocabulary as much as to reach a nativelike level. Above all, a learner should be able to develop specialized vocabulary to a level that might even supersede the "average" native speaker's vocabulary. Low-frequent specialized vocabulary is often based on cognates which could, together with personal interest and usefulness, enhance the motivated learner in the process towards a rich and varied vocabulary. In this chapter the role of the background languages of multilinguals (cross-linguistic influence resulting in positive transfer) has been touched upon as well as literacy level, both factors that can probably enhance lexical acquisition. There are certainly other factors that have not been explored here, such as e.g., motivation, residence in a second-language environment, communicative competence and anxiety. In theory, there should be no limits as to the size of a learner's vocabulary, although processing restrictions will probably always determine the speed of access to words in on line production of a non-native language. Hypothetically, the control that determines the speed of access, retrieval and encoding/decoding capacities is the component of lexical knowledge and use that is the last to become native-like.

Concerning the native speaker as a norm or a benchmark for vocabulary learning, we have seen that the criterion of the adult native speaker is not always straightforward (cf. Cook 2002, 2003; Davies, 2003). This can be noted for example when it comes to precise knowledge of a word, but also in the case of knowledge and use of low-frequent words and collocations. As Read (2004: 213) points out, "knowledge of specialized, low-frequency vocabulary reflects in the first instance a person's level and field of education but also their social background, occupation, personal interests and so on", and maybe not their lexical proficiency in terms of acquisitional development on the non-native – native continuum.

Acknowledgements

I wish to thank several people for commenting on earlier versions of this chapter, first of all David Singleton, Jim Milton and Batia Laufer. I also thank the group of researchers in the AAA program, for many fruitful discussions, especially Christina Lindqvist, who also read and commented on this chapter. Obviously, any and all remaining errors and/or inadvertent misrepresentations are completely my own.

References

Abrahamsson, N. & K. Hyltenstam. 2008. The robustness of aptitude effects in near-native second language acquisition. *Studies in Second Language Acquisition*, 30/4. 481–509.

Abrahamsson, N. & K. Hyltenstam. 2009. Age of onset and nativelikeness in a second language: Listener perception versus linguistic scrutiny. *Language Learning*, 58/2. 249–306.

Aitchison, J. 2003. *Words in the Mind. An Introduction to the Mental Lexicon*. 3rd ed. Oxford: Blackwell.

Albrechtsen, D., K. Haastrup, & B. Henriksen. 2008. *Vocabulary and Writing in a First and Second Language: Process and Development*. Basingstoke: Palgrave Macmillan.

Anderson, R. C. & P. Freebody. 1981. Vocabulary knowledge. In: J. T. Guthrie (ed.), *Comprehension and Teaching: Research Reviews*. Newark, DE: International Reading Association. 77–117.

Arnaud, P. J. L. & S. J. Savignon. 1997. Rare words, complex lexical units and the advanced learner. In: J. Coady & T. Huckin (eds.), *Second Language Vocabulary Acquisition. A Rationale for Pedagogy*. Cambridge: Cambridge University Press. 157–173.

Aronin, L. & B. Hufeisen. 2009. *The Exploration of Multilingualism: Development of Research on L3, Multilingualism and Multiple Language Acquisition*. Amsterdam: John Benjamins.

Bardel, C. 2004. La pragmatica in Italiano L2. L'uso dei segnali discorsivi. Atti del convegno nazionale Il parlato italiano, Napoli, 13–15 febbraio, 2003. CD–ROM. Napoli: M. D'Auria Aditore.

Bardel, C. & C. Lindqvist. 2007. The role of proficiency and psychotypology in lexical cross-linguistic influence. A study of a multilingual learner of Italian L3. In: M. Chini, P. Desideri, M. E. Favilla, & G. Pallotti (eds.), *Atti del VI Congresso Internazionale dell'Associazione Italiana di Linguistica Applicata, Napoli, 9–10 febbraio 2006*. Perugia: Guerra Editore. 123–145.

Bardel, C. & C. Lindqvist. 2011. Developing a lexical profiler for spoken French and Italian L2. The role of frequency, cognates and thematic vocabulary. In: L. Roberts, G. Pallotti, & C. Bettoni (eds.), *EUROSLA Yearbook*, 11. Amsterdam: John Benjamins. 75–93.

Bardel, C., A. Gudmundson, & C. Lindqvist. 2012. Aspects of lexical sophistication in advanced learners' oral production. Vocabulary acquisition and use in L2 French and Italian. In: N. Abrahamsson & K. Hyltenstam (eds.), *High-level L2 Acquisition, Learning and Use*. Thematic issue of *Studies in Second Language Acquisition*, 34. 269–290.

Bardel, C., C. Lindqvist, & B. Laufer (eds.). 2013. L2 *Vocabulary Acquisition, Knowledge and Use. New Perspectives on Assessment and Corpus Analysis. Eurosla Monograph Series*, 2. The European Second Language Association.

Birdsong, D. 2005. Nativelikeness and non-nativelikeness in L2A research. *International Review of Applied Linguistics in Language Teaching*, 43/4. 319–328.

Bogaards, P. 2000. Testing L2 vocabulary knowledge at a high level: the case of the Euralex French Tests. *Applied Linguistics*, 21/4. 490–516.

de Bot, K. 2004. The multilingual lexicon: Modelling selection and control. *International Journal of Multilingualism*, 1/1. 17–32.

Bulté, B. & A. Housen. 2012. Defining and operationalising L2 complexity. In: A. Housen, V. Kuiken, & I. Vedder (eds.), *Dimensions of L2 Performance and Proficiency: Complexity, Accuracy and Fluency in SLA*. Amsterdam: John Benjamins.

Carter, R. & M. MacCarthy. 1988. *Vocabulary and Language Teaching*. London: Longman.

Cenoz, J. 2003. The role of typology in the organization of the multilingual lexicon. In: J. Cenoz, B. Hufeisen, & U. Jessner (eds.), *The Multilingual Lexicon*. Dordrecht: Kluwer. 103–116.

Cenoz, J., B. Hufeisen, & U. Jessner. (eds.). 2001. *Cross-Linguistic Influence in Third Language Acquisition. Psycholinguistic Perspectives*. Clevedon: Multilingual Matters.

Cenoz, J., B. Hufeisen, & U. Jessner. (eds.). 2003. *The Multilingual Lexicon*. Dordrecht: Kluwer.

Chacón-Beltran, R., C. Abello-Contesse, & M. del Mar Torreblanca-López. 2010. Vocabulary teaching and learning: Introduction and overview. In: R. Chacón-Beltran, C. Abello-Contesse, & M. del Mar Torreblanca-López (eds.), *Insights into Non-Native Vocabulary Teaching and Learning*. Bristol: Multilingual Matters. 1–12.

Coady, J. & T. Huckin (eds.). 1997. *Second Language Vocabulary Acquisition*. Cambridge: Cambridge University Press.

Cobb, T. & M. Horst. 2004. Is there room for an academic word list in French? In: P. Bogaards & B. Laufer (eds.), *Vocabulary in a Second Language. Selection, Acquisition and Testing*. Amsterdam: Benjamins. 15–38.

Cook, V. J. 1991a. *Second Language Learning and Language Teaching*. London: Edward Arnold.

Cook, V. J. 1991b. The poverty-of-the-stimulus argument and multi-competence. *Second Language Research*, 7/2. 103–117.

Cook, V. J. 2002. Background to the L2 user perspective. In: V. J. Cook (ed.), *Portraits of the L2 User*. Clevedon: Multilingual Matters. 1–31.

Cook, V. J. 2003. Introduction: The changing L1 in the L2 user's mind. In: V. J. Cook (ed.), *Effects of the Second Language on the First*. Clevedon: Multilingual Matters. 1–18.

Council of Europe. 2001. *Common European Framework of Reference for Languages: Learning, Teaching, Assessment*. Cambridge: Cambridge University Press.

Daller, H., J. Milton, & J. Treffers-Daller. 2007. Editors' introduction. Conventions, terminology and an overview of the book. In: H. Daller, J. Milton, & J. Treffers-Daller (eds.), *Modelling and Assessing Vocabulary Knowledge*. Cambridge: Cambridge University Press. 1–32.

Daller, H., J. Milton, & J. Treffers-Daller (eds.). *Modelling and Assessing Vocabulary Knowledge*. Cambridge: Cambridge University Press.

Davies, A. 2003. *The Native Speaker: Myth and Reality*. Clevedon: Multilingual Matters.

De Angelis, G. 2007. *Third or Additional Language Acquisition*. Clevedon: Multilingual Matters.

De Mauro, T. 2000. *Il dizionario della lingua italiana*. Torino: Paravia.

De Mauro, T. 2005. *La fabbrica delle parole. Il lessico e problemi di lessicologia*. Torino: Utet.

Dewaele, J.M. 2001. Activation or inhibition? The interaction of L1, L2 and L3 on the Language Mode Continuum. In: J. Cenoz, B. Hufeisen, & U. Jessner (eds.), *Cross-Linguistic Influence in Third Language Acquisition. Psycholinguistic Perspectives*. Clevedon: Multilingual Matters. 69–89.

Dijkstra, T. 2003. Lexical processing in bilinguals and multilinguals: the word selection problem. In: J. Cenoz, B. Hufeisen, & U. Jessner (eds.), 2003. *The Multilingual Lexicon*. Dordrecht: Kluwer. 11–26.

Ellis, N. 1997. Vocabulary acquisition: Word structure, collocation, word-class, and meaning. In: N. Schmitt & M. McCarthy (eds.), *Vocabulary: Description, Acquisition and Pedagogy*. Cambridge: Cambridge University Press. 122–139.

Ellis, N. 2002. Frequency effects in language processing: A review with implications for theories of implicit and explicit language acquisition. *Studies in Second Language Acquisition*. 24/2. 143–188.

Enström, I. 2004. Ordförråd och ordinlärning: med särskilt fokus på avancerade inlärare [Vocabulary and vocabulary learning: with a special focus on advanced learners]. In: K. Hyltenstam & I. Lindberg (eds.), *Svenska som andraspråk – i forskning, undervisning och samhälle* [Swedish as a L2 – in Research, Teaching and Society]. Lund: Studentlitteratur. 171–195.

Erman, B., F. Forsberg Lundell, & M. Lewis this volume. Formulaic language in advanced second language acquisition and use.

Fant, L. this volume. Pragmatic markers in high-level second language use.

Fitzpatrick, T. 2006. Habits and rabbits. Word associations and the L2 lexicon. *Eurosla Yearbook*, 6, 121–145.

Fitzpatrick, T. 2007. Word association patterns: unpacking the assumptions. *International Journal of Applied Linguistics*, 17/ 3. 319–331.

Fitzpatrick, T. & C. Izura 2011. Word association in L1 and L2. An exploratory study of response types, response times and interlingual mediation. *Studies in Second Language Acquisition*, 33/3. 373–398.

Gass, S., M. & A. Mackey. 2002. Frequency effects and second language acquisition. A complex picture? *Studies in Second Language Acquisition*, 24/2. 249–260.

Goulden, R., P. Nation, & J. Read. 1990. How large can a receptive vocabulary be? *Applied Linguistics*, 11/4. 341–363.

Green, D. 1986. Control, activation and resource: A framework and a model for the control of speech in bilinguals. *Brain and Language*, 27. 210–223.

Greidanus, T., P. Bogaards, E. van der Linden, L. Nienhuis, & T. de Wolf. 2004. The construction and validation of a deep knowledge test for advanced learners of French. In: P. Bogaards & B. Laufer (eds.), *Vocabulary in a Second Language. Selection, Acquisition and Testing*. Amsterdam: Benjamins. 191–208.

Grosjean, F. 2001. The bilingual's language modes. In: J. Nicol (ed.), *One Mind, Two Languages: Bilingual language processing*. Oxford: Blackwell. 1–25.

Gyllstad, H. 2013. Looking at L2 vocabulary knowledge dimensions from an assessment perspective – challenges and potential solutions. In: C. Bardel, C. Lindqvist, & B. Laufer (eds.), *L2 Vocabulary Acquisition, Knowledge and Use. New Perspectives on Assessment and Corpus Analysis. Eurosla Monograph Series*, 2. EuroSLA. The European Second Language Association. 11–28.

Haastrup, K. 1991. *Lexical Inferencing Procedures or Talking about Words*. Tübingen: Günter Narr.

Hammarberg, B. 2009. *Processes in Third Language Acquisition*. Edinburgh: Edinburgh University Press.

Herwig, A. 2001. Plurilingual lexical organisation: Evidence from lexical processing in L1–L2–L3–L4 translation. In: J. Cenoz, B. Hufeisen, & U. Jessner (eds.), *Cross-Linguistic Influence in Third Language Acquisition. Psycholinguistic Perspectives*. Clevedon: Multilingual Matters. 115–137.

Hilton, H. 2008. The link between vocabulary knowledge and spoken L2 fluency. *Language Learning Journal*, 36/2. 153–166.

Hirsch, D. & P. Nation. 1992. What vocabulary size is needed to read unsimplified texts for pleasure? *Reading in a Foreign Language*, 8/2. 689–696.

Housen, A., B. Bulté, M. Pierrard, & S. Van Daele. 2008. Investigating lexical proficiency development over time – the case of Dutch-speaking learners of French in Brussels. *Journal of French Language Studies*, 18. 277–298.

Hulstijn, J. H. & C. Tangelder. 1993. Semantic and phonological interference in the mental lexicon of learners of English as a foreign language and native speakers of English. In: J. Chapelle & M.-T. Claes (eds.), *Actes: 1er Congrès international: mémoire et mémorisation dans l'acquisition et l'apprentissage des Langues/Proceedings: 1st international congress: memory and memorization in acquiring and learning languages*. Lovain-la-Neuve: CLL. 143–164.

Hyltenstam, K. 1988. Lexical characteristics of near-native second-language learners of Swedish. *Journal of Multilingual and Multicultural Development*, 9/1–2. 67–84.

Hyltenstam, K. & N. Abrahamsson. 2003. Maturational constraints in SLA. In: C. J. Doughty & M. H. Long (eds.), *Handbook of Second Language Acquisition*, Oxford: Blackwell. 539–588.

Jarvis, S. & A. Pavlenko. 2008. *Crosslinguistic Influence in Language and Cognition*. New York: Routledge.

Jarvis, S. & M. Daller. 2013. *Vocabulary Knowledge: Human Ratings and Automated Measures*. Amsterdam: John Benjamins.

Laufer, B. 1988. The concept of "synforms" (similar lexical forms) in vocabulary acquisition. *Language and Education*, 2/2. 113–132.

Laufer, B. 1997. What's in a word that makes it hard or easy: Some intralexical factors that affect the learning of words. In: N. Schmitt & M. McCarthy (eds.), *Vocabulary: Description, Acquisition and Pedagogy*. Cambridge: Cambridge University Press. 140–155.

Laufer, B. 2003. The influence of L2 on L1 collocational knowledge and on L1 lexical diversity in free written expression. In: V.J. Cook (ed.), *Effects on the Second Language on the First*. Clevedon: Multilingual Matters. 19–31.

Laufer, B. & P. Nation. 1995. Vocabulary size and use: Lexical richness in L2 written production. *Applied Linguistics*, 16/3. 307–322.

Laufer, B. & Z. Goldstein 2004. Testing vocabulary knowledge: size, strength, and computer adaptiveness. *Language Learning*, 54: 469–523.

Laufer, B. & G. Ravenhorst-Kalovski. 2010. Lexical Threshold revisited: Lexical text coverage, learners' vocabulary size and reading comprehension. *Reading in a Foreign Language*, 22. 15C30.

Levelt, W. J. M. 1989. *Speaking. From Intention to Articulation*. Cambridge, Massachusetts: The MIT Press.

Lindqvist, C. 2006. *L'influence translinguistique dans l'interlangue française. Étude de la production orale d'apprenants plurilingues. Cahiers de la recherche*, 33. Doctoral dissertation. Stockholms University.

Lindqvist, C. 2010a. Inter- and intralingual influences in advanced learners' French L3 oral production. In: C. Bardel & C. Lindqvist (eds.), *Approaches to Third Language Acquisition*. Special issue of *International Review of Applied Linguistics in Language Teaching*, 48/2–3. 131–157.

Lindqvist, C. 2010b. La richesse lexicale chez l'apprenant avancé de français. *Canadian Modern Language Review*, 66/3. 393–420.

Lindqvist, C. 2012. Advanced learners' word choices in French L3 oral production. In J. Cabrelli Amaro, S. Flynn, & J. Rothman (eds.), *Third Language Acquisition in Adulthood*. Amsterdam: John Benjamins. 255–280.

Lindqvist, C., C. Bardel, & A. Gudmundson. 2011. Lexical richness in the advanced learner's oral production of French and Italian L2. *International Review of Applied Linguistics in Language Teaching*, 49/3. 221–240.

Linnarud, M. 1986. *Lexis in Composition. A Performance Analysis of Swedish Learners' Written English. Lund Studies in English*, 74. Doctoral dissertation. Lund: CWK Gleerup.

Linell, Per. 2005. *The Written Language Bias in Linguistics. Its Nature, Origins, and Transformations*. London: Routledge.

Long, M. H. & J. C. Richards. 1997. Series editors' preface. In: J. Coady & T. Huckin (eds.), *Second Language Vocabulary Acquisition. A rationale for Pedagogy*. Cambridge: Cambridge University Press. IX–X.

Malvern, D., B. Richards, N. Chipere, & P. Durán. 2004. *Lexical Diversity and Language Development*. New York: Palgrave Macmillan.

McCarthy, P. M. & S. Jarvis. 2007. vocd: A theoretical and empirical evaluation. *Language Testing*, 24/4. 459–488.

McCarthy, P. M. & S. Jarvis. 2010. MTLD, vocd-D, and HD-D: A validation study of sophisticated approaches to lexical diversity assessment. *Behavior Research Methods*, 42/2. 381–292.

Meara, P. 1978. Learners' word associations in French. *Interlanguage Studies Bulletin*, 3/1. 192–211.

Meara, P. 1992. *Euralex French Tests*. Swansea: Centre for Applied Language Studies.

Meara, P. 1996. The vocabulary knowledge framework. Unpublished paper. Available online at http://www.lognostics.co.uk/vlibrary/meara1996c.pdf.

Melka, F. 1997. Receptive vs. productive aspects of vocabulary acquisition. In: N. Schmitt & M. McCarthy (eds.), *Vocabulary: Description, Acquisition and Pedagogy*. Cambridge: Cambridge University Press. 84–102.

Milton, J. 2007. Lexical profiles, learning styles and the construct validity of lexical size tests. In: H. Daller, J. Milton, & J. Treffers-Daller (eds.), *Modelling and Assessing Vocabulary Knowledge*. Cambridge: Cambridge University Press. 47–58.

Milton, J. 2008. French vocabulary breadth among learners in the British school and university system: comparing knowledge over time. *Journal of French Language Studies*, 18. 333–348.

Milton, J. 2009. *Measuring Second Language Vocabulary Acquisition*. Bristol: Multilingual Matters.

Milton, J. 2013. Measuring the contribution of vocabulary knowledge to proficiency in the four skills. In: C. Bardel, C. Lindqvist, & B. Laufer (eds.), *L2 Vocabulary Acquisition, Knowledge and Use. New Perspectives on Assessment and Corpus Analysis. Eurosla Monograph Series*, 2. EuroSLA. The European Second Language Association. 57–78.

Milton, J. & T. Alexiou. 2009. Vocabulary size and the Common European Framework of Reference for Languages. In: B. Richards, H. M. Daller, D. Malvern, P. Meara, J. Milton, & J. Treffers-Daller (eds.), *Vocabulary Studies in First and Second Language Acquisition: The Interface between Theory and Application*. Basingstoke: Palgrave. 194–211.

Milton, J., J. Wade, & N. Hopkins. 2010. Aural word recognition and oral competence in English as a foreign language. In: R. Chacón-Beltran, C. Abello-Contesse, & M. del Mar Torreblanca-López (eds.), *Insights into Non-Native Vocabulary Teaching and Learning*. Bristol: Multilingual Matters. 83–98.

Moon, R. 1997. Vocabulary connections: Multi-word items in English. In: N. Schmitt & M. McCarthy (eds.), *Vocabulary: Description, Acquisition and Pedagogy*. Cambridge: Cambridge University Press. 40–63.

Nagy, W. E. 1997. The role of context in first- and second-language vocabulary learning. In: N. Schmitt & M. McCarthy (eds.), *Vocabulary: Description, Acquisition and Pedagogy*. Cambridge: Cambridge University Press. 64–83.

Namei, S. 2002. *The Bilingual Lexicon from a Developmental Perspective. A Word Association Study of Persian–Swedish Bilinguals*. Doctoral dissertation. Stockholm University.

Nation, P. 1983. Testing and teaching vocabulary. *Guidelines*, 5/1. 12–25.

Nation, P. 2001. *Learning Vocabulary in Another Language*. Cambridge: Cambridge University Press.

Nation, P. 2004. A study of the most frequent word families in the British National Corpus. In: P. Bogaards & B. Laufer (eds.), *Vocabulary in a Second Language. Selection, Acquisition and Testing*. Amsterdam: Benjamins. 3–13.

Nation, P. 2006. How large a vocabulary is needed for reading and listening? *The Canadian Modern Language Review/La Revue canadienne des langues vivantes*, 63/1. 59–82.

Nation, P. & D. Beglar. 2007. A vocabulary size test. *The Language Teacher*, 31/7. 9–13.

Nation, P. & R. Waring 1997. Vocabulary size, text coverage and word lists. In: N. Schmitt & M. McCarthy (eds.), *Vocabulary: Description, Acquisition and Pedagogy*. Cambridge: Cambridge University Press. 6–19.

Nurweni, A. & J. Read. 1999. The English vocabulary knowledge of Indonesian university students. *English for Specific Purposes*, 18/2. 161–175.

Nystedt, J., C. Bardel, & A. Gudmundson. 2007. Il lessico nella produzione orale dell'italiano L2 e il Vocabolario di Base. Studio pilota su due apprendenti universitari svedesi messi a confronto con un parlante nativo. *Linguistica e letteratura*, 1–2. 151–183.

Paquot, M. 2014. Cross-linguistic influence and formulaic language: Recurrent word sequences in French learner writing. *Eurosla Yearbook*, 14. 240–261.

Paradis, M. 2009. *Declarative and Procedural Determinants of Second Languages*. Amsterdam: John Benjamins.

Pauletto, F. & C. Bardel submitted. Pointing backwards and forwards: be'-prefaced responsive turns in Italian L2. A developmental perspective.

Poulisse, N. 1999. *Slips of the Tongue. Speech Errors in First and Second Language Production*. Amsterdam: Benjamins.

Read, J. 2000. *Assessing Vocabulary*. Cambridge: Cambridge University Press.

Read, J. 2004. Plumbing the depths: How should the construct of vocabulary knowledge be defined? In: P. Bogaards & B. Laufer (eds.), *Vocabulary in a Second Language. Selection, Acquisition and Testing*. Amsterdam: Benjamins. 209–227.

Ringbom, H. 2001. Lexical transfer in L3 production. In: J. Cenoz, B. Hufeisen, & U. Jessner (eds.), *Cross-Linguistic Influence in Third Language Acquisition. Psycholinguistic Perspectives*. Clevedon: Multilingual Matters. 59–68.

Ringbom, H. 2007. *Cross-Linguistic Similarity in Foreign Language Learning*. Clevedon: Multilingual Matters.

Singleton, D. 1999. *Exploring the Second Language Mental Lexicon*. Cambridge: Cambridge University Press.

Singleton, D. 2006. Lexical transfer: Interlexical or intralexical? In: J. Arabski, (ed.), *Cross-linguistic Influences in the Second Language Lexicon*. Clevedon: Multilingual Matters. 130–143.

Swan, M. 1997. The influence of the mother tongue on second language vocabulary acquisition and use. In: N. Schmitt & M. McCarthy (eds.), *Vocabulary: Description, Acquisition and Pedagogy*. Cambridge: Cambridge University Press. 156–180.

Stæhr, L. Stenius. 2008. Vocabulary size and the skills of listening, reading and writing. *Language Learning Journal*, 36/2. 139–152.

Stæhr, L. Stenius. 2009. Vocabulary knowledge and advanced listening comprehension in English as a foreign language. *Studies in Second Language Acquisition*, 31/4. 577–607.

Stroud, C. 1979. Kontrastiv lexikologi. In: K. Hyltenstam (ed.), *Svenska i invandrarperspektiv. Kontrastiv analys och språktypologi*. Lund: Gleerups. 174–218.

Söderman, T. 1993. Word associations of foreign language learners and native speakers: the phenomenon of a shift in response type and its relevance for lexical development. In: H. Ringbom (ed.), *Near-Native Proficiency in English*. Åbo: Åbo Akademi, 91–182.

Tidball, F. & J. Treffers-Daller. 2008. Analyzing lexical richness in French learner language: what frequency can tell us about basic and advanced words. *Journal of French Language Studies*, 18. 299–313.

Treffers-Daller, J., H. Daller, D. Malvern, B. Richards, P. Meara, & J Milton. 2008. Introduction: Special issue on knowledge and use of the lexicon in French as a second language. *Journal of French Language Studies*, 18. 269–276.

Ure, J. 1971. Lexical density and register differentiation. In: G. E. Perren & J. L. M. Trim (eds.), *Applications of Linguistics*. Cambridge: Cambridge University Press.

Vermeer, A. 2001. Breadth and depth of vocabulary in relation to L1/L2 acquisition and frequency of input. *Applied Psycholinguistics*, 22/2. 217–234.

Vermeer, A. 2004. The relation between lexical richness and vocabulary size in Dutch L1 and L2 children. In: P. Bogaards & B. Laufer (eds.), *Vocabulary in a Second Language. Selection, Acquisition and Testing*. Amsterdam: Benjamins. 173–189.

Wesche, M. B. & T. S. Paribakht. 1996. Assessing vocabulary knowledge: Depth vs. breadth. *Canadian Modern Language Review*, 53. 13–40.

Wilks, C. & P. Meara. 2007. Implementing graph theory approaches to the exploration of density and structure in L1 and L2 word association networks. In: H. Daller, J. Milton, & J. Treffers-Daller (eds.), *Modelling and Assessing Vocabulary Knowledge*. Cambridge: Cambridge University Press. 167–181.

Witalisz, E. 2007. Vocabulary assessment in writing: Lexical statistics. In: Z. Lengyel & J. Navracsics. (eds.), *Second Language Lexical Processes. Applied linguistics and Psycholinguistic Perspectives*, Clevedon: Multilingual Matters. 101–116.

Wolter, B. 2001. Comparing the L1 and the L2 mental lexicon: A depth of individual word knowledge model. *Studies in Second Language Acquisition*, 23/1. 41–69.

Wolter, B. & H. Gyllstad. 2011. Collocational links in the L2 mental lexicon and the influence of L1 intralexical knowledge. *Applied Linguistics*, 21/4. 430–449.

Britt Erman, Fanny Forsberg Lundell, and Margareta Lewis
4 Formulaic language in advanced second language acquisition and use

1 Introduction

Being highly proficient in a language means not only knowing how to combine words according to their selectional and morpho-syntactic restrictions but also knowing what linguistic expressions to use in what situations and contexts, i.e. a high level of proficiency is closely linked to a high level of idiomaticity. The number of studies on idiomaticity has increased concurrently with increasing access to large text corpora, and new insights have brought about a more inclusive view of idiomaticity. The basic assumption of this chapter is that the notion of idiomaticity must be extended to encompass any nativelike selection of expression, including all of what a native speaker of a language knows beyond single words and grammatical rules (cf. Fillmore, Kay and O'Connor 1988). Results from studies of recurrent patterns in text corpora give clear evidence that there is a large store of multi-word units that constitutes an important part of what should be included in the notion of idiomaticity. Multi-word-patterns reflecting this extended view of idiomaticity are commonly referred to as 'formulaic language' (Wray 2002; Schmitt 2004; Adolphs and Durow 2004; Boers et al. 2014), or with more transparent terms such as 'conventionalized word combinations' (Foster, Bolibaugh and Kotula 2014).

At the very core of research on formulaic language is the idea that meaning, broadly speaking, is not only represented by single words. Lexical units in actual discourse are typically multi-word sequences, the meanings of which arise in interaction. Although the meanings of many multi-word sequences are transparent, these are not deducible from the meanings of the component parts in any straightforward way. In other words, they have become conventionalized.

It is generally acknowledged that appropriate use of formulaic language is one of the big stumbling blocks in the attainment of nativelike L2 proficiency (Granger 1998; Howarth 1998; Wray 2002). In fact, measures of the quantity and quality of formulaic language have been shown to be good indicators of the level of a learner's second language proficiency and used to distinguish more nativelike from what is less so (cf. Wiktorsson 2003; Forsberg 2008; Boers et al. 2006; Lewis 2009; Foster, Bolibaugh and Kotula 2014). The awareness of the

Britt Erman, Fanny Forsberg Lundell and Margareta Lewis, Stockholm University

important role of formulaic language for language proficiency has generated new areas of research, the results of which having repercussions for theory as well as practice of foreign language learning and teaching.

A substantial part of this chapter will be concerned with presenting those linguistic theories and methods that take formulaic language into account, not as peripheral but as a core phenomenon[1]. The remainder of the chapter is devoted to a presentation and discussion of empirical research on formulaic language from the perspective of second language acquisition. The linguistic theories presented and discussed in the first section are particularly relevant to the field of advanced second language acquisition. This will be further discussed and problematized.

2 Formulaic language

'Formulaic language' is a cover term for a plethora of multiword sequences. It is an abstract concept, whose instantiations are frequently referred to as 'formulaic sequences' (Schmitt 2004). Formulaic sequences can be of many different kinds. Some are well-established lexical units including lexicalized phrases, e.g. *on the other hand, by and large, let alone, all of a sudden, to all intents and purposes*, all of which could best be described as "long words with internal spaces", which, although written as sequences of words, normally have no internal variation (Fillmore 2007). Some are phraseological units, usually containing an element with a specialized and/or metaphorical sense, e.g. *heave a sigh, blow your own trumpet* (Cowie 1998; Howarth 1998). Many clausal formulaic sequences are routines or phatic expressions, e.g. *Nice weather today, What's up, So what*, typically serving pragmatic functions. In between these groups there are many formulaic sequences with unitary meanings, some of which fulfil 'lexical functions' (in Mel'čuk's framework; 1996, 1998) e.g. *carry out a project, ride a bus, infinite patience, legislative power*; others are the outcomes of social institutions and shared moral values e.g. *write a cheque, a free country, shared responsibility, appropriate behaviour*. The two last mentioned groups are commonly referred to as 'collocations', and are typically transparent, having few syntactic constraints. Yet others may function as sentence stems that can be expanded and inflected (Pawley and Syder 1983), e.g. *I'm (so) sorry to keep/have kept you waiting*, as

---

[1] Generative theories will thus be left out of this discussion foremost because formulaic language is epiphenomenal to this strand of theories, and when addressed it is so in terms of idioms (e.g. Radford 2009: 199–201, 213–214).

lexical bundles (Biber, Conrad and Leech 2002), e.g. *and here we have* (attention-catcher), as sentence launchers, e.g. *I don't know why* typically followed by a clause, or as discourse markers, e.g. *I think, you know, I mean* appearing in many different contexts and with different functions. Regardless of the category ascribed to them, all of these sequences are formulaic, in so far as they match conventionalized concepts. Many of the formulaic sequences exemplified here are not to be found in dictionaries, or only indirectly, viz., when occurring as typical examples of co-texts in which the entry word may occur. Finally, there are numerous sequences and patterns yet to be discovered, notably the outcomes of 'semantic prosodies', e.g. the verb *face* charged with traces of negative contexts: *facing problems, difficulties, consequences*, as apparent in text corpora. Indeed, the actual use of word combinations in corpora gives evidence that there is far less syntagmatic choice than the paradigm is actually capable of creating (Sinclair 1997; Stubbs 2002).

Formulaic language serves both the speaker's and hearer's interests by facilitating production and comprehension, thus ensuring efficient communication (Wray 2002). Indeed, formulaic language meets a multitude of communicative needs, such as encoding, decoding, and being fluent, efficient and idiomatic, to mention a few. It is not surprising therefore that formulaic language makes up a large part of any discourse.

In the next section we will discuss formulaic language from three main perspectives: a statistical, a psychological-cognitive, and a linguistic, all of course intertwined and interdependent.

3 Statistical approaches

Ways of exploring large quantities of spoken and written language usage have been facilitated by sophisticated software and computerized corpora of ever-increasing sizes. Frequency and co-occurring words and patterns are in focus in corpora studies. Sinclair (1991) was among the first to show that words are frequently distributed according to certain patterns and that meaning is seldom conveyed by an individual word. Thus certain words frequently co-occur and grammar and vocabulary interact. In fact, according to Sinclair (1991: 108), most discourse (spoken and written) is made up of syntagmatic multi-word sequences, i.e. everyday expressions used in standard patterns. This insight led him to formulate his idiom principle to the effect that most meanings require the presence of more than one word for their normal realization (see Sinclair 1991; see Section 4.1 below).

A more explicit approach to a corpus-based investigation of the interaction between grammar and lexis is the notion of collocational frameworks. Renouf and Sinclair discuss discontinuous sequences (1991: 129), e.g. *be* + ? + *to, too* + ? + *to* and *a* + ? + *of, an* + ? + *of*, showing that words are not random in a given frame but typically belong to particular semantic classes associated with the framework in question. For instance, *too* + ? + *to* is predominantly filled with non-verbal adjectives such as *easy, good, late* and *young*. Hunston and Francis (2000) developed the notion 'pattern grammar', e.g. patterns emerging around specific sets of verbs. A special kind of frequency-based statistical method to extract words and constructions is the collostructional analysis method (Stefanowitsch and Gries 2009). As the name suggests this method is concerned with the extraction and comparison of patterns and constructions. It incorporates a great number of syntactic and semantic features to explore different patterns of clusters and their dispersion over domains and genres within corpora.

An approach that has gained considerable interest in recent years is the 'lexical bundles' approach. Lexical bundles are multi-word sequences that recur frequently and are distributed widely across different texts (Biber 2010: 170). The lexical bundles framework is largely data-driven and retrieval can be fully automatized and applied to sizeable text corpora. This has the effect that although lexical bundles do not represent complete structural units they have been found to serve important functions, especially in academic discourse (Biber and Barbieri 2007: 270).

Of the multiword sequences, patterns, and lexical bundles mentioned above, collocations, in terms of frequent combinations of lexical items, are no doubt the greatest challenge for any linguist interested in phraseology (Mel'čuk 1998), since "every word is primed for collocational use" (Hoey 2005: 8). Collocations are combinations of words "that a native speaker would use without thinking much, without an active search for the right word" (Yorio 1989: 66–67). In our view these descriptions not only capture collocations but also formulaic language generally and is at the core of idiomaticity. Stubbs defines collocation as "a lexical relation between two or more words which have a tendency to co-occur within a few words of each other in running text" (2002: 24), and Lewis as "the way in which words co-occur in natural text in statistically significant ways" (2000: 132). Indeed, with corpus linguistics an array of statistical association measurements to establish the degree of association between words, e.g. Mutual information and Log-likelihood, appeared.

3.1 Mutual information and the Log-likelihood formula

Both Mutual information (MI) and Log-likelihood, along with several other formulas, arise from significance testing. Furthermore, thresholds are usually chosen heuristically rather than in any principled way (Inkpen and Hirst 2002); for example, MI association values above 6–7 are considered to indicate a fairly strong collocational bonding. In other words, an MI value should be seen as an indication rather than as evidence (Ellis 2006b). MI was developed by Church and Hanks (1991) and is widely used for establishing collocational status. The MI formula involves three parameters: the size of the corpus, the domains represented in the corpus, and the co-occurrence of the 'node' (the word form that is being investigated) and 'collocate' (the word form with which the node co-occurs) within a certain span in the corpus. However, a problem with the MI score is that a word of low frequency in a corpus might, by chance, occur as a collocate or node to another word and this would yield a high MI score. Therefore another statistical measurement to meet this obvious limitation of the MI score, the Log-likelihood, is sometimes used. The Log-likelihood formula could thus be seen as a complement to MI, since the latter is considered less reliable for low frequency words. Nevertheless, of the two statistical measurements MI seems to be more widely used.

3.1.1 Research methodologies of extracting collocations

The research methodologies of two studies, explicitly focussed on collocations, will be briefly described, viz. Kennedy (2003) and Hoffmann and Lehmann (2000); both studies are based on the British National Corpus (BNC). The BNC is a corpus of mainly (90%) written texts fully equipped with several statistical measurements, among them MI and Log-likelihood. The advantages of using a corpus like the BNC are, first of all that it is of considerable size, and also, like other corpora, it was designed for automatic extraction and is therefore tagged.

Using an MI threshold above two, Kennedy (2003) examined how a set of amplifiers collocate with particular words in the BNC. A five-word window span including the node, i.e. the amplifier, was used. Apart from collocational bonding as apparent in high MI scores each amplifier is shown to have preferences for words with particular grammatical and semantic characteristics. Above all he found that some amplifiers do not seem to fit comfortably with particular adjectives (e.g. ?*heavily frustrating*, ?*fully classical*[2]). Kennedy states that, although

---

[2] Paradis (1997) discusses maximisers and adjectives using the notions of boundedness and scalarity within a cognitive framework clariyfing why, e.g., a combination such as *fully classical* is inappropriate. *Classical* is schematically a non-gradable adjective, which usually rejects degree modifiers (see also Erman 2014 for using the notions of boundedness and scalarity to explain similar adverb-adjective combinations).

some amplifiers appear to be interchangeable at first glance, closer examination revealed that this is not the case.

Hoffmann and Lehmann (2000) also used the BNC for their study, but instead of MI they used the Log-likelihood statistic. Their aim, to establish whether there is a link between familiarity and low-frequency word combinations, as well as their methodology were rather different from those of Kennedy. Their results showed that some word pairs were familiar exclusively to the native speakers, but more importantly, frequency is only one of several factors explaining a native speaker's linguistic knowledge.

Above we considered methodologies aimed at extracting node-collocate pairs. Using the same retrieval procedure we can also reach patterns consisting of any number of words, so-called *n*-grams. Lindquist and Levin (2008) and Lindquist (2009) have studied the n-grams around frequent key-words such as the nouns *foot*, *mouth*, and *hand*, and found that such frequent lemmas also tend to be part of frequent phrases, some of which are quite entrenched in our lexicon (*at hand*) while others occur as metaphorical or metonymic extensions (*put one's foot down*), all recognizable and presumably readily accessible in the mental lexicon. Questions pertaining to storage and retrieval of formulaic sequences, i.e. formulaic language from a psychological-cognitive perspective, will be dealt with in the next section.

4 Psychological-cognitive approaches

4.1 The mental lexicon

The store of linguistic units of multi-word size in the mental lexicon presumably is very large. This constitutes one of the core assumptions in the usage-based approach to Mental Grammar (Langacker 1987; Bybee 1998), as well as in early language acquisition (cf. Tomasello 2000; Wray 2002), and is implied in Sinclair's idiom principle (Sinclair 1991). As early as the mid-seventies Bolinger emphasized memory's great potential and refers to the large number of nerve cells and their connections that we were meant to use by saying: "[I]f we didn't need 'em, they wouldn't be there" (1976: 13). Wray's "needs-only analysis" (2002: 130-132) suggests that we do not analyze more than there is need for in the situation at hand. This is in accordance with Sinclair's idiom principle (1991), implying that phrases and collocations constitute single choices. This, of course, does not mean that the components of a formulaic phrase like *I'm afraid* are not processed separately should there be a need for it.

Formulaic language is a prerequisite for fluency and automaticity, because the very concept suggests that it consists of ready-made chunks which are easily retrievable. This is of special interest when dealing with second language acquisition, which, in this respect, according to Ellis, (2006a) is no different from first language acquisition. The language learner experiences instances of language use that become part of her/his mental lexicon, and each time they are heard and used they become further entrenched. Repetition is the mother of learning as it strengthens the associations in long-term memory, whether it concerns driving or language learning (Ellis 1996; see also Boers et al. 2014 and Peters 2014 regarding the positive effect of repetition for learning).

In the following sections we will briefly consider some current ideas about how formulaic language is integrated in our mental lexicon, viz., through chunking, lexical priming and noticing. We will then discuss the Lexical Hypothesis proposed by Levelt (1989), with lexis determining grammar. A brief discussion of the Usage-Based Model concludes the section.

4.2 Chunking based on frequency

Sequences of any kind are central in acquiring both a first and a second language. Sequences of sounds result in words, and sequences of words give rise to collocations and other kinds of formulaic language. Units experienced together result in what Ellis (1996) refers to as chunking. Chunking is described by Ellis as "the development of permanent sets of associative connections in long-term memory that underlies the attainment of automaticity and fluency in language" (1996: 107). Associations reflect language development, from the phonological level of language ("*bitter* → 'litter'"), to the syntagmatic level ("*bitter* → 'taste'") and finally the paradigmatic level (substitutions of the same grammatical class, "*on* → 'off', *swift* → 'fast'") in L1 and L2 alike (Ellis 1996: 93).

Results from computer simulations of language learning, applying connectionist models based on rich data input for statistical extraction of regularities, suggest that language learning is driven by statistics and frequency rather than logic. Frequency counts are implicit and automatic but thousands of hours are needed for acquisition of language to take place (Ellis 2002; see also Langacker 1991: 6). Although frequency is an important variable in determining learning and accessibility, there are other factors to consider. Salience and usefulness are equally important factors, as is the context (Ellis 2002).

4.3 Hoey's Lexical priming

Associative learning, frequency and context are important factors also in Hoey's account of lexical priming (2005). Lexical priming involves the interaction between the experience of language and the mental lexicon (2005). It results in specific contextual features that are part of the characteristics of words and word sequences stored in the mental lexicon. Priming may result in *nesting*, i.e. "the product of priming becomes itself primed in ways that do not apply to the individual words making up the combination" (2005: 8), and the extended combination is in turn a carrier of the co-text and context where it was acquired. Although the word is used as a starting point to exemplify priming, initially, stretches of sounds and letters are primed to co-occur thereby reflecting meaning (2005).

Meaning can be expressed in a number of grammatical ways, but the use of collocations adequate for the context makes language performance sound natural, with each word inherently linked to another one (Hoey 2005: 7). Marked language use may express the same meaning; but with few and weak collocations, unexpected vocabulary for the context and unusual grammar, it will sound unnatural. Hoey defines a collocation from a psycholinguistic and corpus linguistic perspective as follows: "a psychological association between words (rather than lemmas) up to four words apart /.../ evidenced by their occurrence together in corpora more often than is explicable in terms of random distribution" (2005: 5). The reason why collocations are pervasive in language, according to Hoey, is that each word is *primed* to occur with certain other words in our mental lexicon due to our experience of the word in certain co-texts and contexts. This has the implication that priming is domain specific, for instance *research* is primed to collocate with *recent* in academic writing (2005: 10).

In sum, Hoey's account of lexical priming seeks to illustrate that our mental lexicon is conditioned by language experience. Words and word sequences are carriers of contextual features from where they were encountered. At times, there are subtle differences concerning usage to which the human mind is sensitive. However, the L2 learner's opportunities of language experience in the target language (and thus for priming to take place) is in general limited and of a different kind compared with the exposure to her/his native tongue.

4.4 Levelt's Lexical Hypothesis

The Lexical Hypothesis presupposes interaction between a preverbal message and an appropriate match in the mental lexicon. Contrary to the traditional view that grammar provides the framework for lexis, Levelt's lexical hypothesis (1989: 181) implies that lexis contains grammatical information. In Levelt's model of processing speech, a preverbal message (intentions and information) is generated in the Conceptualizer that is used as input to the Formulator. A match to the preverbal message is accessed in the lexicon. Each entry in the lexicon has four kinds of linguistic features (meaning, syntax, morphology and phonology), which are interrelated. Semantic and syntactic information is specified in the lemma part of the entry, and morphological and phonological information is provided in the form part. Additional information concerning usage, e.g. context, register and style, is, according to Levelt, presumably also part of the entry in the lexicon (1989: 183). The relevance of Levelt's Lexical Hypothesis for our purposes here is that it also explains how associative relations between lexical entries which are frequently used together give rise to collocations and phrases (Levelt 1989: 184).

4.5 Cognitive processes

Related to priming evoked by lexemes as discussed above (i.e. 'lexical priming'; cf. Hoey 2005) is priming taking place on a cognitive/conceptual level. The idea that language is driven by cognitive and discourse functions and shaped through actual use is a basic tenet in Cognitive Grammar and is most apparent in the Usage-Based Model.

4.5.1 The Usage-Based Model

The term 'Usage-Based Model' was coined by Bybee (1985) and is one of the key notions in Cognitive Grammar. Langacker (1999) emphasizes the interactive nature of this model. Bybee (1985) views collocational as well as morphological structures as the outcomes of networks of connections as opposed to discrete building blocks. As the term suggests the Usage-Based Model springs from the actual use of the linguistic system and a speaker's knowledge of its conventions (Langacker 1999). In other words, the Usage-Based Model manifests a 'bottom-up', 'maximalist' framework implying that schemas (and hence the formation of rules) emerge from actual input and usage. Lower-level schemas characterized by regularities of only limited scope may be more essential to language structure than high-level schemas representing the broadest generalizations (Langacker 1999). The importance of Langacker's framework for formulaic language is clear: the bottom-up approach allows for irregularities and idiosyncracies typical of many conventionalized linguistic expressions, whether single words, collocations, or other combinations of words, but also for perfectly regular patterns to be acquired. Furthermore, when a composite expression is learnt as an unanalyzed whole, the extent to which individual components (whether collocational or morphological) become activated seems to make little difference in this dynamic approach, which is also one of the core assumptions in research on formulaic language. In the same vein, the extent to which the component parts of composite expressions are conceptually integrated, and their meanings compositional, should be seen in terms of degree rather than as either-or dichotomies.

Next we will consider a closely related and partly overlapping approach, notably a linguistic one, where the focus is not on the cognitive processes for the emergence and entrenchment of structures, as in usage-based models, but rather on instances of language use. Obviously, cognition is as much involved in both frameworks, but there is a shift of perspective.

5 Linguistic approaches

In the following few sections we will review models and theories that seek to explain formulaic language as a linguistic reality. More specifically, we will look at approaches which aim to explain linguistic expressions as forming part of and being dependent on superordinate structures for interpretation, as in Frame Semantics (Fillmore et al. 1988) and Construction Grammar (Croft and Cruse 2004), or restricting lexical choices as in the Lexical Functional framework (Mel'čuk 1998). As in Cognitive Grammar these approaches are largely based on instances of language use. Following these we will review and evaluate the phraseological approach (Howarth 1998), and, finally, we will account for an attempt at making formulaic sequences in texts visible (Erman and Warren 2000).

5.1 Frame Semantics

The foremost function of frames as laid out in Frame Semantics (Fillmore 1985) is to describe understanding based on usage. Knowing and understanding any one of the words linked to a frame presupposes knowledge and understanding of the entire frame. The concept of 'frame' in Frame Semantics shares, with other approaches to knowledge, e.g. Schank and Abelson's 'script' (1977) and Minsky's 'frame' (1977), the idea that familiar, stereotyped situations evoke specific expectations related to them. However, the notion of 'frame' in Frame Semantics is linguistic, in that frames are evoked by words. The notion of a frame could be illustrated through the Commercial Transaction Frame. This frame holds several elements including a buyer, a seller, goods, money, etc., and all the words related to them. Furthermore, words linked to a particular frame focus on different aspects of it. For example, the verb *buy* in the commercial transaction frame focuses on the buyer, *sell* on the seller, etc.

In Frame Semantics a word is defined only in relation to other words being part of and constituting its background frame; in this framework syntagmatic relationships are in the foreground. This contrasts with semantic field theory where it is paradigmatic relationships that are foregrounded. The relevance of Frame Semantics for formulaic language should be clear. The formulaic language approach rests on the assumption that the meanings of specific linguistic prefabricated structures and 'sequences' can only be understood against the background of the frames that evoke them, i.e. against knowledge of the familiar situations in which they are repeatedly being used. Additionally, a frame may hold subframes, i.e. frames evoked by the lexico-syntactic patterns in which the frame-bearing element occurs. Consider, for example, the frame, or knowledge structure, of 'environment'. Corpus searches show that this structure is associated with at least three general notions, viz., 'protection', 'harm' and 'change', which, when used in combination with the frame-bearing element *environment*, have specific lexemes linked to them. For example, for the notion of 'protection' we get *control, safeguard, save, preserve, conserve*. All of these words, when combined with the word *environment*, make up combinations with collocational status (Erman 2009).

An application of Frame Semantics is apparent in the area of dictionary making and lexicography (e.g. Fillmore and Atkins 1992, 1994; Fillmore 2003, 2007). The Berkeley FrameNet Project is an on-line lexical resource for English based on Frame Semantics and supported by corpus evidence, and is continuously updated.

5.2 Construction Grammar

Very close to both Frame Semantics and Cognitive Grammar is the framework outlined in Construction Grammar (Croft and Cruse 2004). They share the idea that there is no division between the lexicon and syntax. Croft and Cruse claim that general schematic constructions (the basic rules of grammar) and fully substantive constructions with filled slots (the idioms and idiosyncrasies of the language) are part, although at the bipolar ends, of the same lexico-grammatical cline, and derived through language use.

5.3 Lexical Functions

Closely related to Frame Semantics is Mel'čuk's Meaning-Text Theory (MTT), which has its roots in the Russian phraseological tradition (1996, 1998). Mel'čuk was in fact the first to take a more systematic approach to collocations through his work on 'phrasemes' (1996, 1998). According to Mel'čuk phrasemes are "the numerically predominant lexical unit" and outnumber single words by ten to one (Mel'čuk 1998: 24). Although this is a strong claim, there is as yet no contrary evidence. The vast majority of phrasemes are made up of collocations. Collocations are described within a Lexical Functional framework. Lexical Functions are abstract categories that can take a variety of linguistic forms. For instance, the lexical function 'Magn' (the extreme point on a scale) can be lexically expressed in many ways: as 'stark' in *stark naked*, as 'infinite' in *infinite patience*, as 'highly' in *highly appreciated*, and 'cutthroat' as in *cutthroat competition*. In contrast to Frame Semantics, which sees choice of lexis (whether single words or composite structures) as the outcome of an interplay between language and the external world, Lexical Functions (Mel'čuk 1996, 1998) should be seen as language internal phenomena. Common to these two frameworks is the notion of a keyword. The keyword is assumed to be a word combination's main meaning-bearing element (Mel'čuk 1996: 39). A collocation's keyword is semantically chosen whereas its collocates are lexically dependent choices imposed by it. So, in our examples above *naked, patience,* and *appreciated* are keywords, and the intensifying expressions (*stark, infinite, highly*) are lexically restricted to them. The examples are meant to illustrate the specific syntagmatic relations that keywords can enter into through the operation of Lexical Functions.

The Lexical Function framework has its most direct applications within translation and lexicography, but is also applied to automatic extraction of collocations.

5.4 Phraseology

Proponents of the phraseological approach have pursued the ideas of the Russian phraseologists from the 1940s, 50s and 60s. Russian phraseology is largely oriented towards fixed and semi-fixed expressions, at the same time offering a comprehensive framework for the whole spectrum of phraseology, using criteria such as degree of restrictedness of the expression's component parts. Informed by the Russian approach, Howarth (1998) suggests a continuum of idiomaticity, ranging from free collocations at one end over restricted collocations, which are partly compositional, and figurative idioms, which are non-compositional, to pure idioms, which are completely opaque, at the other end. Only the last three are phraseological because, although some are transparent and analysable, at least one of the members of the collocation has a specialized or figurative sense.

Rather than focussing on a collocation's inherent, or intrinsic, features, i.e. its meaning and function in the context of situation, or frame, to which it would typically belong, phraseologists focus on extrinsic factors, such as restricted choice of members, and degree of compositionality (cf. Nesselhauf 2003). In fact, limiting collocations to 'restricted' ones would leave out a sequence like *blow the trumpet* (used literally), and the majority of similar multiword expressions, on the grounds that there is no restriction on the nominal object the verb *blow* can take and that neither member is used in a specialized or figurative sense (cf. Howarth 1998). This contrasts with a cognitive approach, according to which a sequence like *blow the trumpet* can only be understood and correctly used against a background frame involving a special instrument, a special technique or activity, a special sound, etc. and is thus considered as a unit with unitary meaning (cf. Fillmore 1985: 229).

In response to the needs of the L2 learner the formal requirements for phraseological status of combinations of words have been relaxed, but the fact remains that few of the definitions or criteria in their framework strictly speaking take a learner perspective (Erman 2009). In fact, studies on the L2 learner's knowledge of target language collocations have shown that the L2 learner has difficulties with collocations that allow considerable variation at least as often as with collocations with a medium degree of restrictions (Nesselhauf 2003).

5.5 Linguistic evidence in texts

So far we have discussed multiword patterns based on frequency, frames and constructions. With a view to establishing the proportion of conventionalized sequences in samples of spoken and written texts, an attempt at making them visible and at categorizing them was made by Erman and Warren (2000). With an orientation towards Sinclair's two main principles in processing texts, the idiom principle and the open choice principle, the main aim of the study was to gain an impression of the impact that the alternation between these two principles has on the structure of texts. To achieve this, a mode of analysis identifying multiword sequences was worked out revealing how multiword combinations combine with each other and interact with words called up according to the open choice principle. Another contribution of the study was the revelation that there is a large amount of prefabricated language in native spoken and written texts, on average around half of the texts, or between 50% and 60%. Prefabricated structures, or prefabs, were found to serve lexical, grammatical and pragmatic (or discourse) functions. Lexical prefabs refer to some extralingusitic entity or phenomenon, but also include more general expressions, such as *on these grounds, in reply to*; grammatical prefabs are intralinguistic text-forming items rather than referring units (e.g. quantifiers and existential constructions), and pragmatic prefabs (e.g. discourse markers) function largely outside the syntactic structure, many of them confined to spoken language and mainly emerging in interaction.

Investigating the proportion and distribution over the types and categories accounted for above in L2 production and comparing these with native production and level of proficiency, Wiktorsson (2003) and Lewis (2009) showed that although the learners in some respects approached native levels, appropriateness sometimes failed, at times due to transfer from L1. In addition, the amount of formulaic language in L2 production was found to correspond well with seat time (from upper secondary to university level) (cf. Forsberg 2008), and grades (Lewis 2009). Knowledge and use of formulaic language was thus a good indicator of proficiency.

5.6 Summary of different perspectives on formulaic language

Following the brief summary of the theories aimed at accounting for formulaic language described above, we propose a linguistic perspective that we find fruitful for second language acquisition with particular focus on idiomaticity in (very) advanced language learners. This is followed by a brief discussion of the assumed differences between natural and formal learning, as well as the sometimes apparent mismatch between native and non-native word combinations and the implications this has for teaching.

While there is broad consensus regarding criteria as well as definitions for many syntactic, semantic and phonological phenomena, definitions and criteria for formulaic language are still controversial. For instance, there is no consensus as to exactly what should be incorporated in the notion of formulaic language, although it is pervasive in everyday language production. Formulaic language is a pervasive yet at the same time 'elusive' phenomenon. Its elusive character can in part be explained by its relative nature reflecting local, cultural as well as global concerns and foci in society (Lewis 2009: 1). Nevertheless, it seems reasonable to assume that a core set of conventionalized, and thus formulaic, language units are shared by most speakers in a language community. It is tempting to say that many conventional combinations of words are just the way ideas and thoughts are habitually expressed. As discussed in the previous sections, attempts have been made to identify and analyze formulaic language in more principled ways.

As we have seen in the review of the literature above, several theories incorporate conventionalized expressions and combinations of words. For instance, Mel'čuk's lexical functions take us a long way towards identifying many collocations (if not the majority of them), which make up the largest category of conventionalized expressions. Frame Semantics, informed by Mel'čuk's and his collaborators' work (Fillmore 2003), is perhaps the first cognitive theory approaching the meaning and understanding of multiword expressions arising through knowledge frames. Cognitive Grammar and the Usage-Based Model (Langacker 1999; Bybee 1998) have great explanatory power in approaching cognitive processes, as well as emergence and storage of multiword expressions. Frequency-based models maintain that the frequency of, and exposure to, word combinations play an important role in language acquisition. Most of the theories incorporating formulaic language acknowledge that multiword expressions, like other features of language, are usage-based. In view of this it is hard to pick out the "one and only" theory or method for the analysis of formulaic language. Nevertheless, for the identification and analysis of formulaic language in all its different realizations we hold that Frame Semantics and the lexical function framework have proven to be the most helpful. The basic assumption in Frame Semantics is that each frame has one meaning-bearing element, or head, which in turn selects related lexemes evoked by it. As mentioned above frames and lexical functions make substantial contributions to identifying and explaining collocations. What makes Construction Grammar particularly well suited for the understanding of formulaic language is that it first of all captures the idea of form-meaning pairings, or "stored pairings of form and function" (Goldberg 2003), and secondly that it incorporates constructions with different degrees of lexical specification, from partly schematic to fully specified. Croft and Cruse suggest a gradient of lexical specification ranging from lexically unspecified to fully lexically specified constructions (Croft and Cruse 2004: 247). Only those constructions that are partly or fully lexically specified match our definition of formulaic language, i.e. instantiated as a formulaic sequence consisting of at least two continuous or discontinuous words selected by native speakers in preference to an alternative combination that could have been selected had there been no conventionalization (Erman and Warren 2000). The above review of literature incorporating the description of formulaic language shows that formulaic language is not specifically linked to or explained through one single theory, method or model, but is incorporated in theories aimed at describing language usage.

Links between linguistic theory with a focus on formulaic language and second language acquisition are at times weak. The perspectives that have been linked to SLA are the generative and phraseological ones. The former is directed towards the extraction of rules through exposure and usage, whereas the latter is concerned with those restrictions imposed by the language system that are assumed to cause specific problems for learners. As suggested above, the theories that ought to be fruitful in SLA research are the cognitive and usage-based ones, such as Frame Semantics/Construction Grammar, and Cognitive Grammar. Fortunately, the implications of these theories in relation to second language research are beginning to be investigated and discussed, especially by psychologists interested in SLA (cf. Robinson and Ellis 2008; Ellis 2006a, b). The next few sections will provide an overview of research on formulaic language and second language acquisition.

6 Formulaic language and SLA

6.1 Introduction

Since the 1970s L1 as well as L2 acquisition research has been interested in the notion of formulaic language. The research can roughly be divided into three main strands: (1) formulaic language as a basis for creative rule development (Clark 1974; Wong-Fillmore 1976; Peters 1983, Myles, Mitchell and Hooper 1998, 1999), (2) formulaic language as a fluency device (Raupach 1984; Towell, Hawkins, and Bazergui 1996; Wood 2006), and (3) formulaic language as a yardstick of second language performance (Yorio 1980, 1989; Granger 1998; Kecskés 2002; Wiktorsson 2003, Forsberg 2008; Lewis 2009). It is important, however, to emphasize that *formulaic language* as used by SLA researchers does not always refer to the same phenomenon in the three strands of research, or correspond to the notion described in the theoretical overview above. Scholars interested in the relationship between formulaic language and rule development mostly refer to 'sequences learned as wholes', without application of grammatical rules. For instance, Myles, Mitchell and Hooper (1998), suggested that the sequences *j'aime* ('I like') and *j'adore* ('I love') produced by beginner learners in their L2 French corpus were learnt as formulaic chunks. These sequences were later segmented and contributed to creative rule development. It seems clear that these sequences are quite different from those described by e.g. the phraseologists discussed above. Researchers investigating the connection between spoken fluency and formulaic language are often interested in discourse markers and 'fillers' (cf. Raupach 1984). Lastly, those who are interested in the link between formulaic language and idiomaticity will be more interested in collocations, such as verb+noun combinations, since they have been found to constitute a difficulty even for advanced learners (Warren 2005; Forsberg 2008; Erman 2009).

Given the diversity of formulaic sequences, why bring them together under one label? According to Wray (2002) they all pertain to the same mechanism, the holistic processing mode, which is said to be the preferred mode, as opposed to the analytic mode. Wray proposed a definition of formulaic sequence to the effect that it is an unanalyzed sequence stored and retrieved whole. This obviously applies both to 'holophrases' learnt in the early stages of acquisition, such as *my name is X* and idiomatic expressions such as *take a look at sth*. The present review, however, focuses on advanced and near-native use of a second language, which implies that we will not discuss formulaic language as a basis for rule extraction, but rather as an inherent part of idiomaticity. It seems reasonable to assume that the last stages of L2 acquisition are characterized, partly, by the emergence of targetlike idiomaticity. As we all know, the L2 learner has a long way to go, or in N. Ellis' words "nativelike fluency and idiomaticity require an awful lot of figuring out which words go together" (Ellis 2002: 157). Language idiomaticity is characterized by the use of conventional combinations by native speakers, and it is reasonable to assume that L2 speakers need to get a huge amount of authentic input to perceive and acquire these combinations. Some of the studies reviewed below (e.g. Dörnyei, Durow and Khawla 2004; Adolphs and Durow 2004; Forsberg Lundell and Sandgren 2013) investigate the correlation between individual factors, e.g. motivation, aptitude, anxiety, sociocultural integration, and the use of formulaic sequences.

The next section discusses studies on formulaic language and advanced/near-native L2 use. It is divided into three sub-sections, based on the different modes and methodologies used in the literature: spoken production (Section 6.2.1), written production (Section 6.2.2) and finally elicitation and psycholinguistic experiments (Section 6.2.3).

6.2 Advanced or very advanced L2 acquisition

This section reviews previous studies on the acquisition and use of formulaic sequences by advanced L2 speakers. The first problem to acknowledge when speaking of advanced L2 acquisition and/or use, is that there does not seem to exist any well-established definition of this notion (but see for example Bartning, this volume). Moreover, many authors are unclear regarding their informants' proficiency level, often simply labelling them as advanced university students, at times including TOEFL scores or the number of years studying the language. Furthermore, the notion of 'advanced' is problematic given that several target languages as well as several L1s may be involved. For example, in Swedish society the 'advanced' university student of English will be more proficient than the 'advanced' university student of French. This can be explained by English being a Germanic language like Swedish as well as having a special status in Sweden. A more language neutral definition of the 'advanced learner' is proposed by Hyltenstam, Bartning and Fant (2005), notably someone whose mastery of an L2 language is close to that of native speakers, but who is still distinguished as a non-native speaker. Although this definition seems reasonable, it does not apply to the studies reviewed here, since it has not to date been possible to control for the proficiency of informants fulfilling such a definition.

When selecting literature on advanced L2 acquisition for review in this chapter, we have followed Bartning's (1997) definition of the 'advanced learner', which is oriented towards the learner's socio-cultural profile, i.e. defined as an educated person, who has studied the second language for several years in school, and who has pursued studies in this language at university level, and, furthermore, is a semi-formal learner, having spent some time in the target language country. The studies included in this review section are consequently those where the informants have been labelled 'advanced university students', approximating Bartning's (1997) definition of an advanced learner. Additionally, we have included studies where the learners are labelled as near-native (Ekberg 2013, Mizrahi and Laufer 2010) or very advanced (Forsberg 2008; Kecskés 2002; Forsberg Lundell and Lindqvist 2012). Formulaic language at advanced levels has mainly been studied focussing on two aspects: formulaic sequences as a fluency device and formulaic sequences characterizing language idiomaticity and, thus, proficiency. In what follows, we will discuss three sources of data: spoken and written production, elicitation, and psycholinguistic experiments.

6.2.1 Advanced spoken (spontaneous) production

Formulaic sequences in spoken production have been studied with regard to both fluency and idiomaticity, both aspects considered as inherent qualities of formulaic language (Wray 2002).

One of the first and best known studies is Raupach's study (1984) of German university students of L2 French before and after a study-abroad period in France, with special regard to gains in fluency. Using a psycholinguistic method, Raupach (1984) found that learners made use of a considerable number of formulae (the term used by Raupach) in order to maintain fluency. The identification of formulae is based on hesitation phenomena, e.g. pauses, prolonged syllables, false starts, and drawls. He proposed that the sequences appearing between these hesitation phenomena are to be considered as formulae. A criterion often cited for the identification of formulaic sequences is phonological coherence (Weinert 1995; Wray 2002). Raupach divides the formulae into the subcategories of organizers and fillers/modifiers. The first category includes sequences such as *c'est, il y a, d'une part...d'autre part* and are thus textual organizing devices. Fillers and modifiers are what would be equivalent to "own-speech management" markers (Allwood, Nivre, and Ahlsén 1989), functioning as 'zones of safety' and modalizing markers. Examples given are *je crois, je pense*, and *mais*. The last word, *mais*, is a single word, not a multi-word expression as the others, and it is worth noting that Raupach believes that single words can also qualify as formulae. One of the major findings of Raupach's (1984) study is that these learners, especially after their stay in France, overuse both types, as compared to the native speaker control group.

The development of second language fluency, and the linguistic resources that contribute to fluency are apparent also in Towell, Hawkins and Bazergui's study (1996). Like Raupach (1984), they measured gains in fluency in L2 French after a study-abroad period in France. They discovered that fluency gains are not due to speed but to longer and more complex utterances, characteristic of spoken French. These are for example clefts, pseudo-clefts and the presentation devices *il y a* and *c'est*, the latter being the most frequent chunk in spoken French (Forsberg 2008). Furthermore, Towell, Hawkins and Bazergui (1996) found a substantial number of 'situational lexicalized phrases', also contributing to the gains in fluency observed after the students' stay in France.

Hancock (2000) and De Cock (2004) studied one subcategory of formulaic sequences, i.e. discourse markers, Hancock in L2 French and De Cock in L2 English. Hancock (2000) following Raupach (1984) and Towell, Hawkins and Bazergui (1996) proposed that discourse markers are used as a production strategy – compensatory fluency – in the L2. Hancock (2000) studied the use of single word discourse markers (e.g. *mais*) as well as multiword discourse markers (e.g. *parce que, je crois/pense/trouve que*) in the production of advanced university students of French and that of native speakers. She found that learners significantly overused some discourse markers (e.g. *parce que, mais*), but also that the function of particular discourse markers might vary between learners and native speakers.

Studying francophone learners of L2 English, De Cock (2004) found that learners and native speakers tended to use the same quantity of formulaic language, but learners used fewer interactive markers and more discourse structuring devices. One of her main findings is the lack of 'attenuation markers' (*kind of, sort of*) in these learners' production. De Cock interprets this lack as a failure on the part of the learner to master the informal register. Consequently, whereas Hancock (2000) notices an overuse by the learners, De Cock notices that certain structures are underused. In these two studies formulaic discourse markers are viewed from two perspectives: as fluency devices, and as markers dependent on register. This may explain why the researchers arrived at different conclusions. Foster (2001) studied lexicalized sequences in speech. Her results showed that not only learners but also native speakers use *I think* very frequently, although the latter not to the same extent.

Ekberg (2013) studied oral picture descriptions by near-native L2 speakers of Swedish, as compared to native speakers performing the same task. She found that in the bilingual/near-native group there was more individual variation in the way they described the pictures. On the basis of this the non-native speaker group can be said to be less uniform and hence less idiomatic than the Swedish native speakers, and her results can be seen as a first indication of the difficulty that idiomaticity (in terms of certain Swedish lexicalized patterns) presents for the non-native speaker, even if they are very proficient and live in the target language community. The participants in Ekberg's study, in contrast to many of those in the other studies reviewed here, were not L2 learners in a formal setting, but teenagers in a multicultural suburb in Sweden.

Boers et al. (2006) investigated whether there is an observable correlation between the use of formulaic sequences and perceived oral proficiency. The spoken production of a group of advanced university students of L2 English, elicited through interviews, was judged by two independent judges with regard to fluency, accuracy and range of expression. Two other judges, familiar with the literature on formulaic sequences, were assigned to manually identify the number of formulaic sequences in these interviews. Boers et al. (2006) found correlations between the number of formulaic sequences produced and the perceived oral proficiency in terms of fluency and range of expression. However, this is a small-scale experiment, and the methodology is questionable, since it is based on the judges' intuitions regarding proficiency as well as the identification of formulaic sequences.

A similar study was conducted by Stengers et al. (2011). This study included not only L2 English but also L2 Spanish, in order to investigate whether language typology played a role for the link between proficiency and use of formulaic sequences. Proficiency was gauged by means of judges who used the CEFR scale and formulaic sequences were identified in the same manner as in Boers et al. (2006). The results confirmed those of Boers et al., viz. there is indeed a significant correlation between proficiency and formulaic sequence use, although the correlation was stronger for English than for Spanish. The authors suggest that the weaker link found in the Spanish data could be due to the fact that the Spanish oral productions, in general, contain more morphosyntactic errors and that the productions may thus have been perceived as less proficient i.e. that the positive impact of formulaic sequences may have been overshadowed by a high rate of errors.

Forsberg (2008) studied the use of formulaic sequences at four different proficiency levels as compared to native speaker production, from beginners to very advanced users of L2 French. The aim of the study was to find out whether the use of formulaic sequences in speech is indicative of second language development. Indeed, there is an increase in the quantity of formulaic language as the learner progresses, so that the largest amount was found in the very advanced learners' and in the native speakers' production. Forsberg's categorization distinguishes those categories of formulaic language that are learnt early from those categories that are learnt late (Forsberg 2008). The most difficult category to acquire for L2 learners appears to be that of Lexical formulaic sequences (Forsberg 2008; Lewis 2009). In Forsberg's study this category is only used to the same extent as the native speakers by the very advanced users who had lived in France for at least 5 years. Another noticeable difference between the advanced and the very advanced users was also found. Whereas advanced university students overused discourse markers, also observed by Raupach (1984) and Hancock (2000), very advanced users displayed a proportion closer to the native target. The most important finding of the study was that the use of formulaic language develops over time and that some features tend to be characteristic of advanced, very advanced and nativelike usage. Especially the use of lexical formulaic sequences seems to be an indicator of second language proficiency (Forsberg 2008). In order to identify formulaic sequences, Forsberg (2008) used Erman and Warren's (2000) methodology of 'restricted exchangeability', i.e. no member of the sequence could be exchanged for a synonymous word without a change in idiomaticity.

All of the studies reported on above had as their main focus the use of formulaic sequences at various learner levels. Dörnyei, Durow, and Khawla (2004) also investigated how factors such as socio-cultural integration and motivation influence acquisition and use of formulaic sequences. This qualitative study follows seven foreign post-graduate students at the University of Nottingham during one semester. The methodology was that of content analysis of interviews, combined with tests on motivation, language aptitude, language anxiety, and attitudes towards the target language community and towards integration. Three factors turned out to be favourable to the acquisition and use of formulaic sequences: motivation, language aptitude and socio-cultural integration. However, the last mentioned factor is the most important one, since socio-cultural adaptation turned out to override lower scores on the first two learner characteristics. And, conversely, it was found that the learner needs extremely high scores on motivation and language aptitude to compensate for low socio-cultural integration scores. Adolphs and Durow (2004), working partly with the same data as Dörnyei, Durow, and Khawla (2004), concentrate on the effect of socio-cultural integration, acquisition and use of formulaic sequences. The results from both studies suggest that there is a relationship between the quantity and quality of socio-cultural integration and the development of formulaic competence.

6.2.2 Advanced written production

Yorio (1980, 1989) was among the first to acknowledge the importance of formulaic language in written texts and how it can be considered as a measure of second language proficiency. Whereas spoken production has been studied both with regard to fluency and idiomaticity, written production has been examined foremost from the perspective of second language idiomaticity. The results generally converge; there are, not surprisingly, differences between advanced university students and native speakers, and L1 influence is often observed. Granger (1998) and Howarth (1998) were among the first to examine the use of collocations in learner corpora. Studying *–ly* intensifiers + adjective (*perfectly possible*), Granger (1998) found that the learners used some of these collocations (e.g. *absolutely, totally*) in a nativelike proportion, whereas others (e.g. *highly, deeply*) were underused by the learners. She also stresses the importance of L1 influence on collocation production in that the learners tended to use word combinations that were non-existent or unusual in L2. Howarth (1998) studied non-native and native speakers' use of collocations in a written corpus, focussing on verb + object combinations. Adhering to the phraseological paradigm he proposes a continuum ranging from free combinations, over restricted collocations, to idioms. Howarth found that learners had more difficulty with the middle category, i.e. restricted collocations, than with the two other categories. These findings were confirmed by Nesselhauf (2003), who, studying L1 German learners of L2 English, used Howarth's classification of collocations, thus adopting a phraseological approach, i.e. with combinatorial restriction as the main criterion. Her aim was to get a better understanding of learners' use of collocations and to improve teaching methods. Nesselhauf concluded that learners produce as many collocations as native speakers, but 24% (255/1072) of the collocations they produced were either found to be wrong in the context or deviant (i.e. incorrect or questionable). Furthermore, she examined the nature of these deviances in detail, and found that the learners' mistakes were most commonly due to a lack of congruence between the expressions the learner used in L2 and the corresponding expression commonly used in L1. Like Granger (1998), she observed that there was cross-linguistic influence in the learners' use of collocations. She also noticed, like Howarth (1998), that the degree of restriction affects learners' difficulty with collocations. The role of cross-linguistic influence in the use of idiomatic language was discussed already in the 1970's by Eric Kellerman (1978), who suggested that learners tend to transfer 'core' meanings of words from their L1 to their L2 rather than their idiomatic or metaphorical meanings. He also proposed that cross-linguistic influence might prevent full development of lexical knowledge in the L2.

Verb + noun collocations that are restricted, but still allow variability, i.e. the verb can be combined with many nouns, appear to be more difficult for learners, than collocations whose members display a smaller combinatorial spectrum. Nesselhauf (2003) suggests that this might be due to teaching students to focus on the more restricted collocations. Furthermore, according to Nesselhauf, length of stay in the target language community seems to have a slightly positive effect on the accuracy of use, whereas the number of years studying the language does not seem to have any measurable effect (Nesselhauf 2003). This, however, goes counter to results from other studies (Forsberg 2008; Lewis 2009).

Wiktorsson (2003) examined prefabs, applying Erman and Warren's mode of classification (2000; see Section 5.5). Wiktorsson's informants were Swedish learners of English (high school and university students), who were compared to native speakers at university level. The compositions investigated were argumentative and narrative, but not considered samples of academic writing. She found that the high school students produced fewer prefabs than the university students, illustrating a natural L2 development, while there were no significant differences between the advanced university students and the native speakers in terms of the quantity of prefabs used. The only observable difference found was of a stylistic character, the learners using prefabs pertaining to the oral register to a larger extent than the native speakers.

Bolly (2009) studied the collocations of two high-frequency verbs *prendre* and *donner*, in the writings of Anglophone L2 French learners and native speakers of French. Her main findings were that the learners tended to overuse verb + noun collocations with *donner* and underuse verb + noun collocations with *prendre*. Furthermore, she found that deviances affected either the verb or the collocation as a whole in the context.

Erman (2009) studied written argumentative essays by a group of first-term university students of English and a group of native English speakers for control. The study examined the use of collocations, especially verb+noun combinations, divided into three subcategories: collocations performing Lexical functions or pertaining to Frames (Mel'čuk 1996, 1998; Fillmore 1985), those that are socio-culturally motivated, and those that are topically induced. The results showed that the non-native group tended to have a good command of collocations, but also that that their collocational range was narrower and that non-target collocations occurred.

Siyanova and Schmitt (2008) investigated written argumentative essays of advanced Russian learners of English, who had studied English 6–12 years, and spent 2 weeks–2 months in the target language country, as compared to the same type of productions by native speakers of English. In both corpora, all adjective + noun combinations (e.g. *social services*) were extracted manually in order to determine whether the non-native and native speakers produced the same number of appropriate collocations. These adjective + noun combinations were further checked for frequency and mutual information (MI) scores in the BNC (British National Corpus). The results show that 45.5% of the learners' adjective-noun combinations were frequent and with high MI, as compared to 48% in the native speakers' production. The difference is not significant, which suggests that advanced L2 learners are capable of producing a large number of appropriate collocations. However, as the authors themselves point out, this is only valid for adjective-noun combinations, since other combinations (e.g. verb-noun and noun-noun) were not included.

Taking a more qualitative approach to learners' use of collocations in L2 English writing, Durrant and Schmitt (2009), show that although learners use collocations extensively in writing they are often qualitatively different from those used by native speakers. Learners use more high-frequency collocations (e.g. *strong coffee*), whereas native speakers use more low-frequency combinations, which are characterized by a high MI-score (see Section 3.1) (e.g. *densely populated*). These characteristics would explain why non-native writing might seem to lack idiomaticity, even though appropriate collocations are used.

Results from a study by Laufer and Waldman (2011) investigating collocational use in argumentative and descriptive essays at three proficiency levels in L2 English point in the same direction. The data revealed that learners at all three proficiency levels produced significantly fewer collocations than native speakers, that the number of collocations increased only at the advanced level, and that collocational errors, particularly due to L1 influence, continued to persist even at advanced levels of proficiency.

Formulaic language in written academic discourse has been gaining interest in the last couple of years and in particular lexical bundles (Cortes 2004; Chen and Baker 2010; Ädel and Erman 2012). Ädel and Erman (2012) investigated four-word lexical bundles in English academic essays by a group of undergraduate Swedish and a group of undergraduate English writers, written within the discipline of linguistics. They found that the native English group had a larger number of types of lexical bundles, which were also more varied than those of the Swedish group, such as 'unattended' *this*-headed bundles (e.g. *this would suggest that, this may be because*), and *there*-headed bundles (e.g. *there is evidence of*). Furthermore, some lexical bundles were underrepresented in the Swedish group, especially bundles involving negations with *not* and *no* (e.g. the bundles *may or may not, that there is no*), and some, especially lexical bundles with a hedging function, were missing (e.g. *there appears to be, this may be because*). In sum, certain lexical bundles are underused by non-native writers, while others are overused, such as *I/we* framed constructions (e.g. *I claim that, we could say that* reported in Granger 1998) and generalizing bundles such as *all over the world* reported by Chen and Baker (2010: 30), less appropriate for academic discourse.

To conclude, it seems that results are somewhat mixed as regards the extent to which advanced learners are capable of producing formulaic language at native-like levels. Some studies suggest that at a quantitative level it is indeed possible (e.g. Siyanova and Schmitt 2008; Forsberg 2008), whereas some do not report nativelike attainment either for quantity or for quality (Laufer and Waldman, 2011). One explanation could be that there is a lack of consistency as regards proficiency measurements, i.e. we cannot be certain that the highly advanced learners in all of these studies are really at the same level of L2 attainment. Another possible explanation is that typological similarities between L1 and L2 will have a positive effect on L2 speakers' use of collocations. However, all the studies seem to agree that non-native and native speakers differ as regards qualitative aspects of collocational production, specific constructions and lexical bundles.

6.2.3 Elicitation and psycholinguistic experiments with advanced learners

In the sections above it has been shown that the majority of studies on formulaic language in advanced L2 learning have dealt with written production, often through the use of large computerized corpora (Granger 1998; Nesselhauf 2003). Apart from production data and corpus studies, there has been an increase in experimental studies. Among these, there is an increased interest in testing the validity of Wray's (2002) claim that formulaic sequences are processed and retrieved as wholes. There has been a shift in research from the usage to the processing and storing of formulaic sequences. Another branch of research focuses on learners' knowledge of formulaic sequences as elicited in a given context (Lewis 2009). These studies will be accounted for next followed by reports on research carried out through psycholinguistic experiments.

Kecskés (2002) studied a particular group of formulaic sequences, which he calls situation-bound utterances (SBUs henceforth). SBUs are "highly conventionalized, prefabricated units whose occurrences are tied to more or less standardized communicative situations" (Kecskés 2002: 1). An example of an SBU in American English would be: – *How are you? – I'm fine thanks /Fine, thanks* (taken from Kecskés 2002). The answers elicited might seem obvious, but Kecskés found that L2 speakers are not always aware of the short response required (indeed, this example is only another way of saying "hi"), but tend to expand on the answer in unexpected ways. To test L2 speakers' knowledge of SBUs, Kecskés used discourse completion tests, problem solving tests and a dialogue interpretation test. His main hypothesis was that the L2 speaker relies on L1 norms when choosing SBUs in the target language. The informants were non-native speakers who had lived for 1–3 years in the target country and native speakers of English. Kecskés (2002) had his hypothesis confirmed, viz. that non-native speakers do not have the same mastery of SBUs as native speakers. Furthermore, length of stay does not always seem to be a determining factor, although the learners who had stayed longer in the US generally performed better; at the same time individual and cultural differences seem to play an important part. Forsberg Lundell and Erman (2012) in their study of requests found that the non-native speakers of English and French underused morphosyntactic as well lexical downtoners compared to the native speakers.

Edmonds (2010)[3] studied the representation of conventional expressions in terms of naturalness judgments and reaction times (similar to Kecskes situation-bound utterances or social/conversational routines) in L2 French speakers and native French speakers. The non-native speakers had a mean of 9 years of formal study of French and short (approx. 4 months) or long stays (1 year or more) in France. Proficiency was not controlled for, but Edmonds considered them high proficiency users. This would also explain the result that when asked to judge the acceptability of social routines, there were no differences between native and non-native speakers, either in the short stay or long stay group. Edmonds

---

3 Several similar studies on L2 English have been conducted by Bardovi-Harlig (2009) and Bardovi-Harlig and Bastos (2011), but the levels of the learners in those studies are not deemed to be advanced enough to contribute to our understanding of high-level L2 acquisition.

thus suggests that the L2 users in her study are well on their way to acquiring target language pragmatic competence.

Schmitt et al. (2004), like Kecskés (2002), used completion tests. Their study was designed to measure both productive and receptive knowledge of a determined number of formulaic sequences. In addition, they examined development over time, testing participants at the beginning and at the end of a semester. The results were correlated with scores regarding motivation, aptitude and attitudes. In order to test the informants' productive knowledge, they constructed a test with gaps to be filled in with formulaic sequences which were included in a running text. Receptive knowledge was measured by using a text where entire formulaic sequences were left out, and the participants were to choose the adequate sequence from a multiple-choice questionnaire. The main findings were that the students (non-native postgraduate students at an English university) were fairly proficient as regards productive and receptive knowledge of formulaic sequences. They also improved during the semester, although it is impossible to say whether this is due to input in general or to the instruction they received.

A similar type of completion test was constructed by Lewis (2009), modelled on a gap test from the reading comprehension part of the National Test of English in Sweden. The 320 informants had to understand the content of the sentence(s) before filling in the appropriate word, which was part of a formulaic sequence. As a result, the written production was minimal but based on and triggered by reading and understanding the sentences. However, the formulaic sequence had to be known in order to be triggered by the context. The results showed that there was a strong correspondence between the results of the gap test and proficiency levels in English. More specifically, there were strong correlations between the gap results and the grades and significant differences between the language levels from upper secondary to university level.

Even if learners seem to have an important stock of formulaic sequences, how do we know that they are processed holistically by non-native speakers? Psycholinguistic experiments have been carried out to further investigate this question. Underwood, Schmitt and Galpin (2004) used eye-tracking methodology to examine whether formulaic sequences are processed more quickly than words that are not part of formulaic sequences. They found that the words in final position in formulaic sequences were processed more quickly than the same words in a non-formulaic context. This evidence suggests that formulaic sequences are processed 'holistically' or at least with less effort than non-formulaic strings of words. These observations were made for both native and non-native speakers, but non-native speakers' processing was found to be slower than that of native speakers. Although the learners were quite proficient (postgraduate students at an English university), this is hardly surprising.

Two fairly recent studies have tested productive collocational knowledge in highly advanced L2 speakers. Mizrahi and Laufer (2010) found that, although speakers who self-identified as near-native in L2 English performed in a nativelike way on a productive vocabulary size test, a minority of them performed in a nativelike way on a productive collocation test. Forsberg Lundell and Lindqvist (2012) tested highly advanced L2 French speakers on four different vocabulary aspects. Just as in Mizrahi and Laufer (2010), significant between-group differences were found between native and non-native speakers on a similar productive collocation test. On the other hand they performed in a nativelike way on a social routine test, based on Edmonds's test (2010) (see above).

Research on this issue has also been carried out by Schmitt and Underwood (2004) and Conklin and Schmitt (2008). Both studies use a self-paced reading task, and the main research questions for both were whether formulaic sequences are read faster than non-formulaic sequences of words, and whether there were differences between native and non-native speakers. The first study yielded somewhat puzzling results. Processing by native speakers tended to be quicker than that by non-native speakers, which was expected, and, according to the authors could probably be explained by better reading abilities in the L1 of both groups. However, the last words in the formulaic strings were not read significantly faster than the last words in the non-formulaic strings by either group, which was unexpected. This result would then suggest that there is no difference in terms of processing gains between formulaic and non-formulaic language. The authors stress, however, that the word-by-word self-paced reading methodology used in this study, where one word is presented at a time, might not be ideal for formulaic language, since the participant probably has to see the whole sequence to benefit from processing gains. In the second study, Conklin and Schmitt (2008) investigated the reading speed of the whole formulaic vs. non-formulaic string of words (i.e. not word-by-word as in the previously mentioned study), this time also choosing only well-established formulaic sequences. They found that both the native and non-native speakers processed formulaic strings faster, but that processing by native speakers was still faster compared to the non-native speakers.

Schmitt, Grandage and Adolphs (2004) used a dictation methodology to investigate the question of holistic storage. The main purpose of their study was to verify whether sequences of words that are identified as recurrent clusters in a corpus are also psychologically valid as chunks. Sequences included were, for example, *in a variety of, aim of the study, as a matter of fact*. 34 native and 45 proficient non-native speakers were included. The results were quite interesting in that the native speakers reproduced some of the sequences incorrectly, suggesting that not all formulaic sequences are stored holistically. There were also important individual differences, indicating that the formulaicity of a string ultimately depends on the speaker's phraseolect. Not surprisingly, the non-native speakers had even more problems reproducing the sequences and only a few of them were in fact correctly reproduced.

The last study to be reported in this review is Ellis, Simpson-Vlach, and Maynard (2008). They also set out to investigate processing differences of formulaic sequences between native speakers and advanced L2 speakers. The main aim was to see what factors affect the processing of formulaic sequences the most: frequency of occurrence (in a number of large corpora), MI (Mutual Information, the degree to which the words are associated), Length (3, 4, 5 words) and Source (spoken or written language). Interestingly, they found that the processing speed of the sequences is determined by different factors for native and non-native speakers. For native speakers the MI score is the most important factor, whereas for non-native speakers the frequency of the whole sequence is the determining factor. These results are presumably in accordance with Ellis' theory of frequency effects, viz. developing sensitivity as to which words appear together (MI) takes a very long time. Furthermore, in line with this theory, the most frequent elements in language generally would be more easily acquired. These results were corroborated by Durrant and Schmitt's (2009) study on L2 writing, where native speakers used more collocations with high MI-scores than the non-native counterparts.

The studies carried out in order to investigate the processing of formulaic sequences through e.g. frequency and association have in common that they investigate a limited set of carefully selected sequences based on their frequency and/or MI score in large corpora such as the BNC. These investigations are thus quite different from those of e.g. Wiktorsson (2003), Forsberg (2008) and Lewis (2009), who aspire to map learners' actual use of formulaic sequences in entire texts. As a consequence discussions of problems with the identification and delimitation of formulaic sequences are usually lacking in the psycholinguistic literature on formulaicity, since only well-established idioms and sequences are taken into account. However, the different methodologies used could also be seen as complementary in so far as experimental studies give information about learners' knowledge, whereas the non-native writers' texts give us information about what learners are in fact capable of producing with regard to formulaic language.

Results reviewed in this section show that there are indeed differences between native speakers and advanced non-native speakers in terms of the processing of formulaic sequences, as well as other factors affecting the reception and production of formulaic language. Factors like these will probably have an influence on the way formulaic language is handled by even very advanced learners, and especially in productive impromptu situations where processing demands, presumably, are high.

7 Summing up of literature regarding advanced learners' use of formulaic sequences and topics for future research

The review of the literature on theories as well as empirical studies of formulaic language has revealed that few researchers have studied very advanced or near-native L2 varieties, which means that there is little material available for comparison. As for spoken production, the focus has been on fluency, and only a few studies have examined idiomaticity, defined as nativelike selection of word combinations. However, Boers et al.'s (2006), Stengers et al.'s (2011) and Forsberg's (2008) results indicate that there is indeed a strong link between proficiency and idiomaticity in oral production. Regarding written production, results are more numerous and fairly unanimous: advanced learners and native speakers differ with regard to their use of formulaic language. Cross-linguistic features seem to influence the L2 production of collocations. The degree of combinatorial restriction also has an effect on the difficulty that collocations may present for learners. Furthermore, overuse and underuse of formulaic language seem to apply even to advanced, and very advanced learners. The only study not reporting any significant differences is Siyanova and Schmitt (2008), where the learners and the native speakers produced similar numbers of appropriate collocations. However, a more detailed study of type and distribution of formulaic language reveals differences between the two groups. As was shown in Wiktorsson (2003) and Forsberg (2008) there were no differences in quantity of formulaic sequences between the two groups, but qualitative differences were found, just as in Durrant and Schmitt (2009). Indeed, regardless of the method used, the results regarding differences in the use of formulaic sequences between native and advanced non-native users seem to converge. For example, if we compare the phraseological approach (e.g. Howarth 1998) and the lexical bundles approach (Chen and Baker 2010; Ädel and Erman 2012) we see that the fundamental findings concerning the use of formulaic language in native and non-native speaker populations overlap. All seem to agree that there are quantitative as well as qualitative differences between native and non-native speakers in their use of formulaic language.

Elicitation tests show that formulaic sequences are processed more quickly than non-formulaic ones, by both native and non-native speakers, but that non-native speakers process them more slowly than native speakers. This could partly be explained through Ellis's theory of chunking as a result of frequency effects, which suggests that the connections between the words in the formulaic sequence are not as entrenched in non-native as in native speakers of a language. Moreover, extralinguistic factors such as socio-cultural adaptation were shown to have an effect on the use of formulaic language (Dörnyei, Durow, and Khawla 2004; Kecskés 2002), even though one study did not yield any significant results regarding this parameter (Schmitt et al. 2004).

Based on results reported in this review, we should expect differences between native and non-native speakers regarding degree of automatization and ease of processing, which should ultimately become evident in language production in general. It is also reasonable to believe that even very proficient L2 speakers suffer from processing constraints (Conklin and Schmitt 2008). In those communicative situations where processing constraints are high and formulaic sequences need to be recalled and produced quickly, not only in well recognized genres as those of auctioneers and sports commentators (Kuiper 2004), but in traditional SLA tasks, such as simultaneous on-line retelling, even very advanced non-native speakers turn out to have more processing problems than native speakers. In future research, it is important to investigate the very advanced/near-native L2 user in several communicative situations, since their performance can be close to that of native speakers in some domains, while not in others (Forsberg 2008). One assumption in this research was that the type of task would have an impact on the L2 speakers' use of appropriate formulaic sequences. To be able to establish this, late L2 performance needs to be scrutinized in much more detail using a variety of different parameters and communicative situations. This turned out to be quite an effective way of assessing general proficiency as reported in Abrahamsson and Hyltenstam (2009); they used ten different tests and tasks in order to measure near-native speakers' knowledge and production of L2 Swedish. Foster, Bolibaugh and Kotula (2014) in their investigation of Polish L2 users of English in the United Kingdom and in Poland using several parameters found that an early start (age of onset <13) was a necessary but not sufficient condition to reach nativelike levels of attainment.

This chapter has also revealed that there are few studies from the SLA field connecting current linguistic theories on formulaic language with L2 acquisition. Many of the studies reviewed use either a phraseological approach (Section 5.4) or a statistical one (Section 3) for the identification of formulaic sequences. However, we noted in Section 5.6 that connections between cognitive linguistics and second language acquisition have been identified (Robinson and Ellis 2008).

Summing up, it has been argued that cognitive theories can provide a useful complement for the explanation, identification and understanding of formulaic sequences along with statistical retrieval methods and psycholinguistic studies. It is particularly fruitful to link cognitive theories to the performance of very advanced L2 speakers from the aspect of formulaic language.

Acknowledgements

A special thanks to Alan McMillion for proofreading our chapter.

References

Abrahamsson, N. & K. Hyltenstam. 2009. Age of onset and nativelikeness in a second language: Listener perception versus linguistic scrutiny. *Language Learning*, 58/2. 249–306.

Ädel, A. & B. Erman. 2012. Recurrent word combinations in academic writing by native and non-native speakers of English; a lexical bundles approach. *English for Specific Purposes*, 31/2. 81–92.

Adolphs, S. & V. Durow. 2004. Socio-cultural integration and the development of formulaic sequences. In: N. Schmitt (ed.), *Formulaic Sequences: Acquisition, Processing, and Use*. Amsterdam: Benjamins. 107–126.

Allwood, J., J. Nivre, & E. Ahlsén. 1989. Speech management. On the non-written life of speech. *Gothenburg Papers in Theoretical Linguistics*, 58. University of Gothenburg, Dept. of Linguistics.

Bardovi-Harlig, K. 2009. Conventional expressions as a pragmalinguistic resource: Recognition and production of conventional expressions in L2 pragmatics. *Language Learning*, 59/4. 755–795.

Bardovi-Harlig, K. & M.-T. Bastos. 2011. Proficiency, length of stay, and intensity of interaction and the acquisition of conventional expressions in L2 pragmatics. *Intercultural Pragmatics*, 8/3. 347–384.

Bartning, I. 1997. L'apprenant dit avancé et son acquisition d'une langue étrangère. *AILE*, 9. 9–50.

Bartning, I. this volume. Morphosyntax and discourse in high-level second language use.

Biber, D. 2010. Corpus-based and corpus-driven analyses of language variation and use. In: B. Heine & H. Narrog (eds.), *The Oxford Handbook of Linguistic Analysis*. Oxford: Oxford University Press. 159–191.

Biber, D., S. Conrad, & G. Leech. 2002. *Longman Student Grammar of Spoken and Written English*. London: Pearson Education.

Biber, D. & F. Barbieri. 2007. Lexical bundles in university spoken and written registers. *English for Specific Purposes*, 26. 263–286.

Boers, F., J. Eyckmans, J. Kappel, H. Stengers, & M. Demecheleer. 2006. Formulaic sequences and perceived oral proficiency: Putting a lexical approach to the test. *Language Teaching Research*, 10/3. 245–261.

Boers, F., M. Demecheleer, A. Coxhead, & S. Webb. 2014. Gauging the effects of exercises on verb-noun collocations. *Language Teaching Research*, 18/1. 54–74.

Bolinger, D. 1976. Meaning and memory. *Forum Linguisticum*, I. 1–14.

Bolly, C. 2009. The acquisition of phraseological units by advanced learners of French as an L2: High frequency verbs and learner corpora. In: E. Labeau & F. Myles (eds.), *Revisiting Advanced Learner Varieties: The Case of French*. Oxford: Peter Lang.

Bybee, J. 1985. *Morphology: A Study of the Relation between Meaning and Form*. Amsterdam: John Benjamins.

Bybee, J. 1998. The emergent lexicon. In: M. C. Gruber, C. D. Higgins, K. S. Olson, & T. Wysocki, (eds.), *CLS 34: The panels*. Chicago: Chicago Linguistics Society. 421–435.

Chen, Y.-H. & P. Baker. 2010. Lexical bundles in L1 and L2 academic writing. *Language Learning and Technology*, 14/2. 30–49.

Church, K. & Hanks, P. 1991. Word Association Norms, Mutual Information and Lexicography. *Computational Linguistics*, 16/1. 22–29.

Clark, R. 1974. Performing without competence. *Journal of Child Language*, 1. 1–10.

Conklin, K. & N. Schmitt. 2008. Formulaic sequences: Are they processed more quickly than nonformulaic language by native and nonnative speakers? *Applied Linguistics*, 29/1. 72–89.

Cortes, V. 2004. Lexical bundles in published and student disciplinary writing: Examples from history and biology. *English for Specific Purposes*, 23/4. 397–423.

Cowie, A. P. (ed.). 1998. *Phraseology: Theory, Analysis, and Applications*. Oxford: Oxford University Press.

Croft, W. & D. A. Cruse. 2004. *Cognitive Linguistics*. Cambridge: Cambridge University Press.

De Cock, S. 2004. Preferred sequences of words in NS and NNS speech. *BELL: Belgian Journal of English Language and Literatures. New Series*, 2. 225–246.

Durrant, P. & N. Schmitt. 2009. To what extent do native and non-native writers make use of collocations? *International Review of Applied Linguistics in Language Teaching*, 47/2. 157–177.

Dörnyei, Z., V. Durow, & Z. Khawla. 2004. Individual differences and their effects on formulaic sequence acquisition. In: N. Schmitt (ed.), *Formulaic Sequences: Acquisition, Processing, and Use*. Amsterdam: John Benjamins. 87–106.

Edmonds, A. 2010. *On the Representation of Conventional Expressions in L1-English L2-French*. Doctoral dissertation, Indiana University.

Ekberg, L. 2013. Grammatik och lexikon i svenska som andraspråk på nästan infödd nivå [Grammar and lexis in Swedish as a second language on a near- native level]. In: K. Hyltenstam & I. Lindberg (eds.), *Svenska som andraspråk: I forskning, undervisning och samhälle*, 2:a upplagan [Swedish as a Second language: In research, education, and society, 2nd ed.]. Lund: Studentlitteratur. 259–279.

Ellis, N. C. 1996. Sequencing in SLA, phonological memory, chunking, and points of order. *Studies in Second Language Acquisition*, 18/1. 91–126.

Ellis, N. C. 2002. Frequency effects in language processing. *Studies in Second Language Acquisition*, 24. 143–188.

Ellis, N. C. 2006a. Cognitive perspectives on SLA: The associative-cognitive CREED. In: K. Bardovi-Harlig & Z. Dörnyei (eds.). *AILA Review*, 19. 100–121.

Ellis, N. C. 2006b. Usage-based language acquisition. Paper presented at FAS Seminar, Friday 28 April, 2006. Stockholm: Stockholm University.

Ellis, N. C., R. Simpson-Vlach & C. Maynard. 2008. Formulaic language in native and second language speakers: Psycholinguistics, corpus linguistics and TESOL. *TESOL Quarterly*, 42/3. 375–396.

Erman, B. 2009. Formulaic language from a learner perspective: What the learner needs to know. In: R. Corrigan, E. A. Moravcsik, H. Quali, & K. M. Wheatley (eds.), *Formulaic Language, Volume* 2. Amsterdam: John Benjamins. 323–347.

Erman, B. 2014. There is no such thing as a free combination: a usage-based study of specific construals in adverb-adjective combinations. *English Language and Linguistics*, 18/1. 109–132.

Erman, B. & B. Warren. 2000. The idiom principle and the open choice principle. *Text*, 20/1. 29–62.

Fillmore, C. 1985. Frames and the semantics of understanding. *Quaderni di Semantica*, 6/2. 222–254.

Fillmore, C. 2003. A maximalist view of multiword expressions. Paper read at the conference "Collocations and idioms linguistic, computational, and psycholinguistic perspectives", 18–20 September, 2003, Berlin.

Fillmore, C. 2007. The detection, annotation and representation of non-core grammatical constructions. Paper read at the Formulaic Symposium, University Wisconsin Milwaukee, 18–21 April, 2007.

Fillmore, C., P. Kay, & M. C. O'Connor. 1988. Regularity and idiomaticity in grammatical constructions: The case of let alone. *Language*, 64. 501–538.

Fillmore, C. & B. T. S. Atkins. 1992. Towards a frame-based organization of the lexicon, the semantics of risk and its neighbors. In: A. Lehrer & E. Kittay (eds.), *Frames, Fields, and Contrasts: New Essays in Semantics and Lexical Organization*. Hillsdale: Lawrence Erlbaum. 75–102.

Fillmore, C. & B. T. S. Atkins. 1994. Starting where the dictionaries s A. Zampolli (eds.), *Computational Approaches to the Lexicon*. Oxford: Oxford University Press. 349–393.

Forsberg, F. 2008. *Le Langage préfabriqué: Formes, fonctions et fréquences en français parlé L2 et L1*. Bern: Peter Lang.

Forsberg Lundell, F. & B. Erman. 2012. High-level requests: A study of long residency L2 users of English and French and native speakers. *Journal of Pragmatics*, 44. 756–775.

Forsberg Lundell, F. & C. Lindqvist. 2012. Vocabulary development in advanced L2 French: do formulaic sequences and lexical richness develop at the same rate? *Language, Interaction, Acquisition*, 3/1. 73–92.

Forsberg Lundell, F. & M. Sandgren. 2013. High-level proficiency in late L2 acquisition – relationships between collocational production, language aptitude and personality. In: G. Granena & M. Long (eds.), *Sensitive Periods, Aptitudes and Ultimate Attainment in L2*. Benjamins: Amsterdam. 231–258.

Foster, P., C. Bolibaugh, & A. Kotula. 2014. Knowledge of nativelike selections in a L2: The influence of exposure, memory, age of onset, and motivation in foreign language and immersion settings. *Studies in Second Language Acquisition*, 36. 101–132.

Foster, P. 2001. Rules and routines: A consideration of their role in the task-based language production of native and non-native speakers. In: M. Bygate, P. Skehan, & M. Swain (eds.), *Researching Pedagogic Tasks: Second Language Learning, Teaching, and Testing*. London: Longman. 75–93.

Goldberg, A. 2003. Constructions: a new theoretical approach to language. *TRENDS in Cognitive Sciences*, 7/5. 219–224.

Granger, S. 1998. Prefabricated patterns in advanced EFL writings: collocations and formulae. In: A. P. Cowie (ed.), *Phraseology: Theory, Analysis and Applications*. Oxford: Clarendon Press. 145–160.

Hancock, V. 2000. *Quelques connecteurs et modalisateurs dans le français parlé d'apprenants universitaires. Cahiers de la recherché*, 16. Stockholm University.

Hoey, M. 2005. *Lexical Priming: A New Theory of Words and Language.* London: Routledge.

Hoffmann, S. & H. M. Lehmann. 2000. Collocational evidence from the British National Corpus. In: J. M. Kirk (ed.), *Corpora Galore: Analyses and Techniques in Describing English.* Amsterdam: Radopi. 17–32.

Howarth, P. 1998. Phraseology and second language proficiency, *Applied Linguistics*, 19/1. 24–44.

Hunston, S. & G. Francis. 2000. *Pattern Grammar: A Corpus-Driven Approach to the Lexical Grammar of English. Amsterdam*: John Benjamins.

Hyltenstam, K., I. Bartning, & L. Fant. 2005. High level proficiency in second language use. Grant application, Stockholm University.

Inkpen, D. Z. & G. Hirst. 2002. Acquiring collocations for lexical choice between near-synonyms. In: *Unsupervised Lexical Acquisition; Proceedings of the Workshop of the ACL Special Interest Group on the Lexicon (SIGLEX)*, 67–76.

Kecskés, I. 2002. *Situation-Bound Utterances in L1 and L2.* Berlin: Mouton de Gruyter.

Kellerman, E. 1978. Giving learners a break: Native language intuitions as a source of predictions about transferability. *Working Papers in Bilingualism*, 15. 309–315.

Kennedy, G. 2003. Amplifier collocations in the British National Corpus: Implications for English language teaching. *TESOL Quarterly*, 37/3. 467–87.

Kuiper, K. 2004. Formulaic performance in conventionalized varieties of speech. In: N. Schmitt (ed.), *Formulaic Sequences: Acquisition, Processing, and Use.* Amsterdam: John Benjamins. 37–54.

Langacker, W. R. 1987. *Foundations of Cognitive Grammar: Theoretical Prerequisites.* Stanford: Stanford University Press.

Langacker, W. R. 1991. *Foundations of Cognitive Grammar.* Stanford: Stanford University Press.

Langacker, W. R. 1999. A dynamic usage-based model. In: S. Kemmer & M. Barlow (eds.), *A Usage-based Conception of Language.* Stanford: CSLI Publications. 1–63.

Laufer, B. & T. Waldman. 2011. Verb-noun collocations in second language writing: A corpus analysis of learners' English. *Language Learning*, 61/2. 647–672.

Levelt, W. J. M. 1989. *Speaking: From Intention to Articulation.* Cambridge, MA: MIT Press.

Lewis, Margareta. 2009. *The Idiom Principle in L2 English: Assessing Elusive Formulaic Sequences as Indicators of Idiomaticity, Fluency, and Proficiency.* Saarbrücken: VDM Verlag.

Lewis, Michael. 2000. *Teaching Collocation: Further Developments in the Lexical Approach.* Hove: Language teaching publications.

Lindquist, H. 2009. A corpus study of lexicalized formulaic sequences with preposition + *hand*. In: R. Corrigan, E. A. Moravcsik, H. Ouali, & K. M. Wheatley (eds.), *Formulaic Language. Volume 1. Distribution and Historical Change.* Amsterdam: John Benjamins. 239–256.

Lindquist, H. & M. Levin. 2008. Foot and mouth: The phrasal patterns of two frequent nouns. In: S. Granger & F. Meunier (eds.), *Phraseology: An Interdisciplinary Perspective.* Amsterdam: John Benjamins. 143–158.

Mel'čuk, I. 1996. Lexical functions: A tool for the description of lexical relations in the lexicon. In: L. Wanner (ed.), *Lexical Functions in Lexicography and Natural Language Processing.* Amsterdam: John Benjamins. 37–102.

Mel'čuk, I. 1998. Collocations and lexical functions. In: A. P. Cowie (ed.), *Phraseology: Theory, Analysis, and Applications.* Oxford: Clarendon Press. 23–53.

Minsky, M. 1977. Frame-system theory. In: P. Johnson-Laird & P. Wason (eds.), *Thinking: Readings in Cognitive Science*. Cambridge: Cambridge University Press. 355–376.

Mizrahi, E. & B. Laufer. 2010. Lexical competence of highly advanced L2 users: is their collocation knowledge as good as their productive vocabulary size? Paper presented at Eurosla 20, Reggio Emilia, Italy.

Myles, F., R. Mitchell, & J. Hooper. 1998. Rote or rule? Exploring the role of formulaic language in classroom foreign language learning. *Language Learning*, 48/3. 323–363.

Myles, F., R. Mitchell, & J. Hooper. 1999. Interrogative chunks in French L2. A basis for creative construction? *Studies in Second Language Acquisition*, 21. 49–80.

Nesselhauf, N. 2003. The use of collocations by advanced learners of English and some implications for teaching. *Applied Linguistics*, 24/2. 223–242.

Paradis, C. 1997. *Degree Modifiers of Adjectives in Spoken British English. Lund Studies in English*, 92. Lund: Lund University Press.

Pawley, A. & F. Syder. 1983. Two puzzles for linguistic theory: Nativelike selection and nativelike fluency. In: J. C. Richards & R. W. Schmidt (eds.), *Language and Communication*. London: Longman. 191–226.

Peters, A. 1983. *The Units of Language Acquisition*. Cambridge: Cambridge University Press.

Peters, E. 2014. The effect of repetition and time of post-test administration on EFL learners' recall of single words and collocations. *Language Teaching Research*, 18/1. 75–94.

Raupach, M. 1984. Formulae in second language speech production. In: H. W. Dechert, D. Möhle, & M. Raupach (eds.), *Second Language Production*. Tübingen: Gunter Narr. 114–137.

Radford, A. 2009. *An Introduction to English Sentence Structure*. Cambridge: Cambridge University Press.

Renouf, A. & J. Sinclair. 1991. Collocational frameworks in English. In: K. Aijmer & B. Altenberg (eds.), *English Corpus Linguistics: Studies in Honour of Jan Svartvik*. London: Longman. 128–144.

Robinson, P. & N. C. Ellis (eds.). 2008. *Handbook of Cognitive Linguistics and Second Language Acquisition*. New York: Routledge.

Schank, R. C. & R. P. Abelson. 1977. *Scripts, Plans, Goals, and Understanding*. Hillsdale: Lawrence Erlbaum.

Schmitt, N. (ed.). 2004. *Formulaic Sequences: Acquisition, Processing, and Use*, Amsterdam: John Benjamins.

Schmitt, N., Z. Dörnyei, S. Adolphs, & V. Durow. 2004. Knowledge and acquisition of formulaic sequences: A longitudinal study. In: N. Schmitt (ed.), *Formulaic Sequences: Acquisition, Processing, and Use*. Amsterdam: John Benjamins. 55–87.

Schmitt, N., S. Grandage, & S. Adolphs. 2004. Are corpus-driven recurrent clusters psycholinguistically valid? In: N. Schmitt (ed.), *Formulaic Sequences: Acquisition, Processing, and Use*. Amsterdam: John Benjamins. 127–152.

Schmitt, N. & G. Underwood. 2004. Exploring the processing of formulaic sequences through a self-paced reading task. In: N. Schmitt (ed.), *Formulaic Sequences: Acquisition, Processing, and Use*. Amsterdam: John Benjamins. 173–190.

Sinclair, J. 1991. *Corpus, Concordance, Collocation*. Oxford: Oxford University Press.

Sinclair, J. 1997. The lexical item. University of Birmingham and The Tuscan Word Centre, Italy. (ms).

Siyanova, A. & N. Schmitt. 2008. L2 learner production and processing of collocation: A multistudy perspective. *Canadian Modern Language Review*, 64/3. 429–458.

Stefanowitsch, A. & S. T. Gries. 2009. Corpora and grammar. In: A. Lüdeling & M. Kytö (eds.), *Corpus Linguistics: An International Handbook, Vol. 2*. Berlin: Mouton de Gruyter. 933–951.

Stengers, H., F. Boers, A. Housen, & J. Eyckmans. 2011. Formulaic sequences and L2 oral proficiency. Does the type of target language influence the association? *International Review of Applied Linguistics in Language Teaching*, 49/4. 321–343.

Stubbs, M. 2002. *Words and Phrases*. Oxford: Blackwell Publishing.

Tomasello, M. 2000. First steps toward a usage-based theory of language acquisition. *Cognitive Linguistics*, 11/1–2. 61–82.

Towell, R., R. Hawkins, & N. Bazergui. 1996. The development of fluency in advanced learners of French. *Applied Linguistics*, 17/1. 84–119.

Underwood, G., N. Schmitt, & A. Galpin. 2004. The eyes have it: An eye-movement study into the processing of formulaic sequences. In: N. Schmitt (ed.), *Formulaic Sequences: Acquisition, Processing, and Use*. Amsterdam: John Benjamins. 153–172.

Warren, B. 2005. A model of idiomaticity. *Nordic Journal of English Studies*, 4/1. 35–54.

Weinert, R. 1995. The role of formulaic language in second language acquisition: a review. *Applied Linguistics*, 16/2. 180–205.

Wiktorsson, M. 2003. Learning Idiomaticity: A Corpus-Based Study of Idiomatic Expressions in Learners' Written Production. *Lund Studies in English*, 105. Lund: Lund University.

Wong-Fillmore, L. M. 1976. *The Second Time Around: Cognitive and Social Strategies in Second Language Acquisition*. Doctoral dissertation, Stanford University.

Wood, D. 2006. Uses and functions of formulaic sequences in second language speech: An exploration of the foundations of fluency. *Canadian Modern Language Review*, 63/1. 13–33.

Wray, A. 2002. *Formulaic Language and the Lexicon*. New York: Cambridge University Press.

Yorio, C. 1980. Conventionalized language forms and the development of communicative competence. *TESOL Quarterly*, 14/4. 433–442.

Yorio, C. 1989. Idiomaticity as an indicator of second language proficiency. In: K. Hyltenstam & L. Obler (eds.), *Bilingualism across the Lifespan*. Cambridge: Cambridge University Press. 55–72.

Alan McMillion and Philip Shaw
5 Reading proficiency in advanced L2 users

1 Introduction

This chapter is concerned with reading proficiency among advanced adult L2 users. Although the literature relevant to L2 reading is substantial, focus on quite advanced readers, those who have reading proficiencies close to those of L1 readers, allows for a set of intrinsically interesting questions not always raised within more general L2 reading research. This set would include at least the following general questions: (1) the extent to which advanced L2 readers achieve native-like reading proficiency levels in terms of comprehension (product), (2) qualitative similarities and differences of processing between L1 and L2 readers who are equivalent in terms of product, and (3) specifically the extent to which advanced L2 readers rely on compensatory processing and are therefore more dependent on contextual information. In addition, there are questions that specifically relate to the situation of many university students who use their L2 as the medium of instruction, either wholly or partially. This is a growing group of advanced L2 readers who are often assumed to be proficient readers in the L2.

In this chapter we give an overview of the research area, although some of its later parts are based on our own research participants whose L1 is Swedish and who may be considered advanced L2 readers of English. Much of the extensive reading research literature naturally concerns L1 readers, and much work on L2 readers has concerned children or less advanced readers (usually both). In addition, much of the research on advanced adult L2 readers concerns readers whose L1s are remote linguistically and in terms of writing system from their L2 (Fraser 2007; Koda 2004). Correspondingly, the research on speakers of related languages such as Dutch and English or Spanish and English mostly concerns children of school age. Our concentration on adult advanced L2 readers of a closely related language allows for a focus on subtle differences in product and processing between the advanced L2 and the L1 readers that might not otherwise be possible.

This focus on advanced readers provides a view of L2 readers when they perform at levels close to those of equivalent L1 readers. From this vantage point processing differences underlying the minimally different or identical products of the L1 and L2 readers can be measured. Investigating such differences should

---

Alan McMillion and Philip Shaw, Stockholm University

also inform us about any basic strategy differences between L1 and the L2 users, such as compensation strategies. The focus on closely related L1 and L2 languages also means that it is likely that many L1 reading processes and strategies can be transferred and used more or less 'off the shelf' in L2 reading. The range of process types that could potentially be transferred is quite broad, going from specific visual letter-feature recognition through alphabetic or holistic recognition strategies and coherence building processes to recognition of generic patterns. Such study may open up discussion of compensatory processing in a more precise fashion than hitherto.

The language processing types, however, constitute only a subset of a rather complex set of issues, many of which are social-pedagogical. Reading always takes place in a context (Gee 2001) and contexts differ in the types of readers they favour and the types of skill they require. The immediate context of our own work is becoming increasingly common at present: L2 English used in tertiary education world-wide. Undergraduate courses taught in the local language increasingly make use of 'international' textbooks written in English (Ward 2009; Arnbjörnsdóttir and Ingvarsdóttir 2015), and at postgraduate levels nearly all reading is in English in many subjects. In fact a growing number of university programs in such countries are actually being offered entirely in English (Wilkinson 2013; Smit & Dafouz, 2012; Byun, Chu, Kim, et al. 2011). An underlying expectation is that students who have studied English as a foreign language for ten years at the primary and secondary levels will have sufficient receptive proficiency to both read English textbooks and follow lectures given in English more or less on a par with L1 students (Graddol 2006). Our current research on the advanced L2 reader is part of a project to find out in what senses this is the case.

In this chapter 'L2 reader' refers to a reader who is fully literate in a wide variety of domains and genres in a first language (typically the language of early upbringing) but is reading in another, in which he/she is presumably less proficient. 'L1 reader' refers to a reader who is fully literate in a wide variety of domains and genres in a first language, and is reading in that language. We do not discuss the possibly more frequent cases in which literacy is not predominantly in the language of early upbringing (as might arise in post-colonial states or among ethnic minorities), or in which language-of-upbringing literacy is limited to a few domains, or in which literacy has been acquired in parallel in two languages. This restriction naturally limits the scope of our analysis, but brings it into line with the definitions used elsewhere in this volume.

Further restrictions on the scope of this review are inevitable, given the enormous quantity of research on reading. We do not discuss the development of L1 or L2 reading skills at any level in children or language learners, focusing instead on the systems which have been acquired. We do not discuss any issues to do with reading as a means of language or vocabulary acquisition. Nor do we discuss issues mainly associated with L2 readers of relatively low proficiency.

The chapter is organized in the following way. Section 2 creates a framework by examining widely-discussed distinctions concerning the notions of *reading*, *proficiency* and *advanced* and how they relate to other aspects of L2 use. Following this discussion a simplified consensus model of the reading process is presented, and research into the various levels at which L1 readers have been shown to differ from one another is discussed.

Section 3 examines several types of differences between L2 readers and their L1 counterparts. These are differences due to:
– different cultural practices and culture-specific knowledge.
– L2 readers' multilingual status; they have knowledge and skills from reading in L1, so that transfer, both positive and negative, is likely.
– the extent to which advanced L2 readers have automated various processes compared to L1 users.
– meta-cognitive influences, covering such aspects as task types, reading strategies, and motivation.

In section 4 we briefly review methods used in current L2 reading research. Section 5 looks at issues related to the widespread use of advanced L2 English in what may be referred to as lingua-franca environments. In section 6 our own current research questions concerning the advanced L2 reader will be presented, followed by a description of our research methods. Finally we outline a few results.

2 Modeling reading

2.1 Definitions

To understand *reading proficiency* we may examine the notions of *reading* and *proficiency* individually. *Reading* can be used in quite a broad way, so that reading comprehension is merely one aspect which can be contrasted with reading fluency (ability to read aloud without errors or hesitation) for example (Crosson and Lesaux 2010). However here we use the term to mean a set of processes that enable the reader to decode marks on a page and eventually end up with a mental representation that approximates what other skilled readers infer to be the intended mental representation of the writer. The notion of *proficiency* takes on different senses depending on what skill is being scrutinized. For advanced L2 use generally, proficiency is commonly associated with speaking or writing skill, and good proficiency means that the L2 user comes close to L1 norms of speaking or writing. By analogy, and using the definition of reading above, advanced L2 reading proficiency would imply that the L2 reader ends up with a representation corresponding to what skilled L1 readers take as the intended one.

This definition raises at least three issues. The first is that language proficiency is not uniform across skills. One reason for the common association between proficiency and production is that reception often precedes production developmentally and so it is assumed that a user who has advanced speaking and/or writing skills must have receptive skills at a similarly advanced level. But this need not be the case. In fact, measurements of speaking, writing, listening and reading may reveal different patterns of skill for any particular L2 user, as is clear from the varied profiles produced by international tests like TOEFL and IELTS. Since an L2 user's productive proficiency may not be identical to their receptive proficiency, L2 users could be designated *native-like* in their reading and/or listening skills but not in their spoken or written production, or vice versa. Clearly, we must view advanced L2 reading proficiency as a separate measure from both some broad measure of overall L2 proficiency and L2 productive proficiency.

The second issue raised by our definition of L2 reading proficiency concerns target proficiencies for L2 reading. In terms of productive syntactic and phonological accuracy any native speaker of the standard variety meets the criteria for the target (at least in the model favored in this volume). But this is not true for reading. Both natives and non-natives will exhibit the full range of reading skills, from illiteracy to professional skills. Consequently the target for reading has to be an educated native. So *native-like* has to mean 'within the range of natives with an equivalent educational (etc.) background'.

The third issue is that the definition given above of advanced L2 reading defines a type of communicative rather than linguistic proficiency. Communicative 'competence' is usually characterized as the ability to communicate content and attitudes in a particular language, and is thus defined in productive terms. Most models include components of pragmatic competence (functional and sociolinguistic), strategic competence, and textual knowledge alongside linguistic proficiency (Canale and Swain 1980, Bachman and Palmer 1996). Although non-natives rarely become identical to native speakers in phonological, idiomatic or grammatical terms (as several papers in this volume demonstrate), it is not unusual for a second-language user to be a better communicator than a first-language user. (It is usual to cite second-language writers like Nabokov or Conrad as examples, but anyone who lectures effectively in a second language is a better communicator than someone who lectures ineffectively in their first.) The strategic component of communicative competence is related to the possession and use of metalinguistic knowledge, such as strategies for dealing with reading problems or communication breakdown (Foster and Tavakoli 2009). The reading literature often refers to meta linguistic knowledge and awareness (for example Stevenson, Schoonen and de Glopper 2007) and this generally refers to the strategic and textual components of communicative competence. Such meta linguistic knowledge appears to be complementary to linguistic processes such as decoding, word recognition, parsing, and text-base construction processes. Many L2 readers may be better able to marshal reading strategies, textual knowledge, and pragmatic skills than L1 readers with equivalent background knowledge and education, even if they do not show the same level of skill in parsing or comprehending decontextualized L2 language samples or in recognizing L2 vocabulary.

Definitions of proficiency in a particular skill may thus be either narrowly linguistic or more broadly communicative. Linguistic proficiency may tend to be defined in terms of native-speaker competence, while communicative proficiency should be defined in terms of effective communication. Linguistically-oriented descriptions of proficiency in reading skills will thus have to focus on tasks which most native speakers can carry out unproblematically, as Hulstijn's (2007) "core reading proficiency" does. Our concern, however, is with the advanced user and this must be someone who has gone beyond that level. Our definition of the advanced reader will therefore be based on communicative competence in the broad sense: a reader is advanced if they can extract the same meaning from a sophisticated text as an L1 user of the same educational background.

2.2 A model of L1 reading processes

The definition of advanced L2 reading above makes it necessary to consider what the sub-skills of reading are likely to be. There is evidence that many of the sub-skills used in L2 reading are general language processing skills that are common to both L1 and L2 reception processes (e.g. Gough, Juel and Griffith 1992:36, Koda 2004, Perfetti 1985:4). In this section we describe first-language reading to provide a framework for discussing the L2 process in the next.

One often-cited model of reading is Kintsch's construction-integration model of comprehension (Kintsch 1998; Nassaji 2007, 2014; Perfetti 1999). This model implies that in normal L1 reading processes we recognize words and parse sentences autonomously, generating propositions which are then linked to one another syntagmatically and hierarchically to form a text-base of information. As this base develops it activates related propositions in the wider knowledge of the reader and integration with this activated background knowledge creates a situation model which can be said to be the reader's comprehension of the text.

A construction-integration model stands in contrast to a schema-theoretic model (Rumelhart 1980) which would argue that pre-existing knowledge structures determine the reading process from the beginning. Where empirical research on background-knowledge use in reading allows a distinction to be made between the two models, it favours the construction-integration model. For example Chen and Donin (1997) found that domain-specific knowledge affected the higher levels of reading in both L1 and L2, but had little effect on lower-level processes. This is not to say that textbase construction is modularized in the sense used in the psycholinguistic literature, but merely that skilled readers normally form a textbase before integrating it with their background knowledge, however structured.

Figure 1 below presents a simplified model of the reading process showing the various information sources that a reader would be expected to use for

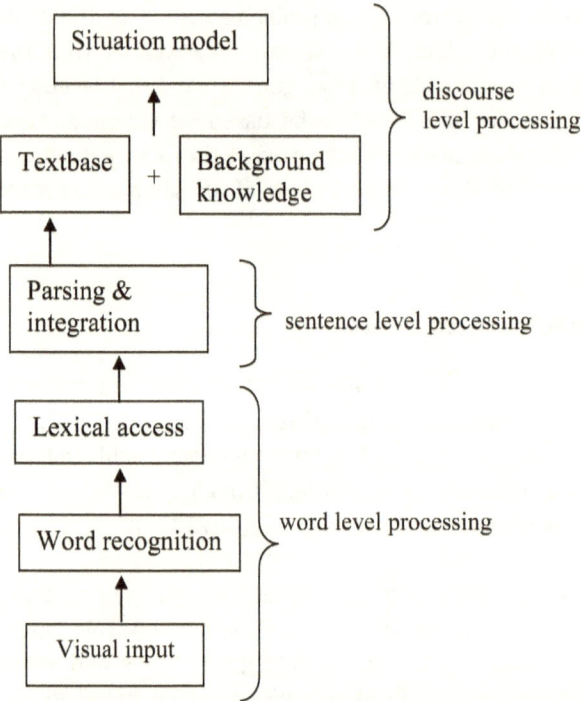

Figure 1: Simplified overview of reading processing

comprehension. The figure shows that visual input in the form of sequences of letters is recognized (and related to both phonological and orthographic representations of words in working memory). Lexical access probably results in activation of all meanings of the accessed word (Gernsbacher 1990), and crucially also of all meanings of words of the current form in all non-dormant languages known to the reader (Bialystok 2007). Many of these meanings must be suppressed by top-down mechanisms based on local and global context. The accessed words are then integrated. Parsing allows access to constructional and grammatical meaning and allows working memory to establish a new proposition or develop the proposition of the preceding text. These propositions are then integrated in working memory into the text base, which represents the reader's interpretation of the propositional content of the text. This in turn is integrated into the situation-model, the reader's construction of the content, which makes use of background knowledge and real-world inferencing (see Hannon and Daneman 2001). Figure 1 and the following sections describe the process in slightly more detail.

2.2.1 Low-level processes

Within the Verbal Efficiency Theory framework, Perfetti (1985, 1999) formulated a model which argues that automaticity of the lower-level processes (visual input) is a prerequisite for effective reading because it allows resources to be allocated to higher level processing. He divides the processes involved in reading into three general phases: (1) the visual, (2) the processes that change the visual input into some kind of linguistic representation, and (3) the processes that operate on the encoded representation (Perfetti 1999: 167). He claims that the initial visual phase is not strictly a reading process and that the third phase may be shared with other language processes (such as listening comprehension), rendering it non-unique to reading. Consequently, the processes that are unique to reading would seem to be those that convert the visual representation to linguistic forms and include at least word recognition.

The nature of the visual representation is a key variable in L1 reading. In reading the eye fixes on a certain point and then saccades to the next fixation point. The span of characters perceived in a single fixation is called the perceptual span and this is somewhat longer and extended in the direction of reading of the fixation in more skilled readers (Rayner and Pollatsek 1989). A typical adult perceptual span covers more characters than most words (at least in English) and so skilled readers start to process the next word 'parafoveally' before their eyes fixate it. Skilled readers are thus able to read considerably faster than unskilled ones even at this low level (Ashby 2006). Speed of reading is also affected by familiarity with vocabulary items. Very familiar words or those which are predictable as a result of conventionalized phraseology are usually fixated for less than the usual quarter-second, and unfamiliar words for longer (Ashby 2006). Since words become familiar through reading, speed may be expected to be closely associated with exposure to print.

As noted above, the visual array is quickly processed in working memory and access to lexical entries achieved via multiple routes, so that both homophones and homographs are activated and must be suppressed (Gernsbacher 1990, Rayner and Pollatsek 1989: 92). Concurrent with these lexical processes, there are also parsing processes. These are also relatively autonomous, unless problems arise and controlled processing takes over. These processes result in propositions, which are handed to the less automatized higher levels.

2.2.2 Discourse processes

Discourse processes include a number of sub-processes, such as proposition creation and linking, schema retrieval, inferencing, and others. As we have seen, in the Kintsch and Perfetti models the surface representation is converted into propositional form and then becomes part of the semantic representation referred to as the text-base. This develops gradually, sentence by sentence, and as the text-base develops, it interacts with background knowledge to produce another level of representation, the situation model. There is evidence that the situation model level is psychologically real (Zwaan and Radvansky 1998; van den Broek et al. 2002). In addition, inferences are used to fill in where explicitly stated information leaves off. Bridging inferences (necessary, integrative) are those that are made in order to impose coherence on the text. Some researchers claim that such inferences are made automatically (McKoon & Ratcliff 1992). Elaborative inferences (predictive) are those that are made to enrich an interpretation. There is evidence that these are made at the time of recall rather than during initial reading (e.g. Singer 1994)

Once L1 readers have mastered basic skills, higher-level processes account for most of the variance in comprehension (Hannon and Daneman 2001; Jackson and McClelland 1979). Models need to include a number of components, given the evidence that several higher-level processes make independent contributions to comprehension, such as prior or background knowledge (Haenggi & Perfetti 1994) and inference generation.

A general cognitive mechanism of suppression is believed to be central in the process of situation model construction (Gernsbacher and Faust 1991), and varying efficiency of this mechanism is responsible for individual differences in reading comprehension. Poor L1 comprehenders have an inefficient suppression mechanism which prevents them from inhibiting irrelevant information. This causes disorderly structure building and smaller and less coherent representational structures. Difficulty in suppression of irrelevant information could be due to lack of capacity in working memory, itself perhaps a result of inefficient decoding which drains resources.

A number of factors are known to affect inference generation during text processing (Koda 2004). For causal bridging inferences, for example, the physical proximity of the propositional units that are to be conjoined is a critical factor for inference generation. On the other hand, sentences that contain surprises are more likely to remain active in working memory and thereby facilitate inference generation in spite of non-adjacency (Koda 2004: 133). Other factors involved in inference generation include text structure and the thematic status of individual text ideas. In addition to text-based factors the reader factors of working-memory capacity and background knowledge are important for inference generation. While the advanced L2 reader may be affected negatively by a shortage of working memory resources, good background knowledge – whether topic specific or general – will certainly be a compensatory resource (discussed below).

2.2.3 General, domain, and genre knowledge

Readers benefit from general knowledge, domain-specific knowledge, and knowledge of the genre they are reading. According to the construction-integration model, there is little direct influence of background knowledge on lower-level processes, although it is clear that background knowledge is beneficial to comprehension as a whole. Background knowledge can be drawn on strategically to fill gaps in the textbase and is doubtless often necessary for creating a situation model (Zwaan and Radvansky 1998).

In fact, reading proficiency and background knowledge are mutually compensatory. For example, Adams, Bell, and Perfetti (1995) investigated the relation between children's knowledge of a specific domain (football) and reading skill in text comprehension among fourth to seventh graders. Their conclusion was that reading skill and domain knowledge make complementary contributions to reading comprehension and reading speed. High-skilled readers with little domain knowledge compensate for their lack of knowledge by relying on their general reading skill, and low-skilled readers with high domain knowledge compensate for poorer reading skills by relying on their specific domain knowledge. Another aspect of L1 reading proficiency which is a general source of compensation for L2 readers is genre knowledge. It has been shown, for example, that adults read genre-conforming texts more easily than genre-violating ones (Vaughan and Dillon 2005) and that children's ability to identify and describe genres develops with their reading proficiency (Harmon, Martinez, and Deckard 2003).

2.3 Metacognitive (strategic) influences

The L1 reading model schematized above does not include any metacognitive influences on the reading process. Such influences would include reading task types and strategies, motivation, and individual differences,

Reading tasks differ in the demands made on metacognitive proficiency. Carver (1990) defined five levels of reading, each with its own appropriate speed:

1. *Scanning* for an individual word, which requires only lexical access or word recognition.
2. *Skimming for gist*, which involves word recognition and access to meaning in the general context, but not sentence integration.
3. *Normal casual reading (rauding)*, in which all words are read and a text base and situation model constructed as described above without conscious effort or planning.
4. *Reading to learn (study reading)*, in which the reader not only constructs a situation model, but also monitors the process to ensure that it will be remembered, and therefore regresses or concentrates on particular terms longer, etc. (This is also the strategy adopted with difficult sentences which the normal casual reading process fails to integrate into the textbase or situation model without special attention.)
5. *Memorization reading*, with frequent pauses and regressions to allow rehearsal of details.

The level of reading is chosen according to the text, the reader's purpose, and the reader's background knowledge. Different text types invite different types of reading. One may, for example, expect that tasks relatable to Hulstijn's core reading proficiency (2007), i.e. what any L1 user can reasonably be expected to do, such as reading the newspaper, will mainly require normal casual reading, the default reading style. Textbooks, on the other hand, may be designed for reading to learn. But according to one's purpose one may read a textbook less intensively: skim it or read it casually. Different levels of background or vocabulary knowledge will also lead to different reading levels: what is a demanding reading-to-learn-task for one reader may be casual reading for another.

Different reading styles require different processing. Processing time and the number of eye-fixations and regressions increase when the text is difficult for the reader or when the text contains inconsistencies which hinder the development of a textbase (Rayner, Chace, Slattery, and Ashby 2006). In Carver's terms they shift down from casual reading (rauding) to reading to learn. At this level readers start to behave strategically, adopting conscious behaviors to manage reading difficulties, and these strategies may be more or less effective. The range of strategies available to effective and ineffective readers is reported to be quite similar, but effective readers are those who adopt appropriate strategies for the problem in hand and are flexible (Stavans and Oded 1993). However, inappropriate reading that ignores rhetorical cues can be a response to texts that are too difficult rather than evidence of missing strategic knowledge; excessive difficulty leads to inappropriate strategy use (Haswell et al. 1999).

2.4 Effects of motivation, style, and intellectual ability

The intensity of exercise of metacognitive skills, the level of reading employed (see Carver's 1990 reading levels above), and the quality of cognitive processing are affected by the reader's beliefs and attitudes. However these factors affect L1 and L2 readers in similar ways and so it is not necessary to examine them closely, except that as they are determined at least in part by individual experience they are likely to vary across cultures.

One group of constructs relates to general motivation to read. First, Guthrie and Wigfield (1999) mention task-mastery goals, the extent to which one wants to achieve full understanding (van den Broek, Risden, and Husebye-Hartman 1995; Kardash and Noel 2000). Although on any particular occasion a reader may be more or less motivated to extract meaning from a particular text, it seems to be the case that readers have general levels of comprehension (that vary for various text types) that they habitually attain and feel satisfied with. A related concept enhancing comprehension over a range of texts is intrinsic motivation, the level of enjoyment experienced in reading tasks in general. Another factor influencing comprehension in general is self-efficacy, one's belief that one can read effectively (Schunk 2003). Otherwise the category of readers' beliefs relates to perceptions of the reading process, such as whether one views reading as transmission or transaction. The scale in this area is between transmission beliefs (the view that the text gives the reader meaning) and transaction beliefs (the view that reader and text are mutually interactive in constructing meaning (Schraw 2000)). Socially oriented researchers question the notion that a particular reader may have a single reading proficiency that is brought to the reading task, independent of text-type and genre. They argue that reading is so embedded in domain knowledge and social practices that it cannot be abstracted from them (Street 1993). It is certainly true that reading behaviour is extremely dependent on task factors (Haswell et al. 1999; Fransson 1984).

Cognitive ability must affect all reading proficiency, and language aptitude (Abrahamsson and Hyltenstam 2008) must affect L2 proficiency and hence L2 reading proficiency, but their effects will not be discussed here. Aptitude only affects L2 reading indirectly, and the construct 'verbal intelligence' seems to be operationalized as scores on instruments which are virtually tests of reading comprehension. Hence to claim that verbal intelligence is associated with success in reading comprehension would be tautologous.

3 A view of L2 processing

As noted above, L1 readers require automatized and strategic skills on a variety of levels. L2 readers require the same range of skills, but they also have difficulties specific to their reading situation. In this section we focus on the particular characteristics of L2 readers with adequate or good L1 reading skills and relatively high proficiency in L2. On the basis of the literature (e.g. Koda 2004,), we can group the ways in which L2 readers' experience is different into three types: (1) those due to not sharing the cultural background of L1 readers (differences in cultural practices and background knowledge), (2) those due to greater knowledge of their L1 than of the L2 (transfer at various levels), and (3) those due to lack of familiarity with the L2 (knowledge and processing factors, including automaticity and capacity limitation). We treat these three types in the three following sections, although the distinctions are not always clear-cut.

3.1 Differences in cultural practices and background knowledge

These factors are grouped together as non-linguistic, although they are frequently associated with linguistic difference. On the simplest level, linguistic knowledge and cultural membership are often congruent, and L2 readers may simply not have cultural information necessary to interpret a text written in another culture. Steffenson and Joag-Dev (1984) illustrate this by showing that texts presupposing knowledge of conventions around weddings in Indian culture are incomprehensible to Americans, but even between closely related cultures like those of Britain and the US cultural knowledge can be a barrier. Different cultures also have different genre conventions and genre repertoires (e.g. Hinds 1990), so that L2 readers may encounter unfamiliar forms and have difficulty interpreting them. Of course L1 readers frequently encounter unfamiliar genres and have to learn to interpret them, but readers in a new culture have the specific problem that they encounter what appear to be familiar genres (such as newspaper leader articles, lonely-hearts ads, or academic articles) which have unfamiliar conventions. L2 readers may also bring with them different strategies of reading, which may even derive from the skills required for the L1 writing system (Koda 2004, Abbott 2006), and thus actually be cases of linguistic transfer.

The motivational and attitudinal characteristics discussed in section 2.4 are determined at least in part by experience of upbringing and education. Since educational practices differ across cultures, it is highly likely that these characteristics vary across cultures, as other attitudinal (Hofstede 2001) and cognitive (Berry 1993) traits have been shown to do. However, individuals within cultures also vary on these dimensions and research on the scale necessary to establish group differences relevant to reading comprehension has not been done, and perhaps cannot be done, given the confounding factors of language and educational level.

3.2 Differences due to the presence of transfer, positive and negative

On the basis of a literature survey on a wide variety of language pairs, Koda (1994, 2004) suggests three basic differences between L2 and L1 reading. First, the L1 reader learns basic literacy at the same time as he or she learns to read, but the L2 reader has prior experience of reading and thus brings strategies and skills to the task. Second, L2 reading is cross-linguistic, in the sense of involving more than one language system, and there will be positive and negative transfer of literacy. Third, L2 readers generally have less knowledge of the target language (vocabulary, phraseology, syntax) than L1 readers (discussed in 3.3).

The first two differences involve transfer. Research in second language acquisition shows that L2 performance is generally influenced by features of L1 performance (Odlin 1989).[1] This type of transfer is also normal in second

---

[1] The evidence that linguistic code features can be transferred from an L2 to an L3 suggests that the same might happen to reading practices, but no research that we are aware of has been done on this.

language reading (Koda 1994, 2004) and operates at all levels, from character and word recognition to parsing, inferencing and reading strategies. Positive and negative transfer occur at all these levels and lead to qualitatively different processing in L2 reading (Hahne 2001; Tan et al. 2003).

At the level of character recognition, for example, related writing systems provide a great deal of facilitation, i.e. positive transfer, to L2 readers, but they also lead to some obstruction, i.e. negative transfer of reading practices. Altenberg and Smith-Cairns (1983), for example, reported that German readers of English process letter sequences which are possible words of German but not of English as quickly as sequences which are indeed possible words of English. This is completely in line with modern psycholinguistic findings that both language systems of the bilingual are active even though only one is being used (Bialystok 2007). The L1 system interferes with the L2 and slows processing.

Where languages are as similar as English and German, there will be many features which will stimulate transfer, both positive and negative. But transfer has to be 'transfer to somewhere' (Andersen 1983), so if languages are very different there are no concrete triggers and transfer remains at more abstract or higher levels. Thus, although there is no transfer of concrete character recognition from roman-alphabet reading to reading Chinese characters or vice-versa, there is evidence of transfer of strategies of character recognition. A number of studies show that Chinese readers are more easily distracted from the meaning of English number words by the size of the font than L1 English readers. This is ascribed to a strategy of paying attention to the overall form of the written word transferred from Chinese (Tzeng and Wang 1983; Haynes and Carr 1990).

Successful L2 reading correlates with successful L1 reading (Bernhardt 2005). In the Swedish university entrance test, *Högskoleprovet*, for example, L1 Swedish-language reading comprehension correlates with L2 English-language reading comprehension more highly than with any other component, even Swedish vocabulary size (Stage 2003). Carson et al. (1990) found correlations of around 0.5 for L1 and L2 English reading for both Chinese and Japanese subjects. Levels of correlation vary with language proficiency, but for advanced second-language users there must be transfer at the levels of strategy choice, model-building, and perhaps text-base formation, however dissimilar the language systems. Furthermore, this transfer is generally positive (if it were not, L1 reading success would not correlate positively with L2 reading success). If we think of 'literacy' as the ability to handle written texts efficiently (cf., for example, Stanovich 1986), then we can say that elements of L1 literacy can be transferred to L2 reading.

This might suggest that high-level processes are independent of language pair. Cognitive skills like coherence building, inferencing, situation modeling, and integration of background knowledge are likely to depend on individual characteristics that are not language-specific (van Gelderen et al. 2003, 2004). Indeed a good deal of educational policy is based on the well-supported belief that literacy is best acquired in L1 and will relatively easily be transferred to L2 (Cummins 1979).

However, on the level of strategy it appears that different language pairs may produce different transfer effects which may be more or less effective in any given situation. Readers of English with Arabic L1 have been shown to perform relatively better on comprehension questions involving "skimming, connecting, and inferring" while readers with Chinese L1 performed better on "items involving breaking a word into smaller parts, scanning, paraphrasing, and matching" (Abbott 2006: 655). This has been ascribed both to language teaching practices in the respective regions, and to the strategies required by the respective scripts, with Arabic requiring a top-down approach to insert the correct vocalism in words, while Chinese script represents morphemes rather directly. The two groups are thus predisposed by L1 linguistic and cultural features to different English reading strategies, which may not always be optimal.

A similar conclusion can be arrived at for knowledge or expectations of text structure and genre. Transfer from one European language to another will be overwhelmingly positive, but as cultures diverge from one another so do text structures, and the proportion of negative textual knowledge-transfer increases (Hinds 1990, Koda 2004). However, Yamashita (2002) shows that the value attributed to reading tended to be similar for L1 and L2 reading even for Japanese and English, suggesting that very high-level factors like attitude are transferrable.

Thus we conclude that Koda's first and second differences between L1 and L2 readers listed above (i.e. that L1 readers learn literacy and decoding at the same time, and that L2 readers have literacy in another language prior to learning to decode the L2) are essentially the same in terms of the reading practices of the advanced L2 reader: both are transfers of L1 practices, but at different levels. Transfer may be positive or negative. Negative transfer can impair L2 readers' processing speed or even product, either because inappropriate practices yield wrong information or because the reader has to devote attention to inhibiting such practices. But positive transfer of 'metalinguistic knowledge' outweighs this factor (Cummins 1979). Transfer is a possible cause of differences in processing between L1 and L2 readers rather than a characterization of the nature of L2 processing.

3.3 Differences due to the L2 status of processing and knowledge

3.3.1 Types of difference

Koda's third type of difference is in knowledge, primarily language knowledge. L2 readers can be assumed not to differ systematically from L1 readers in the transferable non-linguistic aspects of their L1 reading skills (such as inferencing skills or working memory span), motivation, or personality. Differences in background knowledge reflect cultural, not linguistic, differences. This means that the essential differences are all broadly linguistic, either knowledge (Koda 2004) or processing (Perfetti 1999). L2 readers' knowledge of target-language lexis, syntax, characters, etc. may be incomplete and lead to miscomprehension, and even when L2 knowledge is fairly complete, processing may be slower or qualitatively different. In short, differences between L2 and L1 readers may be:
1. differences due to limited linguistic knowledge, both explicit and implicit
2. differences in processing (fluency), due to
    - the influence of automatized procedures transferred from L1 (which may enhance L2 processing or may need to be inhibited)
    - L2 processing being less automatic (Paradis 2009)
    - the effects of multilingualism as such on processing (de Bot 2012)

This analysis is consonant with the three groups of component skills conceptualized by workers in the NELSON project: (1) language knowledge, (2) speed of access to language knowledge, and (3) metacognitive knowledge (Fukkink, Hulstijn, and Simis 2005). Metacognitive knowledge is regarded as representing language-independent, higher-order processing skills which are transferable (normally with positive results) from L1 to L2 reading. The higher-order processing skills are of course not all language-independent, some being only shared across related languages, as discussed in section 3.2.

3.3.2 L2 knowledge

L2 knowledge comprises knowledge of character systems and orthography, vocabulary and phraseology, morpho-syntax and elements of pragmatics such as information structure. Character recognition ability – knowledge of written characters – is an important factor in lower-level reading where L2 uses a different writing system (Koda 1992). Advanced users can be assumed to be familiar with the character set of the L2 and the linguistic units they represent (though complete knowledge is less likely for Chinese with thousands of characters than for an alphabetically-written language). In languages with a shallow orthography, like Spanish, recognition of vocabulary known orally is simple, in languages with a deeper one like English it is more complex, but probably no longer a problem at the advanced level.

Vocabulary size is an important predictor of reading comprehension in both L1 (Farley and Elmore 1992) and L2 (Laufer 1992, 2010; Bernhardt 2005, Henriksen, Albrechtsen and Haastrup 2004) but one may speculate that the underlying reasons are different. The key issue is the relation of vocabulary size to literacy practices. Exposure to print gives both higher-order literacy skills and lower-order automaticity (Cipielewski and Stanovich 1992), and it is also the main source of new vocabulary in the L1 (Huckin and Coady 1999). A large L1 vocabulary (in the domains that are usually tested) would usually be acquired by extensive exposure to print and would therefore be directly associated with good literacy skills and automaticity. L1 users with a small L1 vocabulary are likely to have had limited exposure to print (Farley and Elmore 1992) and hence to have poor reading practices and low automaticity. Consequently, their unsuccessful reading is due to a considerable extent to these poor practices and not solely to failing to understand the words in the text. Being an L1 user of a language implies high proficiency in the syntax, semantics, phonology etc. of the language, but not familiarity with infrequent or academic words, which is largely the result of reading and schooling. Consequently, L1 vocabulary size is indexical of L1 literacy skills, not language proficiency and automaticity in general.

In L2, however, vocabulary size is very closely linked to L2 proficiency and often considered a good measure of it (Alderson 2005). By contrast, vocabulary size in L2 is only very indirectly related to literacy skills, many of which have been acquired in L1 and transferred. Second language learners of the types discussed here have an amount N of exposure to print in L1 and an amount n in L2. Their transferable literacy skills derive from the total amount of exposure to print $N+n$ while their vocabulary derives only from n and their lower-order automaticity also from n (plus a certain amount of transfer if writing systems or vocabulary roots are similar). Hence their L2 literacy skills are associated with a smaller vocabulary and lower automaticity than that available to an L1 reader of that language with those literacy skills. Successful L2 reading comprehension is dependent on an adequate vocabulary and can be quite difficult if less than 95% of the words encountered are familiar (Nation 2001). Thus L2 vocabulary size is related to L2 reading comprehension because it is indexical of L2 proficiency (and because word knowledge is needed for comprehension), not primarily because of a link to overall reading skills. L2 readers can thus have literacy skills which are greater than those typical of an L1 reader with a similar vocabulary size, and they may be able to use them to overcome their vocabulary deficiencies (Bernhardt 2005) and read better than L1 readers with a comparable vocabulary size.

There is currently an increasing recognition of the importance of formulaic sequences – stretches of language which often recur and are presumably stored as units, and of mutual activation of words (Wray 2002, Gyllstad 2007, Erman, Forsberg Lundell, and Lewis this volume). Such sequences may or may not be lexicalized. Lexicalized sequences are vocabulary items that have to be learned, and it is likely that L1 users have a better command than L2 users, and thus a comprehension advantage. Non-lexicalized collocational sequences probably offer a fluency advantage rather than a knowledge advantage to L1 users, that is to say, they do not require special knowledge for processing, but there is evidence that they are processed faster (Conklin and Schmitt 2008).

Knowledge of syntax predicts a smaller part of reading comprehension success (in terms of comprehension product, Ulijn and Strother 1990). Bernhardt (2005) summarized studies suggesting that only 3% of variance in comprehension product could be accounted for by what she calls syntactic knowledge. August (2006) found that 8% of the variance in adult Spanish-speakers' performance reading English could be explained by L2 syntax.

In spite of the relatively few studies concerned with L2 coherence building, there is, as would be expected, evidence that the ability to make use of explicit connective devices and logical connectors varies among L2 readers (Koda 2004). Apparently, many comprehension errors among L2 readers stem from not fully understanding inter-sentential relations or over-applying causal interpretations when inferring a connection between two successive statements. Studies showing, somewhat counter-intuitively, that less explicit marking of propositional relations can enhance comprehension and recall for good L1 readers with relevant background knowledge (O'Reilly and McNamara 2007) have obvious relevance for L2 readers: do advanced L2 readers with relevant background knowledge gain in the same way?

As noted above, text-structures and pragmatic expectations about explicitness are known to vary across cultures and languages (Hinds 1990; Clyne 1983) so that inadequate knowledge of the expectations of the culture envisaged by the author might create difficulties in comprehension. Tests tend to show that this effect is fairly weak, however (Chu, Swaffar and Charney 2002). The conclusion is that the most important component of linguistic knowledge for advanced L2 reading is vocabulary, presumably including formulaic sequences.

3.3.3 Processing (fluency)

Alongside vocabulary knowledge, the construct 'reading fluency' is often found to correlate with comprehension in studies of children acquiring reading L2. Thus Crosson and Lesaux (2010) used a measure of text-reading fluency based on the time taken for error-free reading aloud of texts at various levels of difficulty and found that it explained a significant (though not very large) proportion of the variance in reading comprehension for Spanish-speaking school students.

Advanced L2 users often read more slowly in L2 than in L1 (for French-English bilinguals, cf. Segalowitz, Poulsen, and Komoda 1991). L2 users' processing on various levels is usually slower than L1 users' (Shaw and McMillion 2008 for Swedish-English. and Fraser 2007 for Chinese-English), but this is dependent on the type of bilingualism or biliteracy: in some societies bilinguals may be faster in the L2 even when fully literate in L1 (Kumar and Chengappa 2015). Slower overall reading in L2 is not always associated with inferior comprehension. Some evidence (Biancarosa 2005) suggests that slow reading puts a burden on working memory and implies inefficient processes leading to poor product, but Walczyk (2000) suggests that weaker readers may simply need more time to reach a product that may be fully adequate. Gaps in language knowledge could make a task which L1 readers tackle at a leisure reading speed into a slower reading-to-learn task for L2 readers (Fraser 2007: 374), but there is no necessary link between reading comprehension success and processing speed.

The slower whole-skill rates usually found for L2 readers of the type addressed here are often regarded as meaning that L1 users have more automatized decoding that requires less attention and thus leaves more capacity free for higher cognitive processing (Geva and Ryan 1993). Segalowitz and Hulstijn (2005) point out that faster processing is not necessarily due to automatization, so that the L1 advantage may include faster controlled processes as well as more automatization. Slower whole-skill reading is certainly partly due to slower low-level processing. It is a very robust finding of word recognition studies that L2 users process individual uncontextualized words more slowly (Fukkink, Hulstijn and Simis 2005).

Collocations (mutually predicting words) are processed relatively faster than strings with less mutual prediction by both L1 and L2 users (Conklin and Schmitt 2008). However, it can also be shown (Erman et al. this volume) that L2 users do not have the same command of phraseology as L1 users, and there can be no processing-speed advantage for a formulaic sequence one does not know. Presumably, L1 users process many collocations faster than L2 users because the collocational links are stronger for them than for the L2 users.

Concerning parsing speed, Hopp (2006) found that L1 English and Dutch near-native speakers of German parse to 'native-like degrees' (2006: 394), while the merely 'advanced users' did not. This suggests that it is certainly possible for near-native L2 users to converge on native syntactic processing, but that informants with even slightly lower levels of L2 proficiency differ qualitatively from peers with L1 proficiency. Hahne (2001) compared highly proficient L2 learners listening to sentences containing a breach of selectional restrictions with L1 listeners. She found that while both displayed a P600 ERP (event related potential) which can be related to late syntactic processes (Hahne and Friederici 1999), the L2 users failed to show the early anterior negativity ERP pattern, which is associated with automatic, first-pass syntactic parsing.

Differences among readers in working memory span may be particularly significant for L2 reading, if it is less automatized than the L1 equivalent. Individual working memory span is important for all reading (Haarmann, Davelaar and Usher 2003, Abu-Rabia and Siegel 2002), since it facilitates the cumulative development of the textbase and situation model. Slower and non-automatized working memory dependent processes could therefore impair higher-order processing. Non-automatized processing among L2 readers may imply that L2 readers experience more demands on memory, which would constitute another difference between L1 and L2 readers.

These lower-level processing differences account for varying amounts of variance in the overall quality of L2 reading. L1 reading researchers (Perfetti 1985, 1988; Baker and Brown 2000; Pressley and Afflerback 1995) generally find a correlation of reading rate (though this is often 'oral reading fluency' of children, see Crosson and Lesaux 2010) and quality of product. This is interpreted as meaning that inefficient low-level processing depletes resources in working memory and reduces the efficiency of high-level processing, and that slow processing inhibits cumulation of the textbase and situation model. On the other hand, as noted above, Walczyk (2000) found that slower readers could use controlled processes to compensate for deficiencies in low-level processing. Word-recognition speed is more closely related to reading success in beginners than in advanced L2 readers (Nassaji 2014).

A central issue in the study of processing in advanced L2 users is the extent to which processing is controlled by explicit (conscious, declarative) knowledge and the extent to which aspects of the processing have been automated and are consequently implicit and proceduralized (Paradis 2009). On the one hand, faster processing may indicate that proceduralization has taken place, but, on the other, it may simply be a result of speeded-up explicit processing. Teasing these apart can be a formidable challenge. Segalowitz and Hulstijn (2005) suggest that if the standard deviation for response times decreases as the response time mean decreases, automatization or proceduralization may have taken place. The idea (coefficient of variation) is simply that proceduralization implies unconscious, ballistic processing with no direct influence from metalinguistic knowledge and consequently will show little variance in repeated tasks.

4 Investigatory procedures

The instruments available for analyzing adult reading operate at a variety of levels and are capable of giving different qualities, quantities and types of information. The levels range from the word to the whole text. Some instruments aim to capture the knowledge underlying reading, for example knowledge of vocabulary or syntax (Shiotsu and Weir 2007), other instruments try to capture the comprehension process on-line (as indicated by patterns or locations of brain activity, eye-tracking, response times, or reading speeds), and yet others to capture the product of reading, the mental model or textbase. The on-line instruments tend to be analytic, aiming at identifying parts of the process, while the product instruments are holistic, assessing the overall result of more or less naturalistic reading (Zwaan and Singer 2003). Studies comparing L1 and L2 reading may be made within subjects across languages (the same subjects reading in their L1 and their L2) or within languages across subjects (reading in a given language by subjects for whom it is L1 or L2).

The most qualitative and holistic data are obtainable from reader accounts of their strategies and experience of reading texts in a naturalistic way. Think-aloud protocols have been used, in which readers verbalize the processes they go through in reading and understanding a text. To some extent such approaches may distort the processes they investigate ('reactivity', Yoshida 2008). They are also less useful for examining unconscious processes, which are not available to introspection or verbalization, than for examining strategies and problem-solving. If a reader reads a text in a rauding style (Carver 1990) and does not encounter any difficulties, a think-aloud protocol may only contain silence. Nevertheless, useful information can often be obtained. For example, Stevenson, Schoonen and de Glopper (2007) used think-aloud protocols to compare (within subjects) the strategies of Dutch high-school students reading in L1 and L2. They found that gaps in L2 knowledge neither inhibited higher-level processes nor caused over-reliance on them.

Neurolinguistic investigation of brain and mental processes is relevant to analytically-oriented reading research. Decoding and parsing processes may be different for L1 and L2 recipients, and this may be demonstrated by a variety of instruments. Functional Magnetic Resonance Imaging (fMRI) brain scans give information about the location in the brain of activity, without particularly good time resolution. For example, Rüschemeyer, Zysset and Friederici (2006) used fMRI scans of L1 and L2 readers processing sentences with or without semantic or syntactic anomalies (a common task in neurolinguistic investigations) and found that L1 and L2 readers use the same cortical network to process language, but the L2 readers show higher activation in certain areas, which is consistent with lower automatization.

In contrast, event-related potentials (ERP) give good time-resolution but no indication of the location of activity. A recent controversy concerned the reading of sentences like *He greeted the wife of the diplomat who liked dogs* and the level in the syntactic tree at which constituents are linked. L1 readers of English show 'low attachment', tending to attach the relative clause to the second NP while L1 readers of Greek, Spanish, German and French show 'high attachment', tending to attach it to the first. Clahsen and Felser (2006) have used ERPs and found cases where L2 readers have no preference for either type of attachment – interpreted as shallower processing, making use of semantic and pragmatic cues in preference to parsing (see also Felser, Roberts, Marinis and Gross 2003). If this is the correct interpretation, it may illustrate inferior processing, presumably due to lack of automaticity at some low level. But other researchers found both transfer and native-like attachment. It may be a simple matter of L2 knowledge: Dussias (2003) and Frenck-Mestre (2002; 2005) found that advanced English users of L2 French showed French-style high attachment preferences, while less advanced ones had English-style low attachment.

Frenck-Mestre (2005) gives details of the well-established approach that uses eye-tracking equipment in which subjects read a text on screen while the movements of their eyes (saccades, fixations and regressions) are tracked by small cameras. This can be extremely revealing of difficulties in processing particular texts, but of course the instruments used affect one's results. For example, Frenck-Mestre (2002) not only reports failure to find eye-tracking equivalents of the evidence for different attachment strategies found by some ERP workers but also shows that one reason for the slower performance of proficient L2 readers in holistic reading tasks is that they frequently re-read sentences; she takes this to be a strategy inherited from their less proficient days, implying that it is not necessary now but still maintained.

Another type of on-line instrument, technologically simpler but less informative, is the self-paced reading task in which subjects see a segment of text on a computer screen, read it, and press a key to move on to the next segment. For example, Hoover and Dwivadi (1998) used this technique to show that faster

L2 readers were faster both at word-recognition and at parsing. If one segment takes longer than another, one can assume that there is something in the segment (syntax, phraseology, lexis, or content) or in its discourse location that causes processing difficulty. This task is a good example of the analytic nature of some on-line instruments: subjects are unable to make use of normal holistic strategies like previewing, re-reading etc. Even if the rest of the text is indicated by dashes of some kind, so that the reader has a sense of overall structure, the intervention severely distorts the process. The information gained is about linguistic processes, not reading as a communicative activity.

Another group of on-line instruments, somewhat more remote from communicative reading, is the activation tasks (as used by Altenberg and Smith-Cairns 1983). These instruments measure the speed of activation of a representation, along with the speed of a decision as to its well-formedness.

Tasks in which subjects are simply asked to name (read out loud) the word presented are pure activation measures. However, they are hardly appropriate for second-language readers because they are vulnerable to mere phonological reading of the word form and hence may not be measuring the speed of lexical access. The most common task is lexical decision, in which subjects have to press a key to show whether a string of letters presented to them is a well-formed word of the target language or not. Non-words may be orthographically possible ('legal') or impossible ('illegal') in the target language, for example *lut* as 'legal' and *tlu* as 'illegal' in English. The time taken to press the appropriate key to record the decision represents the sum of (1) the time taken to identify the word, (2) the time taken to switch from word recognition to result recording, and (3) the time taken to press the key. All three times vary across individuals, but only the lexical decision time should vary systematically with language background, so that given a reasonably large sample, differences in time should reflect differences in degrees of automaticity of lexical access. L1 readers reject illegal non-words much faster than legal ones (Altenberg and Smith-Cairns 1983, see 3.2 above).

An analogous 'sentence-verification' model can be applied to sentences and even to short discourses: the text can be presented and the subject asked to judge how far it is sensible or linguistically well-formed. However, the longer the text the more naturalistic the process is and hence the more vulnerable to conscious processes and strategies. For example, in a short-text reading task some readers will have a strategy of quick response, others will have a strategy of re-reading, and this may be linked to L1/L2 status (Frenck-Mestre 2002).

Familiar instruments like tests of content and summary tasks look at the issue more holistically or as communication. There are many test formats, each evoking a construct which is not exactly the product of naturalistic reading. Thus, for example, free recall, in which readers write down or verbally retell what they have understood from the reading, tests many skills other than reading, such as memory and productive proficiency but has the advantage that it does not draw readers' attention unnaturally to particular points. By contrast, multiple-choice tests require readers to have the same interpretation as the test writer and are vulnerable to test-wise strategies, but they more purely test reading comprehension. Batteries of tests are probably required to get an accurate picture for research purposes.

August (2006) gave non-academic adult L2 readers multiple-choice tests of L1 (Spanish) and L2 (English) reading and L2 grammar and showed, as expected, contributions from L1 literacy and L2 proficiency. She concludes that her subjects needed more instruction in L2 literacy skills because they had less to transfer from L1 literacy. However, because she used different tests for L1 and L2 she could not estimate whether reading skills or speeds were superior in one language or the other. This problem can be overcome by using translation-equivalent texts in L1 and L2. A major project in the Netherlands, the NELSON project, examines L1 and L2 reading in a closely related pair of languages (Dutch and English), but does so in secondary-school pupils (Snellings, van Gelderen and de Glopper 2002, van Gelderen, Schoonen and de Glopper et al. 2003, 2004; Stevenson, Schoonen and de Glopper 2007). Their results are useful in the context of our project, which also examines closely related languages (Swedish and English), but they are not directly relevant to adult L2 reading. The NELSON research paradigm is to examine the performance of readers on translation-equivalent texts in L1 and in L2, and to carry out a within-subjects analysis, focusing on the contribution of linguistic nativeness where individual characteristics such as metalinguistic knowledge and strategy choice are controlled for. As noted above, they find support for a three-component model (L1 literacy, L2 knowledge, metalinguistic knowledge) along with faster reading in L1 than in L2.

In a similar framework, but examining advanced adults, Fraser (2007) used several tests for different levels of reading (from scanning to reading for memorization, Carver 1990), including multiple-choice tests to elicit study reading (reading to learn) and recall to elicit memorization. She found that at all of Carver's levels Chinese graduate students read considerably more slowly in L2 English than in L1 Chinese. Furthermore the gap was considerably larger than previous workers had found for the language-pair French-English, confirming the effect of typological difference between languages (more positive transfer to English from French, more negative and less positive from Chinese). She ascribes the difference to slower processing in L2; even though the Chinese readers experienced the English-language texts as easy and achieved good comprehension, they were slower. Reading speed did not correlate with language proficiency, presumably because it was a function of higher-level processing speed and not language knowledge. Fraser infers from her results that while reading speed and reading success often correlate for L1 schoolchildren, in accordance with the predictions of Verbal Efficiency Theory (Perfetti 1988), in a case like hers controlled processes, though inevitably slower than automatized ones, are fully developed and able to produce an acceptable result given time (cf. Walczyk 2000).

These are within-subjects studies, however, and do not directly answer the question of whether L2 readers are in fact disadvantaged in relation to L1 readers, given that both groups show a range of reading proficiency levels, and if they are disadvantaged, in what ways. This question is particularly important in an ideological context where it is asserted that L1 users of English are not to be regarded as models for production and therefore not as 'owning' the language. This issue is addressed in the following section.

5 L2 reading research in a lingua-franca environment

Our own research is focused on English, a language in relation to which the notion of native-speaker core proficiency has been problematized. L1 speakers of most languages are more accurate users by definition because the norm for accuracy is L1 use. In some cases, however, accuracy and L1 use are not so intimately linked. This is obviously true of dead languages, where the norms are purely those of the standard, probably evolved during the period when the language did have L1 users. It may not be true of languages which have a majority of users who are not first-language users in the above sense. In such cases the norms would be contested and the majority might define other norms than those of the natives, a process which is claimed to have started for English (Graddol 2006). This makes it politically and theoretically difficult to define proficiency for English in terms of L1 norms (Jenkins 2000, Mauranen 2012). For example, L1 oral core proficiency in Southern British English may not provide efficient and effective performance in conversation in either American or Indian English. Conversely, in India it is likely that core proficiency in Indian English, even where it is not technically L1, is more effective and efficient than its 'true'

L1 equivalent. This is as true of genre expectations and cultural knowledge as of core proficiency.

In this situation it is argued that the English of advanced L2 users has equal status to that of L1 users (Seidlhofer 2001). This means that to ask how L2 users compensate for their disadvantage may seem a meaningless question, since it presupposes that L2 use is a deficit rather than a difference.

However, there seem to be important empirical issues. If in fact L2 readers in an environment where English is used as a lingua-franca medium of instruction approach the reading rate and quality of their L1 peers, then their use of English is indeed of equal status with L1 users. But if their reading rates are lower and quality is inferior, then it is misleading to call the situation one of difference.

Although the literature on L1 reading is enormous and that concerning L2 reading is growing, it is only recently that researchers have started trying to make connections between low-level processing in L2 and whole-skill performance. The general issue concerns the nature of compensation. Given that advanced L2 readers are generally effective on a communicative level – they get the meaning of the text eventually – but possibly deficient in language knowledge and slow on low-level processing, how do they compensate? How far does slow and non-automatized low-level processing inhibit higher-level processes, and how far do effective high-level processes compensate for it (Stevenson, Schoonen and de Glopper 2007; van Gelderen, Schoonen and de Glopper et al. 2003, 2004)?

Another area of interest is the relation between vocabulary size and reading comprehension in L1 and L2 readers. As we noted above, many L2 users who have a given level of vocabulary size in relevant domains can be expected to have better literacy skills than L1 users at that vocabulary level, and so are likely to perform better overall in comprehension tasks. This prediction, as far as we are aware, has not been investigated and it is one of the aims of our own research to test it. Note that the hypothesis here is that literacy skills transferred from L1 compensate for inadequate L2 vocabulary knowledge and automaticity, which is a different hypothesis than that background knowledge can compensate for inadequate L2 proficiency. This is related to the exposure-to-print issue because L1 readers with a large vocabulary presumably have acquired it from extensive exposure to print.

6 Our Programme

The research program that we propose in order to look at these questions involves developing profiles of L1 and L2 readers with similar academic backgrounds, maturity, etc., and who face similar reading tasks in either an L1 English or a

Table 1: Research instruments used in our own study

A. **Whole-skills reading tasks** for all or a subset of informants
   1. short newspaper reports to be matched with summary sentences under time pressure (adapted from Bonnet 1988),
   2. a traditional timed multiple-choice test using texts intended for well-educated L1 general readers.
   3. an extract from a relevant textbook to be read and summarized in writing from memory.
B. **Vocabulary size and quality** for all or a subset of informants
   1. words from the Academic Word List (Coxhead 2000) in a fill-in-the-blank style test.
   2. multiple-choice synonym and antonym questions with no context adapted from a test designed to discriminate among L1 English students.
   3. an adaptation to timed computer administration of Gyllstad's Collocation Test (2007) which requires readers to discriminate between correct and incorrect collocations.
C. **Grammatical knowledge** was tested a subset through a similar timed grammaticality judgement test
D. **Processing** was assessed by reaction-time tests like those described in section 4 above:
   1. Lexical discrimination tasks measuring speeds for real-word recognition.
   2. Sentence-verification tasks involved judging whether two-clause sentences were logically coherent (*he ate lunch because he was hungry*) or not (*he ate lunch although he was hungry*). This draws almost entirely on controlled processing or declarative knowledge.
   3. Sentence verification tasks with context. First two sentences were shown on the screen. When the mouse button was pressed, the sentence disappeared and a third appeared. Together the sentences built a scenario or simple situation. The task was to decide whether the third sentence was coherent with the preceding two sentences. This is somewhat closer to naturalistic sentence processing

parallel-language environment like that of the modern Scandinavian university (Norén 2006). The profiles are derived from batteries of tests as in van Gelderen et al. (2004).

Our subjects were first-year university students of biology in Britain and Sweden. They were comparable in age, gender make-up, social class and educational level. It is assumed by some Swedish authority that the Swedish students are comparable in reading skills to L1 readers, since they are required to read the same book as the British students: Sadava, Oriana, Purves and Craig's basic textbook (2007).

The most natural form of reading is Carver's middle level, so-called rauding, but this is hard to investigate, since any test of the reading product converts the task into reading to learn or study reading. Reading to learn is, however, a very important form of reading and the one most relevant to L2 readers in a lingua-franca environment, since what they are required to do is learn from the same textbooks as L1 readers. Different methods of product assessment distort the results in different ways and it is therefore appropriate to assess it in different ways.

Pilot tests showed that most L1 readers, and many Swedish readers of English, perform at ceiling levels on standard tests of reading and vocabulary intended for L2 readers. We therefore decided to use a standard reading test intended for native speakers – the Nelson-Denny Test (Brown, Fishco and Hanna 1993), which incorporates a vocabulary test, and at the same time develop tests which were appropriate for our subjects and our construct of reading proficiency. We asked a subset of the subjects to take a test of Swedish reading proficiency derived from the Swedish university entrance test *Högskoleprovet*, so that we could assess the influence of L1 literacy on their L2 achievement. The other tests used are summarized in Table 1.

7 Some findings

In Shaw and McMillion 2008, McMillion and Shaw 2009, Shaw and McMillion 2011 we report some initial general findings. One that is little discussed in the literature, which tends to treat L1 and L2 readers as completely separate categories, is that there was overlap between L1 and L2 readers on all measures of speed and accuracy. Many L2 users scored within the L1 range not only on holistic tasks like the multiple-choice reading test but also on sub-skill tests like word-recognition speed which presumably assess purely linguistic receptive proficiency. This is an area in which advanced second-language users may well outdo L1 users.

Like other contributors to this volume, we wanted to analyze equivalent L1 and L2 groups, but equivalence is a slippery concept. The widest interpretation would be to take seriously the idea that all literacy is situated and compare L1 and L2 readers who are able in their respective situations to learn successfully from the same textbooks. We could thus compare first-year biology students in Sweden with peers in an English-speaking country, in this case Scotland. This comparison is also motivated by the discourse used by the informants which suggests that 'English and Swedish are the same' for them, that the choice of language for reading is motivated purely by convenience and not by any sense of ease or difficulty (Mežek 2013).

In such a comparison, unsurprisingly, nativeness does seem to matter, though in reading it seems to be a matter of greater exposure to print than of any critical-period effects. In general the lowest scorers on tests were L2 users and the majority of the highest scorers were L1 users. The range of scores was greater for L2 users than for L1 users. Interviews with L2 participants who scored high in the L1 range showed that they had indeed had very much exposure to print in L2, though not necessarily much active use. Correspondingly many Swedish university students report that they read very little of set texts (Pecorari et al. 2011). These advanced L2 users read significantly slower than L1 peers, and this was in fact the main reason for lower scores on timed tests. Like Stevenson et al. (2007) we found little evidence that L2 and L1 participants of similar educational and relatively similar cultural backgrounds use different reading strategies. Scores on a test of inferencing with little linguistic difficulty or time pressure were equivalent, for example, and the patterns of answers to multiple-choice questions targeting different reading subskills were also comparable.

A narrower view of equivalence is that broadly taken by other contributors to this volume: equivalent informants are those who can perform communicative tasks in similar contexts with similar success. At this level we can compare L1 and L2 readers who score at similar levels on standardized tests. Here we find significant differences in vocabulary size (given uncontextualized prompts) and in uncontextualized word-recognition speed and accuracy between the two, but not in contextualized sentence discrimination. The implication is that the L2 readers are indeed compensating for less automatized processes by using superior higher-level skills. It should be noted that L2 readers who score in the L1 range on unsituated reading comprehension tests are likely to perform better on situated literacy tasks like learning biology than L1 readers with the same test scores.

An even narrower view of equivalence would take it to mean similar vocabulary size or uncontextualized word-recognition reaction-time. Our results show that the relatively few L2 readers who perform like L1 users on these uncontextualized measures score, on average, above the levels of their L1 peers on the (relatively more contextualized) reading test. Thus although fewer and fewer L2 readers score equivalently to L1 readers as the tasks become less situated and holistic, those that do score equivalently on decontextualized tasks perform better than L1 equivalents on more situated and holistic activities.

8 Conclusion

Reading is a notoriously complex area and, although there is a vast amount of research, there is relatively little which examines whole-skill reading in relation to measures of both processing and knowledge in advanced L2 readers. Because reading involves so many skills at so many levels, there are multiple opportunities both for compensation and for strategic choice.

In response to the first question posed in the introduction, whether advanced L2 readers can achieve native-like reading proficiency, the literature broadly indicates that even very advanced L2 readers normally read slower in their second language. Our research suggests, however, that a proportion of very advanced L2 readers do achieve reading proficiency levels at or above the average of L1 peers.

Concerning the second question, there seems to be a consensus that the products of L1 and very advanced L2 readers are virtually indistinguishable, although the L2 readers are usually slower. However, the question can be turned the other way round: L2 readers who perform at any given L1 level on uncontextualized tasks like word-recognition and vocabulary size can be expected to perform better than equivalent L1 users on communicative tasks.

The third question brings many of the key issues to the fore. There are many indications that very advanced L2 readers do rely on compensatory processing, given the similarity of the reading product with that of comparable L1 readers alongside smaller vocabularies and slower processing.

As universities become internationalized under a linguistic world order that currently prescribes English as their lingua franca, it becomes more and more important to get a nuanced view of what might be going on when young adults study in their home country but in a foreign language.

References

Abbott M. L. 2006. ESL reading strategies: differences in Arabic and Mandarin speaker test performance. *Language Learning*, 56/4. 633–670.

Abrahamsson, N. & K. Hyltenstam. 2008. The robustness of aptitude effects in near-native second language acquisition. *Studies in Second Language Acquisition*, 30. 481–509.

Abu-Rabia, S. & L. S. Siegel. 2002. Reading, syntactic, orthographic, and working memory skills of bilingual Arabic-English Speaking Canadian children. *Journal of Psycholinguistic Research*, 31/6. 661–678.

Adams, B. C., L. C. Bell, & C. A Perfetti. 1995. A trading relationship between reading skill and domain knowledge in children's text comprehension. *Discourse Processes*, 20. 307–323.

Alderson, J. C. 2005. *Diagnosing Foreign Language Proficiency: The Interface Between Learning and Assessment*. London: Continuum.

Altenberg, E. P. & H. Smith Cairns. 1983. The effects of phonotactic constraints on lexical processing in bilingual and monolingual subjects. *Journal of Verbal Learning and Verbal Behavior*, 22. 174–188.

Andersen, R. 1983. Transfer to somewhere. In: S. Gass & L. Selinker (eds.), *Language Transfer in Language Learning*. Boston: Newbury House Publishers. 177–201.

Arnbjörnsdóttir, B. & H. Ingvarsdóttir, Hafdis. 2015. Simultaneous parallel code use: using English in university studies in Iceland. In: A. Fabricius & B. Preisler (eds.), *Transcultural Interaction and Linguistic Diversity in Higher Education: The Student Experience*. London: Palgrave. 142–163.

Ashby, J. 2006. Prosody in skilled silent reading: evidence from eye movements. *Journal of Research in Reading*, 29/3. 318–333.
August, G. 2006. So what's behind adult English second language reading? *Bilingual Research Journal*, 30/2. 245–264.
Bachman L. & A. Palmer. 1996. *Language Testing in Practice.* New York: Oxford University Press.
Baker, L. & A. Brown. 2000. Metacognitive skills and reading. In: P. D. Pearson, R. Barr, M. L. Kamil, & P. Mosenthal (eds.), *Handbook of Reading Research, volume 1.* New York: Longman. 353–394.
Berry, J.W. 1993. An ecological approach to understanding cognition across cultures. In: J. Altarriba (ed.), *Cognition and Culture: A Cross-Cultural Approach to Cognitive Psychology.* Oxford, UK: Elsevier. 361–375.
Bernhardt, E. 2005. Progress and procrastination in second language reading. *Annual Review of Applied Linguistics*, 25. 133–150.
Bialystok, E. 2007. Cognitive effects of bilingualism: how linguistic experience leads to cognitive change. *International Journal of Bilingual Education and Bilingualism*, 10/3. 210–223.
Biancarosa, G. 2005. Speed and time, texts and sentence: Choosing the best metric for relating reading rate to comprehension. *Written Language & Literacy*, 8/2. 79–100.
Bonnet G. 1988. *The Effectiveness of the Teaching of English in the European Union; Report of the Colloquium and Background Documents.* Paris: Ministère de l'éducation nationale: DFD Edition diffusion.
Brown, J. I., V. V. Fishco, & G. Hanna. 1993. *The Nelson Denny Reading Test.* Chicago, IL: The Riverside Publishing Company.
Byun,K., H. Chu, M. Kim, I. Park, S. Kim, & J. Jung. 2011. English-medium teaching in Korean higher education: Policy debates and reality. *Higher Education*, 62/4. 431–449.
Canale, M. & M. Swain. 1980. Theoretical bases of communicative approaches to second language teaching and testing. *Applied Linguistics*, 1. 1–47.
Carson, J. E., P. L., Carrell, S. Silberstein, B. Kroll, & P. Kuehn. 1990. Reading-writing relationships in first and second language. *TESOL Quarterly*, 24. 245–266.
Carver, R. P. 1990. *Reading Rate: A Review of Research and Theory.* San Diego: Academic Press.
Chen, Q. & J. Donin. 1997. Discourse processing of first and second language biology text: Effects of language proficiency and domain-specific knowledge. *Modern Language Journal*, 81. 209–227.
Chu, H.-C. J., J. Swaffar & D. H. Charney. 2002. Cultural representations of rhetorical conventions: the effects on reading recall. *TESOL Quarterly*, 36/4. 511–541.
Cipielewski, J. & K. Stanovich. 1992. Predicting growth in reading ability from children's exposure to print. *Journal of Experimental Child Psychology*, 54. 74–89.
Clahsen, H. & C. Felser. 2006. Grammatical processing in first and second language learners. *Applied Psycholinguistics*, 27. 3–42.
Clyne, M. 1983. Culture and discourse structure. In: L. E. Smith (ed.), *Readings in English as an International Language.* London: Pergamon. 163–167.
Conklin, K. & N. Schmitt. 2008. Formulaic sequences: are they processed more quickly than nonformulaic language by native and nonnative speakers. *Applied Linguistics*, 29/1. 72–89.
Coxhead, A. 2000. A new academic word list. *TESOL Quarterly*, 34/2. 213–238.
Crosson, A. C. & N. K. Lesaux. 2010. Revisiting assumptions about the relationship of fluent reading to comprehension: Spanish-speakers' text-reading fluency in English. *Reading and Writing*, 23. 475–494.

Cummins, J. 1979. Linguistic interdependence and the educational development of bilingual children. *Review of Educational Research*, 49. 222–251.

de Bot, K. 2012. Rethinking multilingual processing. In: S. Flynn, J. Rothman, & J. Cabrelli Amara (eds.), *Third Language Acquisition in Adulthood*. Amsterdam: John Benjamins Publishers. 79–93.

Dussias, P. E. 2003. Syntactic ambiguity resolution in second language learners: Some effects of bilinguality on L1 and L2 processing strategies. *Studies in Second Language Learning*, 25. 529–557.

Erman, B., F. Forsberg Lundell, & M. Lewis. this volume. Formulaic language in advanced second language acquisition and use.

Farley, M. J. & P. B. Elmore. 1992. The relationship of reading comprehension to critical thinking skills, cognitive ability, and vocabulary for a sample of underachieving college freshmen. *Educational and Psychological Measurement*, 52/4. 921–931.

Felser, C., L. Roberts, T. Marinis, & R. Gross. 2003. The processing of ambiguous sentences by first and second language learners of English. *Applied Psycholinguistics*, 24. 453–89.

Foster, P. & P. Tavakoli. 2009. Native speakers and task performance: comparing effects on complexity, fluency, and lexical diversity. *Language Learning*, 59/4. 866–896.

Fransson, A. 1984. Cramming or understanding? Effects of intrinsic and extrinsic motivation on approach to learning and test performance. In: C. J. Alderson & A. H. Urquhart (eds.), *Reading in a Foreign Language*. London: Longman. 86–121.

Fraser, C. A. 2007. Reading rate in L1 Mandarin Chinese and L2 English across five reading tasks. *Modern Language Journal*, 91/3. 372–394.

Frenck-Mestre, C. 2002. An on-line look at sentence processing in the second language In: R. R. Heredia & J. Altarriba (eds.), *Bilingual Sentence Processing*. Amsterdam: Elsevier Science. 217–236.

Frenck-Mestre, C. 2005. Eye-movement recording as a tool for studying syntactic processing in a second language: a review of methodologies and experimental findings. *Second Language Research*, 21/2. 175–198.

Fukkink, R. G., J. Hulstijn & A. Simis. 2005. Does training in second-language word recognition skills affect reading comprehension? An experimental study. *The Modern Language Journal*, 89/1. 54–75.

Gee, J. P. 2001. Reading as situated language: A sociocognitive perspective. *Journal of Adolescent & Adult Literacy*, 44/8. 714–725.

Gernsbacher, M. A. 1990. *Language Comprehension as Structure Building*. Hillsdale, NJ: Erlbaum.

Gernsbacher, M. A. & M. E. Faust. 1991. The mechanism of suppression: A component of general comprehension skill. *Journal of Experimental Psychology: Learning, Memory, and Cognition*, 17. 245–262.

Geva, E. & E. B. Ryan. 1993. Linguistic and cognitive correlates of academic skills in first and second languages. *Language Learning*, 43/1. 5–42.

Gough, P., C. Juel, & P. Griffith. 1992. Reading, spelling, and the orthographic cipher. In: P. Gough, L. C. Ehri, & R. Treiman (eds.), *Reading Acquisition*. Hillsdale, NJ: Lawrence Erlbaum Associates. 35–48.

Graddol, D. 2006. *English Next*. London: British Council.

Guthrie, J. T. & A. Wigfield. 1999. How motivation fits into a science of reading. *Scientific Studies of English*, 3/3. 199–205.

Guthrie, J. T., A. Wigfield, K. C. Perencevich, A. Taboada, N. M. Humenick & P. Barbosa. 2006. Influences of stimulating tasks on reading motivation and comprehension. *The Journal of Educational Research*, 99/4. 232–245.

Gyllstad, H. 2007. *Testing English collocations: Developing receptive tests for use with advanced Swedish learners*. Doctoral Dissertation. Lund: Lund University Press.

Haarmann H. J., E. J. Davelaar, & M. Usher. 2003. Individual differences in semantic short-term memory capacity and reading comprehension. *Journal of Memory and Language*, 48/2. 320–345.

Haenggi, D. & C. A. Perfetti. 1994. Processing components of college-level reading comprehension. *Discourse Processes*, 17/1. 83–104.

Hahne, A. & A. D. Friederici. 1999. Electrophysiological evidence for two steps in syntactic analysis: early automatic and late controlled processes. *Journal of Cognitive Neuroscience*, 11. 193–204.

Hahne, A. 2001. What's different in second language processing? Evidence from event-related brain potentials. *Journal of Psycholinguistic Research*, 30. 251–266.

Hannon, B. & M. Daneman. 2001. Susceptibility to semantic illusions: An individual-differences perspective. *Memory & Cognition*, 29/3. 449–461.

Harmon, J. M., M. G. Martinez & A. Deckard. 2003. Children's strategic awareness for reading different genres and text types. In: J. Worthy, B. Maloch, J. Hoffman, D. Schallert, & C. Fairbanks (eds.), *53rd Yearbook of the National Reading Conference*. Oak Creek, WI: National Reading Conference. 218–232.

Haswell R. H., T. L. Briggs, J. A. Fay, N. K. Gillen, R. Harrill, A. M. Shupala, & S. S. Trevino. 1999. Context and rhetorical reading strategies. *Written Communication*, 16/1. 3–27.

Haynes, M. & T. H Carr. 1990. Writing system background and second language reading: A component skills analysis of English reading by native-speaking readers of Chinese. In: T. H. Carr & B. A. Levy (eds.), *Reading and its Development: Component Skills Approaches*. San Diego: Academic Press. 375–421.

Henriksen, B., D. Albrechtsen, & K. Haastrup. 2004. The relationship between vocabulary size and reading comprehension in the L2. In: B. Henriksen, D. Albrechtsen, & K. Haastrup (eds.), *Writing and Vocabulary in Foreign Language Acquisition*. Copenhagen: Museum Tusculanum Press. 129–140.

Hinds, J. 1990. Inductive, deductive, quasi-inductive: Expository writing in Japanese, Korean, Chinese, and Thai. In: U. Connor & A. M. Johns (eds.), *Coherence in Writing: Research and Pedagogical Perspectives*. Alexandria, VA: TESOL. 87–109.

Hofstede, G. 2001. *Culture's Consequences: Comparing Values, Behaviors, Institutions and Organizations across Nations* (2nd ed.). Thousand Oaks, CA: Sage.

Hoover, M. L. & V. D. Dwivedi. 1998. Syntactic processing by skilled bilinguals. *Language Learning*, 48. 1–29.

Hopp, H. 2006. Syntactic features and reanalysis in near-native processing. *Second Language Research*, 22/3. 369–397.

Huckin, T. & J. Coady. 1999. Incidental vocabulary acquisition in a second language. *Studies in Second Language Acquisition*, 21. 181–193.

Hulstijn, J. 2007. The shaky ground beneath the CEFR: Quantitative and qualitative dimensions of language proficiency. *The Modern Language Journal*, 91/1. 663–667.

Jackson, M. D. & J. L. McClelland. 1979. Processing determinants of reading speed. *Journal of Experimental Psychology: General*, 108. 151–181.

Jenkins, J. 2000. *The Phonology of English as an International Language*. Oxford: Oxford University Press.

Kardash, C. M., & Noel, L. K. 2000. How organizational signals, need for cognition, and verbal ability affect text recall and recognition. *Contemporary Educational Psychology*, 25. 317–331.

Kintsch, W. 1998. *Comprehension: A Paradigm for Cognition*. New York: Cambridge University Press.

Koda, K. 1992. The effects of lower-level processing skills on the development of second language reading. *Modern Language Journal*, 76. 502–512.

Koda, K. 1994. Second language reading research: Problems and possibilities. *Applied Psycholinguistics*, 15. 1–28.

Koda, K. 2004. *Insights into Second Language Reading: A Cross-Linguistic Approach*. Cambridge: Cambridge University Press.

Kumar, R. S. & S. Chengappa. 2015. Sentence processing in high proficient Kannada-English bilinguals: a reaction time study. *International Journal of Multilingualism*, 12. 376–392.

Laufer, B. 1992. Reading in a foreign language: How does L2 lexical knowledge interact with the reader's general academic ability. *Journal of Research in Reading*, 15/2. 95–103.

Laufer, B. 2010. Lexical threshold revisited: Lexical text coverage, learners' vocabulary size and reading comprehension. *Reading in a Foreign Language*, 22/1. 15–30.

Mauranen, A. 2012. *Exploring ELF: Academic English Shaped by Non-Native Speakers*. Cambridge: Cambridge University Press.

McKoon, G. & R. Ratcliff. 1992. Inference during reading. *Psychological Review*, 99/3. 440–466.

McMillion, A. & P. Shaw. 2009. Compensation and compensatory processes in advanced L2 readers. In: C. Brantmeier (ed.), *Crossing Languages and Research Methods: Analyses of Adult Foreign Language Reading*. Charlotte, NC: Information Age Publishing. 123–146.

Mežek, Š. 2013. Multilingual reading proficiency in an emerging parallel-language environment. *Journal of English for Academic Purposes*, 12/3. 166–179.

Nassaji, H. 2007. Schema theory and knowledge-based processes in second language reading comprehension: a need for alternative perspectives. *Language Learning*, 57/1. 79–113.

Nassaji, H. 2014. State-of-the-Art Article: The role and importance of lower-level processes in second language reading. *Language Testing*, 47/1. 1–37.

Nation, I. S. P. 2001. *Learning Vocabulary in Another Language*. Cambridge: Cambridge University Press.

Norén, K. 2006. Universiteten väljer språk. *Språkvård*, 2006/1. 26–29.

Odlin, T. 1989. *Language Transfer: Cross-Linguistic Influence in Language Learning*. New York: Cambridge University Press.

O'Reilly, T. & D. S. McNamara. 2007. Reversing the reverse cohesion effect: Good texts can be better for strategic, high-knowledge readers. *Discourse Processes*, 43/2. 121–152.

Parry, K. 1997. Vocabulary and comprehension: Two portraits. In: J. Coady & T. Huckin (eds.), *Second Language Vocabulary Acquisition*. Cambridge: Cambridge University Press. 55–68.

Paradis, M. 2009. *Declarative and Procedural Determinants of Second Languages*. Amsterdam: John Benjamins Publishing Company.

Pecorari, D., P. Shaw, A. Irvine, & H. Malmström. 2011. English textbooks in parallel-language tertiary education. *TESOL Quarterly*, 45/2. 313–333.

Perfetti, C. A. 1985. *Reading Ability*. New York: Oxford University Press.

Perfetti, C. A. 1988. *Verbal efficiency in reading ability. Reading Research: Advances in Theory and Practice. Volume 6*. New York: Academic Press.

Perfetti, C. A. 1999. Comprehending written language: A blueprint of the reader. In: C. M. Brown & P. Hagoort (eds.), *The Neurocognition of Language*. Oxford: Oxford University Press. 167–208.

Petty, R. E. & J. T. Cacioppo. 1996. *Attitudes and Persuasion: Classic and Contemporary Approaches*. New York: Westview Press Inc.

Pressler, M. & P. Afflerbach. 1995. *Verbal Protocols of Reading: The Nature or Constructively Responsive Reading.* Mahwah, NJ: Lawrence Erlbaum.
Rayner, K. & A. Pollatsek. 1989. *The Psychology of Reading.* Englewood Cliffs, NJ: Prentice Hall Rayner, K., K. H. Chace, T. J. Slattery, & J. Ashby. 2006. Eye movements as reflections of comprehension processes in reading. *Scientific Studies of Reading*, 10. 241–255.
Rüschemeyer, S.-A., S. Zysset, & A. D. Friederici. 2006. Native and non-native reading of sentences: An fMRI experiment. *Neuroimage*, 31/1. 354–365.
Rumelhart, D. 1980. Schemata: the building blocks of cognition. In: R. J. Spiro, B. Bruce, & W. Brewer (eds.), *Theoretical Issues in Reading Comprehension.* Hillsdale, N.J.: Lawrence Erlbaum. 33–58.
Sadava, D., H. C. Heller, G. H. Orians, W. K. Purves, & D. M. Hillis. 2007. *Life: The Science of Biology. Vol. II: Evolution, Diversity and Ecology.* (8th ed.). London: Palgrave Macmillan.
Schraw, G. 2000. Reader beliefs and reading instruction in narrative text. *Journal of Educational Psychology*, 92. 96–106.
Schunk D. H. 2003. Self-efficacy for reading and writing: influence of modeling, goal setting, and self-evaluation, *Reading & Writing Quarterly*, 19. 159–172.
Segalowitz, N. S., C. Poulsen, & M. Komoda. 1991. Lower level components or reading skill in higher level bilinguals: Implications for reading instruction. *AILA Review*, 8. 15–30.
Segalowitz, N. S. & J. Hulstijn. 2005. Automaticity in bilingualism and second language learning. In: J. Kroll & A. M. B. de Groot (eds.), *Handbook of Bilingualism, Psycholinguistic Approaches.* Oxford: Oxford University Press. 371–388.
Seidlhofer, B. 2001. Closing a conceptual gap: the case for a description of English as a lingua franca. *International Journal of Applied Linguistics*, 11/2. 133–158.
Singer, M. 1994. Discourse inference processes. In: M. Gernsbacher (ed.), *Handbook of Psycholinguistics.* San Diego, CA: Academic Press. 479–516.
Shaw, P. & A. McMillion. 2008. Proficiency effects and compensation in advanced second-language reading. *Nordic Journal of English Studies*, 7/3. 124–144.
Shaw, P. & A. McMillion. 2011. Components of success in academic reading tasks for Swedish students. *Ibérica*, 22. 141–162.
Shiotsu, T. & C. J. Weir. 2007. The relative significance of syntactic knowledge and vocabulary breadth in the prediction of reading comprehension test performance. *Language Testing*, 24. 99–128.
Smit, U. & E. Dafouz. 2012. Integrating content and language in higher education: An introduction to English-medium policies, conceptual issues and research practices across Europe. *AILA Review*, 25/1. 1–12.
Snellings, P., A. van Gelderen, & K. de Glopper. 2002. Lexical retrieval: an aspect of fluent second language production that can be enhanced. *Language Learning*, 52/4. 723–754.
Stage, C. 2003. *Normering, ekvivalering eller kalibrering av delar av högskoleprovet.* Umeå: Umeå University.
Stanovich, K. E. 1986. Matthew effects in reading: Some consequences of individual differences in the acquisition of literacy. *Reading Research Quarterly*, 21/4. 360–406.
Stavans, A. & B. Oded. 1993. Assessing EFL reading comprehension: The case of Ethiopian learners. *System*, 21/4. 481–494.
Steffensen, M. & C. Joag-Dev. 1984. Cultural knowledge and reading. In: C. Alderson & S. H. Urquhart (eds.), *Reading in a Foreign Language.* London: Longman. 48–62.
Stevenson, M., R. Schoonen, & K. de Glopper. 2007. Inhibition or compensation? A multidimensional comparison of reading processes in Dutch and English. *Language Learning*, 57/1. 115–154.

Street, B. 1993. The new literacy studies. *Journal of Research in Reading*, 16/2. 81–97.
Tan L. H., J. A. Spinks, C.-M. Feng, W. T. Siok, C. A. Perfetti, J. Xiang, P. T. Fox, & J.-H. Gao. 2003. Neural systems of second language reading are shaped by native language. *Human Brain Mapping*, 18/3. 158–166.
Tzeng, O. J. L. & W. S.-Y. Wang. 1983. The first two R's: The way different languages reduce speech to script affects how visual information is processed in the brain. *American Scientist*, 71. 238–243.
Ulijn, J. M. & J. B. Strother. 1990. The effects of syntactic simplification on reading EST texts as L1 and L2. *Journal of Research in Reading*, 13. 38–54.
van den Broek, P., K. Risden, & E. Husebye-Hartmann. 1995. The role of readers' standards for coherence in the generation of inferences during reading. In: R. F. Lorch, Jr. & E. J. O'Brien. (eds.), *Sources of Coherence in Reading*. Hillsdale, NJ: Lawrence Erlbaum. 353–373.
van den Broek, P., S. Virtue, M. Gaddy Everson, Y. Sung, & Y.-C. Tzeng. 2002. Comprehension and memory of science texts: inferential processes and the construction of a mental representation. In: J. Otero (ed.), *Psychology of Science Text Comprehension*. Mahwah, NJ: Lawrence Erlbaum. 131–154.
van Gelderen, A., R. Schoonen, K. de Glopper, J. Hulstijn, P. Snellings, A. Simis, & M. Stevenson. 2003. Roles of linguistic knowledge, metacognitive knowledge, and processing speed in L3 L2, and L1 reading comprehension: a structural equation modeling approach. *International Journal of Bilingualism*, 7/1. 7–25.
van Gelderen, A., R. Schoonen, K. de Glopper, J. Hulstijn, A. Simis, P. Snellings, & M. Stevenson. 2004. Linguistic knowledge, processing speed, and metacognitive knowledge in first- and second-language reading comprehension: a componential analysis. *Journal of Educational Psychology*, 96/1. 19–30.
Vaughan, M. & A. Dillon. 2000. Why structure and genre matter for users of digital information: a longitudinal experiment with readers of a web-based newspaper. *International Journal of Human-Computer Studies*, 64/6. 502–526.
Walczyk, J. J. 2000. The interplay between automatic and control processes in reading. *Reading Research Quarterly*, 35/4. 554–566.
Ward, J. 2009. EAP reading and lexis for Thai engineering undergraduates. *Journal of English for Academic Purposes*, 8/4. 294–301.
Wilkinson, R. 2013. English-medium instruction at a Dutch university: Challenges and pitfalls. In: A. Doiz, D. Lasagabaster, & J. M. Sierra (eds.), *English-Medium Instruction at Universities: Global Challenges*. Clevedon: Multilingual Matters. 3–24.
Wray, A. 2002. *Formulaic Language and the Lexicon*. Cambridge: Cambridge University Press.
Yamashita, J. 2002. Mutual compensation between L1 reading ability and L2 language proficiency in L2 reading comprehension. *Journal of Research in Reading*, 25/1. 81–95.
Yoshida, M. 2008. Think-aloud protocols and type of reading task: The issue of reactivity. In: M. Bowles (ed.), *L2 Reading Research. Selected Proceedings of the 2007 Second Language Research Forum*. Somerville, MA: Cascadilla Proceedings Project. 199–209.
Zwaan, R. A. & M. Singer. 2003. Text comprehension. In: A. C. Graesser, M. A. Gernsbacher, & S. R. Goldman (eds.), *Handbook of Discourse Processes*. Mahwah, NJ: Erlbaum. 83–122.
Zwaan, R. A. & G. A. Radvansky. 1998. Situation models in language comprehension and memory. *Psychological Bulletin*, 123/2. 162–185.

Kingsley Bolton
6 Linguistic outsourcing and native-like performance in international call centres: An overview

1 Introduction

This chapter is intended to provide an overview of the research project in the Stockholm University research programme on "High-level Proficiency in Second-language Use", entitled "Linguistic outsourcing and native-like performance in international call centres and Business Process Outsourcing (BPO) operations". In the following discussion, I present a survey of the theoretical and methodological issues involved with this research, as well as a discussion of a number of preliminary findings, which may shape the direction of continued research in this area.

1.1 Linguistic outsourcing

The motivation for this study was derived partly from the realisation that the use of English as an international language in call centres in India and the Philippines has the potential to inform a range of issues relating to bilingualism, second language acquisition, sociolinguistics, world Englishes and related topics. By the early 2000s, it had become evident that large numbers of clerical, data management and other jobs were being exported from "native" English-speaking societies, such as the UK and US to societies such as India and the Philippines, where there were evidently sufficient numbers of proficient language users able to perform tasks previously reserved for American and British employees. For the last two decades, many linguists have made the claim that English was no longer the sole possession of Britain and America, that it was truly a world language. Now it seemed that such a claim was being vindicated, even at the cost of tens of thousands of jobs, as these were outsourced to such exotic destinations as Bangalore and Manila.

This new outsourcing of back-office clerical work also caught the imagination of such established social commentators in the US as Thomas L. Friedman

Kingsley Bolton, Nanyang Technological University, Singapore

and Susan Sonntag. Part of the inspiration for Friedman's best-selling book, *The World is Flat: A Brief History of the Twenty-First Century* (first published in 2005), was inspired by visits Friedman made to the Indian information technology companies *Infosys* and *WiPro* in Bangalore, India, in the early 2000s. Here, he witnessed the work that these companies were doing in writing computer software for US and European businesses and running the back offices of multinational companies, all of which involved such disparate tasks as computer maintenance, high-tech research, answering customer calls from all over the world and dealing with a range of other BPO (Business Process Outsourcing). Following a visit to the "24/7" call centre in Bangalore, Friedman noted that:

> There are currently about 245,000 Indians answering phones from all over the world or dialling out to solicit people for credit cards or cell phone bargains or overdue bills. These call centre jobs are low-wage, low-prestige jobs in America, but when shifted to India they become high-wage, high-prestige jobs. The esprit de corps at 24/7 and other call centre I visited seemed quite high, and the young people were all eager to share some of the bizarre phone conversations they've had with Americans who dialed 1-800-HELP, thinking they would wind up talking to someone around the block, not around the world. (Friedman 2006: 24)

One major feature of the training of new recruits, he added, was the "accent neutralisation class", and Friedman describes how the teacher "dressed in a traditional Indian sari" conducted the class, and "moved seamlessly among British, American and Canadian accents" (2006: 27).

A few years earlier, the renowned literary and social critic Susan Sontag had also been moved to refer to such trends in the 2002 The St. Jerome Lecture on Literary Translation, entitled "The World as India", which was subsequently published in the *Times Literary Supplement*. In this essay, Sontag noted that in India and elsewhere, the "global preeminence" of English had been reinforced by the popularity of computers and English media, which contributed to the "unique success" of English, noting that: "English is now advancing in every part of the world, through the dominance of English-speaking media – which means media in which English is spoken with an American accent – and the need for business people and scientists to communicate in a common tongue" (Sontag 2002). For Sontag, Indian call centres were interesting because they raised questions concerning authenticity in more than one language, and here (at some intellectual distance from literary translation), Sontag mused on the Indian call centre, where telephone inquiries to companies like IBM, American Express, GE, Delta Airlines, and numerous hotel chains were now being handled by young Indians:

> From large floors of office buildings in Bangalore or Bombay or New Delhi, call after call is answered by young Indians seated in rows of small booths [...] each equipped with a computer that allows them to summon with a few clicks the relevant information to make a reservation, maps to give information about the best highway route, weather forecasts, and so forth. [...] Nancy, or Mary Lou, Betty, Sally Jane, Megan, Bill, Jim, Wally, Frank – these cheerful voices had first to be trained for months, by instructors and by tapes, to acquire a pleasant middle-American (not an educated American) accent, and to learn basic American slang, informal idioms (including regional ones), and elementary mass-culture references (TV personalities and the plots and protagonists of the main sitcoms, the latest blockbuster in the multiplex, fresh baseball and basketball scores, and such), so that if the exchange with the client in the United States becomes prolonged, they will not falter with the small talk and will have the means to continue to pass for Americans. (Sontag 2002)

Some ten years on, the views of many western commentators in the UK and US on the international call centre phenomenon are far less sanguine than those early thoughts of both Friedman and Sontag. In the US, the outsourcing of clerical, back-office and telephone voice work to Asia has become bundled together with a swathe of issues related to the outsourcing of US manufacturing industries overseas and the decline of "middle-class" jobs in the US economy. In the UK media, call centres have been adversely associated with consumer difficulties in contacting retailers or service providers, as well as prolonged delays in telephone calls, where the consumers themselves have to foot the bill for lengthy waiting times.

From an academic perspective, however, the use of English in international call centres and BPOs also connects with several other debates on such issues as the "language and identity", "language ideologies", "language politics", "the native speaker", and "world Englishes". The operation of English-language call centres in India and the Philippines thus provide important sites for the investigation of language and globalisation, in a region where localised varieties of Asian Englishes e.g. Indian English, Malaysian English, Singapore English, and Philippines English have become rather firmly established over recent decades.

1.2 Asian Englishes

One basic distinction relating to English in the Asian region is the well-established dichotomy between "Outer Circle" English-using societies, where English is, sociolinguistically at least, a second language with important intranational uses, and "Expanding Circle" countries, where English has traditionally had the status of a foreign language (Kachru 1997). The major Outer Circle Asian societies include such South Asian nations as Bangladesh, Bhutan, India, Nepal, Pakistan, and Sri Lanka, and Southeast Asian societies such as Brunei, Malaysia, the

Philippines, and Singapore, as well as Hong Kong in East Asia. Even here, however, the distinction between Outer Circle and Expanding Circle is now becoming somewhat blurred (Kirkpatrick 2008).

Historically, all the Outer Circle Asian societies are former colonies of Anglophone colonial powers. In most cases, these were British colonies, as in the case of Brunei, Hong Kong, greater India, Malaysia, Myanmar, and Singapore, most of whom achieved independence between 1947 and 1963, although it was not until 1997 that China regained sovereignty over Hong Kong. The one US colony in Asia was the Philippines, which was under Spanish colonial rule from the 1560s until 1898, followed by American control until 1946. In most of these societies, English has been retained for important internal purposes after independence, and in most Outer Circle countries there is a *de jure* recognition of English in such domains as government, law, education, the mass media and creative writing. The map in Figure 1 illustrates the distinction between Outer Circle and Expanding Circle societies.

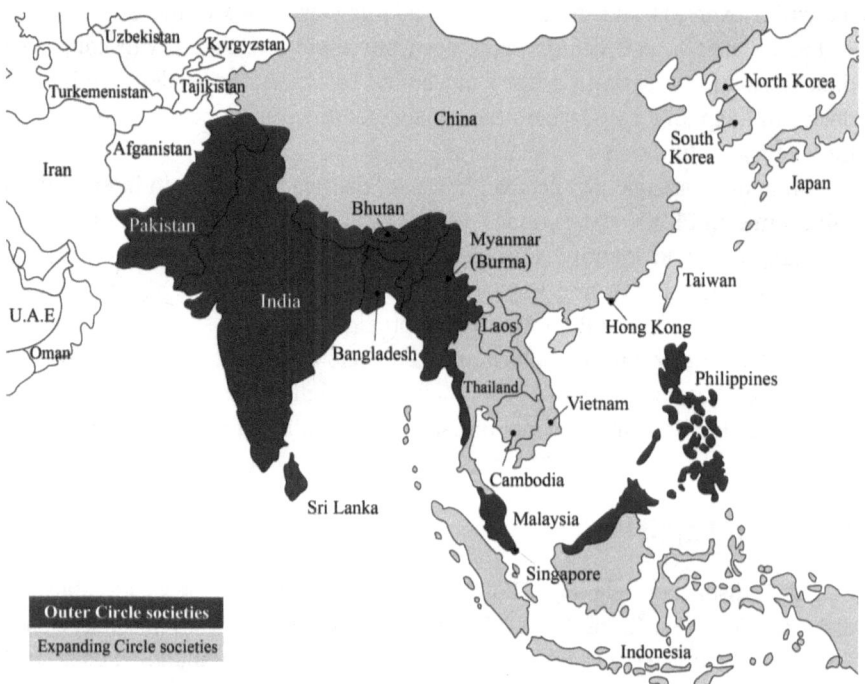

Figure 1: Outer Circle and Expanding Circle societies in South, Southeast, and East Asia

The statistics of English worldwide is a crudely inexact science, but there can be little doubt that the numbers of learners and users in the Asian region is simply staggering. In India alone, estimates of English-knowing bilinguals currently range from 15% to 30% of the population, suggesting totals between 200 and 400 million people, and even in China today it is calculated more than 400 million have studied English up to junior secondary level (Graddol 2010; Bolton and Graddol 2012). English is not only widely used in the major Outer Circle Asian societies, but also has an increasing presence in domains of business, education, and media of such Expanding Circle societies as China, Indonesia, South Korea, Thailand, etc. In such Outer Circle societies as Hong Kong, India, Malaysia and the Philippines, the varieties of English acquired and used there have become increasingly "nativized", and have developed their own distinctive features, at the levels of accent, vocabulary, and grammar. Despite the groundbreaking interest in individual Asian Englishes over the last thirty years, the degree of acceptance that such varieties have gained has varied a great deal. While academics and linguists have often revelled in the task of identifying and describing distinct varieties of English, the reactions of the educational, political and business elites have often been less than enthusiastic.

As with statistics concerning the spread of English in the region, hard evidence relating to comparative levels of proficiency is hard to come by. One potentially useful source of data are the results of international tests, such as those for the Test of English as a Foreign Language (TOEFL) examinations, which are available on the Internet (TOEFL 2006, 2007). An earlier article (Bolton 2008) compared the TOEFL scores for individual Asian societies for the years 2005–06, and the data from this study are presented in Table 1, together a somewhat ad hoc ranking of these societies (based on "paper-based" and "computer-based" results). There are, however, severe limitations on the extent to which we can draw sound inferences on the basis of such figures, and these scores are not claimed by the TOEFL organisation (the Educational Testing Service) itself to represent comparative national proficiency levels. Crucially, we lack detailed information about the demographic, educational, and social characteristics of candidates in the societies concerned, greatly reducing the validity of comparisons between national groups. Nevertheless, despite these limitations, the results are interesting at even an impressionistic level. At the higher end of the table we find Singapore, India, Malaysia, Pakistan, and the Philippines, which generally tallies with anecdotal perceptions of English use in such societies. At the lower end, we find such countries as Japan, Thailand, Cambodia, Burma, and Taiwan.

Table 1: TOEFL scores for individual Asian societies, 2005–06

Rank	Country	Paper-based (computer based)
1	Singapore	– (255)
2	India	586 (236)
3	Malaysia	572 (232)
4	Philippines	566 (238)
5	Pakistan	562 (238)
6	Bangladesh	557 (228)
7	China	557 (216)
8	Sri Lanka	548 (234)
9	Hong Kong	539 (216)
10	South Korea	538 (218)
11	Nepal	535 (218)
12	Indonesia	535 (214)
13	Vietnam	534 (207)
14	Taiwan	530 (206)
15	Burma (Myanmar)	518 (206)
16	Cambodia	– (206)
17	Thailand	500 (200)
18	Japan	497 (192)

(Bolton 2008: 10)

Apart from these broad comments, however, few sound conclusions can be drawn from such fragmentary data. Aside from the limitations of the data, there are also profound issues about how "proficiency" might best be measured in Asian societies, given that many traditional proficiency tests are benchmarked in various ways against Inner Circle (UK or US) "native speaker" patterns of performance, and yet ignore the multilingual proficiency of many Asian users of English.

What does seem likely, however, is that, across Asia, as economies move up the "value-added" chain from labour-intensive into knowledge-intensive, high-tech, and service-related industries, the demand for higher-level English skills has grown. Here, one may wish to reconsider the relationship between localised varieties of English ("Asian Englishes") and international "standard" varieties. For example, in India and the Philippines, one obvious question is whether the BPOs and international call centres bring with them (as many believe) a re-orientation of linguistic performance away from localised, intranational norms towards a "native-like" performance in British and American English? After decades of "de-centring" from the UK and US, are Asian Englishes about to re-centre their linguistic norms? To what extent, are such expectations of "native-like" or "near-native" proficiency realistic, or ever achieved, for that matter? These are some of the questions highlighted by such developments.[1]

If nothing else, the issue of proficiency may also serve to re-awaken – and to re-configure – research into individual bilingualism (and multilingualism) within Outer Circle societies. For a number of years, approaches to such questions seem to have polarised researchers in second-language acquisition versus those employing a world Englishes approach. In the past, second-language acquisition research has often been dominated by approaches concerned with the adaptation of immigrants to host societies such as the US, where a standard language ideology tends to view monolingualism as the default norm (and the speech of second-language learners characterised by interlanguage approximations to a native-speaker target norm). In contrast, the "varieties-based" approach to world Englishes – with its focus on "features" rather than "errors" – has been built on an extrapolation (and idealisation) from the individual choices made by individual language users in selecting from the "features pool" they have available to them (Mufwene 2001). In a reconfigured approach to individual bilingualism, the challenge for second-language acquisition research is to recognise that, in many Asian societies, individual language learning takes place in complex multilingual and functionally-differentiated settings (Kirkpatrick 2008). This is certainly so in many parts of India and the Philippines, where language users are usually trilingual, and also in most Asian settings, where there is a typical home-school or home-office language switch, at the very least.

Conversely, the challenge for the world Englishes researcher may be to re-examine the notion of "native speaker" within localised settings, and to provide psycholinguistic and sociolinguistic descriptions of the native speaker of Philippine English or Indian English, for example, not least in order to investigate what it is this may tell us about the native speaker of British or American English, as well as the ontological status of this rather controversial term. To recast this in simple terms, it has to be understood that the study of second-language varieties in Outer Circle English-using societies has been influenced by two rather different, and at times "incommensurable", sets of approaches and discourses, those of second-language acquisition studies on the one hand (usually emanating from Inner Circle as well as EFL researchers), and world Englishes (typically from Outer Circle linguists), on the other. Few attempts to

---

[1] A related question, outside the scope of the present project, would be the extent to which the globalisation of English-language media such as the film, DVDs, television, the Internet, etc., are similarly having an impact in spreading standard or non-standard (for example, "hip-hop") norms from, in particular, the US to Asia and other regions of the world.

reconcile these two approaches have been made, although Davies' (1989) paper on "international English" as an "interlanguage" did attempt to open up these issues for consideration.[2]

2 The current study

This section of the chapter provides an overview related to the analysis of high-proficiency performance in international call centres, with specific reference to the sociological background, previous research from second-language acquisition and sociolinguistic perspectives, and the methodology of the current research.

2.1 General background

The broad aim of the current study on "linguistic outsourcing" was to investigate the notion of "native speaker" and "near-native performance" with specific reference to the linguistic performance of call centre agents or "customer service representatives" (CSRs) in two major locations, India and the Philippines, and to describe and analyse the perception and reality of linguistic behaviour in such call centre situations. For various reasons, however, the primary focus of fieldwork investigation became the Philippine call centre industry, as is explained below.

As indicated earlier, since the late 1990s, many European and American businesses have begun outsourcing a range of back-office operations to off-shore locations through a strategy known as "Business Process Outsourcing" (BPO). A significant part of outsourcing has involved the establishment of call centres that deal with customer inquiries by telephone and email, although outsourcing can also take a variety of other forms, including back-office operations, data

---

[2] In this article, Davies discusses the differences between *English as an international language* (EIL) and *interlanguage* (IL). In today's debate, "English as an international language" would more likely be glossed as "world Englishes". Despite this, many of the points raised in this article are of continuing relevance. For example, in introducing the scope of discussion, he notes: "International English [aka world Englishes] and interlanguage are both concerned with language learning and language use: with the *psycholinguistic*, that is, the study of language in relation to cognition and learning, and with the *sociolinguistic*, that is, the use of language in the world, the social use of language. They turn upside down the normal process-product relation: On the surface, EIL is seen as a recognizable thing, whereas IL is seen as a development process" (Davies 1989: 448).

entry, engineering design, legal and medical transcription, and even film animation. Currently, the two most important locations for international call centres are India and the Philippines, which are both developing societies that have traditionally had large-scale poverty coupled with massive developmental and employment problems. In the Philippines the industry grew rapidly from 1,000 employees in the year 2000 to 40,000 employees in 2004, to 100,000 in 2005, and 300,000 in 2007 (Sañez 2008). Astonishingly, in 2015, it is estimated that over one million Filipinos are now employed in call centres and related BPO operations. This accounts for an estimated 10% of the Philippine economy, all of which has led to recent reports now describing the Philippines as "the call centre capital of the world" (Lee 2015). The range of services provided by Philippine call centre companies includes call-in queries, technical support, travel and consumer services, and medical and legal transcriptions; while many Indian centres specialise in banking and financial services.

The economic background to the operation of international call centres in India and the Philippines thus involves the rapid emergence of BPO activities from the late 1990s, and their crucial economic importance to these two developing countries, where English is largely learnt as a second language, predominantly through education and the media, as well as other domains. This in turn leads one to consider a number of theoretical approaches, ranging from second-language acquisition perspectives to those of sociolinguistics and discourse analysis.

2.2 Second-language acquisition perspectives

Given the importance of the notion of "native speaker" and "near-native performance" to the current research project, second-language acquisition perspectives are highly relevant. Hyltenstam and Abrahamsson (2003) review a range of current debates amongst psycholinguists and second-language acquisition researchers, noting that at the core of current arguments are various controversies concerning the effects of maturational constraints related to the age of second-language learners. Many of the arguments relating to this turn on the importance of the "critical period hypothesis" (CPH) in explaining the different outcomes of individual learners in acquiring proficiency in a second or foreign language (Lenneberg 1967). In its strong form, CPH theory argues that puberty represents a critical point in acquisitional potential, that after puberty foreign languages can only be learned through "conscious and laboured effort" and that foreign accents can rarely be mastered with any degree of accuracy (Lenneberg 1967: 176).[3]

The importance of age of onset in determining the extent to which second-language speakers of a particular language are perceived as "native-like" has been established by a significant body of detailed research (Abrahamsson and Hyltenstam 2009), from which at least two broad conclusions may be drawn. First, that in many second language contexts, the aspiration towards a "native-like" second language proficiency is essentially unrealistic and unattainable. Second, that, given the fact that the "age of onset" is of such importance in determining whether second-language learners achieved a native-like command of the language, other factors such as education and language training are unlikely to enable learners to perform equally with native speakers of a particular language. Hyltenstam and Abrahamsson's work has not been unchallenged, and other researchers have been concerned to present contrasting views, very often noting the attainment of high levels of second-language proficiency among some relatively "late" language learners (Birdsong 2006). However, this chapter is less interested in the particulars of the debate within second-language acquisition research than with the implications of such research for a sociolinguistic approach.

2.3 Sociolinguistic perspectives

In addition to second-language acquisition perspectives, there are a range of sociolinguistic approaches that might be relevant to the analysis of call centre communication. One central theoretical issue here – from multiple perspectives – is the concept of "native speaker". Davies (2003), for example, classifies current perspectives on the native speaker as including psycholinguistic, linguistic, and sociolinguistic approaches. After evaluating a range of views on the native speaker, essentially from sociolinguistic and applied linguistic perspectives, he

---

[3] Hyltenstam and Abrahamsson (2003) review various challenges to the CPH hypothesis, including (i) the work of Krashen et al. (1979) and Long (1990) who mention that adults may have short-term advantages over children in second language acquisition; (ii) the work of Bongaerts (1999) and others who document cases where adults do achieve native-like proficiency (Birdsong, 1999); and (iii) research challenging the belief that the critical period is closely tied to puberty (e.g. Bialystok and Hakuta 1994; Flege 1999). After evaluating such research, Hyltenstam and Abrahamsson conclude that "none of the challenges to the CPH pose a serious threat to the hypothesis" and that while it may be the case that some late learners of second languages do achieve high levels of proficiency, it seems doubtful that such levels can be equated with a native command of the language (pp. 162–163).

concludes that "it is not likely that many second-language learners become native speakers of their target language" (Davies 2003: 212). Davies' survey of this issue also includes mention of societies (such as in Nigeria, Kenya, India, Singapore and the Philippines) where English is used as an additional language, and where localized varieties or "New Englishes" have emerged, raising the question of whether we can now talk about the native speaker of Indian English, Philippine English, or other varieties of world Englishes (p. 166).

Another sociolinguistic perspective of direct relevance to this current project is that presented by Piller (2002). Her study focuses on native-speaker performance rather than competence, and identifies and discusses the "passing" strategies of high-level second language users of English and German. She found that one third of her informants claimed that they were able to pass for native speakers in various situations. Her emphasis here is to highlight "insider's accounts of expert L2 uses and their linguistic passing processes", arguing that "passing is much more frequent than linguistic research and particularly work in ultimate attainment tends to suggest" (Piller 2002: 181–182). In her commentary, Piller notes that passing is "typical of first encounters, often service interactions, and each encounter may present a new challenge to test one's performance" (Piller 2002: 191). Although the concept of "passing" has been widely applied in both gender studies and ethnic studies, Piller's use of the term here is innovative, and certainly has an obvious potential for use in studies of call centre activities and linguistic outsourcing of the type discussed above, where factors such as "personal motivation, choice and agency" may enable language-users to operate with "native-like" or at least "near-native" proficiency (*ibid.*: 201).

2.4 Previous research on call centre communication

Hitherto, there have been relatively few studies of call centre communication from the perspective of the linguistic sciences and related disciplines, although rather more research has been carried out from various social scientific perspectives, including sociology (Taylor and Bain 2004, 2005; Taylor, D'Cruz, Noronha and Scholarios 2009). Linguistically-oriented studies have grown in number in recent years with relatively early studies including the work of Cowie (2007) on accent training in the Indian context, as well as Friginal's (2007) study of Philippine call centres. Friginal's study based on his (2008) PhD research, focused on the effectiveness of training methods employed at a Philippine call centre, and concluded that the "interplay of product knowledge, intercultural communication skills, service personalities and language skills" was more important than "high-level English" in this type of work (Friginal 2007: 344).

Other research on the Philippine context has included that of Bolton (2010, 2013), but perhaps the most detailed studies of international call centre communication hitherto carried out have been those of Forey and Lockwood (2007), Lockwood et al. (2008), and Forey and Lockwood (2010). In their 2007 article, Forey and Lockwood use a systemic-functional approach to discourse analysis to identify and describe a "generic model" of a call centre interaction. At the core of this model, are chains of macro speech acts, which are described in terms of "stages", as illustrated in Table 2 below:

Table 2: Generic stages in call centre communication (adapted from Forey and Lockwood, 2007)

Generic stage	Function of stage
Opening	Greetings, etc.
Purpose	Identifying purpose of call
Gathering information	Collecting and checking information, etc.
Establishing purpose	Clarification, empathising, apologising, etc.
Servicing the customer	Providing clear explanations and descriptions, etc.
Summarising	Summarising key points
Closing	Closing down the communication

Another set of sociolinguistically-oriented insights into call centre communication, from a rather different provenance, is provided by Deborah Cameron's pioneering research on British call centres, which, broadly speaking, adopted a "critical discourse analysis" (CDA) perspective. In her (2000a) study of call centre operations, Cameron characterizes call centres as "factories", where *codification* and *surveillance* are two overarching principles. Cameron notes the essential contradiction in UK call centres between the demand that staff interact with customers in an "authentic", "caring", and "sincere" fashion, and "the call centre regime [that] imposes on workers the demand to present themselves in a way that the company determines, down to the last detail", resulting quite often in significant levels of frustration and stress (2000a: 101). She also notes the attempt to impose "linguistic uniformity" in a variety of ways, including the use of standard greetings, call centre scripts, and a variety of other practices promoted by call centre training. In her second paper (2000b), Cameron suggests that the emotionally expressive style of speech (associated with caring and empathy) promoted by call centres displays characteristics often associated with the speech of women. Thus, Cameron argues that the style required in telephone conversation interaction with call centre customers in some senses constitutes a form of "women's language", with cadences associated not only with caring, empathy, and rapport, but also with a feminised variety of "emotional labour" (Hochschild 1983). These insights also have a relevance to the situation in the call centre industry in both India and the Philippines, where the vast majority of those employed for so-called "voice work" are women (for a further review of the literature see Bolton 2010, 2013).

2.5 Research issues and methodology

2.5.1 Research issues

As stated earlier above, the broad aims of the current study are to describe the linguistic practices of selected international call centres and BPOs (Business Process Outsourcing), particularly in the Philippines and India and to investigate the extent to which "native-like" linguistic behaviour is regularly expected of, and achieved by, call centre staff (or "agents") in such locations. More specific research questions include the following: (i) What expectations do employers have of native-like performance from their staff? (ii) How is such performance defined (and judged) by employers? (iii) What is the profile of successful call centre agents (in terms of language background, education, etc.)? (iv) What strategies do agents use to pass as native users of the language? and (v) What are the characteristics of successful versus unsuccessful communication in such contexts? In order to investigate these issues, fieldwork was carried out in both Bangalore, India, and Manila, Philippines.

2.5.2 Methodology

The methodology adopted for this study involved a broad-based sociolinguistic research methodology, including extensive interviews with call centre managers and trainers and call centre staff; attendance at call centre industry events; as well as the collection of recorded call centre conversations. After initial exploratory visits to both India and the Philippines, it was decided to concentrate the initial stage of research on call centre operations in the Philippines. The main reasons for this were essentially practical and pragmatic. During my two visits to Bangalore, access to call centres in the city was found to be heavily restricted, and despite having colleagues in the city with industry contacts, it was difficult to gain access to call centres during visits there. This was not the case in Manila, Philippines, where I gained relatively easy access to a number of Manila call centres, call centre agents, and, eventually, obtained a substantial corpus of actually-occurring telephone conversation data.

The linguistic data collected were of two broad types. First, a series of semi-structured interviews were carried out with call centre agents or "CSRs" (customer service representatives), as they are most commonly referred to. These interviews surveyed call centre employees on their personal backgrounds, as well as details of their training and work experience. All interviews were recorded and later transcribed. Second, a corpus of authentic telephone conversations – involving a total of 1412 telephone conversations in all – was obtained from a major Philippine call centre. These telephone conversations have now been transcribed, and the next stage of research will involve further analysis of this data. A number of initial findings relating to this research are discussed in the following section.

3 Initial findings relating to the Philippine call centre communication

In this section of the chapter, a number of initial findings derived from fieldwork research are discussed with specific reference to the call centre industry in Manila, the capital city of the Philippines, the features of Philippine English and the analysis of call centre interactions.

3.1 Philippine English and the Philippine call centre industry

The English language is relatively well established in the Philippines, where it has a wide range of functions in this Outer Circle society, including its use as a co-official language of government, law, and education, as well as its extensive use in the business sector, mass media and entertainment (Bautista and Bolton 2008). However, the story of English in the Philippines is one greatly coloured by the effects of colonialism and its aftermath. Indeed, the Philippines experienced almost 400 years of colonial rule, first, from Spanish from 1565 till 1898, and then from the US from 1898 to 1946 as noted earlier. American colonial rule started with a brutal war which was then succeeded by the establishment of the first system of mass education that the Philippine islands had known, with elementary schools established throughout the length and breadth of the country. The medium of instruction in all schools was English, and, remarkably, as early as 1918, some 47% of the population claimed to be able to speak English. In the period following Philippine independence from the US in 1946, English-medium education in the schools gave way to a bilingual system, made official in 1987, which persists to the present. Nevertheless, as noted earlier, a large proportion of Filipinos claim to speak English, with some 76% reporting they understand the spoken language and 75% claiming to read in English.

The linguistic features of Philippine English have been described in some detail in the research literature, and these include distinctive feature at the major levels of language, including phonology, lexis, and grammar. Phonological features include the devoicing of sibilant consonants in words like *beige, pleasure, seize, bees*, and *cities*, which are articulated as [s], and the rendering of "th" sounds as [t], [d], in words such as *this* [dis], *thin* [tin]. With vowels, other features may occur including a loss of distinction between long and short vowels in such pairs as *sheep/ship, full/fool, boat/bought*, etc.; the [æ] vowel, in *bat, cat, fat, hat*, etc., may be replaced by the central low vowel [a]; while many speakers deploy a reduced vowel inventory compared with American English. At the supra-segmental level, intonation is typically "syllable-timed" with distinctive patterns occurring in words such as *elígible, estáblish, cerémony*.

At the lexical level, Philippine English has borrowed extensively from Spanish (*asalto* 'surprise party', *bienvenida* 'welcome party', *despedida* 'farewell party', *estafa* 'fraud, scandal', *merienda* 'mid-afternoon tea', *querida* 'mistress'), and Tagalog (*boondock* 'mountain', *kundiman* 'love song', *tao* 'the common man'. Loan translations are also widely used including *open the light/radio* for "turn on the light/radio", *joke only* "I'm teasing you", and *you don't only know* "you just don't realise". Local coinages include such items as *to carnap, high blood, hold-upper*, and *topnotcher*, while archaic items derived from late nineteenth century American English include *comfort room (CR), solon*, and *viand* (Bolton and Butler 2008). At the grammatical level, we find variable third-person singular marking, the over-use of the progressive, the variable use of articles, and variation in tense and aspect as in *We have done it yesterday* (versus "We did it yesterday") and *He lived here since 1996* (compared to "He has lived here since 1996"). Other features include variation in transitivity and the use of prepositions (Bautista 2008).

However, the frequency and distribution of such features varies greatly according to social class and education, and linguists have long noted the existence of "edulects" in Philippine society. *Acrolectal Philippine English* is associated with academics, bilinguals from English-speaking homes, and English majors at university level. Thus, acrolectal Philippine English is perceived as approximating to "near-standard" American English. *Mesolectal Philippine English* is spoken by professionals who are non-English majors and who mostly use English in the workplace, and who display a noticeably Philippine accent. *Basilectal Philippine English* is said to be spoken by such people as janitors and taxi-drivers, and is associated with a broad Philippine accent and a rather low level of education (Tayao 2008).

In a society where poverty is rife and unemployment endemic, where some ten per cent of the population work abroad as "Overseas Foreign Workers" in jobs as engineers, technicians, seamen or as nurses, carers and domestic helpers, the growth of the BPO industry has been hailed as a "sunshine industry". Jobs in call centres are low paid compared with their equivalents in North America or the UK, but in Manila, a starting salary of 20,000 pesos (approx. US $430) is comparable to that received by a bank clerk or management trainee (AuxBreak 2015). The time difference between Manila and the East Coast of the US is 12 hours, and so the vast majority of CSRs work the night shift between mid-evening and early morning. The work is often demanding and stressful, and the industry suffers from high turnover, with an attrition rate of 30 per cent annually, as well as frequent reports of such health problems as fatigue, high strain, back pain and respiratory diseases (Torres 2014).

Within the telephone call centres, operations are typically of two kinds. Usually, staff is deployed to handle either *inbound* calls or *outbound* calls. As the name suggests, *inbound* refers to answering incoming inquiries, dealing with various aspects of customer service for a wide variety of products and services, ranging from financial services to various kinds of technical help. In those call centres that were visited by this researcher in the initial stages of research, 2006–8, the majority of call centre staff (some 80–90%) were involved in handling inbound calls. By contrast, *outbound* calls essentially involve calling customers or potential customers for sales and telemarketing purposes or even for matters of billing and debt collection. Outbound calls are much less popular among call centre staff, as handling such calls often involves high levels of stress dealing with rather angry customers.

Typically, in the observations and interviews that were carried out by this researcher, my judgement (and the judgement of Philippine linguists I discussed with) was that call centre staff typically spoke varieties of English that ranged from mid-level to high-level mesolectal Philippine English, and that the majority of call centre agents interviewed spoke English with what might be perceived as a distinctive Philippine accent marked by a number of the features discussed above, including the characteristic stress timing associated with Philippine English speech. However, despite the existence of the *de facto* norm of educated Philippine English in use by many call centre agents, a great deal of time and effort was spent in providing new recruits to the industry with courses on "accent neutralisation", which in practice meant instructing new staff in the basics of American English phonology. Other elements in induction training included grammar practice; an introduction to American culture and society; and a course dealing with customer service management.[4]

After training, the performance of individual CSRs (customer service representatives) within the call centre is continually monitored by their superiors, who are identified by such job titles as "team leader", "line manager", and "supervisor". The ability to deal with customers on the telephone quickly and efficiently in English is highly valued by the employers and CSRs who score highly in the various metrics applied to their work are often promoted rather quickly to positions of greater authority. In this, a high proficiency of English is a key merit, although it is not the only criterion involved in staff assessment.

3.2 A corpus of authentic call centre conversations

As noted above, the types of data collected by this researcher included two varieties of recorded data. The first type of data were collected from interview research with a group of 50 CSRs working for call centres in Manila, the characteristics of which are discussed in Section 3.3 below. The second type of recorded data was secured from a major telephone company in the Philippines, which comprised recordings of more than 1400 telephone conversations from a leading call centre. These telephone conversations were systematically transcribed and a corpus of this material organised.

An examination of the specific characteristics of the data set indicate that in total there are 1412 complete interactions in the corpus. The vast majority of these, some 980, are inbound conversations where US customers are dealing with Philippine CSRs with queries regarding such goods and services as cable television subscriptions, cameras, computer parts, computer printers, computer software, credit card charges, digital cameras, hotel reservations, and laptop computers. What is noteworthy from the initial investigation of the corpus is that only in very few of the calls is there anything approximating to a breakdown of communication between customers and CSRs. In the vast majority of

---

[4] For example, one call centre's basic training course for new staff (on "Call Centre Fundamentals") comprised a 108-hour curriculum, which devoted 42 hours to "Intensive English" (English grammar practice); 18 hours to "America 101" (US culture and society); 24 hours to "Customer Service Management" (communication and interpersonal skills, including such things as "handling of complaints"); and 24 hours to "Oral Communication with Accent Neutralisation" (training in standard spoken American English). In Philippine call centre training, therefore, the use of a Philippine variety of English is often seen as problematic, and whatever the *de facto* speech norms of established call centre staff, proficiency in this context is typically defined according to native-speaker criteria.

cases, the linguistic and communicative skills of CSRs are sufficient to deal with customers' inquiries, product orders, and service requests. The transcription below of an inbound query about a cable television bill is not untypical of a standard call centre interaction in this particular call centre.[5] In this interaction, the CSR is a speaker using an educated variety of Philippine English, approximating to that style of speech associated with an upper-range speaker of mesolectal PE. Her caller is apparently an older Southern US speaker of American English, who is calling to query a billing statement that he has received for a cable television service. The telephone call is quite short, and lasts 5 minutes and 30 seconds. The line numbers next to the speaker identifications indicate the line number of the transcript for purposes of reference.

Transcript: Incoming call querying a billing statement for cable television

1	CSR:	Thank you for calling ——. My name is Faye. Can I have your first and last name?
2	Caller:	——.
3	CSR:	Thank you. Can I have your telephone number, please?
4	Caller:	My phone number is ——.
5	CSR:	Thank you. And how may we help you today, Mr ——?
6	Caller:	Well, uh … I … I've got this kind of bill here … and … and … I mean, we … we get this card in the mail and we paid … uh … like … what … 69 dollars or something to start with or whatever. And when I hooked it up and then we ain't had it hooked up two weeks and … uh … anyway we get this rebate we … we just got … we got the mail in here (?) but then, our first two months was supposed to be free. We're supposed to get like 59 dollars back, from that 60 something that we paid to begin with. And we've already got a 31 dollar bill … 31.40 cents.
15	CSR:	Okay, I'll be glad to assist you with your concern today, Mr ——. So you got a bill for 31 dollars and 47 cents, and this is for two months from April 11th until June 10th. Well, we got a payment from you of 49 dollars and 99 cents and this …
19	Caller:	We are supposed … yeah, they said we will get that back.
20	CSR:	Yes, it did. On page two of your bill, you will see that you were credited for 49 dollars and 99 cents.
22	Caller:	Page two? Page two? I don't …
23	CSR:	Yes.

---

5 This text has earlier been discussed at some length in Bolton (2010: 555–557).

24 Caller:	I can't figure … I don't even …	
25 CSR:	On the back of page one.	
26 Caller:	Uh … okay, let's see. (sighs). Credit … Uh, where would that be … I don't know …	
28 CSR:	Do you see … yes.	
29 Caller:	Uh …. I see credit adjustment … 49.99. Okay, and then … all right. So where's … all right. So what was it all together … to start with … 87 … what's this 87.95?	
32 CSR:	Okay, that is if you'll include the 49.99. But your monthly charge is 58.97, but you have to less 12 dollars and 99 cents for this part because this part is free until July 10th, and then you have to less 5 dollars and 99 cents for the home protection plan because this is free for 18 months. So your total monthly rate is 39 dollars and 99 cents, and you mentioned a while ago that you already have the redemption form. And you have 60 days from installation to send it back together with a copy of your first bill and the first 10 dollar credit will kick in after 8 to 10 weeks after you have submitted the redemption form. So if you'll apply the 10 dollar credit to your account for ten months, your monthly rate will be 29 dollars and 99 cents.	
44 Caller:	Uh … 29.99?	
45 CSR:	Yes, that's right.	
46 Caller:	Okay, I thought it was … uh. I thought it was … according to that … to that card … that flyer, the card we got in the mail, it was supposed to be like 19.99 a month or …	
49 CSR:	Well you can … that is only for the America's Top 100. The regular price of the America's Top 100 is 29.99.	
51 Caller:	Right, but I mean, wouldn't it be 19.99 for the first 10 months? With rebate?	
53 CSR:	Well, you, because you have other charges. So the America's Top 100 with rebate will be 19 dollars and 99 cents, plus 5 dollars for your local channels, plus 5 dollars for the additional receiver fee. So that would be 29 dollars and 99 cents for 10 months.	
57 Caller:	Uh … okay. Well, we was misled, so …	
58 CSR:	I apologize for that.	
59 Caller:	Uh … I guess that happens. Uh … so, so we owe this is for 3 months, 31.47?	
61 CSR:	That's correct. So, if you'll pay 31 dollars and 47 cents, then that will make you good until June 10th.	

63 Caller:	And we won't get a payment for June 10th, right?	
64 CSR:	That's right. And the next bill will be sent out on May 26th, but that will cover from June 11th until July 10th.	
66 Caller:	And that'll be 29.99?	
67 CSR:	That's correct. Uh ... no, it would be 39.99. It will only be 29.99 once the 10 dollar credit will ... begins to appear on your bill. So you have to submit the redemption form for you to have 29.99.	
70 Caller:	Well, that will be sent out tomorrow morning then.	
71 CSR:	Okay. So don't forget to include a copy of your first bill. Just a copy, don't include your payment with it.	
73 Caller:	Don't include your payment with it ... just a copy of the first bill.	
74 CSR:	That's right and would you like to take care of your bill now, Mr —?	
75 Caller:	Uh no, not right at this point.	
76 CSR:	Okay, not a problem.	
77 Caller:	All right. Well, I just needed to know what was going on.	
78 CSR:	Okay, is there anything else I can help you with?	
79 Caller:	No, thank you.	
80 CSR:	All right, so are we good now?	
81 Caller:	Yeah, I guess we have to be. Ha, ha! So thank you very much.	
82 CSR:	You're welcome. Thank you for calling. Have a nice day.	
83 Caller:	Uh huh.	
84 CSR:	Bye bye.	
85 Caller:	Bye.	

If one applies the framework suggested by Forey and Lockwood (2007) in Section 2.4 above, one can then identify lines 1–4 as forming the *Opening* stage, lines 5–12 as the *Purpose* stage, 15–18 as *Gathering Information*; 19–31 as *Establishing Purpose*; 32–65 as *Servicing the Customer*; 66–73 as *Summarising*; and lines 74–85 as *Closing Down the Communication*. Forey and Lockwood's model of 'generic stages' in call centre interactions thus seems to explain the discourse structure rather well, at least in broad transactional terms.

It is interesting to note that the 'native' speech of the US caller is marked by a greater number of non-standard grammatical features than that of the "non-native" call centre agent. These include the non-marking of *get* for past tense in line 7, the use of *ain't* in line 9, and *we was* in line 57. In contrast, there appears to be only one deviation from "standard English" grammar in the CSR's, which occurs in line 33, when *less* is used as a verb (instead of "subtract"). Indeed, in terms of standardised grammatical features, Faye's speech is largely error-free, despite the use of a distinct Philippine intonation. What is most noticeable from this encounter, moreover, is the considerable cognitive and linguistic skill exercised by the CSR as she guides her somewhat confused customer through a complex explanation of the charges he has incurred for his cable TV subscription. Throughout the interaction, Faye maintains a helpful and polite tone, as she deals with a potentially irate caller, who is initially angered at what he assumes to be an incorrect billing statement. One particularly interesting exchange is set out on lines 20–25, when Faye asks her customer to refer to page 2 of his billing statement. In response to his bewildered query of where this might be found, she gently points out that this may be found "On the back of page one". In the *Closing* section, after dealing with other queries, Faye skilfully, and again gently, inquires "Alright, so are we good now?" which actually succeeds in eliciting an almost cheery "Yeah, I guess we have to be", from her now compliant and somewhat reassured customer.

The corpus of call centre conversations represents an important data set for the study of international call centres, and it is anticipated that further analysis will produce more interesting results, of relevance to not only call centre communication but also to the study of bilingual language proficiency and performance in wider perspective.

3.3 Interviews with call centre agents

A second strand of the research methodology employed in the study comprised a total of 51 detailed semi-structured interviews, which were carried out with call centre employees in Manila, Philippines. The questions asked in the interviews covered a wide range of topics, including agents' personal histories, on-the-job training, the agents' experience of working in call centres, the use of American (and other native-like) accents, difficulties in handling calls, health issues, attitudes to the call centre industry, and the perception of gender-related issues.

A number of interesting findings came out of these interviews. In broad terms, it appears that from the data, the "typical" Philippine call centre agent is a female graduate in her mid-twenties, who has attended private schools and college or university, and who comes from a lower-middle or middle-class family. Interestingly, many of these call centre agents reported having started learning English at a relatively early age (i.e. having an early onset time in the learning of English as a second language). Of this group of 51 CSRs, some 38% reported learning English before the age of 5, and 82% before the age of 7, with the vast majority reporting having come from bilingual and multilingual homes. A clear majority of those interviewed also expressed positive attitudes to English and also to the industry in which they were working, expressing opinions such as the following:

> I think it it's a big help ... if you are a graduate of a 4 year course and you don't have a job for now it's always an option ... just go to a call centre. You apply, for sure you'll have a job. So I think it it's a big help somehow. (CSR7, female, 24 years)

> It is [positive] because it's a money making industry ... [and] I see right now at least people are getting reacquainted with the English language although some patriotic people or nationalistic people are gonna say that we're not using our language properly anymore but then again we just have to be realistic. English is a universal language. (CSR40, female, 22 years)

> [The] call centre industry can help our economy uh to boost so that's the important thing right now, and uh it could provide uh jobs to people ... as long as we can speak English, I mean we have we have plus points to have or to ah to enter a call centre industry. So basic skills, basic computer skills, you know how to speak English then you have a way of a having a work in a call centre industry so that's it I mean it boosts our economy and then it helps many people here in the Philippines to have a job. A decent one. That's the important thing. (CSR12, male, 25 years)

> I think uh we contribute a lot to the economy ... I think we can contribute and there's a lot of opportunity ... I'm just a housewife but I got the position, so there's a lot of opportunity with call centres. (CSR4, female, 38 years)

Not all comments from CSRs were totally positive, however, and a number of those interviewed discussed the stresses and strains of night work, and the resultant health problems that occur as a result of prolonged employment in the industry. Some of those interviewed also expressed clearly ambivalent views on their work conditions, and cited problems with sleep, health issues, and family life. Cameron's (2000b) comments concerning the gendered nature of call centre communication also emerge from such interviews, when female agents discuss the ways in which they often need to placate irritated or "irate" (a much used adjective) callers.

Some of the most interesting interviews, however, were neither with the female call centre employees nor the males, but actually with three interviewees, who self-identified themselves as "gays" (Bolton 2010).[6] A number of interviewees reported that the call centres provided a employment space for cross-dressing Philippine gays to gain work and to express themselves in work. One gay call centre CSR explained the attractions of work in this industry thus:

---

[6] The use of "gay" here is not uncontested, as in the Philippines the term is often used to conflate homosexuality, transvestism and transgenderism. The use of the term here however is motivated by the fact that the interviewees, two of whom were participants in transvestite (or *bakla* culture), actually referred to themselves using the English word "gay".

> We've been through a very rough time and we have this motivation and ... call centre jobs are the cream of the crop ... we've been through a lot of challenges growing up ... and we're up for the workload ... we seek for a place in which we're widely accepted. And we find it very amusing to work in a call centre, because anything goes. We are not prejudiced by being gay. All we have to do is to just meet our metrics. And that's why a lot of gays are doing their best to be in this job that we're currently at. Because we are not threatened ... we can act naturally. We can say our thoughts. We can express. We can talk to people. (CSR26, Chris, gay, 26 years)

Another gay informant, James, reported that at work he usually used a female name, "Sunshine", when talking to customers, which he found immensely useful in calming down angry clients, who often assumed that he was a Latina living in the US.

> It's 80% sometimes they think that I'm Latina. Which is a good thing that I don't sound like a Filipino, because ... they hate Filipinos. But usually I sound like American 80%, 'cause when in calls my voice sounds soft and modulated and they don't know ... that I'm not a Filipino ... they call me Ma'am. And they don't know that I'm a boy ... sometimes they won't even know that I'm a guy. Sometimes they always call me like B-I-T-C-H! (CSR37, James)

What is easily notable from the discourse of the call centre gay informants was not only their own descriptions of their call centre experiences, but also their references to the explicit elements of performativity in their workplace linguistic behaviour. For example, James directly linked his performance in dance and theatre to the performativity of his call centre work and the abilities of "Sunshine", his stage self, to pass as female, and to cross linguistic and cultural boundaries. Such discourses thus link not only to Piller's (2002) insights on "passing" and second language acquisition, but also to other theorisations of "crossing" and "performativity" that have had a major impact on various branches of linguistics in recent years (Auer 2006; Butler 1990).[7]

---

[7] "[P]assing is an act, something they do, a performance that may be put on ... a performance that is typical of first encounters, often service interactions, and each new encounter may present a new challenge to test one's performance" (Piller 2002: 191); "Crossing is a particular kind of code-switching in which speakers 'transgress' into a language or variety which ... is not generally thought to 'belong' to them" (Auer 2006: 490; see also Rampton 1995); while, in discussing performativity, Butler explains that "There is no gender identity behind the expressions of gender; ... identity is performatively constituted by the very "expressions" that are said to be its results" (Butler 1990: 25).

4 Conclusion

This chapter has attempted to provide an overview of a wide range of questions that connect to the investigation of high-level second language proficiency in Asian call centres, with particular reference to the Philippines. What emerges, I would argue, from this overview of the research terrain, is the awareness of multi-layered possibilities in researching language use in the call centre context.

As may be evident from the range of discussion in this chapter, it is possible to examine the phenomenon of such linguistic outsourcing from a broad range of perspectives, including those of world Englishes, second language acquisition, and sociolinguistics. In western societies such as the US and UK, call centre work of the kind described here is often seen as of low prestige and status. Within Britain, the call centre industry has expanded rapidly since the mid-1980s, and now employs many people in areas previously associated with heavy manufacturing, such as Scotland, the North East, Yorkshire and the North West, where the closure of traditional industries since the nineteen-sixties has provided a ready workforce of around 1 million relatively low-paid employees, working in conditions that some see as the "modern-day equivalents of the factory production line" (BBC 2011). In the US there are currently around 3 million workers employed in call centres across the country, again in relatively low-paid jobs. In the Asian countries, the numbers employed in voice-related call centres are much smaller than the US or even the UK, with an estimated 350,000 Indian CSRs, compared to 400,000 in the Philippines (Site Selection Group 2015).[8] Despite this, such jobs in the Philippines (and also in India) are often regarded as very attractive for young men and, far more commonly, young women seeking employment in relatively poor developing societies. The issue of call centre work as a gendered occupation is highlighted not only by the numerical predominance of women in this sector, but also, and interestingly, by the liminal, yet apparently successful, role of Philippine gays in the Manila call centre industry.

Nevertheless, at the heart of call centre operations is the managerial rationalisation of work processes, often referred to as "Taylorism", after the work of F. W. Taylor (1964), the advocate of "scientific managerialism". In the US, the systematic routing of customer inquiries and communications through banks of telephones located in specially-designed spaces (i.e. "call centres" or "contact centres"), engineered to facilitate surveillance and monitoring, was initially motivated by the desire to cut costs and maximise profits. By the early 2000s,

---

[8] These numbers evidently refer only to "voice work", not to other BPO operations, such as animation, documentation archiving, legal transcription, medical transcription, etc.

cost-cutting also came to promote outsourcing, and the transfer of call centre work from western societies to sites in India and the Philippines. In India, Taylor and Bain problematize several aspects of the call centre industry, including the predominance of night work, working conditions, workplace culture, and the stress placed on many call centre staff when they are required to deal with western customers. Specifically, they note that, "[t]he widespread adoption of anglicized pseudonyms, of having to conceal their Indian locations, and the obligation to speak in "neutral accents", or even emulate their customers" dialects, contribute greatly to a pressurized working experience" (Taylor and Bain 2005: 273), conditions which also routinely exist in Philippine call centre operations.

A recent article by Hultgren (2011) points out that call centres, as an "organizational prototype" were first developed in the US from the 1960s onwards as a means of rationalising customer service interactions across a range of industries. As a result, the operational procedures, staff protocols, and the industry's technologies in India and the Philippines are usually derived from US sources, and, additionally, the company-authorised scripts that are adopted in such centres are also of similar origin. This in turn has contributed to a particular approach to controlling and "styling" such interactions across many societies in the world, where style may then be vernacularized to a greater or lesser extent as a genre that cuts across language boundaries (Cameron 2000b). Within the call centre industry today, managers and trainers may emphasise such attributes as empathy, friendliness, and rapport, but the bottom line for the call centre industry as a whole is cutting costs, and maximising efficiency and profits, in a fashion pioneered by US business managers. Thus, as part of this, the globally prescribed speech style derived from the US call centre industry has now been exported worldwide, although its instantiation in practice, and across languages, may vary greatly (Hultgren 2011: 60).

The effects of globalisation are played out in other ways as well. When call centres first attracted attention in the early 2000s, newspaper reports claimed that Indian call centre agents would answer British calls with "flawless British accents", while US callers would be dealt with by agents with "American accents" (Ringshaw 2003).

> A telephone call to a British bank or insurer is as likely to be answered in Delhi as Reading by staff with flawless British accents. The level of sophistication in some call centres is remarkable: US callers are routed to operators with American accents, British callers to those with British tones. (Ringshaw 2003: 8)

The overwhelming bulk of evidence from India and the Philippines has shown that this simply is not true. Call centre agents in both localities speak English, and perform in English, with varying degrees of local accents. The accidental and accentual advantage of the Philippines appears to be two-fold. Historically, it was American English that was transported to the Philippine Islands and taught and learnt in Philippine public schools, and, secondly, perhaps as the result of substrate language influence, as well as the legacy of 300 years of Spanish colonialism, Philippine English is often perceived by American listeners as a variety of Hispanic-American English (as noted by James in the previous section of this chapter). This anecdotal explanation was re-iterated mid-way through my own fieldwork, by the female chief executive of one of the largest telecommunications companies in the Philippines, who commented that one secret of her company's success in the industry was because her call centre agents were blessed with "pleasing Latino accents". Given that a significant proportion of Hispanic Americans work in service industries, one obvious inference here might be that such accents are generally positively perceived by US customers as appropriate for call centre service work, although this would in turn warrant further investigation.

From a linguistic perspective, the existence and relative success of Asian call centres raises a number of questions related to proficiency and "native-like" performance in using English as an international language. In Outer Circle societies such in India and the Philippines, many young people grow up in bilingual or multilingual settings, acquiring English from a very early age, along with the other languages of the home or society. In contexts such as these, traditional models of bilingualism and second language acquisition are open to challenge on both psycholinguistic and sociolinguistic grounds, suggesting that stock conceptualisations of "native-like" proficiency derived from research in many western societies may need to shift in order to create the space for alternative models of multilingual acquisition and performativity.

References

Abrahamsson, N. & K. Hyltenstam. 2009. Age of acquisition and nativelikeness in a second language: Listener perception vs. linguistic scrutiny. *Language Learning*, 59/2. 249–306.
Auer, P. 2006. Sociolinguistic crossing. In: K. Brown (ed.), *Encyclopedia of Language and Linguistics* (2nd edition). Oxford: Elsevier. 490–492.
AuxBreak. 2015. The highest paying call center companies in the Philippines. http://www.auxbreak.com/highest-paying-call-center-companies-in-the-philippines/#sthash.FlZpKSkp.16NjgqFp.dpbs (accessed September 30, 2015).
Bautista, M. L. S. 2008. Investigating the grammatical features of Philippine English. In: M. L. S. Bautista & K. Bolton (eds.), *Philippine English: Linguistic and Literary Perspectives*. Hong Kong: Hong Kong University Press. 201–218.

Bautista, M. L. S. & K. Bolton (eds.). 2008. *Philippine English: Linguistic and Literary Perspectives*. Hong Kong: Hong Kong University Press.
BBC. 2011. Are call centres the factories of the 21st century? http://www.bbc.co.uk/news/magazine-12691704 (accessed September 30, 2015).
Bialystok, E. & K. Hakuta. 1994. *In Other Words: The Science and Psychology of Second-Language Acquisition*. New York: Basic Books.
Birdsong, D. 1999. Nativelikeness and non-nativelikeness in L2A research. *International Review of Applied Linguistics in Language Teaching*, 43/3. 319–328.
Birdsong, D. 1999. Introduction: Whys and why nots of the critical period hypothesis for second language acquisition. In: D. Birdsong (ed.), *Second Language Acquisition and the Critical Period Hypothesis*. Mahwah, N.J.: Lawrence Erlbaum. 1–22.
Birdsong, D. 2006. Age and second language acquisition and processing: A selective overview. *Language Learning*, 56/s1. 9–49.
Bolton, K. 2008. English in Asia, Asian Englishes, and the issue of proficiency. *English Today*, 24/2. 3–12.
Bolton, K. 2010. "Thank you for calling": Asian Englishes and "native-like" performance in Asian call centres. In: A. Kirkpatrick (ed.), *The Routledge Handbook of World Englishes*. London: Routledge. 550–564.
Bolton, K. 2013. World Englishes and international call centres. *World Englishes*, 32/4. 495–502.
Bolton, K. & S. Butler. 2008. Lexicography and the description of Philippine English vocabulary. In: M. L. S. Bautista & K. Bolton (eds.), *Philippine English: Linguistic and Literary Perspectives*. Hong Kong: Hong Kong University Press. 175–218.
Bolton, K. & D. Graddol. 2012. English in China today. *English Today*, 28/3. 3–9.
Bongaerts, T. 1999. Ultimate attainment in L2 pronunciation: The case of very advanced late L2 learners. In: D. Birdsong (ed.), *Second Language Acquisition and the Critical Period Hypothesis*. Mahwah, N.J.: Lawrence Erlbaum. 133–159.
Butler, J. 1990. *Gender Trouble: Feminism and the Subversion of Identity*. London: Routledge.
Cameron, D. 2000a. *Good to Talk? Living and Working in a Communication Culture*. London: Sage.
Cameron, D. 2000b. Styling the worker: gender and the commodification of language in the globalized service economy. *Journal of Sociolinguistics*, 4/3. 323–347.
Cowie, C. 2007. The accents of outsourcing: the meanings of "neutral" in the Indian call centre industry. *World Englishes*, 26/3. 316–330.
Davies, A. 1989. Is international English an interlanguage? *TESOL Quarterly*, 23/3. 447–467.
Davies, A. 2003. *The Native Speaker: Myth and Reality*. Clevedon: Multilingual Matters Ltd.
Flege, J. E. 1999. Age of learning and second language speech. In: D. Birdsong (ed.), *Second Language Acquisition and the Critical Period Hypothesis*. Mahwah, N.J.: Lawrence Erlbaum. 101–131.
Forey, G. & J. Lockwood. 2007. "I'd love to put someone in jail for this": An initial investigation of English in the business processing outsourcing (BPO) industry. *English for Specific Purposes*, 26. 308–326.
Forey, G. & J. Lockwood (eds.). 2010. *Globalisation, Communication and the Workplace*. London: Continuum.
Friedman, T. L. 2006. *The World is Flat: A Brief History of the Twenty-First Century*. 2nd edition. New York: Farrar, Straus and Giroux.

Friginal, E. 2007. Outsourced call centers and English in the Philippines. *World Englishes*, 26/3. 331–345.
Friginal, E. 2008. *The Language of Outsourced Call Centres: A Corpus-Based Study of Cross-Cultural Interaction.* Doctoral dissertation. San Francisco: Northern Arizona University.
Graddol, D. 2010. *English Next India. The Future of English in India.* London: British Council.
Hochschild, A. 1983. *The Managed Heart: The Commercialization of Human Feeling.* Berkeley: University of California Press.
Hultgren, A. K. 2011. "Building rapport" with customers across the world: The global diffusion of a call centre speech style. *Journal of Sociolinguistics*, 15/1. 36–64.
Hyltenstam, K. & N. Abrahamsson. 2003. Maturational constraints in SLA. In: C. J. Doughty & M. H. Long (eds.), *Handbook of Second Language Acquisition*. Oxford: Blackwell. 539–588.
Kachru, B. B. 1997. English as an Asian language. In M. L. S. Bautista (ed.), *English is an Asian Language: The Philippine Context*. New South Wales, Australia: Macquarie Library. 1–23.
Kirkpatrick, A. 2008. English as the official working language of the Association of Southeast Asian Nations (ASEAN): Features and strategies. *English Today*, 24/2. 27–34.
Krashen, S. D., M. Long, & R. Scarcella. 1979. Age, rate, and eventual attainment in second language acquisition. *TESOL Quarterly*, 13. 573–582.
Lee, D. 2015. The Philippines has become the call-center capital of the world. *Los Angeles Times*. February 1, 2015. http://www.latimes.com/business/la-fi-philippines-economy-20150202-story.html (accessed 30 September, 2015).
Lenneberg, E. 1967. *Biological Foundations of Language*. New York: Wiley & Sons.
Lockwood, J., G. Forey & H. Price. 2008. English in the Philippine call centers and BPO operations: Issues, opportunities and research. In M. L. S. Bautista & K. Bolton (eds.), *Philippine English: Linguistic and Literary Perspectives*. Hong Kong: Hong Kong University Press. 219–241.
Long, M. 1990. Maturational constraints on language development. *Studies in Second Language Acquisition*, 12. 251–285.
Mufwene, S. S. 2001. *The Ecology of Language Evolution*. Cambridge: Cambridge University Press.
Piller, I. 2002. Passing for a native speaker: Identity and success in second language learning. *Journal of Sociolinguistics*, 6/2. 179–206.
Rampton, B. 1995. *Crossing: Language and Ethnicity among Adolescents*. London: Longman.
Ringshaw, G. 2003. Call centres take the passage to India. *Sunday Telegraph*, May 25th, 2003, 8.
Sañez, O. 2008. Driving "breakthrough" growth in Philippines O&O: Roadmap 2010. FUSE General Assembly Meeting. March 25, 2008.
Site Selection Group. 2015. How big is the U.S call center industry compared to India and the Philippines. http://info.siteselectiongroup.com/blog/how-big-is-the-us-call-center-industry-compared-to-india-and-philippines (accessed September 30, 2015).
Sontag, S. 2002. The world as India. The St. Jerome Lecture on Literary Translation. http://www.susansontag.com/prize/onTranslation.shtml (accessed September 30, 2015).
Tayao, M. L. G. 2008. A lectal description of the phonological features of Philippine English. In M. L. S. Bautista & K. Bolton (eds.), *Philippine English: Linguistic and Literary Perspectives*. Hong Kong: Hong Kong University Press. 157–174.
Taylor, F. W. 1964. *Scientific Management*. New York: Harper and Row.
Taylor, P. & P. Bain. 2004. Call centre offshoring to India: The revenge of history? *Labour & Industry*, 14/3. 15–38.

Taylor, P. & P. Bain. 2005. "India calling to the far away towns": The call centre labour process and globalization. *Work, Employment and Society*, 19/2. 261–282.

Taylor, P., P. D'Cruz, E. Noronha, & D. Scholarios. 2009. Indian call centres and business process outsourcing: a study in union formation. *New Technology, Work and Employment*, 24/1. 19–42.

Taylor, P., G. Mulvey, J. Hyman, & P. Bain. 2002. Work organisation, control and the experience of work in call centres. *Work, Employment and Society*, 16/1. 133–150.

TOEFL 2006. Test and score data summary for TOEFL internet-based test: 2005-06 test year. https://www.ets.org/Media/Research/pdf/TOEFL-SUM-0506-CBT.pdf (accessed September 30, 2015).

TOEFL. 2007. Test and score data summary for TOEFL internet-based test: September 2005–December 2006. Princeton, NJ: Educational Testing Service. https://www.ets.org/Media/Research/pdf/TOEFL-SUM-0506-iBT.pdf (accessed September 30, 2015).

Torres, E. 2014. Philippines: A magna carta for call centre workers. http://www.equaltimes.org/philippines-a-magna-carta-forcall?lang=en#.VgurELQ ri -J (accessed September 30, 2015).

Kenneth Hyltenstam
7 The polyglot – an initial characterization on the basis of multiple anecdotal accounts

1 Background

People frequently add one, two, or, less commonly, even three or four languages to the linguistic repertoire they developed as children. Given the opportunity, favourable conditions for acquisition and practice, and a degree of commitment on behalf of the individual, there is nothing particularly exceptional in mastering a handful of languages at a high level of proficiency. In rare cases, however, single individuals acquire 10, 20, or even more languages and maintain their ability to use most of them over their lifespan. When accounted for in the literature, these people are generally called *polyglots* (from Greek *polys* 'many' and *glotta* 'tongue', 'language') or sometimes *hyperpolyglots*, as suggested by Richard Hudson.[1] Hudson proposed the tentative definition of a hyperpolyglot as "one who can speak six or more languages fluently". He based this criterion on the fact that the limit for what he calls community multilingualism, i.e. highly multilingual settings in which "everyone speaks a lot of languages", seems to be five or six languages (Hudson 2012: 24). I have opted to simply use the term polyglot rather than hyperpolyglot. A polyglot is thus here distinguished from a multilingual or bilingual speaker.[2]

---

[1] The year 2003 is mentioned in different sources as a date for Hudson's coinage of this term, but as I was unable to locate the reference, I contacted Richard Hudson personally to ask. He replied, referring to memory failure: "I'm afraid I'm stumped by 'Hudson 2003'" (personal communication 1 October 2009). Nevertheless, in a question to LINGUIST List on 26 October 2003, he used the term (see Erard 2012: 281), and in Hudson (2012) he writes about "the great and exceptional language learners (for whom I've coined the term 'hyperpolyglot')" (p. 24).

[2] The notion of *polyglot* was used predominantly in the 19th and early 20th centuries to refer to people who speak "more [than two] languages fluently" (Paradis 1989: 117). It was sometimes used in contrast to the notion of *bilingual*, i.e. a person who speaks *two* languages fluently, but these two terms have also been used as synonyms in many contexts. The notion of polyglot was used especially in medical, psychological, and linguistic accounts of aphasic patients (cf. Paradis 1983). Later, when the idea of absolute fluency and equal command of two languages was challenged as an untenable defining criterion for what should be counted as bilingualism, the terms *bilingual* and *multilingual* were adopted – and often used interchangeably – to refer to the communicative-functional use of two or *more* languages without any claims to a specific level of fluency or proficiency. The notion of polyglot seems to have become more or less obsolete in the modern literature on bilingualism or multilingualism, so there is room for reviving it for the specific type of language user focused on in the present chapter.

Kenneth Hyltenstam, Stockholm University

The discussion in this chapter is restricted to individuals who have added at least six languages to their repertoire after puberty and attained a high level of proficiency in these languages. The theoretical motivation for the age criterion is based on current knowledge of the differences between child and adult L2 learners (Hyltenstam and Abrahamsson 2003; Birdsong 2005; DeKeyser and Larson-Hall 2005; Long 2005, 2007; Abrahamsson and Hyltenstam 2009; Hyltenstam 2012), and the fact that it is obviously a more spectacular feat to attain high levels in several languages for late learners than it is for early learners.

Polyglots have only minimally been the focus of systematic research in the field of second language acquisition (SLA). This is paradoxical, since polyglots excel in acquiring new languages and, accordingly, could potentially reveal new knowledge concerning several phenomena that are involved in second language acquisition and use. Questions such as the following are directly implicated: Is it possible to add new languages to those you have already acquired throughout the lifespan, and what is the result of language acquisition at different ages? Is it true that the acquisition of additional languages becomes increasingly easier, as often claimed? Is a certain degree of aptitude or other personal traits necessary for learning several languages to a high degree of proficiency, and how does aptitude interact with age? What are the motivational factors necessary for acquiring additional languages? Are polyglots special language learners, or do they use the same strategies and techniques, and invest as much effort, in acquiring a new language as anybody else? Are polyglots able to maintain a high level of proficiency in several languages in spite of limited exposure to each of them, i.e. are polyglots different from other language users with respect to language maintenance and attrition?

At a more general level of consideration than that concerned specifically with SLA, it is of interest to ask whether there are specific kinds of intellectual functioning that are characteristic of people who develop polyglotism. Can polyglotism be grouped with other exceptional abilities in mathematics, music, or art? Does it rely on such exceptional abilities that are involved in the so-called Geschwind-Galaburda syndrome, as has been suggested by Novoa, Fein, and Obler (1988)? Or is it an effect of a condition of the Asperger or (high functioning) autism type (for the link between autism and exceptional ability, see Fitzgerald 2004)? In relation to these questions, a central issue concerns variability among polyglots, i.e. whether it is possible to describe polyglotism in the framework of one specific type of cognitive functioning or whether polyglotism can arise in different mental environments.

The existence of exceptionally multilingual individuals is well attested anecdotally. Among other examples, Baker and Prys Jones (1997: 19) mention a Dr. Harold Williams (1876–1928) of New Zealand who spoke 58 languages, reporting that Williams attended a meeting at the League of Nations in Switzerland and was able to address each delegate in their own language. Baker and Prys Jones also mention the example of Pope John Paul II, who was fluent in Polish, Latin, Italian, English, Spanish, French, Russian, and German, but who also knew several other languages to various degrees. His ability to learn languages rapidly was demonstrated when he learnt Japanese in 1991 before a visit to Japan and spoke it so well that he "surprised some missionaries who had not managed to learn as much during many years in Japan" (p. 21). Harold Williams and John Paul II are but two examples of those names often referred to in various lists of polyglots that appear in print and, in particular, on net-based sites.[3]

There is a handful of individuals about whom more extensive life histories specifically focussing on the person's polyglot abilities are available. Harold Williams is one of these (Tyrkova-Williams 1935). Others are Alexander Schwartz (Schwartz 2003), Kató Lomb (Alkire 2008; Krashen and Kiss 1996), and Erik Gunnemark (Gethin and Gunnemark 1996). All these references are valuable sources of information, but they are lacking in terms of generalizability. A collection of five life histories (Laurén 2006) gives a more systematic account of one particular issue: explicit versus implicit language learning strategies.

In the following sections, we will focus on and systematize existing anecdotal information. As an introduction to this section and in order to give flesh and blood to the notion of polyglot, we will present two life histories. Then, by comparing anecdotal information concerning polyglots from various sources, we will be able to discern particular recurring patterns that are suggestive for a more formal characterization of polyglots.

In a separate chapter (Hyltenstam this volume b), the literature on four individuals will be referred to and reviewed: CJ, Emil Krebs, Daniel Tammet, and Christopher Taylor. These polyglots belong to a small group of individuals who have been the focus of controlled empirical research. Other cases in this group, such as the one referred to by the pseudonym "Ann" (Biedroń and Szczepaniak 2009), could potentially have been included in the discussion, but although "Ann" is obviously a highly talented 21-year-old language learner, five of the

---

[3] It is generally inappropriate and unethical in scientific texts to disclose the identity of cases that are referred to. The present context is different in that the identities of individuals are already public, appearing previously as they have in various public sources (print and other media). This is true also of some of the cases that are described in the scientific literature that we will discuss specifically in chapter 8 (Hyltenstam this volume b), such as Daniel Tammet: "His identity can be disclosed because he has written an autobiography (Tammet 2006) and he agreed to take part in a television documentary" (Baron-Cohen, Bor, Billington, Asher, Wheelwright, and Ashwin 2007: 240).

eight languages she was reported to have learnt were still only at an elementary or communicative level. Thus, she does not meet the polyglot criteria applied here, and cases like hers will not be dealt with further. As the investigations of the four cases focus on quite distinct issues and employ varying theoretical perspectives (in particular neuroscientific perspectives), they provide quite distinct information to a general characterization of polyglots. Furthermore, as two of those cases concern individuals with neurological conditions (Autism/Asperger Syndrome, Synaesthesia, Savantism), we will discuss the possible link between such polyglots and polyglots among the typically developing (TD) population (for terminology, cf. Wallace 2008).

2 Anecdotal evidence

2.1 Lists of polyglots

Several net-based sources such as Wikipedia, European Direct Navigation, and Answer.com provide lists of polyglots. Polyglots are often listed in relation to how many languages they claim or are reported to know so that we have categories of polyglots knowing 10, 20, 50, and even 100 languages. Many of these lists are exact duplicates of other lists, while others are included as parts of others. It is not unreasonable to suspect that several of the names presented in these lists are repeated uncritically. Therefore, as some of the information is not particularly reliable, these lists must be treated with caution, the most basic problem being that the information has not always been verified, and information about sources is not always provided. In a journalistic follow-up of certain "established" polyglots – or polyglot celebrities – Erard (2012) revealed a wide range of realities, from utterly false claims in certain cases to individuals knowing fewer languages than claimed, and others possessing very restricted types of language skills, for example, only reading comprehension. Moreover, rarely is there any discussion of what it means to *know* a language, nor any general definition of what is counted as a language.[4] Nevertheless, several of the names that appear in such lists are also referred to in other more credible sources. The typical kinds of information provided in the lists are dates of birth (and death, where applicable), occupation, and number of languages known. Sometimes more detailed information is given with regard to a person's proficiency in speaking, understanding, reading and writing, ability to translate, etc. In some cases, we are also told which particular languages a polyglot knows/knew.

---

[4] It is clearly out of the question to consider net-based lists and blogs with idiosyncratic and downright incorrect understandings of the notion of polyglot as reliable sources of information.

The number of different names that currently appear in net-based sources is somewhere between 100 and 150. In the scientific literature, one would find approximately 10 cases, several of which overlap with those of the net-based sources. Nevertheless, the exact number of names is of little importance, as it is not possible to extract information on the incidence of polyglotism from available sources. As the sources mentioned cover a long period of time – from the 15th century up until today – we can conclude that the phenomenon of polyglotism is extremely rare. On the other hand, it is highly likely that the people (both living and dead) who have been mentioned make up only a small number of all existing polyglots during these centuries. The lists are mostly restricted to Western literate societies, and it is conceivable that they are somewhat biased toward people who are celebrities for reasons other than that of being polyglots.

With such caution in mind, a list of 94 names was created for purposes of the discussion in the present chapter (see Appendix 1). Against the problematic nature of the information discussed in the previous paragraph, the names included should only be seen as examples. The criterion for inclusion has been that some kind of converging information was found in independent sources. As can be seen in the Appendix, different sources often give diverging information, for example about how many languages a particular polyglot knows/knew. The list also covers the four well-researched cases and the individuals mentioned above, about whom more extensive life histories are available. In order to present a picture of what polyglotism can entail, we will revisit two of these in more detail in the next section.

2.2 Life histories

2.2.1 Harold Williams

Harold Williams was born in New Zealand, the eldest son of one of the first leaders of the Methodist Church in the country (Tyrkova-Williams 1935). As a schoolboy, Harold had access through his father's library to the New Testament in various languages, among them the Malayo-Polynesian languages Dobuan (Papua New Guinea) and Niuean (Savage Island). A born linguist, and guided by the English version of the Gospel, he constructed a grammar of Dobuan and compiled vocabularies of both Dobuan and Niuean. When Harold was 17 years old, his vocabulary of Niuean, the language of the Niue Islands, which are east of Tonga and south of Samoa, was published in the *Journal of the Polynesian Society* (Williams 1893). Throughout his life, Williams continued to use versions of the *New Testament* written in various languages as a method of studying new languages, figuring out their grammars and vocabularies on the basis of known content.

As a teenager in Auckland, Williams enjoyed visiting ships and wharves, where he gained exposure to Polynesian and Melanesian languages and found opportunities to communicate with native speakers using these languages. After training at the Methodist Ministry, he was sent to the Northern Wairoa district, where he was surrounded by gumdiggers of many nationalities and used the opportunity to learn languages from them through conversation. This was how he became familiar with Polish and Russian. Williams took a particular interest in Russian, inspired especially by the novels of Leo Tolstoy, which he read in their original language. At the age of 23, when he was already proficient in 20 languages, Harold Williams left for Europe to pursue his university studies. Three years later, in 1903, he received his doctorate from Munich University, with a dissertation entitled *Grammatische Skizze der Ilocano Sprache mit Berücksichtigung ihrer Beziehungen zu den anderen Sprachen der Malayo Polynesischen Familie* (Tyrkova-Williams 1935: 16). Instead of becoming a university teacher, which he had considered doing, he became a journalist and continued his in-depth studies of Slavonic languages. In 1905, he began working in Russia, as well as in Turkey, for various British newspapers (*The Times, Manchester Guardian, Daily Chronicle*). He became a leading authority on Russian affairs and reported from every corner of the country, which was facilitated by his acquisition of Finnish, Estonian, Lettish, Georgian, and Tartar. During his time in Russia, he also served as a chief source of information for the British embassy.

After the revolution, Williams was forced to flee Russia. During the following years, without secure employment, he taught himself languages that included Japanese, Irish, Tagalog, Hungarian, Czech, Albanian, Basque, and Chinese. In 1922, he was appointed foreign editor for *The Times*, which came with the responsibility of commenting on political events from all over the world. In the op-eds that he wrote in this position, Williams was able to advocate ideas that he felt were morally right, such as preserving peace and European security. In this manner, he became a politically influential figure of his time.

Several observations are noteworthy in the interpretation of Harold Williams' polyglotism. One extraordinary circumstance is that his ability to learn in general was quite average during early childhood; however, at the age of seven Williams experienced "an explosion in his brain", after which his capacity to learn increased to an extraordinary level, except in the area of mathematics, which remained "perplexing" and "incomprehensible" to him (Tyrkova-Williams 1935: 2). The change in learning ability was especially true for languages and manifested in his learning of Latin, which occurred prior to his "work" on grammars and vocabularies for the languages noted above. Coupled with this is the observation that he was a person with encyclopaedic knowledge. His memory allowed him to retain and access factual detail in a wide range of political and cultural areas. On the other hand, in spite of his augmented learning abilities, he failed at his first attempt to earn a university degree at the University of Auckland because of "an inability to sufficiently master mathematics" (ibid.).

The points we have taken up here could be seen in light of present knowledge, which will be dealt with in more detail in chapter 8 (Hyltenstam this volume b), but is briefly commented on here. First, the "explosion of the brain" issue may be related to new research insights that "savant" or exceptional abilities in areas such as mathematics, calculation, visual representation, music, or rote remembering of calendars and registers can have its onset in brain damage; cases have been observed both with reference to brain damage for external reasons, such as accidents, and internal reasons, such as dementia (Miller, Cummings, Mishkin, Boone, Prince, Ponton, and Cotman 1998). A change in the ability to store and access memories may thus come about for such reasons. Secondly, Harold Williams' difficulties with mathematics may give substance to a common layman conception of a difference between mathematical and linguistic ability, but the existence of such a correspondence in general is contradicted by several cases of calculating prodigies who were also extraordinary second language learners (Smith 1988: 40), notably Daniel Tammet, who has both mathematical and linguistic savant abilities (Tammet 2006), and Alexander Schwartz, to whom we now turn.

2.2.2 Alexander Schwartz

Alexander Schwartz (Baker and Prys Jones 1997; Schwartz 2003) was born in Hungary in 1926. At the age of ten, when he entered a Jewish secondary school (of the European 20th century type, which covered grades 5 to 12), he had already studied four languages, in addition to his native Hungarian: Latin, Hebrew, German, and English. In 1937, at the age of 11, he moved with his family to New York. The high school in Manhattan, which he entered at age 14, required a foreign language, and Alexander chose French; however, his goal was to become an engineer. French and mathematics soon became his favourite subjects "because both require paying attention to a set of rules" (Schwartz 2003: 3).

Schwartz' interest in language directed him during this period to DeViti's textbook of Spanish and the Berlitz textbooks of Spanish and Italian. He started to study these languages on his own, soon adding to this input by reading novels in Spanish and Italian. Through a variety of circumstances, Schwartz came into contact with Esperanto, and he also had the opportunity to brush up on his German. These activities had the character of a hobby as he pursued his plans to become an engineer. When he later studied at Columbia Engineering School in New York, Schwartz worked in various jobs after school, in part because of the economic demands posed by an early marriage and parenthood, and some of these involved translation, which he had had his first experiences with when he was drafted by the U.S. Army and served in an intelligence position.

Seeing the advantages of qualifying for employment in the incipient computer market, he took up studies in mathematics at Columbia and obtained a job in a computing centre, while at the same time taking evening courses in advanced mathematics, which led to a Master's degree in mathematics in 1956. Having completed courses in Italian, Portuguese, Swedish, Norwegian, and Danish in his spare time, Schwartz felt that Russian would be a useful language to know for a mathematician, particularly as many Russian textbooks had not been translated into English. However, despite his experience in studying languages, he found Russian to be too difficult to learn on his own, and in order to gain entry into Slavonic languages, he decided to start instead with Polish, as it was written in the Latin alphabet. Schwartz acquired "a good grounding" in that language. He nevertheless continued to have difficulties with Russian and therefore enrolled in an intensive, five-week course on the language at New York University. After that, he was able to continue studies of the language on his own and eventually was able to read and understand math textbooks written in Russian. After regular working hours at the computer centre, he then started to translate Russian articles into English for the *Soviet Journal of Atomic Energy*.

Having joined the American Translation Association in 1961, Schwartz discovered that the United Nations was in the process of recruiting new translators. After having passed the examination for translators from both French and Spanish into English, he was employed at the English Translation Section of the United Nations in 1962. The work at the organization involved not only full translation of documents but also the task of writing English summaries of letters in many languages that were sent to the U.N. from all over the world.

During this employment, which lasted until 1986, Alexander Schwartz studied many other languages (among these Serbo-Croatian, Bulgarian, Czech, Icelandic, Catalan), mostly on his own, but for the purposes of work. For example, he learnt "enough" Belarusian and Ukrainian to be able to translate credentials of diplomats from these Soviet member states. He also learnt Japanese due to the prospect of a possible mission to Japan. All in all, he translated 31 languages into English, a feat that is recorded in the 1994 Guinness Book of Records. The statement was published after Schwartz' chiefs of service had attested to its validity.

One observation that can be drawn from Schwartz' autobiographical writings is his interest in minute textual details and his attention to formal and factual correctness. He was deeply concerned with the accuracy of translated texts and describes in detail how translations for the English Translation Section were controlled by independent translators at all times. Schwartz also describes how, after his retirement, he did proofreading and fact-checking for the *Guinness Book of Records* on a freelance basis. This indicates not just an interest in language editing but also the encyclopaedic kind of knowledge it takes to be able to detect all kinds of mistakes and inadequacies (Schwartz 2003: 25).

3 Observations based on a list of 94 polyglots – a preliminary picture

The list and the comments it contains (see Appendix 1) lead to several observations, and even allow for the counting of some recurring patterns.

First of all, it is obvious from several of the observations, especially in the life histories, that polyglots invest an immense amount of time and focused attention to the language learning task. This can be seen in the light of several fundamental phenomena that are generally referred to in discussions of success in second language acquisition that include motivation, language awareness, and autonomy. We will come back to these issues more extensively in the next chapter (Hyltenstam this volume b), but a note on motivation is relevant here. Motivation is supposed to explain why people opt for certain activities, as well as how long and how hard they are willing to go on with these activities (Dörnyei and Skehan 2003: 614). In a process-oriented model of motivation, Dörnyei (2000) distinguishes between choice motivation, executive motivation, and motivational retrospection. What is of specific interest here is executive motivation, the actual activities/practices involved in studying, acquiring and maintaining a language. Strong executive motivation may lead a learner to a passionate commitment to specific tasks and strategies. Polyglots seem to take advantage of every conceivable occasion to be occupied with new language data, and many of the observations involve information about permanent motivation to continue their language learning. The notion of choice motivation is also interesting. Several of the polyglots talk about a strong commitment to opt for language learning, even as a perceived necessity. Motivational retrospection may also be cited: With experienced success with second language acquisition generally, polyglots do not seem to hesitate starting with a new language.

A related aspect, as evidenced in certain cases, notably those of Kató Lomb and Erik Gunnemark, is that motivational factors also produce a drive or a mission to inform their environment about the phenomenon of language learning and even to convince others of the correctness of their particular methodological approaches and insights (for many other cases, see Erard 2012). Both Lomb and Gunnemark have published highly personal books about their language learning experiences that provide the reader with innumerable practical recommendations (Lomb 2008; Gethin and Gunnemark 1996). None of the cases bears witness to familiarity with the theoretical literature on SLA. However, Lomb's book has been reviewed by Peek (2008), who analyzes its significance for adult second language learning related to issues of awareness, attitude, aptitude, and personal responsibility.

Looking more specifically, and maybe more concretely, at what the list can tell us, one notes that it includes several people who had successful professional careers in fields other than language arts. Among the historically well-known persons represented in the list, we find the Italian Renaissance philosopher Giovanni Pico della Mirandola (1463–1494), who was said to know 22 languages. Pico della Mirandola is known for his 900 theses – which he formulated at the age of 23 – that summarized the existing knowledge at the time; his *Oration on the Dignity of Man* (1486) was an introduction to these theses. The list also includes two recent popes: John Paul II (1920–2005), who, as mentioned above, became fluent in 11 languages during his lifetime, and his successor, the former head of the Catholic Church, Benedict XVI (1927–), who "speaks at least" 10 languages.

For a great number of the listed people, language is, in fact, the focus of their profession. As a matter of fact, more than a fourth of the 94 names, or 28 individuals, are referred to as professional linguists – or philologists in earlier times and in certain geographical areas. Examples comprise a number of well-known linguists. Danish comparative philologist Rasmus Christian Rask (1787–1832) mastered 25 languages and dialects, and could read in 35 languages. The Sorbonne and Paris V professor André Martinet (1908–1999), prominent scholar in the European structural linguistics tradition, spoke 12 languages. Donald Kenrick (1930–), an expert on Romani languages, is able "to translate from over sixty languages, and [to speak] around thirty of them, more or less fluently" (Gunnemark 2000). Steven Wurm (1922–2001), the Australian specialist of Papua New Guinean languages, had working knowledge of around 50 languages. Perhaps the most well-known professor of linguistics who was also a polyglot was the North American linguist Kenneth Hale (1934–2001), who was said to know over 50 languages, and was an expert in American Indian languages of North and Central America, but also learned and studied aboriginal languages of Australia. Many of the languages he mastered were indigenous minority languages. The dean of the School of Humanities at MIT, where Hale was professor of linguistics, reported that Hale had commented on this fact in the following way: "the problem is that many of the languages I've learned are extinct, or close to extinction, and I have no one to speak them with" (MIT News Office 2001).[5] Hale was particularly attached to Warlpiri, one of the aboriginal languages of Australia, so much so that he decided to raise two of his sons to speak it – and did so successfully.

Another large group of people who have language as a profession consists of translators and interpreters. Among the 94 names, 22 are referred to as translators (19) and/or interpreters (3). Here we find examples such as Erik Gunnemark (1918–2007), István Dabi (1943–), and Alexander Schwartz (1926–). Erik Gunnemark was able to translate nearly 50 languages – claiming that he had to use a dictionary for about 20 of them. Of these 50 languages, he spoke 6 fluently, 7 at an advanced level, and 15 at what he himself called a mini-level (personal communication, 2006; cf. Gethin and Gunnemark 1996: 318). István Dabi translates 103 languages, and the case of Alexander Schwartz translating 31 languages was mentioned above.

It is not only professional linguists and translators/interpreters who can count having language as a profession. Knowledgeable in 12 languages, Jean van Yzendoorn (1932–2015) was a language consultant at a large Finnish company in the iron business and was responsible for international correspondence, among other matters (Laurén 2006). Michael Everson (1963–), a master of 14 languages, is an expert in the writing systems used in the world's languages and works as a consultant with regard to fonts, orthographies, and standards, especially with regard to languages that have only recently begun to be written. Edgardo Donovan (1974–), who has "various levels of proficiency" (www.eddiedonovan.com) in 30 languages or language varieties (such as Brazilian and European Portuguese), 9 of which (where tests were available) have been tested via the *U.S. State Department standardized proficiency exam*, the *Defense Language Proficiency Test* (DLPT), has, among other things, worked as a cryptologic linguist for the National Security Agency of the U.S. Air Force, where he is also an officer.

---

[5] One problem with the category of professional linguists in this context is the following: As professional linguists generally have detailed knowledge *about* many languages (their structure, history, relationships with other languages, their distribution and number of speakers, etc.), they are sometimes mistakenly believed to actually *know* a lot of languages. In discussing the particular case of Ken Hale, and referring to an interview he conducted with Hale in 1996, Erard (2012: 82) questions the number of languages that Hale could actually speak, partly on the basis of this type of misconception. Nevertheless, Hale had a gift for rapid language acquisition and could "say many things in different languages" (ibid.).

Several others are professionals in language in another way, namely, the fairly large groups of writers (15 names) that comprise authors of fiction such as James Joyce, J. R. R. Tolkien, and Anthony Burgess, or journalists such as the previously mentioned Harold Williams. James Joyce (1882–1941) "knew" English, French, Spanish, Italian, Danish, Norwegian, Russian, Latin, classical Greek, Dutch, Slovenian, Croatian, and Irish), and J.R.R. Tolkien (1892–1973) also knew some 13 languages, mostly Germanic languages. Anthony Burgess (1917–1993) was fluent in German, French, Spanish, Italian, Russian, Malay, and Welsh, in addition to his native English, and had some command of Chinese, Hebrew, Japanese, Persian, and Swedish. All three authors created artificial languages that were used in their fictional work (see below).

Finally, the ability and motivation to learn new languages is arguably a great asset for their profession for some polyglots, as in the case of the Finnish diplomat Pertti Laakso (1934–), who knows "at least" 14 languages (Laurén 2006), or the two popes mentioned above.

Interestingly, even though several of the listed people are reported to have taught language courses, none is explicitly referred to as primarily a language teacher by profession; only three have been "teachers" for some part of their career. The other side of the coin is that the majority seem to be mainly self-taught. Individuals seem to take advantage of all kinds of materials and methods they happen to come upon. They specifically study grammars, dictionaries, and various naturally occurring texts such as newspapers and all kinds of media, novels, and signboards. They use recorded materials and take the opportunity to interact verbally with speakers of the target language. For polyglots, the study of languages does not seem characteristically to be a group activity, but rather an individual pleasure.

Obviously, many polyglots have taken their interest in language to a professional level and have made their living on the basis of linguistic knowledge. As will become clear below, it does not seem to be the other way around, i.e. that their professional ambitions have led them into the language learning business. In many cases in which the development of their interest in languages has been commented upon, it is clear that this interest was prior to any professional training, often starting in the early teens or even in childhood.

Those polyglots who are not professionals in language(s) are in most cases highly qualified academics, politicians, or artists. In only two cases in the list, do we find exceptions to this: Arvo Juutilainen (1949–), a former gardener and bibliophile from Finland who can read about 100 languages and speaks 15 of these "more or less fluently", and also knows the vocabulary of at least 50 other languages due to a photographic memory (Gunnemark 2000). Erard (2012: 74) mentions another case, the blacksmith Elihu Burritt (1810–1879), who taught himself 50 languages.

Four of the individuals appearing in the list were creators of artificial languages. First of all, of course, we have the creator of Esperanto himself, 'Dr. Hopeful', the pseudonym of Lazar Zamenhof (1859–1917), who knew 13 languages. Zamenhof was an eye doctor by profession and had the special background of having grown up in a town, Bialystok (then in Russia, now in Poland), where four ethnic groups lived together and where German, Russian, Polish, and Yiddish were spoken. His first publication on the language that he created, which was later called Esperanto, after his pseudonym, appeared in 1887. The other three who made up languages of their own were the polyglot fiction authors Tolkien, Joyce, and Burgess. Tolkien created several varieties of language for fiction purposes (Hostetter 2007; see also The Elvish Linguistic Fellowship, www.elvish.org), a feat that may be seen as a felicitous marriage between his academic linguistic knowledge and creative fiction fantasy. *Finnegans Wake* (1939) by James Joyce was written in a "self-made" mixed language with elements from more than 10 European languages, primarily Nordic languages. Likewise, Burgess invented the Anglo-Russian teen slang Nadsat, which was used in his novel *A Clockwork Orange* (1962) (and in the film), and the "prehistoric" language Ulam for the film *Quest for Fire* (1981).

When information on which languages a certain person knows/knew is provided in the list, it is possible to observe a number of things. First, among the languages that are known, some are very distant in terms of genetic relationship or typology. For example, among the many languages that Giuseppe Mezzofanti (1774–1849) was reported to have known, we find English, Welsh, Hebrew, Persian, Turkish, Russian, Hungarian, and Chinese (Russell 1858 [2013]). Georg Sauerwein (1831–1904) had Modern Greek, Irish, Danish, Albanian, Armenian, and many others in his repertoire, and Alexander Schwartz claims to know, for example, Italian, Serbo-Croat, Icelandic, Chinese, Japanese, and Finnish, among many other languages. Another generalization is that many polyglots also know several closely related languages or language varieties, as in the cases we have just mentioned: Mezzofanti knew Italian, Spanish, and Portuguese, in addition to Danish and Swedish. Sauerwein knew Danish, Icelandic, Norwegian, and Swedish as one group, and Finnish and Estonian as another group, whereas Check, Slovak, Serbian, Croatian, and different dialects of Chinese made up two additional groups. Schwartz learned Swedish (in six months) and then added Norwegian (in two months) and Danish (in two weeks) (Schwartz 2003). Another observation is that many polyglots also learn languages with limited communicative reach: Kenneth Hale's comment on learning extinct or almost extinct languages, as mentioned above, is a case in point. Other examples are Sauerwein's knowledge of Manx Gaelic, Samoan, Hawaiian, and Aneitum (New Hebrides) or Rolf Theil Endresen's ability in Saami (of northern

Scandinavia) and Nizaa (a language of Cameroon), alongside more widely spoken African languages such as Fulfulde or Hausa, and some variety of Romani.

One of the most remarkable pieces of information that can be extracted from the list is the extremely uneven sex distribution among the names of polyglots: Among the 94 names listed, only 3 belong to females. One of these is Kató Lómb (1909–2003), who first graduated with a university degree in physics and chemistry, and then completed a doctorate in chemistry (Krashen and Kiss 1996; Alkire 2008; see also Lomb 2008), but whose special interest for and ability in language learning eventually resulted in a professional life as a translator and interpreter. Before that, she also worked as a language teacher in various languages. The other two women are Helen Abadzi and Eva Toulouze. The high correlation between maleness and polyglotism holds also for the handful of cases that have been described in greater detail or have been the focus of controlled empirical research, all of which have consisted only of male individuals (Hyltenstam this volume b). The male dominance may be seen as particularly surprising given the well-established female advantage in language-related tasks in general (Eriksson, Marschik, Tulviste, Almgren, Perez Pereira, Wehberg, and Gallego 2012).

A final observation is that a handful of the polyglots included in the list of 94 names are said to have special abilities or interests in areas other than language that require special types of memory. We have already mentioned photographic memory in the case of Arvo Juutilainen, which Juutilainen is able to use for learning the vocabularies of different languages from dictionaries, but he is also a book collector who used to have a library of about 40,000 books in 447 different languages (Wilkman 2006). Whether the interest for and handling of this large collection of authors and titles has also depended on a photographic memory ability is not clear, but may well have been the case. Another example is Leofranc Holford-Strevens (1946–), who knows Latin and all the Romance and Germanic languages, as well as Russian. He is the author of *The History of Time* (Holford-Strevens 2005), which demonstrates his special interest in calendar chronologies and the calculation of time. This area of knowledge is also dependent on memorizing and being able to perform calculation. Finally Michael Everson (1963–), who is an expert on writing systems, obviously has an exceptional ability for remembering the specific visual shapes of a variety of characters in all their detail.

This shows that polyglots may have other interests and skills that may be connected to their extraordinary abilities in language. One question that still may arise is whether polyglots are characterized by restricted, perhaps particularly focussed, interests. This does not necessarily seem to be the case. There are several examples in the list of people with quite varied interests and activities, including, for example, Paul Robeson (1898–1976), who was an American actor, singer, writer, athlete, and political and civil rights activist, and was conversant in more than 20 languages. Kenneth Hale was not only a professional linguist but also a successful rodeo bull rider during his years as an undergraduate at the University of Arizona. An amazing example of versatility and top achievement in many areas is that of Edgardo Donovan (1974–), who, in addition to being a polyglot, is an officer in the U.S. Air Force, a former cryptologic linguist for the National Security Service, a former chief web designer for the First-e Group PLC, Dublin, Ireland, which was one of Europe's largest e-Banks during the years 1998–2001, author of essays on topics such as management, technology, international relations, and literature, keyboard player, and former member of the under-18 Italian national team in American football. Donovan seems to be equipped with an extremely competitive orientation, winning honourable awards in almost all his areas of specialization.

4 Conclusion

The preliminary picture of polyglots that emerges from this analysis of multiple anecdotal evidence is the following. Polyglots are highly motivated language learners. They are more often than not self-taught, and some express a high confidence in their own approach to language learning. Like professional linguists they are deeply interested in language as a phenomenon, not least in language as structure. Many polyglots are, in fact, professional linguists or deal with languages professionally in other ways, often as translators, or, to a lesser extent, as interpreters. One would have thought that the profession of language teacher might attract the attention of polyglots, but this turned out explicitly not to be the case. One may speculate that language learning in groups is, perhaps, outside the contexts that polyglots find comfortable for this activity. A number of them are authors of different categories, novelists, poets, journalists, something that very likely reflects a well-developed verbal ability. The interest in constructing artificial languages, manifest in some polyglots, as well as the patterns that can be observed in their selection of languages to learn (often closely related languages or typologically distant languages), talks to a fascination with language structure and a high degree of language awareness. Finally, polyglots are overwhelming male. The reason for this can only be speculated on. This will be done in the next chapter (Hyltenstam this volume b).

References

Abrahamsson, N. & K. Hyltenstam. 2009. Age of onset and nativelikeness in a second language: Listener perception versus linguistic scrutiny. *Language Learning*, 58/2. 249–306.

Alkire, S. 2008. Preface. In: S. Alkire (ed.), *Polyglot. How I learn Languages by Kató Lomb.* Berkeley: TESL-EJ. vii–xiv.

Amunts, K., A. Schleicher, & K. Zilles. 2004. Outstanding language competence and cytoarchitecture in Broca's speech region. *Brain and Language*, 89. 346–353.

Baker, C. & S. Prys Jones (eds.). 1997. *Encyclopedia of Bilingualism and Bilingual Education.* Clevedon: Multilingual Matters.

Baron-Cohen, S., D. Bor, J. Billington, J. Asher, S. Wheelwright & C. Ashwin. 2007. Savant memory in a man with colour form-number synaesthesia and Asperger Syndrome. *Journal of Consciousness Studies*, 14/9–10. 237–251.

Biedroń, A. & A. Szczepaniak. 2009. The cognitive profile of a talented foreign language learner: A case study. *Psychology of Language and Communication*, 13. 53–71.

Birdsong, D. 2005. Interpreting age effects in second language acquisition. In: J. F. Kroll & A. De Groot (eds.), *Handbook of Bilingualism: Psycholinguistic Perspectives.* Oxford: Oxford University Press. 109–127.

DeKeyser, R. & J. Larson-Hall. 2005. What does the critical period really mean? In: J. F. Kroll & A. De Groot (eds.), *Handbook of Bilingualism: Psycholinguistic Approach.* Oxford: Oxford University Press. 88–108.

Dörnyei, Z. 2000. Motivation in action: towards a process-oriented conceptualisation of student motivation. *British Journal of Educational Psychology*, 70. 519–538.

Dörnyei, Z. & P. Skehan. 2003. Individual differences in second language acquisition. In: C. J. Doughty & M. H. Long (eds.), *Handbook of Second Language Acquisition.* Oxford: Blackwell Publishing. 589–630.

Erard, M. 2012. *Babel No More. The Search for the World's Most Extraordinary Language Learners.* New York: Free Press.

Eriksson, M., P. B. Marschik, T. Tulviste, M. Almgren, M. Perez Pereira, S. Wehberg, & C. Gallego. 2012. Differences between girls and boys in emerging language skills: Evidence from 10 language communities. *British Journal of Developmental Psychology*, 30/2. 326–343.

Gethin, A. & E. V. Gunnemark. 1996. *The Art and Science of Learning Languages.* Oxford: Intellect Ltd.

Gunnemark, E. V. 2000. Donald Kenrick as polyglot: Could he be replaced by a machine? In: T. Acton (ed.), *Scholarship and the Gypsy Struggle: Commitment in Romani Studies.* Hatfield: University of Hertfordshire Press. 150–154.

Gunnemark, G. V. 2006. *Polyglottery today* (unpublished manuscript).

Holford-Strevens, L. 2005. *The History of Time: A Very Short Introduction.* Oxford: Oxford University Press.

Hostetter, C. F. 2007. Tolkienian linguistics: The first fifty years. *Tolkien Studies*, 4. 1–46.

Hudson, R. 2012. How many languages can a person learn? In: E. M. Rickerson & B. Hilton (eds.), *The Five-Minute Linguist. Bite-Sized Essays on Language and Languages*, 24. Sheffield: Equinox. 102–105.

Hyltenstam, K. 2012. Critical period. In: C. Chapelle (ed.), *Encyclopedia of Applied Linguistics.* Wiley-Blackwell. DOI: 10.1002/9781405198431.wbeal0285.

Hyltenstam, K. This volume b. The exceptional ability of polyglots to achieve high-level proficiency in numerous languages.
Hyltenstam, K & N. Abrahamsson. 2003. Maturational constraints in SLA. In: C. J. Doughty & M. H. Long (eds.), *Handbook of Second Language Acquisition*. Oxford: Blackwell. 539–588.
Krashen, S. & N. Kiss. 1996. Notes on a polyglot: Kato Lomb. *System*, 24/2. 207–210.
Laurén, C. 2006. *Tidig inlärning av flera språk. Teori och praktik*. Vasa: Vaasan Yliopisto.
Lomb, K. 2008. *Polyglot. How I Learn Languages*. Berkeley: TESL-EJ.
Long, M. 2005. Problems with supposed counter-evidence to the critical period hypothesis. *International Review of Applied Linguistics in Language Teaching*, 43/4. 287–317.
Long, M. H. 2007. *Problems in SLA*. Mahwah, NJ: Erlbaum.
Miller, B. L., J. L. Cummings, F. Mishkin, K. Boone, F. Prince, M. Ponton, & C. Cotman. 1998. Emergence of artistic talent in frontotemporal dementia. *Neurology*, 51. 978–982.
MIT News Office. 2001. Kenneth L. Hale, linguist and activist on behalf of endangered languages, dies. Obituaries. *MIT News*. October 11.
Novoa, L., D. Fein & L. K. Obler. 1988. Talent in foreign languages: A case study. In: L. K. Obler & D. Fein (eds.), *The Exceptional Brain: Neuropsychology of Talent and Special Abilities*. New York: Guilford Press. 294–302.
Paradis, M. (ed.). 1983. *Readings on Aphasia in Bilinguals and Polyglots*. Quebec: Didier.
Paradis, M. 1989. Bilingual and polyglot aphasia. In: F. Boller & J. Grafman (eds.), *Handbook of Neuropsychology II*. Amsterdam: Elsevier Science Publishers. 117–140.
Peek, R. 2008. Languages for ALL. *BISAL*, 3. 77–87.
Russell, C. W. 1858 [2013]. *The life of Cardinal Mezzofanti: With an Introductory Memoir of Eminent Linguists, Ancient and Modern*. London: Forgotten Books.
Schwartz, A. 2003. When bad news is good news or serendipity strikes again ... and again ... and again .... *Translation Journal* 7/3. (Online 3 May 2007).
Smith, N. & I. M. Tsimpli. 1995. *The Mind of a Savant. Language Learning and Modularity*. Oxford: Blackwell.
Smith, S. 1988. Calculating prodigies. In: L. K. Obler & D. Fein (eds.), *The Exceptional Brain: The Neuropsychology of Talent and Special Abilities*. New York: Guilford. 19–47.
Tammet, D. 2006. *Born on a Blue Day. A Memoir of Asperger's and an Extraordinary Mind*. London: Hodder & Stoughton.
Tyrkova-Williams, A. 1935. *Cheerful Giver. The Life of Harold Williams*. London: Peter Davies.
Wallace, G. L. 2008. Neuropsychological studies of savant skills: Can they inform the neuroscience of giftedness? *Roeper Review*, 30. 229–246.
Wilkman, M.-L. 2006. Trädgårdsmästarens böcker söker nytt hem. *Borgåbladet*, 31.3.2006.
Williams, H. 1893. Vocabulary of the language of Niue (Savage Island). *Journal of the Polynesian Society*, 2/1. 17–24.

Appendix 1: List of polyglots

#	Name	Lifespan	# languages	Profession	Source*
1	Giovanni Pico della Mirandola	1463–1494	Said to have known more than 22 lgs.	Italian scholar. Renaissance philosopher.	D
2	James Crichton	1560–1582	Knew 12 lgs.	Scottish musician, sportsman and linguist; (gift for perfect recall).	D
3	Tom Coryat	1577–1617	5+ probably a dozen other lgs	British writer and traveller	P
4	Comenius (Jan Amos Comensky)	1592–1670	Said to have translated his own book into 15 lgs.	Moravian linguist.	D
5	Wojciech Bobowski/ Ali Ufki	1610–1675	Spoke 16 lgs.	Polish dragoman at the court of the Ottoman sultan.	D
6	Sir William Jones	1746–1794	12+ Reported to speak 41 lgs. 28 lgs	British philologist.	B D P
7	Thomas Young	1773–1829	12+	British scientist.	B
8	Giuseppe Mezzofanti	1774–1849	Fluent in 38 lgs., 50 dialects. -"-. 12+ 30	Catholic cardinal.	A H D B P
9	Dic Aberdaron	1780–1843	Reputed to have taught himself 14 lgs.	Welsh linguist.	D
10	Sandor Körsösi Csoma	1784–1842	12+ Could read in 17 lgs.	Hungarian philologist. Hungarian scholar.	B D
11	Rasmus Christian Rask	1787–1832	Could read in 35 lgs.	Danish philologist.	D
12	Jean-François Champollion	1790–1832	12+ Mastered at least 13 lgs.	French egyptologist.	B D

#	Name	Lifespan	# languages	Profession	Source*
13	Sir John Bowring	1792–1872	12+ "In truth knew only" 15 lgs., instrumental knowledge of 35 dialects.	Brittish M.P.	B D
14	George Henry Borrow	1803–1881	Had studied 42 lgs.	British author and traveller (had obsessive-compulsive disorder).	P
15	Hans Conon von der Gabelentz	1807–1874	Described 80 languages. Fluent in 80 lgs (!)	German linguist.	A D
16	Elihu Burritt	1810–1879	Could read 50 languages	American Blacksmith.	P
17	Sir Richard Francis Burton	1821–1890	12+ Spoke 29 lgs. and "countless" dialects.	British explorer, orientalist.	B D
18	Heinrich Schliemann	1822–1890	"Was familiar with" 12 lgs.	German archeologist.	D
19	Joshua Chamberlain	1828–1914	Spoke 10 lgs.	Union army officer during the American Civil War.	D
20	George Sauerwein	1831–1904	Could read, write and speak 60 lgs. Spoke more than 50 lgs.	Publicist, poet, linguist. German linguist.	A D
21	Ármin Vámbéry	1832–1913	12+ Spoke 16 lgs.	Hungarian orientalist. Hungarian linguist.	B F
22	L. L. Zamenhof	1859–1917	Knew 13 lgs.	Eye doctor, philologist and initiator of Esperanto.	D
23	José Rizal	1861–1896	Said to have known 22 lgs.	Philippin eye surgeon and "hero".	D

#	Name	Lifespan	# languages	Profession	Source*
24	Emil Krebs	1867–1930	Perfectly fluent in 68 lgs.; studied 120 others. Fluent in more than 60 lgs. Fluent in 68 lgs, understood more than 50 others. Comments on these with a list of 35 lgs. known to him in 1914.	German diplomat, interpreter, translator, intelligence service.	A C (brain analysis) D L S (life history)
25	Harold Williams	1876–1928	12+ Fluent in 58 lgs. and many dialects.	New Zealandish journalist.	B E Q
26	James Joyce	1882–1941	Knew 13 lgs.	Irish writer.	D
27	Fan S. Noli	1882–1965	Spoke 14 lgs.	Albanian writer, Bishop, Prime Minister.	D
28	Andrzej Gawroński	1885–1827	Spoke and wrote in 40 lgs., understood and could read in about 100.	Polish linguist.	D
29	Alejandro Xul Solar	1887–1963	Spoke 12 lgs.	Argentinian artist.	S
30	Francis Sommer	1890–1978	Fluent in 94 lgs.	Born in Germany. Research librarian, U.S.	D
31	J.R.R. Tolkien	1892–1973	Knew some 13 lgs.	British writer; philologist of ancient Germanic languages, specializing in Old English.	D
32	Georges Dumézil	1898–1986	Knew up to 40 lgs.	French philologist.	D
33	William James Sidis	1898–1944	Knew about 40 lgs.	"Child prodigy."	D

An initial characterization on the basis of multiple anecdotal accounts — 235

#	Name	Lifespan	# languages	Profession	Source*
34	Paul Robeson	1898–1976	Conversant in over 20 lgs.	American actor, athlete, singer, writer and political and civil rights activist.	D
35	Mario Pei	1901–1978	Fluent in 5 lgs., capable of speaking 30 others.	Italian-American linguist.	D
36	Pent Nurmekund	1906–1996	12+ Could translate from about 70 lgs.	Estonian Linguist.	B L
37	João Guimarães Rosa	1908–1967	Spoke more than 12 lgs. fluently, read 18 lgs.	Brazilian writer.	D
38	André Martinet	1908–1999	Spoke 12 lgs.	French linguist.	D
39	Uku Masing	1909–1985	Spoke 65 lgs, translated from 20 lgs.	Estonian philosopher, translator, theologian, folklorist. Estonian linguist.	A D
40	Kató Lomb	1909–2003	Fluent in 9–10 lgs., translated from 6, read a further 11, "earned money with 16 lgs." Spoke 17 lgs, could read in 11 further lgs.	Hungarian translator and interpreter.	D R (polyglot as a lg learner)
41	Géza Képes	1909–1989	Understood 25 lgs.	Hungarian poet, translator.	D
42	Eugen M. Czerniawski	1912–?	Can translate from 40 lgs., speaks 30 of them fluently.	Ukrainian engineer, later translator and teacher.	L
43	Michel Thomas	1914–2005	Spoke at least 10 lgs.	Polish born linguist.	D
44	Anthony Burgess	1917–1993	Spoke 13 lgs. well or fluently.	English writer.	D

#	Name	Lifespan	# languages	Profession	Source*
45	Ferenc Kemény	1917–2008	Understood 40 lgs., wrote in 24 out of them, spoke 12 out of them.	Hungarian translator.	D
46	Erik Gunnemark	1917–2007	Translated from 47 lgs., spoke 6 lgs. fluently, and approximately 7 at an advanced level + 15 at a "mini-level".	Swedish translator and author.	T
47	Pope John Paul II	1920–2005	Learnt 11 lgs. during his lifetime.	Former pope.	D
48	Narasimha Rao	1921–2004	12+. Fluent in 4 lgs., could read and write 17 lgs.	Indian politician. -"- and Prime Minister.	B F
49	Steven Wurm	1922–2001	Working knowledge of around 50 lgs.	Australian linguist.	I
50	Hansrudi Schaffter	1922–2002	Knew 6 lgs.	Swiss clerk, translator, interpreter, restaurateur.	M (life history)
51	Lajos Kada	1924–2001	Spoke at least 10 lgs.	Hungarian Archbishop.	D
52	Alexander Schwartz	1926–	Translates from 31 lgs.	Translater at the UN 1962–1986.	K (autobiography)
53	Otto Back	1926–	Understands written texts in 25 lgs.	Austrian linguist.	M (life history)
54	Herbert Pilch	1927–	Speaks more than 11 lgs.	German scholar.	D
55	Pope Benedict XVI	1927–	Speaks at least 10 lgs.	Present pope.	D
56	Niels Ege	1927–2003	Translated into 6 lgs, interpreted from 15 lgs, knew 5 further lgs.	Danish translator.	D

#	Name	Lifespan	# languages	Profession	Source*
57	Robert Stiller	1928–	Speaks about 60 lgs.	Polish writer, translator and editor.	D
58	Donald Kenrick	1930–	12+ Translates from over 60 lgs, speaks about 30 of them, mostly fluently. Speaks about 30 lgs, reads a further 25 lgs.	British linguist.	B J
59	Barry Farber	1930–	Speaks more than 25 lgs.	Radio talk show host.	S
60	Jean van Yzendoorn	1932–2015	Knew at least 12 lgs.	Language consultant at larger company in the iron branch.	M (life history)
61	Derick Herning	1932–	Knew 22 lgs.; "victory in the first 'Polyglot of Europe' contest" 1990.	From the Shetland Islands.	E
62	Esteban Tollinchi Camacho	1932–2005	Knew 11 lgs.	Puertorican "humanist".	S
63	Pertti Laakso	1934–	Knows at least 14 lgs.	Diplomat.	M (life history)
64	Kenneth Hale	1934–2001	Knew over 50 lgs.	U.S. linguist.	A D
65	Jacques Berg	1935–	Speaks 11 lgs.	French historian and linguist, writer.	D
66	Rolf Theil Endresen	1946–	Knows over 50 lgs.	Norwegian linguist.	D
67	István Dabi	1943–	Fluent in 9 lgs, Translates from 103 lgs. (20 without a dictionary). Knew 18 lgs. at age 18.	Hungarian translator.	A D
68	Sam Sloan	1944–	Speaks or understands 15 lgs.	U.S. chess player.	D

#	Name	Lifespan	# languages	Profession	Source*
69	Greger Granwik	1945–	Knows 6 lgs.	"Adventurer".	M (life history)
70	Carlos do Amaral Freire	1933–	Can communicate in 30 lgs., but can translate, read and write in others; studied more than a hundred; studies 2 new lgs. each year. -"-.	Brazilian translator.	F D U
71	Ivan Argüelles	1939–	14 lgs.	Mexican-American poet.	
72	Leofranc Holford-Strevens	1946–	Knows 40 lgs.	British classicist, editor at the OUP.	D Web-page
73	Arvo Juutilainen	1949–	Can read 100 lgs. Speaks about 15 lgs. more or less fluently, can read nearly 90; knows the vocabulary of at least 50 other lgs. thanks to a photographic memory.	Finnish former. gardener and bibliophile. Received the Unelmien Helsinki award from Helsinki City library in 2001.	G L Helsinki City Webpage.
74	Ziad Fazah	1954–	Speaks 60 lgs. Speaks, reads and understands 58 lgs., most of which he learned before age 20. Speaks 63 lgs.; failure at showing evidence of this.	Guinness: "greatest polyglot" Born in Liberia, raised in Lebanon, lives in Brazil since the 1970s.	A F D P
75	Eva Toulouze	1956–	Speaks or understands 11 lgs.	French academic.	D
76	C.J.	1958–	6 lgs.	U.S. university student.	N (experimental study)
77	Helen Abadzi	1950s–	19 lgs.	Born in Greece, a world bank consultant, interpreter.	P

#	Name	Lifespan	# languages	Profession	Source*
78	Johan Vandewalle	1960–	22 lgs.	Belgian linguist and Civil Engineer Architect.	P
79	Christopher Taylor	1962–	Can read, write and communicate in 15–20 lgs.	British autistic savant.	O
80	Michael Everson	1963–	14 lgs.	Linguist, expert in writing systems in the world.	D
81	Gregg Cox	1963–	64 lgs. (explicitly denied by himself), speaking 14 lgs. fluently.	American, dictionary work.	P
82	Alexander Arguelles	1964–	Can read 38 lgs. (according to his personal web page).	American specialist in foreign languages.	P
83	Graham Cansdale	1965–	22 lgs.	British translator.	P
84	Edgardo Donovan	1974–	Speaks, writes, reads, and understands 9 lgs and 21 related dialects. Speaks, reads and understands 30 lgs, has been officially tested in 8 of them.	American/Italian Webdesigner,, officer, cryptologic linguist	D U
85	Daniel Tammet	1979–	Knows 11 lgs. Learns lgs rapidly.	British high-functioning autistic savant.	A V
86	H.K. Freher	?	Said to have known 36 lgs.	Linguist and singer.	D H
87	Taneda Teruyoto	?	Speaks 20 lgs.	Japanese interpreter, leader of a conference centre.	D
88	Otto Back	?	Speaks at least 10 lgs.	Director of a translators college.	D
89	Mariano Lavid	?	Knows 9 lgs.	Translator.	D

#	Name	Lifespan	# languages	Profession	Source*
90	Gideon Dienes	?	Speaks 11 lgs.	Hungarian consultant.	D
91	Aleksandr Naumenko	?	Speaks 8 lgs, translates from 4 further lgs.	Russian translator.	D
92	Andrew Sugár	?	Speaks 10 lgs, understands 6 more.	Hungarian translator	D
93	Javier Alejandro Díaz Cataño	?	Speaks 14 lgs.	Mexican university teacher and writer.	S
94	Jorge Fernández C	?	Speaks 12 lgs.	Peruvian university teacher.	S

* The source column refers through capital letters to published work and web sites where the individual names are mentioned. Several of these sources include further reference to other work. A legend for the letters is given below. For further bibliographic detail, see reference list of the present chapter.

A = Wikipedia under the term 'polyglot'
B = Wikipedia under the term 'multilingual'
C = Amunts, Schleicher, and Zilles (2004)
D = Wikipedia under 'List of polyglots'
E = Baker and Prys Jones (1997)
F = Wikipedia (Answers.com)
G = Wilkman (2006)
H = Russell (1858 [2013])
I = Academy of the Humanities – Fellows of the Academy Obituaries 2001
J = Gunnemark (2000)
K = Schwartz (2003),
L = Gunnemark (2006)
M = Laurén (2006)
N = Novoa et al. (1988)
O = Smith and Tsimpli (1995)
P = Erard (2012)
Q = The New Zealand Edge
R = Krashen and Kiss (1996)
S = Wikipedia under 'Barry Farber'
T = personal communication, Erik & Dan Gunnemark
U = www.Eddie.Donovan.com
V = Tammet (2006)

Kenneth Hyltenstam
8 The exceptional ability of polyglots to achieve high-level proficiency in numerous languages

1 Introduction

Polyglots have only minimally been the focus of systematic research, even though the existence of exceptionally multilingual individuals is well attested anecdotally, as we saw in the previous chapter (Hyltenstam this volume a). The present chapter reviews and discusses existing studies of polyglots and goes into some depth in accounting for the widely varying theoretical approaches that have been employed in this research. The four studies that will be reviewed have focused on very different aspects of the topic of polyglotism. The first one (Novoa, Fein, and Obler 1988) looks at the neuropsychological and linguistic behaviour of a young man who before the age of 30 already mastered six languages. The second study (Amunts, Schleicher, and Zilles 2004) employs current brain scanning methods to analyze the cytoarchitecture of language areas in the dominant hemisphere and their right hemisphere homologue in a polyglot who was said to speak more than 30 languages during his lifetime. The two remaining cases concern polyglots who are also savants and diagnosed within the autism spectrum, in one of the cases combined with synaesthesia (definitions and explanations will be given below) (Baron-Cohen, Bor, Billington, Asher, Wheelwright, and Ashwin 2007; Smith and Tsimpli 1995). Our focus in this chapter in relation to these last cases is what the cognitive qualities of their conditions have to say about the heightened language learning abilities that can be seen in polyglots in general.

After the individual studies have been reviewed and discussed, the chapter seeks to provide a comprehensive account of current knowledge about polyglots. On the basis of this knowledge, a proposal regarding directions in future research is presented. The chapter will close with a discussion of how notions central to SLA and bilingualism theory can contribute to the portrayal of polyglots.

Kenneth Hyltenstam, Stockholm University

2 Case studies

2.1 Normally[1] functioning polyglots

2.1.1 CJ – excellence in linguistic form rather than in semantic or conceptual dimensions

Using a case study methodology, Novoa et al. (1988) investigated in exhaustive detail the psychological, cognitive, and linguistic traits of a person who had learnt many languages post puberty. CJ, a 29-year-old male in the U.S., studied French, German, Spanish, and Latin during his high school years. In college he majored in French and spent a year in France at age 20. During that year, he visited Germany briefly and merely listening to German "was enough for him to recover his lost fluency" (p. 295). After graduation, he took up a government position in Morocco and learnt Moroccan Arabic. After that he reactivated his Spanish and learnt Italian "in a 'matter of weeks'" (ibid.). Native listeners to each of his languages confirmed that his abilities in each language were perceived as nativelike.

CJ was given a large battery of neuropsychological tests, a language aptitude test, and tests for visuospatial functions, musical ability, memory, and personality. Among other theoretical considerations, the testing was informed by the Geschwind-Galaburda cluster of neuro-immuno-endocrinological factors linked to non-right-handedness and exceptional abilities (Geschwind and Galaburda 1987). Results showed definite strengths in the acquisition of new codes, fluency and vocabulary access. CJ excelled in formal aspects of language but was average in semantic or conceptual dimensions. On the specific language aptitude test that he was given, the *Modern Language Aptitude Test* (Carroll and Sapon 1959), he scored at or near the ceiling for most components.

It was suggested in the study that CJ's exceptional language ability might be dependent on "a more bilateral organization for language than right-handed males as a group show" and that, in a Geschwind-Galaburda cluster interpretation, this in turn might have been caused by an unusual hormonal environment during the third and fourth month of fetal life, which eventually may result in hypertrophy in areas of the right hemisphere that correspond to certain zones in the left hemisphere. The reason this can occur is the fact that during this

---

1 In line with one kind of practice in research on atypical behaviour and functioning in adults, I allow myself here to use the term "normal" for comparative reasons (cf. Boutcher and Bowler 2008: xvii). Otherwise, the more appropriate term 'the typically developing (TD) population' (cf. Wallace 2008) is employed.

period, the right hemisphere of the fetus develops faster than the left and that, due to the specific hormonal factor, cell migration to the left hemisphere is delayed (Geschwind and Galaburda 1987). CJ's left-handedness and homosexuality, as well as his being a twin, were also discussed as features related to the cluster (Novoa et al. 1988: 300).

The Geschwind-Galaburda framework has not been formally applied in later research on polyglots, except in an online survey conducted by Erard (2012). Responses from nearly 400 people who claimed "to know six or more languages" and who had volunteered to provide information "about their background, their language learning and their cognitive styles" (p. 168) were analysed. A statistically significant higher likelihood of homosexuality than would be predicted was reported. Immune diseases were also reported to a higher extent, but this was not the case for left-handedness and twinning, two other features of the cluster. As the author acknowledges, various caveats were attached to this study, not least of all relating to the problematic nature of the online population in general. At most, we can conclude that these results provide weak support, if any, for the applicability of the neuro-immuno-endocrinological background to polyglotism.

2.1.2 Emil Krebs – an exceptional brain

Amunts et al. (2004) analysed aspects of the inter-hemispheric organization in the brain of a polyglot, Emil Krebs (EK), who lived during the years 1867–1930. The analysis was made possible because his brain was preserved as part of the Vogt collection at the University of Düsseldorf. It is of particular value that EK's life and knowledge of languages has been reasonably well documented in published sources, i.e. articles and books by his contemporaries, among them colleagues and other people who had come into contact with him in a variety of situations. All this information is summarized in Matzat (2007). Before reporting the results of the study of EK's brain, a few notes will be presented about his background. This first section is, indeed, parallel to the anecdotally based life histories presented in chapter 7 (Hyltenstam this volume a).

Around age 10, EK, born and raised in Freiburg, had his first experience with a foreign language. He had found a page from an old newspaper and, because it was printed in a language unknown to him, asked his teacher what language it was. The teacher told him it was French and provided the boy with a French dictionary. After a few months, Emil came back to his teacher and "spoke" French. He received some ridicule due to his faulty French pronunciation, but it was apparent that he had figured out much of the grammar of French. He became extremely interested in languages, and in his teens, in addition to the languages he studied at school, Latin and Ancient Greek, EK spent time studying Modern Greek, English, Italian, Spanish, Russian, Polish, Arabic, and Turkish, all on his own. After school, he opted for a career as interpreter and learned Chinese. From documents that have been preserved, it is known that he received his diploma from the Seminar for Oriental languages, Berlin, in 1890. His own goal was to take up his profession as an interpreter in Beijing, but as his knowledge of Turkish was considered sufficient for him to receive his diploma also in that language, the German Foreign Department nearly sent him to Constantinople instead of to China. However, he ultimately began his career in China in 1893, and over the years his excellent knowledge of Chinese was a matter of much commentary. It was claimed that the Chinese widow empress considered him to be "the best speaker of Chinese among the foreigners" (Matzat 2007: 9). In particular, his pronunciation was apparently regarded as excellent.

During his time in China, EK continued to learn new languages from books and through contact with other foreigners in Beijing. His learning of new languages was said to be very rapid; for example, one of his younger colleagues, Werner Otto von Hentig, who came as a young attaché to Beijing, claimed that EK spent approximately ten weeks learning Armenian, "but then he really knew it" (von Hentig 1962: 33). By 1912, at the age of 45, he was said to speak 32 languages fluently.[2]

EK left China in 1917 in connection with China's cancellation of the diplomatic relations with the German "Reich". He spent the last part of his life in continuous negotiations for adequate employment. He had aspirations for an academic career and asked the new professor of Sinology at the University of Berlin, Otto Franke, with whom he had been a student of Chinese, whether he could not be employed as a "Dozent" and suggested that he could teach Japanese, Tibetan, Chinese, and Mongolian there. Professor Franke recognized EK's adequate level of knowledge but declined to secure him an appointment because of serious apprehensions about "die Person des Herrn Krebs", that is, 'Mr Krebs' personality' (Matzat 2007: 13). The employment that he eventually obtained was at a cipher office of the Foreign Department, where he, among

---

[2] Different sources give varying information about how many languages Krebs maximally knew. Numbers range from 50 to 100. His widow claimed soon after his death that the number was 68. In 1914, EK himself produced a list of languages that he could translate into German. This list comprised 33 languages. He also listed the languages that he knew well enough to "correctly" translate from German into these languages: English, French, Italian, Spanish, Russian, Hungarian, Chinese, and Finnish (Matzat 2007: 17).

other duties, translated letters to the state administration and other documents. These obstacles in finding appropriate employment may be understood in relation to other comments on EK's lack of social sensitivity. The many authors of books and articles who commented on his linguistic exceptionality also mention some aspects of his social behaviour. One often repeated characteristic was his uncommunicativeness; for instance, in her memoirs his sister-in-law, Toni Deneke (1965), called him "a learned fellow who kept silent in 45 languages". Deneke, however, also commented that EK was always friendly when interrupted in his language studies but that he was absent-minded (Matzat 2007: 16). This friendliness was not precisely what struck von Hentig (1962), who wrote that "[c]ommunication with Krebs was difficult". EK would return a friendly greeting with phrases such as "What do you want? Leave me alone" or shout "Go to hell!" when disturbed in his afternoon nap (von Hentig 1962: 34).

EK continued to learn new languages over his entire lifespan. He was equally interested in grammatical, phonological, stylistic, lexical, and idiomatic aspects of the languages, but not in the literature of those languages. He spent many hours every day learning new languages and continuously repeated the languages he had already learned. The languages he chose to learn were often closely related, so, for example, after he learnt Russian, he continued with Old Slavic and the other Slavic languages. The same also held true for his study of Chinese and its various historical developments and the modern Sino-Tibetan languages (Matzat 2007: 19). He was not a linguist, however, in the sense of one who takes a scientific interest or even a metalinguistic interest in language. He was not interested in the comparative linguistics of his time and did not write anything about languages.

EK was sufficiently well known for his extraordinary language abilities, as shown by his ability to attract the interest of both the general public of his time and the scientific community. Professor Oscar Vogt at the Kaiser Wilhelm Institute for Brain Research in Berlin obtained permission from his widow the same day that EK died to use his brain for scientific research. Professor Vogt wrote a report for the family after having analysed the brain stating that "it showed no abnormalities whatsoever, but was a particularly well developed, clear and well-organized brain, most similar to that of a mathematician" (my translation from German) (Matzat 2007: 16). In another work (von Häntig 1962), it is claimed that Vogt had indicated that there was an astonishing special development of the language centre of EK's brain.

While the worth of these observations from the 1930s along these lines is debatable, EK's brain was more recently made available for advanced techniques from observer-independent brain analysis (Amunts et al. 2004). The study analysed EK's brain and compared it to 11 male control brains from the body donor programme of the University of Düsseldorf. The cytoarchitecture of Broca's region and its right hemisphere homologue, also known as Brodmann's (1909) areas BA 44 and 45 in each hemisphere, were examined. Furthermore, as an internal control, the visual area BA 18 was studied in all the brains.

It has been well established that Broca's area is specifically involved in grammatical and phonological processing. The role of the right homologue of Broca's region for language processing has been the focus of intense research interest over the last two or three decades. It is now clear that it is essential for affective aspects of prosody, discourse, interpretation of metaphors, and other aspects of non-literal meaning such as jokes, idiomatic expressions, etc. (for a summary of empirical research, see Paradis 2004: 15ff). It is also well established that these areas of the cortex exhibit an inter-hemispheric asymmetry in terms of cytoarchitectonic differences that is held to mirror language dominance (Geschwind and Galaburda 1987).

The analysis carried out by Amunts et al. (2004) concerned the laminar distribution of cell bodies in the cortex. A vertical incision of the cortex exhibits variation in cytoarchitecture, i.e. different layers have different densities of cell bodies and contain different types of cells. Generally accepted anatomic models refer to these layers as layers I–VI. The proportion of cortical volume occupied by cell bodies in the different layers was estimated by a measure of the grey level index, GLI, producing a profile running from the border between layers I and II vertically to the cortex/white matter border. These profiles were the basic units of comparison between brains. Without delving into great detail in the multifaceted analysis that was conducted, which included multivariate statistical measures, it is important to understand that one measure, Mahalanobis distances, provides information about shape differences between profiles from the 12 brains. In each brain, silver-stained for cell bodies, five to ten profiles were taken from each of the three sections in each of the areas BA 44 and 45 from both hemispheres (and similarly for BA 18, it must be assumed, although it was not mentioned explicitly). Another measure, Euclidian distances, provides a measure of the cytoarchitectonic dissimilarity between corresponding areas of the two hemispheres for each brain. This level of dissimilarity was then contrasted between the investigated brains.

The results showed generally that the cytoarchitecture of EK's brain was different from all the control brains in both hemispheres. The difference was significant for both left and right BA 44 and for right BA 45. Comparing the analysis of BA 18, the visual area, there were no significant differences between EK's brain and the controls. In terms of the measure of inter-hemispheric asymmetry, EK's brain also differed from the controls in two ways. The left and right areas of BA 44 were more symmetrical in EK's brain than they were in all the other brains; in fact, there was a minimal difference between the two hemispheres, while the left and right areas of BA 45 were more asymmetrical than in any of the controls. The combination of symmetry for BA 44 and asymmetry for BA 45 was unique for EK's brain.

The authors concluded that the specific cytoarchitectonic arrangement in EK's brain was "presumably caused by local differences in connectivity" (p. 350), i.e. in how nerve cells connect to each other through dendrites and axons, which mirrors memory/learning. This finding would reflect a density of connections specifically in Broca's region. The finding of differences in symmetry pattern is in line with results from other studies of cerebral organization in individuals with exceptional abilities (for music, mathematics, etc.). The authors speculated that since the asymmetry of BA 45 was mainly due to a special cytoarchitecture of the right hemisphere BA 45, this might be correlated with EK's well-documented proficiency in the pronunciation of languages with very different prosody from that of his first language, German. It was also speculated that this was related to his special abilities related to discourse, metaphors, and figurative meanings, all, as mentioned above, right brain-dependent phenomena, which was also documented, especially in his performance in Chinese.

2.2 Savants

2.2.1 Daniel Tammet – exceptionality in language acquisition and mathematical calculations

Daniel Tammet (DT) (1979–), a high-functioning autistic savant, was born as the first son of nine children in a British working-class family. His savant abilities consist of mathematical calculations, calendrical calculations, and language acquisition. In a matter of seconds, he can multiply six-digit numbers and tell the day of the week for a specific date of any year. He holds the European championship for memorizing Pi (conventionally abbreviated as 3.14) to 22,514 decimal places, which took him five hours and nine minutes to recite (and three months to learn). He has mastered 11 languages, including Mänti, which is a language of his own creation based primarily on Estonian and Finnish. He learnt Icelandic in a week and was then subject to public testing of his achievement in a television interview in Icelandic, where he amazed the viewers in being able to converse freely with the interviewer.

At the age of four years, DT had a massive epileptic seizure and was diagnosed with temporal lobe epilepsy. He was treated with anti-seizure medication for three years, which seems to have prevented further fits, as the seizures have never recurred (Tammet 2006: 38ff). DT was diagnosed with Asperger Syndrome (AS), a condition within the autism spectrum, parallel to high-functioning autism, according to some authors (e.g. Fitzgerald 2004).[3] In addition, he has synaesthesia, implying, in his case, that he sees numbers in colours, as well as in three-dimensional shapes and textures. He also sees some words as having colour.

DT is the author of two books: *Born on a Blue Day* (Tammet 2006) is his autobiography and has been translated into 18 languages; in *Embracing the Wide Sky* (Tammet 2009), he reflects on research on autism and the savant syndrome, and links this scientific knowledge to his own experiences. He has appeared in famous television shows (*Late Show with David Letterman*, *ABC News*, *60 Minutes*, and *Good Morning America*) and was featured in the award-winning film *Brainman*. Interviews with him have been published in the larger dailies and weekly magazines all over the world (*Times*, *Guardian*, *Telegraph*, *Independent*, *New York Times*, *International Herald Tribune*, *The Advocate*, *Der Spiegel*, *Le Monde*, and *Dagens Nyheter*). This coverage has resulted in very detailed information about him on the Internet. He has also participated in scientific research conducted by Simon Baron-Cohen and colleagues, and it is from this work that the bulk of the remaining description of his case is drawn.

DT was 26 years old at the time of testing. His self-reported synaesthesia was first confirmed using *The Test of Genuineness-Revised* (Asher, Aitken, Farooqi, Kurmani, and Baron-Cohen 2006). In order to be diagnosed with synaesthesia, a consistency between the individual stimulus and the perception in the "other" mode is a requirement, and DT's degree of consistency was over 90 %. He was diagnosed with AS through two tests. He scored 39 on *The Autism Spectrum Quotient* (Baron-Cohen, Wheelwright, Skinner, Martin, and Clubley 2001), which should be compared to the mean of 35.8 among people with AS and the mean of 16.3 among controls. On *The Empathy Quotient* (Baron-Cohen and Wheelwright 2004), he scored 8 out of a maximum of 80; the mean for people with AS is 20.4 and for controls 45.3.

Furthermore, the researchers used *The Adult Asperger Assessment* (Baron-Cohen, Wheelwright, Robinson, and Woodbury-Smith 2005), which covers the individual's developmental history. Information was given by both DT and his mother. On this instrument, he scored positively on 13 out of a maximum of 18

---

[3] "The differentiation between high-functioning autism and Asperger's syndrome has never been achieved scientifically ... Indeed, Asperger's syndrome is often used as a synonym for high-functioning autism" (Fitzgerald 2004: 12). In the 2013 fifth edition of the Diagnostic and Statistical Manual of Mental Disorders (DSM-5), Asperger's syndrome was eliminated as a diagnosis and included in the autism spectrum disorder (ASD) (see next section).

symptoms. AS is diagnosed if at least 10 symptoms are confirmed. DT's *social difficulties* throughout his development can be exemplified with a lack of friends at school, and the fact that he taught himself eye-contact only at the age of 13 after his mother had suggested to him "to look at others' eyes and not his own feet" (Baron-Cohen, Bor, Billington, Asher, Wheelwright, and Ashwin 2007: 247). He also has a tendency to take things literally and reports that others have told him that he does not notice when somebody is upset. His *obsessions* include strict routines (for example, eating exactly 45 grams of porridge for breakfast every day) and organization (at childhood he had a library at home with a strict alphabetic catalogue).

DT was also given *The Systemizing Quotient* (Baron-Cohen, Richler, Bisarya, Gurunathan, and Wheelwright 2003). His score was 50 out of 80 against the mean of 35.9 for people with AS and 27.2 for controls. This means that his systemizing ability (see below) is far above average. On a standard memory test he scored 11.5 on the visual digit span (mean for controls is 6.5) and 6.5 on the spatial span task (5.3 for controls). His memory for faces expressing basic emotions or neutral was clearly below average; his scores were comparable to those of children at ages 6-8 years.

An interesting fact is that DT as an adult has made "an excellent adjustment" socially, which raises the question of whether he would be helped at all by being diagnosed: "This was discussed with him and on balance he decided he would like the diagnosis because it helped him understand his own development" (ibid. 245). DT himself indeed consistently refers to his AS diagnosis from 2005 in most of his interviews and in his own writing after that time, and also on his home page.

The interpretation proposed by Baron-Cohen et al. (2007) is that DT's three conditions – savantism, autism, and synaesthesia – are linked. The authors regard the first of these, savantism, to be an effect of the other two. For synaesthesia, briefly, it is possible to argue that having a dual perceptual system is favourable for mnemonic enhancement. For autism, or the *Autistic Spectrum Cluster* (ASC) in DT's case, two features are of specific interest. First, systemizing, or even hyper-systemizing (Baron-Cohen 2006), is considered to be a core characteristic of ASC. This can help an autistic individual to more easily grasp systematic patterns, for example, in language data or regularities that are necessary for mathematical calculations. Secondly, autism is characterized by an impairment of what has been called the *Theory of Mind* (Frith 1989; Baron-Cohen, Leslie, and Frith 1985), or mindblindness (Baron-Cohen 1995). The notion of Theory of Mind (Premack and Woodruff 1978) refers to "being able to infer the full range of mental states (beliefs, desires, intentions, imagination, emotions) that cause action. In brief, to be able to reflect on the content of one's own and others' minds" (Baron-Cohen 2000: 3). The theory of mind is supposed to be a domain specific module that is activated around age three. The impairment in "mind-reading" ability implicated in autism has the effect that

> whilst the [autistic] person could think with ease about objects in the world, or about facts and patterns in the world, their idea of what another person might be thinking, and especially of what another person might be thinking about them, might be quite limited. A person with mindblindness might spend hours thinking about a favourite topic, becoming lost in the details and going deeply into it, all the while remaining relatively oblivious of how they appear to others or what others think of their behaviour. (Baron-Cohen et al. 2007: 247)

DT as a schoolchild had no understanding of how he appeared to his peers "when he sat on the carpet during story-time, with his eyes tight shut and his fingers in his ears, picturing numbers in his mind and their shapes and colours, whilst the other children looked at each other or at the teacher and listened to the story" (ibid.). In other words, DT's mindblindness may have allowed him to develop savantism.

2.2.2 Christopher Taylor – language as an island of genius

The case of "Christopher", or Christopher Taylor (CT) as he is called by his real name in the media, has been described in various articles and also in one full book-length account (Smith and Tsimpli 1995). He was born in the U.K. in 1962 and was the youngest of five siblings, all of whom are considerably older than himself. CT's savantism is entirely related to language. He is able to read, write, and communicate between 15 and 20 languages, and can also translate, not only between any of these languages and his first language, English, but also between his various L2s, and "can learn a new one in a matter of weeks" (Hermelin 2001: 24). However, on the definition of a person "whose general personality is so severely subnormal, that the patient is incapable of living an independent life" (ibid., citing a 1957 British Royal Commission report, *The Law as It Relates to Mental Illness and Mental Deficiency*), he is mentally handicapped. His incompetencies comprise visuospatial based abilities such as reliably finding one's way around and recognizing faces, difficulty in conserving number, and poor eye-hand coordination resulting in severe difficulties with many everyday tasks, for example, buttoning his clothing and shaving. He lives in a sheltered community, "where he can lead a reasonably normal life, working in the garden, carding wool, watching television and endlessly studying languages" (Smith and Tsimpli 1995: 2). He stays in close contact with his family members, who consistently provide him with support.

CT's mother was 45 years old at the time of his birth and had contracted rubella early during pregnancy. She also had a bad fall late in the pregnancy and a long labour with probable foetal distress, but no certain correlation between these incidences and CT's condition has been medically confirmed. CT was diagnosed as brain-damaged at the age of six weeks and as mentally retarded at the age of two. Books were his main interest at the early age of three, and his family discovered that he could read advertisements in the daily newspaper already at that age. He never had an interest in fairy tales or fiction, generally, but was fascinated by telephone directories, dictionaries, etc. When he was six or seven, his interest extended to technical papers in foreign languages, which were provided to him by his sister. In school a couple of years later, he correctly identified a printed foreign text that his teacher had encountered as Polish, which he had apparently picked up from the speech of his sister's husband.

CT has been intensely studied by the experimental psychologists Neil O'Connor and Beate Hermelin (see e.g. O'Connor and Hermelin 1991; Hermelin 2001), and the linguists Neil Smith and Ianthi-Maria Tsimpli (see Smith and Tsimpli 1995). These sources also account for his institutional medical records. Medical investigations during his childhood suggested hydrocephaly and showed slow EEG waves in the frontal lobes, and at about age 20 he was diagnosed with "severe neurological impairment of his motor co-ordination, amounting to apraxia" (Smith and Tsimpli 1995: 4). An MRI scan[4] around the same time revealed moderate cerebral atrophy, among other things. However, Smith and Tsimpli fail to see any of these conditions as explanation for his enhanced linguistic performance.

CT has never been formally diagnosed with autism or Asperger Syndrome but exhibits many of the typical behavioural features of these conditions (Hermelin 2001: 64): he avoids eye contact; does not show strong emotions; does not spontaneously engage in conversation, especially small talk; does not understand jokes, irony, or metaphors; and has difficulty understanding the concept of "pretend". As a typical example of the latter, Hermelin refers to a situation in which, as a joke, Neil Smith picked up a banana and pretended to phone a friend by putting it to his ear as he said *Hello, hello* into it and asked questions such as *How are you?* "When he asked Christopher what he had been doing the answer was: *Putting a banana to your ear.* Question: *Why was I doing this?* Answer: *I donno.* Normal three year olds do understand such pretend games, but Christopher did not" (ibid. 65).

---

4 MRI = Magnetic resonance imaging.

From a psychological perspective, the most prominent characteristic is the mismatch between CT's verbal and other cognitive abilities. While his performance IQ is relatively low, his verbal IQ is average or above average. His severe mental handicap is reflected in low scores on performance IQ tests administered at different times (compared to the average of 100 in all cases): *Raven's Matrices*: 75 or 76; the performance part of the *Wechler Scale test WISC-R, UK*: 42, 67, 52; the *Columbia Greystone Mental Maturity Scale*, administered at age 29.2: 68, indicating a mental age of 9.2 and an IQ of 56 (ibid.: 4).

In contrast, on the verbal part of the *WISC-R, UK*, he scored 89, 102, and 98 at different times. On a specifically designed multilingual version of the *Peabody Picture Vocabulary Test* administered to CT in his late 20s (O'Connor and Hermelin 1991), he scored 121 for English, 114 for German, 110 for French, and 89 for Spanish. It should be noted that the average of 100 is computed on native speakers of each language. His performance on the *Gollins figures*, where objects and words have to be identified from partial representations of them, showed that he was much better at words than at figures. In a similar experiment where CT's performance was compared to that of 20 controls (including undergraduate and postgraduate linguistics students), CT "was (by far) the worst on object recognition, but second best on word recognition" (Smith and Tsimpli 1995: 9).

CT's linguistic abilities are quite specific in a wide range of areas. We have already noted that CT was an unusually early reader (age 3). At school age, he could correctly spell any English word he was asked to spell. He clearly shows pleasure and delight when he deals with things to do with language and expresses sheer love for foreign languages. Smith and Tsimpli have investigated in great detail his L1 abilities in English, his L2 abilities in a number of languages he has taught himself over the years, his abilities in learning a new language that he has not encountered before, and his skill in translating between languages. I will briefly review their findings in each of these respects.

First of all, the analysis of L1 data from CT suggests that his knowledge of English is entirely comparable to that of other native speakers. His judgments of well-formedness (thousands of judgments over four years of stimulus sentences as 'good' or 'bad') showed that he could competently deal with structures of a wide range: declaratives, passives, negatives, interrogatives, relatives, clefts, pseudo-clefts, agreement, word-order, the use of polarity items, correct choice of preposition, selectional requirements of the predicate, etc. (ibid.: 44). However, some structures that other people would judge as well-formed, CT would object to, for example, topicalization, left-dislocation, extraposition, and centre embeddings. The investigators believe that his reactions to such sentences do not reflect his grammatical competence but rather processing problems or his intellectual deficit. Sentences like *The horse raced past the barn fell* may be outside his capabilities to judge. These also cause processing difficulties for people with average intellectual capacities, as they cannot easily be judged on immediate intuition, but can generally only be assessed after backtracking and arriving at a coherent interpretation.

With reference to second languages, a remarkable feature is that CT is able to pick up languages from any type of source: "listening to the radio, obtaining foreign newspapers, or being formally taught" (Hermelin 2001: 66). In contrast to his first language, his abilities in other languages are selective in that he has astonishing facility with their lexicons and morphology, whereas his syntax remains "far from native-like in any of his second languages" (Smith and Tsimpli 1995: 121) and can be characterized as "basically English with a range of alternative veneers" (ibid.: 122). Smith and Tsimpli characterize his attention to the orthographic form and morphological makeup of words as "bordering on obsession" (p. 81f.).

As part of the study, CT was taught two new languages. One was Berber, which he had no prior knowledge of, but he acquired it with enthusiasm to a similar level to that of languages he had acquired before.[5] The other was 'Epun', a language constructed solely for the experiment. The grammatical structure of Epun was basically within the range of attested languages in a number of respects and had a transparent relation between phonology and orthography. After CT had been taught "normal" structures of Epun for about nine months, some "impossible" features were presented. One example was "the syntax of emphasis", which was expressed by the element *-nog* suffixed to the third word of the sentence (and *-nogin*, if this word happened to be the last word of the sentence, that is, in final position). Based on the hypothesis that CT possessed an "intact, or enhanced language module in association with some impairment of his central, cognitive faculties" (p. 138), it was hypothesized that he should have no specific problems with normally occurring grammatical features but would be unable to acquire the 'alinguistic' structures that were independent of linguistic structure but were presumably attainable with non-linguistic cognitive processes. The results showed clearly that CT could cope with the linguistic structures reasonably well, but was not able to do so at all with the "impossible" structures, despite their being cognitively quite simple.

In terms of translation, Smith and Tsimpli (1995) first note that CT initially attracted attention because of his extraordinary ability to rapidly translate

---

5 On a later occasion, CT was studied while being taught British Sign Language (Morgan, Smith, Tsimpli, and Woll 2002). As interesting as this study is, not least of all with respect to the acquisition of a language with a different mode of expression, we will not go into its results, as they are not critically different from CT's acquisition of other languages.

between different languages. However, with respect to content, his translations never give more than an approximation to the original texts, irrespective of his level of proficiency in the languages. Briefly, his translations are syntactically characterized by heavy influence of his first language, English, and his selection of vocabulary is not context- or content-sensitive. So, for example, when translating the Swedish sentence *Katten spinner i hennes knä* ('The cat purrs on her lap'), he produces *The cat spins in her knee* in English (p. 160). Even in languages that he handles reasonably well morphologically and semantically in overall ability and understanding, his translation abilities do not at all match this level of proficiency: "It seems that once he has accessed a possible item, the recognition process comes to a full stop and he is content with whatever word constitutes a lexical equivalent of the input" (p. 163).

Among the general theoretical conclusions that the authors draw from CT's dissociation of abilities is that it provides strong support for the modularity hypothesis in linguistics (first proposed by Fodor 1983). In this respect, CT, along with many cases of William Syndrome children that have been investigated, provides evidence that it is possible to master many of the complexities of natural languages and at the same time lack ability in cognitively simple tasks. Furthermore, CT's asymmetric treatment of lexical and syntactic aspects of language provides support for linguistic theories that treat these as separate. The conclusions for second language acquisition that Smith and Tsimpli (1995) draw are in regard to the phenomenon of transfer, especially from the L1. In the data from CT, not merely in translation but also in speaking and making judgments about correctness, or grammatical judgments, there is a pervasive evidence of English influence "confirming the suggestion that he has a single dominant grammar – that of his mother tongue – and a phenomenal facility for acquiring the morphology and lexical items of a host of second languages" (p. 191).

3.3 Summary information gained from scientific studies

Many of the observations made on the basis of the unsystematic anecdotal information from life histories and lists of polyglots (Hyltenstam this volume a) are paralleled by the knowledge obtained from the scientific analysis of the four cases. For example, all four cases have added new languages to their repertoire throughout their lifespan, or up to the point at which they were studied, indicating a high level of motivation or specific types of motivation to learn languages. It is clear that language, in fact, is their main interest, or is at least one of them.

More specifically, all four cases can be described as successful language learners in various respects, not least of all in their ability to learn vast amounts of linguistic material in short periods of time. Thus, high levels of language learning aptitude are either confirmed, as in the case of CJ, or implied. More detailed information about verbal ability comes from three of the four cases. CJ's profile includes enhanced levels of acquisition of new codes, fluency, and vocabulary access, and a specific ease with formal aspects of language as compared to semantic and conceptual dimensions. Emil Krebs likewise had a focused interest in grammar, phonology, stylistics, the lexicon, and idiomaticity, and had a particular ease with prosodic features, but was less attracted to the literary function of language. Christopher Taylor had high scores on verbal aspects of various tests and had a specific ease with the lexicon and morphology. In summary, the results obtained from the four cases point to an interpretation that their exceptional abilities are more related to facility with linguistic form than to conceptual aspects or content, something that is also found in the anecdotal accounts. With regard to the aspect of memory, Daniel Tammet's enhanced memory for verbal material is specifically discussed in relation to his synaesthesia. Implicated in this is a high level of linguistic awareness. The typical pattern that polyglots are self-taught language learners is also seen repeatedly in the scientific studies.

The issue of whether the cerebral organization of polyglots is different from that of non-polyglots come to the fore both in the case of Emil Krebs, for whom hemispheric symmetry/asymmetry patterns have been identified, and for CJ, whose polyglot abilities have been linked to a more bilateral organization of language due to the fetal hormone environment. In Daniel Tammet's case, the possibility that his early childhood epileptic seizure had any consequences for his development of savantism and polyglotism has not been discussed in the empirical investigations referred to above, but plays a role in a different theoretical framework in which his case is often referred to, namely, the *Theory of Privileged Access* to lower level sensory information (Snyder 2004). While the Theory of Mind approach, and other approaches within the same family, such as the *Weak Central Coherence Theory* (Frith 1989), the *Enhanced Perceptual Functioning Theory* (Mottron and Burack 2001), and the *Extreme Male Brain Theory of Autism* (Baron-Cohen 2002), arrive at a position where savants, just as people with Asperger's Syndrome or synaesthesia, are seen to have minds that are differently wired from the typically developing brain, Allan Snyder and colleagues have proposed a theory with the opposite view: that there are, in fact, no cerebral differences at the capacity or storage level (see, for example, Snyder and Mitchell 1999). An Australian expert on geniuses, prodigies, and savants, Snyder considers that savants differ from other people only in that they have "privileged access" to lower level sensory information.[6] Whereas

---

6 In arguing for his own theoretical understanding of savantism, Snyder often refers to the case of Daniel Tammet, on the basis of available documentation.

normal perceptual development involves a successive reliance on concepts, savants maintain the ability to perceive sensory details, so to speak, as they appear in the world. The conceptual "filter" for language sounds, for example, is known to be established already at the age of six months, and visual perception is successively coded by the semantic-linguistic development that takes place during early childhood. Preschool children in general cannot draw natural scenes. They cannot "copy" exactly what they see or draw from memory all the details they have seen, but rather draw from a mental scheme. There are examples of savants, however, such as the mentally retarded[7], autistic child Nadia (Selfe 1977), who, at the age of three and a half, was able to "draw natural scenes ... with astonishing life-like perspective and to do so 'spontaneously' without any training" (Snyder and Mitchell 1999: 587). Snyder refers to cases where "privileged access" rather than having a developmental cause has been acquired through either external reasons, such as accidents, or internal reasons, such as dementia, as was mentioned above. In fact, Snyder and his team have shown that when temporarily simulating such brain impairment in healthy people by the technique of low frequency repetitive transcranial magnetic stimulation (rTMS), significant stylistic change in drawing and also enhanced proofreading ability were achieved (Snyder, Mulcahy, Taylor, Mitchell, Sachdev, and Gandevia 2003). This in turn invokes a link between DT's epileptic seizure and what was mysteriously called "an explosion of the brain" in one of the life story cases referred to in chapter 7, that of Harold Williams (Hyltenstam this volume a).

Nevertheless, much of the information comes from research on savant/autistic polyglots such as DT and CT. The status of Emil Krebs in this dimension can only be speculated on, but there are certainly aspects of it that have been commented on by authors who had first-hand experience with him as a person that might point in the direction of high functioning autism (lack of empathy, not engaging in small talk, etc.). The question remains what bearing this has on non-savant and non-autistic polyglots. As in many other areas of behaviour, extreme, or indeed, pathological cases may sharpen our analytical perception of typical cases. On the other hand, it is worth stressing that it is absolutely clear from all the anecdotal evidence that not all polyglots (potentially) have a diagnosis of this kind. Most of them clearly belong to what is called the typically developing (TD)[8] population. An issue to consider, therefore, is to what extent

---

7 In DSM–5 (2013) 'mentally retardation' is replaced with 'intellectual disability'. Around 2010, when Nadia was 42 years of age, she was classified in the group Severe Mental Retardation', with an IQ estimated to be below 40 (Selfe 2011)
8 For this terminology, see e.g. Wallace (2008).

information about savant – and autistic – polyglots is relevant in an account of their non-savant counterparts.

3.3.1 Savantism and autism

It is obvious that those specific skills or talents that are characteristic of savants to various degrees are also seen in the TD population. This is exemplified in what we have seen above concerning polyglots, given that we interpret the extraordinary talent for acquiring or learning foreign languages as one of those skill areas that are typical of savants. In order to discuss these matters further, we need to go through the relevant terminology and theoretical understanding of the relationship between savant skills and giftedness in TD individuals.

The notion of savant (in earlier writings, idiot-savant, a term now impossibly archaic and pejorative) was traditionally reserved for "individuals with disabilities who nevertheless display remarkable skills" (Wallace 2008: 229), or, with another formulation, "a person of low intelligence who possesses an unusually high skill in some mental task like mental arithmetic, remembering dates or numbers or in performing rote tasks at a remarkably high level" (Grossman 1977). The notion of the savant syndrome is currently used for this condition according to a suggestion by Treffert (1989). There are, thus, certain specific areas where individuals with the savant syndrome exhibit extraordinary skills (cf. Selfe 2011: 116):

1. *Mathematics*: Ability to compute highly complicated calculations in a matter of seconds; also including calendar calculation such as, for example what day of the week a certain date fell in a specific year.
2. *Music*: Among others, perfect pitch and ability, without formal training, to perform complex musical compositions after having listened to them only once.
3. *Language and literacy*: Ease in acquisition of foreign languages; hyperlexia, i.e. the ability, starting at a low age of four or before, among children to read complex texts fluently but without obvious understanding of their content.
4. *Spatial and temporal skills*: Ability to judge exact distances and ease in giving precise directions; ability to indicate the exact time without the aid of a clock.
5. *Drawing and art*: Ability to exactly reproduce in drawing or sculpture a visually experienced impression of objects, for children at an age where the TD developing population has no idea of perspective, 3-D, etc.

It is relevant to note that all these skill areas possess high internal structure. This observation has led to the current conclusion that they all rely on rule-based knowledge, which is in stark contrast to earlier thinking that people with the savant syndrome operate exclusively on the basis of an exceptional rote memory (Wallace 2008: 231). In fact, "the very high level of similarity of special abilities all over the world" (Mottron, Dawson, Soulières, Hubert, and Burack 2006: 36) indicates that they share features that are responsive to savant syndrome functioning, something that we will return to below.

It should be noted that the savant syndrome is extremely rare (one in a million of the total population). It has been stated repeatedly that the savant syndrome is often associated with autism, or rather, with what is now termed the *autism spectrum disorder* (ASD).[9,10] As claimed by Mottron et al., "[s]avant abilities may represent the autistic equivalent of what 'expertise' is for non-autistic individuals" (ibid.). Despite the fact that individuals with ASD make up a minor proportion among people with intellectual impairment, as much as 30–50% of those who display savant skills are also diagnosed with ASD (for reviews of varying estimations, see Selfe 2011: 113f.; Wallace 2008: 230).

In discussing the case of Daniel Tammet, reference was made to the Theory of Mind framework. The later theoretical development by Simon Baron-Cohen, the Extreme Male Brain Theory of Autism, or, under another label that focuses on the two central cognitive processes around which the theory is built, the Empathizing/Systemizing Theory, might have a special relevance in the study of polyglots. This theory has been developed over the last two decades, but a similar perspective was actually held by Hans Asperger already in 1944, when he described the condition that carries his name, Asperger Syndrome, in the following way: "the autistic personality is an extreme variant of male intelligence" (cited in Baron-Cohen 2002: 251).[11] Baron-Cohen's theory is based on the observation mentioned above that ASD is unevenly distributed among the sexes. For classical autism, the male-female distribution is 4:1, and in AS it is "at least" 10:1 (Baron-Cohen 2002: 251). The initial empirical behavioural support for the

---

9 *The International Classification of Diseases* of WHO (ICD – 10); *The Diagnostic and Statistical Manual* of the American Psychiatric Association (DSM-5).
10 One of the leading researchers in the field, Simon Baron-Cohen, has expressed concern over the D (disorder) in the acronym ASD, especially for high-functioning individuals, and has instead suggested ASC (Autism Spectrum Cluster).
11 It may not be coincidental that the reasoning along the line of male-female differences was not seriously pursued until more recently considering the taboo status that the topic underwent during decades. With the ascertaining of brain differences on average between males and females, the interest for behavioural consequences may be less controversial today. (See, however, fn. 12.)

idea of an "extreme-male-brain" condition comes from research results indicating a pattern where there is more/less of x (any behavioural feature) in people with ASD than in the average male, and where average differences by TD males and females are significant. In addition, some anatomical features pattern in ways similar to the behavioural measures: AS individuals have a marked tendency, to a greater extent than average males, of having the fourth finger (ring finger) longer than the second, something that distinguishes average males from average women. Males with AS may also exhibit precocious puberty, coexistent with increased levels of testosterone.

Baron-Cohen interprets the behavioural evidence for the extreme male brain theory in terms of the two cognitive processes of empathizing and systemizing. Empathizing is defined as

> the drive to identify another person's emotions and thoughts, and respond to these with an appropriate emotion. Empathising allows you to predict a person's behaviour, and to care about how others feel. (Baron-Cohen 2002: 248)

Systemizing, on the other hand is

> the drive to analyse the variables in a system, to derive the underlying rules that govern the behaviour of a system, and to control it. (ibid.)

Baron-Cohen observes that all humans have both empathizing and systemizing skills. In some individuals these are equally well developed, as their brains are balanced for these dimensions. What he formally calls the 'female brain' is a type where empathizing is more developed than systemizing, and vice versa for the 'male brain'. Importantly, it is underscored that there is no isomorphism between male/female brains and male/female individuals. The only claim is that male brains are represented more frequently in males and vice versa, which is reason enough for Baron-Cohen to use this stereotypical, and maybe still controversial, terminology. The extreme male brain type has hyper-developed systemizing and hypo-developed empathizing: "they might be talented systemizers but at the same time they can be 'mind-blind'" (Baron-Cohen 2002: 249).[12]

---

[12] Baron-Cohen's theory, albeit strongly influential, has certainly not escaped criticism. Such criticism has concerned both conceptual issues, such as how the central notions of empathizing and systemizing can be measured (Andrew, Cooke, and Muncer 2008), and methodological shortcomings and lack of replication of individual studies (Spelke 2005). From a feminist perspective, although not theoretically explicitly so, Fine (2010) is, perhaps, the single most critical attack of the theory.

The heightened systemizing skills in people with AS explain the existence of certain preferences, narrow interests, and behaviours in that all these involve a monitoring of phenomena with an inherent system, phenomena that are analysable and predictable in a clear input-operation-output manner.

2.3.2 Cerebral organization

Judging from what neuroscience has revealed about the brain with respect to second language acquisition and bilingualism/multilingualism over the past few decades, a reasonable hypothesis is that "the polyglot brain" is special in terms of both structure and function compared to brains that have not been exposed to more than one language. With respect to the much more precise question of differences between brains that have experienced the acquisition/learning of just one or two second languages and brains that have coped with acquiring *many* languages, as in polyglots, we do not have much empirical basis for precise hypotheses (see, however, below for a study investigating differences between bilinguals and multilinguals). Research that has been concerned empirically with cerebral structural issues of a true polyglot is limited to the case study by Amunts et al. (2004) that was referred to above. As already mentioned, this study showed two things: first, a different cytoarchitecture of the traditional language areas in the left hemisphere and its right hemisphere homologues and, second, a specific pattern of asymmetry between these areas compared to 11 control brains. The study of CJ, as we saw above, led Novoa et al. (1988) to suggest a more bilateral organization for language in polyglots on a Geschwind-Galaburda theoretical account.

Lacking data from polyglots (in the present sense of individuals proficient in at least six languages in addition to their L1), the obvious way to proceed is to infer from known differences between monolinguals and bilinguals, i.e. individuals who know one and more than one language respectively. As for language and language processing, generally, neuroimaging research has meant a breakthrough in terms of available facts, although certainly, this field is still in its infancy, and results are in many ways merely suggestive (for overviews, see Reiterer 2009; Golestani 2014).

Recent brain scanning research "supports the idea that use of two or more languages changes the brain" (Green 2013). For example, it was shown in a voxel-based morphometry (VBM) study (Mechelli, Crinion, Noppeney, O'Doherty, Ashburner, Frackowiak, and Price 2004) that participants who had learnt a second language had greater grey matter density in the inferior parietal cortex compared to participants who had no or little experience in second language learning.[13] Furthermore, the level of density correlated negatively with age of onset and positively with level of proficiency in the second language. In another study (Grogan, Parker Jones, Ali, Crinion, Orabona, Mechias, Ramsden, Green, and Price 2012), structural magnetic resonance imaging (MRI) and VBM were used to identify the efficiency of word processing in bilinguals (knowing exactly two languages) compared to multilinguals (knowing more than two languages). There were two new findings in this study. First, the multilinguals had higher grey matter density in the right posterior supramarginal gyrus than the bilinguals. Variation in grey matter density in this locality had previously been established to reflect the "sheer number of words known" (ibid: 1352), which, arguably, would be a greater number for multilinguals than for bilinguals. Secondly, grey matter density in the left pars opercularis in the left posterior inferior frontal cortex (i.e. a subregion of the classical Broca's area) was positively correlated with lexical efficiency in second language use as measured by lexical decision accuracy, lexical decision response time, and verbal fluency.[14] It is known from earlier functional studies that activation during lexical retrieval is higher specifically in the left pars opercularis, and the authors therefore see it as a natural interpretation that these increased demands are what drive plastic changes in grey matter density (ibid.).

While some studies have failed to observe white matter differences between monolingual and bilingual/multilingual speakers, such differences have been observed in several studies. Differences have been documented in adult second language users, for example, in the traditional left hemisphere language areas and their right hemisphere homologues, but also in specific sites in the frontal lobes (Schlegel, Rudelson, and Tse 2012).

Whereas it has thus been made clear that experiential facts change the brain structurally, it has likewise been shown that exposure and learning experience change the brain at the functional level. To illustrate, language processing, like other cognitive tasks, is dependent at a functional level on neural networks that are distributed over highly interconnected specific cortical regions (Prat 2011: 635). Individuals differ with respect to network efficiency so that, for some people, more mental resources are consumed in performing a specific task than for others. This can take the form of more spread activation, i.e. activation

---

[13] This can be the effect of neural dendrites growth and/or neurogenesis, both processes that participate in learning (for references, see Golestani 2012).

[14] This was seen only in the bilingual group. The correlation for the multilingual group was not significant. The explanation offered for this difference between the groups is that the measure for lexical efficiency could be tested in the single second language, English, for the bilingual group, while the multilingual group would have had to be tested for lexical proficiency in all their second languages to arrive at an accurate picture.

spread over a wider cortical area, or more intense activation in a certain area. In all, more efficient individuals use more focal activation and also less activation (ibid: 636). Prat, Mason, and Just (2010) carried out a meta-analysis of five neuroimaging investigations of reading comprehension, all based on the earlier established idea that higher skills correspond to increased efficiency. The more skilled readers turned out to be those who had a larger vocabulary size; vocabulary size was actually the best predictor of brain efficiency. Interestingly, where the skilled readers showed reliably less activation was in the right hemisphere homologues of the left hemisphere language regions. These right hemisphere regions are generally more involved in difficult tasks. In summary, this research demonstrates individual differences at the network functional level, which results from differences in experience with particular tasks.

Does this mean that all variation in brain structure and function is a consequence of external factors? Not at all. As Bates, Elman, Johnson, Karmiloff-Smith, Parisi, and Plunkett (1998) state, "[a]ll reasonable scholars today agree that genes and environment interact to determine complex cognitive outcomes" (p. 590). However, although some progress has been made, there are still very few facts about this interaction that can be considered established, as reflected in recent overviews of the field: "avenues for future research include examining the relative contributions of experience-dependent plasticity, and of factors that may be more 'innate'" (Golestani 2014: 27).

Nevertheless, some neuroimaging research concludes that specific brain differences are innate. One example is a study by Golestani, Price, and Scott (2011), who decided to find out whether expert phoneticians had brain structures that differed from age- and gender-matched controls. The results showed more than one type of difference. One type, as could be expected, was clearly experience-dependent, but there was also another difference that "could have existed before the onset of expertise training" (p. 4218). The experience-dependent changes involved the left pars opercularis, which was larger for the phoneticians. Its size was significantly correlated with the amount of phonetic transcription training the phoneticians had undergone. The other structure that was significantly different in the phoneticians and the controls appeared in the left auditory cortex, where the left transverse gyrus had a different and greater morphology. Other studies have shown that the transverse gyrus is anatomically established at the 31st week of gestational age and that its development is stabilized both morphologically and myelogenetically at age seven. Together with the fact that there was no correlation between the number of years of phonetic transcription training and the morphology of the left transverse gyrus, this led the researchers to interpret this morphology as an innate feature that can be favourable for future work in areas where detailed auditory processing is required, as in phonetics.

Another discussion in this area is whether "innate" differences are genetically induced or dependent on specific hormone exposure during fetal life. Regarding genetic causes for variation, specific language impairment (SLI) in children is now often seen as a genetically induced disorder, in contradistinction to earlier proposals, for example, those from the 1970s that hypothesized causes to be inadequate parenting or subtle brain damage (Bishop 2006). However, as Bishop makes clear, there seems to be a complex of causes for SLI, and only in one case of an intensively studied British three-generation family has a specific gene, *FOXP2*, clearly been identified as causal. Brain imaging studies of affected family members have identified abnormalities in the caudate nuclei and cerebellum, as well as in Broca's area. As for prenatal hormone exposure, one example of a well-established fact is the role that the level of testosterone exposure may contribute to differences in empathizing. For example, in one study (Chapman, Baron-Cohen, Auyeung, Knickmeyer, Taylor, and Hackett 2006), levels of testosterone were measured amniotically during the second trimester of pregnancy in 193 mothers. Six years later, their children (100 males and 93 females) were tested for empathizing on two different tests: children's versions of the *Empathy Quotient (EQ-C)* and *"Reading the Mind in the Eyes" Task (Eyes-C)*. The results showed a significant negative correlation between level of prenatal testosterone and empathizing on both measures.

We will conclude this section by briefly addressing two interrelated issues of specific relevance to the question of brain organization in polyglots. First, would the hemispheric asymmetry in language relevant regions observed in the case of Krebs have anything to do with polyglot talent? Secondly, is it likely, and if so, what evidence is there, that the polyglots' talents in language acquisition are based in a pre-existing cerebral organization?

A difference in symmetry pattern between faster and slower phonetic learners was observed by Golestani, Paus, and Zatorre (2002). These researchers trained 59 individuals to distinguish Hindi dental and retroflex sounds and then identified a learning rate score, which was later correlated with measures of white and grey matter values obtained in a VBM study. Results showed a correlation between the rate of phonetic learning and grey and white matter volumes in the parietal lobe of both hemispheres, but the significance was particularly pronounced in the left hemisphere. However, there was no association between learning rate and grey or white matter density in the primary speech areas. There was also a significant relationship between learning rate and the position of the parieto-occipital sulcus in each hemisphere. The location of this sulcus is always more posterior in the left than in the right hemisphere, but this asymmetry turned out to be greater in the fast than in the slow learners. Admittedly, the asymmetries observed in this study are of a different nature compared to those observed in the case of Krebs, but it may be the case that talent for language is related to various kinds of hemispheric asymmetry.

A number of brain imaging studies have identified correlations between variation in brain structure and function and more and less successful language performance, both in a first and a second language, and also in language learning ability. Among the 25 individual studies concerned with brain structural correlates of individual differences in language related performance that were reviewed by Golestani (2014), approximately 80% show differences in brain structure that are correlated to performance in terms of higher/lower rate of processing, level of fluency, size and depth of vocabulary knowledge, efficiency in learning of non-native features, etc., at different linguistic hierarchical levels. In short, these differences can be coupled with talent in language performance. As "brain structure can be assumed to be more stable, or less malleable, than brain function" (p. 1), the reviewer finds it reasonable to believe that several of these differences are more likely to be genetic and heritable rather than experience-dependent. But again, this is an area that is not well understood at present. Even if researchers agree that "genetics and the environment likely interact" (Golestani 2014: 27), a fact that simultaneously complicates the matter and opens up a potentially productive avenue of future research is that "the environment itself is partly selected based on genetically influenced preferences" (ibid.). This would be a reasonable point of departure for disentangling the interaction between innate talent and environmental influence in the development of polyglotism.

3 Summary and blueprint for research on polyglots

First of all, it is essential to keep in mind that information that has been presented here and in the previous chapter (Hyltenstam this volume a) is not generalizable to the entire polyglot population. For those polyglots that were included in the list of 94 cases, the information is anecdotal, and observations about each of the people mentioned there are arbitrary and unsystematic. The four cases for which we have systematic data are highly diverse, and the analyses have been done from varying perspectives. This means that it is impossible to draw conclusions about what applies across the board and what is limited to certain individuals. Yet, the rich, albeit untidy, data that have been presented indicate recurring patterns and features that might be of interest in describing and explaining polyglotism. The observations easily lend themselves to hypotheses on a wide range of issues in the area of polyglotism. We will summarize the most salient features that might have to do with the polyglots' special ability in language learning and language use.

3.1 Motivation

A large proportion of the individuals that appear in the lists have continued to add new languages to their repertoire throughout their lifespans. In some cases, their specific interest in language started as early as between the ages of 7 and 10, but it seems that late childhood or the early teens are the ages when many polyglots refine and develop their language learning exceptionality. This enduring interest in language and language acquisition implies a high degree of *motivation* to learn languages and to repeatedly start on the trajectory of effort that is required to acquire a language. It is important to note that many polyglots seem to exhibit a special pleasure, fascination, or enthusiasm with language. Their *passion with language* leads to an intense preoccupation with studying and repeating linguistic features and structures. Several accounts note that polyglots may spend many hours every day devoted to language learning, and it is claimed that "[a]ll great polyglots agree that they must constantly read or speak or write foreign languages in order to keep them up" (Gunnemark 1996: 318). Motivation is supposed to explain why people opt for certain actions, and how long and how hard they are willing to go on with certain activities (Dörnyei and Skehan 2003: 614). The process-oriented model of motivation proposed by Dörnyei (2000) may be productive for specifying various aspects of motivation. The fact that polyglots often remember a certain occasion when their interest in language and language learning became explicitly manifest, often without any social pressure or influence, may lead to ideas of cognitive-developmental phases that have an impact on their *choice motivation*. Furthermore, what is of specific interest for research on polyglots is that aspect of motivation that leads a learner to a strong commitment to tasks involved in both learning and maintaining a new language (*executive motivation*). A common observation among polyglots is that their success in language learning motivates them to continue on the same track (*motivational retrospection*). The various dimensions of motivation in polyglots are clearly a point worth addressing in future research.

3.2 Learner autonomy

A common observation referred to above is that polyglots are often self-taught and take total responsibility for and control of their own learning. This is possible because they understand what is needed for a successful language acquisition, which in turn allows them to select effective strategies, such as collecting materials of various kinds, putting up regular and systematic time schedules, and creating opportunities for using and practicing what they have learnt in natural communicative settings. The effectiveness of this autonomy and how it is manifested (Little 1991) are issues worth following up further.

3.3 Aptitude

In many cases, it is obvious that the polyglots' language learning/acquisition results in functional, high-level proficiency levels in a relatively brief time. This fact may reasonably be linked to high levels of *language learning aptitude*, as in the case of CJ, which was reviewed above. The notion of *language learning aptitude* can be defined as a "specific talent for learning languages which exhibits considerable variation between learners" (Dörnyei and Skehan 2003: 590). More generally, language aptitude may be taken to mean facility with language in all perspectives, i.e. the storing of language and the receptive and productive processing in both oral and written mode. Linked to language learning or acquisition, then, language aptitude comprises "a conglomerate of different abilities that can assist in the different stages and processes of language learning" (Kormos 2013: 141). A high level of language learning aptitude has been seen as a requirement for near-native proficiency in post-puberty learners (DeKeyser 2000), but may also play a significant role for L2 acquisition in childhood (Abrahamsson and Hyltenstam 2008) and in L1 maintenance among bilingual children living in a L2-dominant social context (Bylund, Abrahamsson, and Hyltenstam 2010). It seems highly probable that polyglots may rely on a high level of language learning aptitude in the acquisition of new languages, and it may also be the case that aptitude plays a role in their productive and receptive maintenance of languages already acquired.

3.4 Language awareness and metalinguistic knowledge

Of particular interest is the fact that several of the polyglots that have been referred to in the literature are *specifically intrigued by linguistic form* and obviously have a high level of *metalinguistic knowledge*, i.e. an explicit academic linguistic knowledge base. This is exhibited particularly in the case of polyglots who construct(ed) their own languages, but more generally in all those who were/are professional linguists, translators, and interpreters. The concern with linguistic form may also to some degree account for the specific patterns we have observed in polyglots' selection of languages to learn, with the presence of both extremes in relation to linguistic distance represented, i.e. closely related as well as totally unrelated languages. Many of the polyglots obviously use their metalinguistic knowledge when learning new languages, i.e. they apply a formal or explicit approach where the studying of grammars and the use of dictionaries are important tools. Even if it may seem to be the case that the majority of polyglots we have reviewed belong to this category, the five cases described by Laurén (2006), according to the analysis, exemplify language learners along a continuum from formal to informal learners (p. 96). This kind of information, at an anecdotal level, points in the direction that the variation between different individuals in this respect may be considerable, and a closer look at the role of language awareness versus metalinguistic knowledge in polyglots' achievements is warranted.

The notion of language awareness has come into focus over the last 30 years as the central idea of a movement for enhancing the teaching of languages, in both first and second/foreign language contexts, through students' and teachers' conscious reflection about language (Hawkins 1984). The Association for Language Awareness (ALA) defines language awareness broadly as "explicit knowledge about language, and conscious perception and sensitivity in language learning, language teaching and language use" (ALA webpage 10 February 2015). This extensive scope comprises cognitive aspects (consciousness, attention, noticing; explicit vs. implicit knowledge and learning), aspects of teaching methodology, aspects of processing (perception and production; reading and writing), and sociocultural aspects (see Svalberg 2007, 2012). For the present purposes, the cognitive aspects of language awareness, drawing on the terms explicit and conscious from the definition, are most important.

3.5 Systemizing and maleness

The interest in knowledge areas that can be formulated in terms of *systems* seems to be a common feature of many of the polyglots reviewed in this chapter. The interest in language as a system in and of itself is maybe one of the most salient features of the group of polyglots. There is, of course, a direct link between this observation and the characteristic feature among polyglots of a developed metalinguistic knowledge that was mentioned above. Coupled with the fact of heavy male dominance among polyglots, and the discussion of systemizing and maleness in those polyglots who are savants or within the ASC, it is clearly of interest to learn to what extent high systemizing ability is a feature of polyglots in general.

Interests outside of language in which systems play a central role, such as mathematics, technology and natural sciences, may also be considered from this perspective. Many of the individuals we have considered here exhibit an encyclopaedic kind of knowledge of various more or less restricted areas of speciality. One instance of this may be the memorization of lists such as timetables for trains, name-days of the almanac, or dates of historical events in specified areas. This may be linked to the existence of extraordinary memory characteristics (photographic or otherwise enhanced). Related to this is also an interest in compiling and systematizing various kinds of facts in taxonomic lists or catalogues, and collections of various kinds.

A feature common to the authorships of polyglot authors Joyce, Tolkien, and Burgess (Hyltenstam this volume a) is the complex compositions of interacting systems of stories, religions, languages, family, and kinship in a swarm of detail. The handling of this complex elaboration of detail is made possible by their constituting interacting systems in and of themselves.

3.6 Cerebral correlates

From the limited data that exist, we may cautiously suggest that the polyglot brain is different in more than one dimension from brains that have experienced the acquisition and use of one or two languages. A line of neurological descriptive research (identifying the nature of observed differences) is illustrated by the study of the cytoarchitecture and hemispheric symmetry patterns in Emil Krebs' brain by Amunts et al. (2004), but a wider range of neuro-scanning methodologies can be predicted to provide many more details on polyglot-specific cerebral structure and function. The causes for the differences, however, if they exist on a systematic level, are still to be identified. The main issue still is to what extent polyglot brains are different because the language learning experience has changed them and to what extent they are differently predisposed for handling linguistic material from the start, i.e. how does the nurture-nature entanglement or complex interact to create cerebral differences? In the case that nature has a significant role, a further question is what is genetic and what is dependent on the hormonal environment of the developing fetus, specifically considering the various theories of prenatal hormone environment and the effect of heightened testosterone levels (Geschwind and Galaburda 1987; Baron-Cohen 2002). We may expect these central questions to be highlighted considerably in the immediate future. New methodologies in neuroscience are currently developing the knowledge bases on language and bilingualism on an unprecedented scale. This holds promise for answers on the issues considered now, and for the formulation of more detailed questions in the future.

Acknowledgements

I would like to gratefully thank Christopher Stroud for comments on this chapter and on chapter 7, particularly for valuable suggestions related to content structuring.

References

Abrahamsson, N. & K. Hyltenstam. 2008. The robustness of aptitude effects in near-native second language acquisition. *Studies in Second Language Acquisition*, 30/4. 481–509.

Abrahamsson, N. & K. Hyltenstam. 2009. Age of onset and nativelikeness in a second language: Listener perception versus linguistic scrutiny. *Language Learning*, 58/2. 249–306.

Amunts, K., A. Schleicher & K. Zilles. 2004. Outstanding language competence and cytoarchitecture in Broca's speech region. *Brain and Language*, 89. 346–353.

Andrew, J., M. Cooke, & S. J. Muncer. 2008. The relationship between empathy and Machiavellianism: An alternative to empathizing–systemizing theory. *Personality and Individual Differences*, 44/5. 1203–1211.

Asher, J., M. R. F. Aitken, N. Farooqi, S. Kurmani, & S. Baron-Cohen. 2006. Diagnosing and phenotyping visual synaesthesia – a preliminary evaluation of the revised test of genuineness (TOG-R). *Cortex*, 42/2. 137–146.

Baron-Cohen, S. 1995. *Mindblindness. An Essay on Autism and Theory of Mind*. Cambridge, MA: MIT Press.

Baron-Cohen, S. 2000. Theory of mind and autism: A fifteen year review. In: S. Baron-Cohen, H. Tager-Flusberg, & D. C. Cohen (eds.), *Understanding Other Minds*. Oxford: Oxford University Press. 3–20.

Baron-Cohen, S. 2002. The extreme male brain theory of autism. *Trends in Cognitive Science*, 6. 248–254.

Baron-Cohen, S. 2006. The hyper-systemising assortative mating theory of autism. *Progress in Neuro-Psychopharmacology and Biological Psychiatry*, 30. 865–872.

Baron-Cohen, S., D. Bor, J. Billington, J. Asher, S. Wheelwright, & C. Ashwin. 2007. Savant memory in a man with colour form-number synaesthesia and Asperger Syndrome. *Journal of Consciousness Studies*, 14/9–10. 237–251.

Baron-Cohen, S., A. M. Leslie, & U. Frith. 1985. Does the autistic child have a 'theory of mind'? *Cognition*, 21/1. 37–46.

Baron-Cohen, S., J. Richler, D. Bisarya, N. Gurunathan, & S. Wheelwright. 2003. The Systemising Quotient (SQ): An investigation of adults with Asperger Syndrome or High Functioning Autism and normal sex differences. *Philosophical Transactions of the Royal Society*, 358. 361–374.

Baron-Cohen, S. & S. Wheelwright. 2004. The Empathy Quotient (EQ): An investigation of adults with Asperger Syndrome or High Functioning Autism, and normal sex differences. *Journal of Autism and Developmental Disorders*, 34. 163–175.

Baron-Cohen, S., S. Wheelwright, J. Robinson, & M. Woodbury-Smith. 2005. The Adult Asperger Assessment (AAA): A diagnostic method. *Journal of Autism and Developmental Disorders*, 35. 807–819.

Baron-Cohen, S., S. Wheelwright, R. Skinner, J. Martin, & E. Clubley. 2001. The Autism Spectrum Quotient (AQ): Evidence from Asperger Syndrome/High Functioning Autism, males and females, scientists and mathematicians. *Journal of Autism and Developmental Disorders*, 31. 5–17.

Bates, E., J. Elman, M. Johnson, A. Karmiloff-Smith, D. Parisi, & K. Plunkett. 1998. Innateness and emergentism. In: W. Bechtel & G. Graham (eds.), *A Companion to Cognitive Science*. Oxford: Basil Blackwell. 590–601.

Bishop, D. V. M. 2006. What causes specific language impairment in children? *Current Directions in Psychological Science*, 15/5. 217–221.

Boucher, J. & D. Bowler. 2008. *Memory in Autism. Theory and Evidence*. Cambridge: Cambridge University Press.

Brodmann, K. 1909. *Vergleichende Lokalisationslehre der Grosshirnrinde in ihren Prinzipien dargestellt auf Grund des Zellenbaues*. Leipzig: Barth. (English translation available by Laurence Garey as *Brodmann's 'Localization in the cerebral cortex'* (1994).

Bylund, E., N. Abrahamsson, & K. Hyltenstam. 2010. The role of language aptitude in first language attrition: The case of pre-pubescent attriters. *Applied Linguistics*, 31/3. 443–464.

Carroll, J. B. & S. Sapon. 1959. *Modern Language Aptitude Test. Form A*. New York: The Psychological Corporation.

Chapman, E., S. Baron-Cohen, B. Auyeung, R. Knickmeyer, K. Taylor, & G. Hackett. 2006. Fetal testosterone and empathy: Evidence from the empathy quotient (EQ) and the "reading the mind in the eyes" test. *Social Neuroscience*, 1/2. 135–148.

DeKeyser, R. M. 2000. The robustness of critical period effects in second language acquisition. *Studies in Second Language Acquisition*, 22/4. 499–533.

Deneke, T. 1965. *Das Testament – Menschenschicksale um das Haus am Frauenplan*. Weimar: Kiepenheuer Verlag.

Dörnyei, Z. 2000. Motivation in action: Towards a process-oriented conceptualisation of student motivation. *British Journal of Educational Psychology*, 70. 519–538.

Dörnyei, Z. & P. Skehan. 2003. Individual differences in second language acquisition. In: C. J. Doughty & M. H. Long (eds.), *Handbook of Second Language Acquisition*. Oxford: Blackwell Publishing. 589–630.

Erard, M. 2012. *Babel No More. The Search for the World's Most Extraordinary Language Learners*. New York: Free Press.

Fine, C. 2010. *Delusions of Gender: How our Minds, Society, and Neurosexism Create Differences*. New York: W. W. Norton & Company.

Fitzgerald, M. 2004. *Autism and Creativity. Is there a Link between Autism in Men and Exceptional Ability?* Hove and New York: Brunner-Routledge.

Fodor, J. 1983. *The Modularity of Mind*. Cambridge, MA: MIT Press.

Frith, U. 1989. *Autism. Explaining the Enigma*. Oxford: Blackwell.

Geschwind, N. & A. M. Galaburda. 1987. *Cerebral Lateralization. Biological Mechanisms, Associations, and Pathology*. Cambridge, MA: MIT Press/Bradford Books.

Gethin, A. & E. V. Gunnemark. 1996. *The Art and Science of Learning Languages*. Oxford: Intellect Ltd.

Golestani, N. 2014. Brain structural correlates of individual differences at low-to high-levels of the language processing hierarchy: A review of new approaches to imaging research. *International Journal of Bilingualism*, 18/1. 6–34.

Golestani, N., T. Paus & R. J. Zatorre. 2002. Anatomical correlates of learning novel speech sounds. *Neuron*, 35. 997–1010.

Golestani, N., C. J. Price, & S. K. Scott. 2011. Born with an ear for dialects? Structural plasticity in the expert phonetician brain. *The Journal of Neuroscience*, 31/11. 4213–4220.

Green, D. W. 2013. Cognitive control for language switching in bilinguals: A quantitative meta-analysis of functional neuroimaging studies. Abstract for oral presentation at University of Reading, GB.

Grogan, A., O. Parker Jones, N. Ali, J. Crinion, S. Orabona, M. L. Mechias, S. Ramsden, D. W. Green, & C. J. Price. 2012. Structural correlates for lexical efficiency and number of languages in non-native speakers of English. *Neuropsychologia*, 50/7. 1347–1352.

Grossman, H. 1977. *Manual on Terminology and Classification in Mental Retardation*. Washington, DC: American Association on Mental Deficiency.

Gunnemark, E. V. 1996. Polyglots. In: A. Gethin & E. V. Gunnemark 1996. *The Art and Science of Learning Languages*. Oxford: Intellect Ltd. 317–319.

Hawkins, E. W. 1984. *Awareness of Language: An Introduction*. Cambridge: Cambridge University Press.

von Hentig, W. O. 1962. *Mein Leben: eine Dienstreise*. Göttingen: Vandenhoeck & Ruprecht.

Hermelin, B. 2001. *Bright Splinters of the Mind*. London: Jessica Kingsley.

Hyltenstam, K. This volume a. The polyglot – an initial characterization on the basis of multiple anecdotal accounts.

Kormos, J. 2013. New conceptualizations of language aptitude in second language attainment. In: G. Granena & M. Long (eds.), *Sensitive Periods, Language Aptitude, and Ultimate Attainment*. Amsterdam: Benjamins. 131–152.

Laurén, C. 2006. *Tidig inlärning av flera språk. Teori och praktik*. Vasa: Vaasan Yliopisto.

Little, D. 1991. *Learner Autonomy 1: Definitions, Issues and Problems*. Dublin: Authentik.

Lomb, K. 2008. *Polyglot. How I Learn Languages*. Berkeley: TESL-EJ.

Matzat, W. 2007. *Das „Sprachwunder". Emil Krebs. Dolmetscher in Peking und Tsingtau. Eine Lebensskizze*. Creative Commons. (www.tsingtau.org)

Mechelli, A., J. T. Crinion, U. Noppeney, J. O'Doherty, J. Ashburner, R. S. Frackowiak, & C. J. Price. 2004. Neurolinguistics: Structural plasticity in the bilingual brain. *Nature*, 431. 757.

Morgan, G., N. V. Smith, I. M. Tsimpli, & B. Woll. 2002. Language against the odds: The learning of BSL by a polyglot savant. *Journal of Linguistics*, 38. 1–41.

Mottron, L. & J. A. Burack. 2001. Enhanced perceptual functioning in the development of autism. In: J. A. Burack, T. Charman, N. Yirmiya, & P. R. Zelaso (eds.), *The Development of Autism: Perspectives from Theory and Research*. Mahwah, NJ: Erlbaum. 131–148.

Mottron, L., M. Dawson, I. Soulières, B. Hubert, & J. Burack, J. 2006. Enhanced perceptual functioning in autism: An update and eight principles of autistic perception. *Journal of Autism and Developmental Disorders*, 36/1. 27–41.

Novoa, L., D. Fein & L. K. Obler. 1988. Talent in foreign languages: A case study. In: L. K. Obler & D. Fein (eds.), *The Exceptional Brain: Neuropsychology of Talent and Special Abilities*. New York: Guilford Press. 294–302.

O'Connor, N. & B. Hermelin. 1991. A specific linguistic ability. *American Journal of Mental Retardation*, 95. 673–680.

Paradis, M. 2004. *A Neurolinguistic Theory of Bilingualism*. Amsterdam: John Benjamins.

Prat, C. S. 2011. The brain basis of individual differences in language comprehension abilities. *Language and Linguistic Compass*, 5/9. 635–649.

Prat, C. S., R. A. Mason, & M. A. Just. 2010. Right hemisphere contributions to reading: A multi-experiment individual differences investigation. Paper presented at the 16th Annual Meeting of the Organization for Human Brain Mapping, Barcelona, Spain, 6–10 Jun.

Premack, D. & G. Woodruff. 1978. Does the chimpanzee have a theory of mind? *Behavioral and Brain Sciences*, 4. 515–526.

Reiterer, S. M. 2009. Brain and language talent: A synopsis. In: G. Dogil & S. M. Reiterer (eds.), *Language Talent and Brain Activity*. Berlin: Mouton de Gruyter. 155–191.

Schlegel, A. A., J. J. Rudelson, & P. U. Tse. 2012. White matter structure changes as adults learn a second language. *Journal of Cognitive Neuroscience*, 24/8. 1664–1670.

Selfe, L. 1977. *Nadia: A Case of Extraordinary Drawing Ability in an Autistic Child*. London: Academic Press.

Selfe, L. 2011. *Nadia Revisited. A Longitudinal Study of an Autistic Savant*. London: Psychology Press.

Smith, N. & I. M. Tsimpli. 1995. *The Mind of a Savant. Language Learning and Modularity*. Oxford: Blackwell.

Smith, S. 1988. Calculating prodigies. In: L. K. Obler & D. Fein (eds.), *The Exceptional Brain: The Neuropsychology of Talent and Special Abilities*. New York: Guilford. 19–47.

Snyder, A. 2004. Autistic genius? *Nature*, 428. 702–704.

Snyder, A. W. & D. J. Mitchell. 1999. Is integer arithmetic fundamental to mental processing? The mind's secret arithmetic. *Proceedings of the Royal Society. Biological Sciences, London*, 266. 587–592.

Snyder, A. W., E. Mulcahy, J. L. Taylor, D. J. Mitchell, P. Sachdev, & S. C. Gandevia. 2003. Savant-like skills exposed in normal people by suppressing the left fronto-temporal lobe. *Journal of Integrative Neuroscience*, 2/2. 149–158.

Spelke, E. S. 2005. Sex differences in intrinsic aptitude for mathematics and science? A critical review. *American Psychologist*, 60/9. 950–958.

Svalberg, A. M.-L. 2007. Language awareness and language learning. *Language Teaching*, 40/4. 287–308.

Svalberg, A. 2012. Language awareness in language learning and teaching: A research agenda. *Language Teaching*, 45/3. 376–388.

Tammet, D. 2006. *Born on a Blue Day. A Memoir of Asperger's and an Extraordinary Mind*. London: Hodder & Stoughton.

Tammet, D. 2009. *Embracing the Wide Sky. A Tour across the Horizons of the Mind*. London: Hodder & Stoughton.

Treffert, D. 1989. *Extraordinary People. Understanding "Idiots Savants"*. New York: Harper & Row.

Wallace, G. L. 2008. Neuropsychological studies of savant skills: Can they inform the neuroscience of giftedness? *Roeper Review*, 30. 229–246.

Subject index

accuracy 9
– *see also* correctness
acquisition sequences 6
– *see also* developmental sequences
advanced proficiency 5, 43, 57, 128
– *see also* high-level proficiency
age of onset (AO) 7, 194
aptitude 8–9, 127, 255, 266
argumentation management 16, 33
artificial languages 227
Asian Englishes 187
Asperger Syndrome (AS) 248
assessment 2–4, 92
– *see also* testing
autism spectrum cluster (ASC) 249
autism spectrum disorder (ASD) 258
automaticity 155

brain scanning research 260
– *see also* neuroimaging research
breadth of vocabulary 93
– *see also* lexical breadth
Business Process Outsourcing (BPO) 197

CAF (complexity, accuracy, fluency) 9, 52
– *see also* these individual terms
call centre 193
– agents 205
– communication 195
– conversation 201
– industry 198
CEFR scale (Common European Framework of Reference for Language) 3–4, 47
cerebral organization 268
chunking 117
cognateness 92
cognates 90, 98
collocations 91, 114–115, 118, 122–123, 167
– tests of collocations 138, 175
communicative competence 152–153
complexity 9, 29
connectives 17
Construction Grammar 121
Construction-integration model of comprehension 153
corpora studies 113, 115

correctness 9
– *see also* accuracy
coverage 84–85
critical period 7, 193
– *see also* sensitive period
crossing 207
cross-linguistic influence 73, 81, 89, 92, 133
cytoarchitecture
– Broca's region 246

depth of knowledge 93
developmental sequences 45
– *see also* acquisition sequences
developmental stages 6, 45
discourse 53–55, 59

empathizing 259
exceptionality 216, 221
– language ability 242
– cerebral 243
Extreme Male Brain Theory of Autism 258–259

facility with linguistic form 242, 255, 266
fillers 21, 129
fluency 9, 21, 23, 29
– in reading 151, 167
form/function mapping 15, 54
formulaic language 112
formulaic sequences 112–113, 127, 166
frame 120–121
Frame Semantics 120
frequency 84, 95–99, 117, 125

genre 36, 157–158
Geschwind-Galaburda Theory 216, 242

high-functioning autism 247
high-level proficiency 5–7, 75
– *see also* advanced proficiency
hyperpolyglots 215

idiomaticity 23–25, 111, 140
illocutionary function 19
information structure 53
innateness 262
interaction management 16, 31

interlanguage 3, 45, 192
IQ tests 252

L1/L2 reader 150
learner autonomy 265
lemma 78, 99
Levelt's model of speaking 119
lexical breadth 77
– see also breadth of vocabulary
lexical bundles 114, 135
lexical depth 78, 82–83
lexical density 95
lexical diversity 95
Lexical Frequency Profile (LFP) 97, 99
lexical functions 122
lexical priming 118
lexical sophistication 96
lingua-franca environment 173
linguistic outsourcing 185

Meaning-Text Theory 122
memory 80
– photographic 228, 268
– working-memory 155–157, 160
meta-discursive function 19
metalinguistic knowledge 153, 266
modalization 20
modularity hypothesis 254
morphosyntax 43
motivation 26, 131, 159, 223, 265
multi-word sequences 113

nativelikeness 5–8, 43
native speaker 5, 75–76, 191, 194–195
near-native proficiency 5–6, 43, 57, 75, 191
neuroimaging research 261
new Englishes 185
non-native proficiency 5–6
noun phrase morphology 45

own-communication management 16, 32

passing strategies 195
performativity 207
perspective taking 55–56
Philippine English 199
phraseology 122
polyglots 2, 215, 229, 254, 265

– cerebral organization 255, 260, 268
– life histories 219
– lists 218
– male dominance 228, 267
pragmatic markers 15–21
prefabs/prefabricated structures 14, 124
privileged access 255
processing 141, 154, 156, 160, 164, 168, 260–261

reading
– proficiency 151–153
– speed 167

savants 247
savant syndrome 257
schemata 154
sensitive period 7
socio-cultural profile 128
stabilization 4–5, 9
styles of speech 196
synaesthesia 248
systemizing 259
– and maleness 267

targetlike behaviour 27
targetlike selection 23
testing 92
– see also assessment
text-base 154
thematic vocabulary 98
Theory of Mind 249–250
Theory of Privileged Access 255–256
transfer 18, 91, 161–164
– of literacy 161

ultimate attainment 4–5, 7–9, 60
Usage-Based Model 119

Verbal Efficiency Theory 155
verbal morphology 45
vocabulary knowledge 78
– see also word knowledge

word family 78, 99
word knowledge 78–82
– see also vocabulary knowledge
world Englishes 191–192

www.ingramcontent.com/pod-product-compliance
Lightning Source LLC
Chambersburg PA
CBHW030612230426
43661CB00053B/1956